Eclipsing the West

Manchester University Press

Eclipsing the West

China, India and the forging of a new world

Vince Cable

Manchester University Press

Published by Manchester University Press
Oxford Road, Manchester, M13 9PL
www.manchesteruniversitypress.co.uk

British Library Cataloguing-in-Publication Data
A catalogue record for this book is available from the British Library

ISBN 978 1 5261 7982 1 hardback

First published 2025

EU authorised representative for GPSR:
Easy Access System Europe, Mustamäe tee 50, 10621 Tallinn, Estonia
gpsr.requests@easproject.com

Typeset by
Cheshire Typesetting Ltd, Cuddington, Cheshire

'The only questions are whether it is India, China or the United States which will dominate the world by the end of this century.'

William Dalrymple, *The Golden Road*

Contents

Prologue

In September 2014, Xi Jinping flew to Ahmedabad for a meeting with newly elected Indian Prime Minister Narendra Modi. It was the first time the paramount leader of China had visited his country's southern neighbour since taking office a year earlier. Relations between the two countries had been somewhat distant since 1962, when a long-running border dispute escalated into a short war. But now a new relationship was in the process of being established, between two men who were collectively responsible for the lives of almost 3 billion people. There was much to discuss.

The choice of Ahmedabad, rather than New Delhi, represented a break from convention. The most populous city in the western state of Gujarat, it was Modi's hometown and had been the seat of his power during the thirteen years he had spent as Chief Minister of the state, prior to becoming Prime Minister. Ahead of the formal talks, which were to focus on boosting trade and increasing Chinese investment in India, Modi treated his guest to a tour of local sights. Among them was Mahatma Gandhi's ashram, where the two men were photographed sitting cross-legged on the floor beside a traditional spinning wheel once used by the icon of pacifism and Indian independence himself.

Chinese and Indian reporting on the visit was upbeat, verging on celebratory. The *Times of India* informed its readers that 'the chemistry between the two leaders was quite evident as they chatted continuously and looked completely relaxed in each other's company'.[1] *China Daily* noted that discussion points included creating a new industrial park and establishing relations between Ahmedabad and the Chinese city of Guangzhou.[2] By the end of the visit some twelve deals had been agreed, the most significant of which committed China to investing $20 billion (£12.2 billion) in India's infrastructure over five years.[3] The relationship was off to a good start.

It would not be long before tensions began to emerge. Over the next few years, the two countries would clash on a variety of issues, notably China's resistance to India joining the elite Nuclear Suppliers Group in 2016, which was followed by India rejecting an invitation to attend a summit for China's much-vaunted Belt and Road Initiative a year later.[4] The low point would arrive in May 2020, when the border dispute once again erupted into violence. In the midst of the Covid pandemic, Chinese and Indian troops clashed in the mountainous region of the Galwan Valley. The brutal melee lasted several hours. Twenty Indian and at least four Chinese soldiers were killed, with some falling hundreds of feet to their deaths.

The popular reaction in India was intense. Widely circulated videos showed protestors burning Xi in effigy.[5] The government banned numerous Chinese apps, including TikTok, excluded Huawei from Indian telecom networks and launched tax raids on Chinese companies. India also took the step of strengthening its security ties with the USA, short of a formal alliance, including participation in the Quad (Quadrilateral Security Dialogue) with the USA, Australia and Japan.

Despite this, trade has continued to grow. Today China is India's largest trade partner, receiving 30% of its imports from China. Steps have since been taken to reduce the risk of border clashes, leading to a formal agreement on border patrols on the eve of a BRICS summit in Russia in October 2024, when the leaders met again to put diplomatic and economic relations on a better footing. Direct flights resumed.

As this demonstrates, there is a complicated relationship between these two enormous and powerful countries, which, despite their very different political systems and lack of trust, have much in common. Both seek radical reform of international institutions, to reflect their growing economic weight. Both resist Western criticism of their approach to 'human rights' and secessionist movements. Both value close relations with Russia. Both are potentially threatened by President Trump's 'tariff wars'. They are 'frenemies'. As I argue in this book, they are the twenty-first century's new superstates, and they are likely to dominate the world – economically, politically and through their environmental footprint – in the years to come.

*

My interest in the two countries goes back a long way. I first visited India as a student in the mid-1960s, when the afterglow of independence was wearing off, and any remotely observant visitor could see and feel the gulf between the British-educated elite and the villagers, who lived in abject poverty. Passing through North India shortly before the Green Revolution, in a drought year, I witnessed signs of famine. I have returned many times since, on family and professional business. I have reported on and written about the country, and I have witnessed the transformation and India's impressive development at first hand.

In the 1990s I worked for Shell and became their Chief Economist at a time when there was growing awareness of China and India as major emerging sources of energy demand. Senior management was excited by China's growth in the wake of Deng Xiaoping's 'reform and opening up' but nervous about committing large amounts of shareholders' funds to oil, gas and petrochemical projects in a country where the business environment was seen as 'challenging'. There was similar uncertainty about India, which also had a bad reputation for mind-numbing bureaucracy and corruption.

I was asked to carry out major scenario-planning exercises in both countries as a precursor to large-scale investment. Conditions were not ideal. My Chinese collaborator – a young woman with a baby – was imprisoned for reasons that were opaque. The Indian adventure was in the wake of a failed joint venture with a local company that had been found to have unexplained large holes in the accounts. But, in both cases, the logic pointed to making a big commitment in future. Both commitments have been vindicated many times over.

Later, as a member of the Coalition Cabinet, I had a responsibility for developing the UK's rather low trade and investment profile in the big emerging markets, especially China and India. This involved repeat visits to both countries and engagement with politicians, business people and thinkers. In China, my visits were a prelude to the golden era of China–UK relations, which culminated in President Xi's visit in 2015. The UK government in that period was described by critics as 'naive', but as an insider I saw a carefully calibrated and successful balancing of risks and opportunities. Meetings with top Communist Party officials from the President down also taught me that it was possible to engage with them seriously, even on sensitive issues like Tibet or labour unions. And I was able to build good business relationships with big investors like Huawei and Geely.

Communication is easier in India than in China, and it was possible to develop deep relationships with political and business contacts. My visits overlapped the Congress and Bharatiya Janata Party (BJP) governments, which had very different styles. The most fruitful relationships were with big investors like Ratan Tata, whose commitment to British automobiles and steel did much to stabilise our manufacturing sector.

When I left Parliament, I wanted to build on these foundations. During the lockdown I wrote *The Chinese Conundrum*, which made the case for positive engagement with China on economic, environmental and other issues where there was some common ground. Like others trying to understand where the Chinese regime was coming from, I earned the label of being an 'apologist' for China. But since the book was banned in China, despite strenuous efforts by a leading Chinese publisher, I concluded that I had probably got the balance about right.

My Indian journey was in the opposite direction. In the 1980s and 1990s I wrote enthusiastically about India's quickening tempo of development and the resilience of its democracy, but there was widespread indifference in Western political and economic circles. More recently the challenge has been to curb the unrestrained enthusiasm of commentators and investors, who have been carried away by the promise of Modi's India. I continue, nonetheless, to be an optimist about India realising its vast human resource potential.

In this book I look both backwards and forwards. I look backwards to trace how China and India have evolved from the point in the late 1940s when both countries assumed their present political form, with India's independence from Britain and the establishment of the People's Republic of China. And I look forward to a future in which they are centrally important and – perhaps – the dominant economic and political actors on the world stage.

Introduction: the new superstates

When the Soviet Union collapsed at the beginning of the 1990s, the world entered a new period of history, defined by a single, undisputed superpower, the United States, and a set of international institutions and rules that it largely created. Over the next thirty years, this system provided the stability and openness required for an unprecedented process of globalisation. Around the world, there were rapid advances in trade and investment, flows of money and – to a degree – of people.[1] The experience of globalisation was, on balance, hugely beneficial for poor countries and for poverty reduction, though there were inevitably losers as well as winners. Some commentators went as far as to predict that the world of the future would be a borderless one, and that the nation state would soon be a thing of the past.[2]

Today, such dreams of a borderless world seem hopelessly naive. In the wake of the global financial crisis of 2008, political and economic nationalism has emerged as a powerful force across the world. 'Strongman' authoritarian leaders have been swept to power in numerous countries – from China and India to Hungary, Turkey, Russia and Saudi Arabia. In the 'developed' world, populist parties have fuelled xenophobic anti-immigration policies, trade protectionism and suspicions of global 'elites'. The USA, despite robust growth and technological leadership, is preoccupied with its seeming relative decline. Its own strongman leader, Donald Trump, and the political movement he unleashed, has brought into question America's commitment to maintaining the postwar international order. The old world is disappearing, but the shape of the new one remains unclear.

So what might this new world look like? Various economists, politicians and business leaders have argued that the twenty-first century will be the

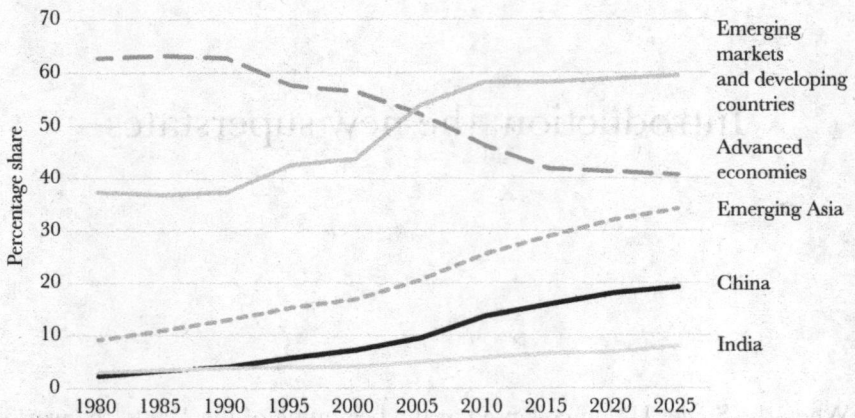

Source: IMF World Economic Outlook Database, October 2024 (www.imf.org)

0.1 Share of the world economy

'Asian century'.[3] This is not a far-fetched claim. Figure 0.1 shows the trend of the last twenty-five years, in which emerging markets, especially in Asia, have displaced the 'advanced' economies as the dominant force within the world economy. Asia already accounts for well over half the world's population and economy and much of the world's economic growth, for good (poverty reduction) or ill (environmental damage).

Continents are not, however, meaningful entities, with their own political, military, economic and cultural identity. Nation states are. And among Asian nation states, two appear to be of pre-eminent importance: China and India.

Superpowers or superstates?

There are various broad measures that capture the significance of these two countries. The most obvious one is population. At 1.4 billion each, China and India collectively account for 36% of the world's population. Added to this, their combined share of the world economy is just over 20% at market exchange rates (17.5% China, 3.2% India) and 27% measured on a purchasing power parity basis (19.1% and 7.8%). China is the world's largest exporter by far – almost 16% of the global total, if you include Hong Kong – while India accounts for another 2.3%. China also dominates manufacturing,

2

with around 32% of total production, while India contributes 3%. There are measurement issues with these indicators, but they capture the scale of the two big Asian countries, albeit with China well ahead for now.

How should we describe these large, powerful states? During the Cold War, the USA and the USSR were labelled 'superpowers'. In reality, and with hindsight, the USSR was a hollow structure that matched the USA in few respects beyond its nuclear weapons. China is now routinely described as a 'superpower',[4] while India has been called a 'superpower of the future'.[5] On a range of measures relevant to the idea of a superpower – stock of human and natural capital, widespread use of the currency for international transactions, scope and scale of military capabilities, 'soft power' – both countries continue to fall short of the US. But that picture is changing fast.

I would argue that a more useful term for the world we are moving into is 'superstate'. The political scientist Alasdair Roberts distinguishes superstates from 'normal' states by 'the expanse of territory, the number and diversity of people and the social and economic capacity'.[6] China and India both meet that definition, as does the US. Other countries – notably Indonesia, Japan, Russia and Brazil – meet some of the criteria but not others. Roberts makes the case for considering the EU a superstate, though its lack of political cohesion means it falls short, at least for now.

Superstates are not (necessarily) superpowers in the old sense, but their sheer size and economic capacity give them tremendous advantages, especially in the more fragmented world that we appear to be entering. China, India and the US all benefit from unified internal markets, reinforced by common infrastructure. They have their own currencies and their own, vast labour markets. China's economic success has rested in significant part on its ability to draw hundreds of millions of migrant workers from the poor, less productive rural interior to the industrial and export-oriented cities of the coastal belt. India, too, has a huge migrant labour force, which moves from poorer states like Bihar to expanding cities and big infrastructure projects. Cross-border immigration on this scale would never be tolerated and is being fiercely resisted even in countries with a long tradition of openness to migration such as the US.

Superstates can also take advantage of powerful network effects from being able to develop transport systems. Notable examples include the high-speed trains in China, the rapidly improving Indian highways and railways and airline connectivity in both countries. There are benefits from large national mobile networks and power grids. Chinese coastal provinces can offset chronic water shortages against water supplies from rivers originating in interior provinces such as Tibet; likewise, Gangetic India with supplies from the Himalayan foothills.

And, not least, superstates have the political advantage of being able to deploy internal security when needed, to make fiscal transfers from a common tax system, to undertake common planning and to minimise the overheads of central administration. All these factors stand in sharp contrast to the diseconomies of a fragmented set of nation states, as in sub-Saharan Africa, the Middle East and much of Latin America.

Superstates and geopolitics: two traps

The emergence of China and India as superstates, combined with the relative decline of the USA and the weakening of global rules and institutions this entails, presents some serious geopolitical challenges. In this book, I consider two in particular: the Thucydides Trap and the Kindleberger Trap.

The Thucydides Trap was formulated by the American political scientist Graham T. Allison in the early 2010s. Named from the Greek historian who chronicled the devastating wars between Athens and Sparta, it describes a situation where a declining power is drawn into conflict with an emerging one that threatens to displace it.[7] The most striking modern example – and a chilling one – is the First World War, which was the culmination of a period of competition between a rising Germany and a declining British Empire. Allison warns of the possibility this will happen between the US and China, and there is good reason to fear this. President Biden used one of his first public appearances after assuming power in 2021 to declare that China would not surpass the US on his watch. President Xi has been equally clear that he regards US hegemony as both unacceptable and transitory.[8]

Historically such conflicts have taken the form of open warfare, with a handful of exceptions where the declining power accepted its diminished role, as in the case of Britain and the United States. But the world today is very different from that of Athens and Sparta, not least in the availability of

4

weapons of mass destruction. The US and the USSR never came to blows for this reason. It is possible to envisage a new form of 'cold war' involving China, covering trade, capital flows, currency, technology, competition for political influence and the formation of new defensive alliances.[9]

India has no direct role to play in this context, though a time may be approaching when it challenges China as an emerging power. For the moment, it is seeking to strengthen its ties with the US, and in Asia with Japan, against the perceived threat of China to its borders and within the Indian Ocean. But there are also contexts in which India works with China against the interests of the USA, as in support for de-dollarisation or for good relations with Putin's Russia as part of a multipolar or 'multi-aligned' approach.

The Kindleberger Trap is named from the American economic historian Charles Kindleberger, a leading architect of the Marshall Plan after the Second World War. This problem arises when a declining power is unable or unwilling to continue supporting 'international public goods', such as the rules around an open trading system, international financial stability, conflict resolution, global pandemics and global environmental problems like climate change. At the same time, the emerging power is unwilling or unable to take on the responsibility.[10] An example can be found in the inter-war period, when the international order under the League of Nations was crumbling. The UK did not have the authority or resources to defend it, while the USA was not strong enough to intervene decisively and, anyway, was heavily influenced by isolationist sentiment.

The same isolationist sentiment is widespread today and effectively represented by Donald Trump. If it prevails, the question will arise again as to which power will champion international public goods. China is often seen as undermining attempts to create strong international rules, as with the Law of the Sea and the repudiation of international norms on human rights. The Chinese government has been at pains to point out that it does understand the Kindleberger Trap and is working to avoid it.[11] It does so by setting out broad principles of global cooperation as in the Global Security Initiative, the Global Development Initiative and the Global Civilisation Initiative, which inevitably reflect a Chinese world view. The Chinese idea of a global order is captured by the concept of 'tianxia' ('all under heaven'), which is peaceful and harmonious but with China at its centre.

5

Perceptions and alternative facts

The discussion so far has assumed that we are dealing with rational state actors who have an objective view of other actors and a clear understanding of their motives and behaviour. That may, however, be wishful thinking. Perceptions and reality can be wildly at odds, which in turn leads to behaviour that reflects basic misunderstandings. The concept of a 'superstate' starts with the seemingly uncontroversial and quantifiable metric of economic size, but there is deep disagreement about what that means.

The world of 'alternative facts' begins with the most basic of economic statistics: gross domestic product (GDP) and what it tells us about the size of nations. GDP is probably the best proxy we can find for economic size, though it fails to account for the stock of capital of a country, including natural resource endowment and the level of education of its population. Some researchers have argued that such omissions seriously understate the relative economic strength of the USA.[12] GDP also tells us nothing about the usefulness or quality of the goods and services produced and the important, unpaid services that are not included. The Soviet Union and its satellites were notorious for producing useless, poor-quality goods, resulting in over-stated GDP levels and growth.

The main statistical arguments about the economies of the USA, China and India concern a different point. Measured at market exchange rates the USA is clearly Number 1 ($27 trillion as against $17.7 trillion for China and a mere $3.7 trillion for India in 2023, according to the IMF). But exchange rates go up and down in response, for example, to interest rate changes, which have nothing to do with underlying economic size and performance. Moreover, Indian and Chinese workers are overwhelmingly paid in local currency, and this enables them to buy considerably more than would be the case with the dollar equivalent converted at the official exchange rate. Correcting for differences in price levels produces GDP at purchasing power parity, and the International Monetary Fund's (IMF) estimate is that China's current GDP in purchasing power parity (PPP) is $33 trillion, the USA's $27 trillion and India's $13 trillion. That paints a very different picture of China as Number 1 and India as Number 3 (and closing the gap). Figure 0.2 illustrates the impact of two alternative measurements across a range of countries.

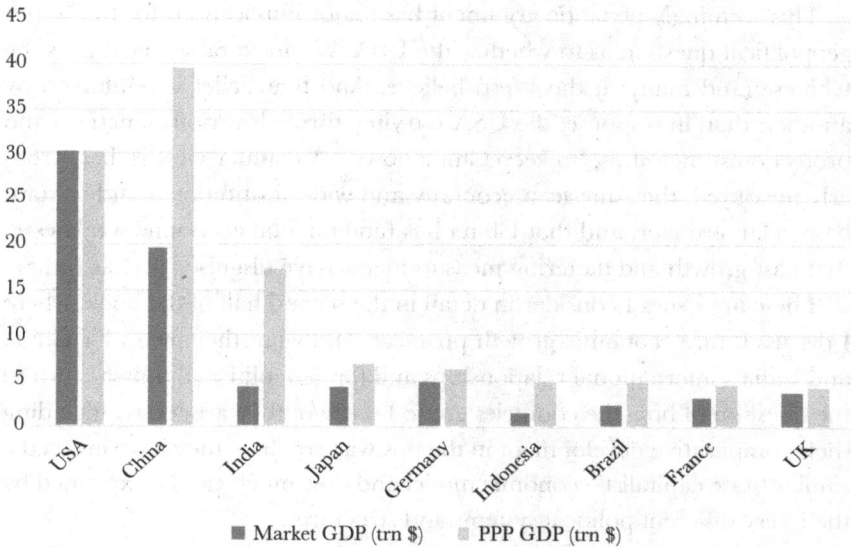

Source: World Bank/IMF (2025 estimate)

0.2 Estimated economic size by country

A vigorous debate has opened between proponents of the two methods. Some argue that, for comparison purposes, the market exchange rate measure should be used, since it reflects performance in those parts of the economy – exports, imports and foreign investments, in and out – where we are dealing with comparable goods and services.[13] Others favour the PPP measure, on the basis that it captures the reality of what the bulk of a country's population produce, consume and are paid.[14] Use of market exchange rates has a particularly negative effect on India, since it has been a more closed economy than China and for longer, and its price level is even more disconnected from world levels.

These alternative facts contribute to quite different narratives. The question of who is Number 1 in economic terms has two different answers. Narratives about the future – which country is 'rising' or 'declining' – also differ. If the recent slowdown in Chinese growth is to levels little higher than the USA, then it may never catch up (in terms of market exchange rates), but if China is already substantially bigger, the same growth rates will lead to a widening of the gap in absolute terms.

7

This seemingly pedantic argument has major implications for the bigger geopolitical question as to whether the USA is in inexorable decline, as the Chinese (and many in the West) believe. And that belief is reinforced by another: that, in response, the USA is trying, through various sanctions and protectionist measures, 'to keep China down'. A counter view is that, properly measured, the American economy and wider institutional and cultural base is far stronger, and that China has fundamental economic weaknesses that past growth and flattering measurements have disguised (as has India).

These are issues I consider in detail in the second half of the book, where I discuss future economic growth prospects and what they mean for China and India's international relationships and for geopolitics. But first I turn to the question of how the countries got to be where they are today, including their comparative development in the postwar era, how they have evolved a similar 'state capitalist' economic model and how much can be explained by their very different political systems and structures.

PART I

Economic development: limping hare and galloping tortoise?

1

Economic and social development

To explain the status of China and India as 'superstates', we have to understand how they got there. As I noted in the previous chapter, the two countries are now, arguably, the first and third (in market prices the second and fifth) biggest economies in the world. China is well ahead on most metrics of development, though India is growing more rapidly. Aesop's fable of the hare and the tortoise is often cited as a metaphor: the Chinese hare bounded off at great speed but is now sleeping while the Indian tortoise catches up. The fable is far-fetched, but it contains elements of truth.

China and India have some uncanny similarities which have long attracted comparative study.[1] Their populations are almost identical – 1.4 billion – though they will diverge in future. Both countries embarked on their present path of development at roughly the same time, with India gaining independence from the British Empire in August 1947, two years before the establishment of the People's Republic of China in October 1949. At the outset, they shared a belief in socialist planning, rapid industrialisation and self-reliance; like Mao Zedong, India's first Prime Minister, Jawaharlal Nehru, took inspiration from Stalin's USSR.[2] And both countries inherited the same level of extreme poverty, with an average per capita income at 10% of UK levels and 6% of US levels.[3] Last but not least, both draw on their history as great civilisations and use it to frame both domestic politics and international relations.

There were and are, inevitably, also significant differences. First, China embarked on uninterrupted, exclusive one-party rule under the Communist Party (CCP). India chose the path of parliamentary democracy and political federation, resulting in several changes of government at the centre and

11

many at state level, as well as other features of a democratic system such as a (more or less) free press and independent judiciary. In fact, the contrast obscures some similarities, including the emergence of new political leadership a decade ago with a more authoritarian approach to government. A second point of comparison, which derives from the first, is that although both countries liberalised their economies in the 1980s and after, opening them up to market disciplines, trade and foreign investment, China did so with far greater speed, intensity and consistency. But in recent years these stereotypes have become blurred, as people have begun to question both India's democratic credentials and China's commitment to reform and opening up.

The re-emergence of China and India

There is little data that allows us to assess the level of development in China and India before the nineteenth century beyond travellers' tales. Adam Smith wrote about both countries in his 1776 *Wealth of Nations*, emphasising their apparent wealth. He said of China that it had long been 'one of the richest, that is most fertile, best cultivated, most industrious and most populous countries in the world', though he added that 'the poverty of the lower ranks of people in China far surpasses the most beggarly nations of Europe'.[4] He judged that India – especially Bengal – was one of the most prosperous regions in the world, but that 'some injudicious restraints imposed by the servants of the East India Company' had led to famine and subsequent economic decline.[5] Historical research has established that the wages paid to weavers in India at that time were roughly the same as those paid to British weavers.[6]

A century and a half on from the apparent prosperity of the Adam Smith era, both India and China had stagnated or declined to abject poverty. This can be explained in part by the fact that they largely missed out on the Industrial Revolution. But there were other disasters too. The British economist Angus Maddison judged that there was no advance on income per head in China between 1820 and 1870 because of the huge loss of life (tens of millions) and destruction during the Taiping Rebellion.[7] This was followed by a spurt of growth, as China sought to emulate the modernisation of the Meiji rulers in Japan. But it ended with the overthrow of the Qing dynasty in

1911, after which conflict between warlords, war with Japan and a civil war between Communists and Nationalists caused widespread destruction and a regression in living standards.

There is continuing debate over the impact of the British Raj on Indian development. But it seems that, despite some additions to infrastructure – notably the railways – and a framework of stability, little overall economic progress occurred. The detailed study of S. Sivasubramonian for the 1900–47 period shows that there was an annual average of 0.9% growth, which was almost entirely offset by population growth.[8] In a book on the origins of global inequality, economist Angus Deaton comments that 'it is possible that the deprivation in childhood of Indians born around mid-century was as severe as any large group in history, all the way back to the Neolithic Revolution and the hunter gatherers that preceded them'.[9] As for the wider economy, it has been summarised as follows: 'stagnant per capita incomes, abysmal standard of living, stunted industrial development and the bulk of the population dependent on stagnating, low productivity, subsistence agriculture'.[10] There are few well-informed assessments of the state of China at the time of the 1949 revolution, and there are widely differing estimates of economic progress in the decades before, but we can reasonably assume that conditions were little better than in India.[11]

China surges ahead

The headline story about the growth of China and India over the last seventy-five years is that, with both starting from a low base, China grew much more rapidly to achieve significantly higher average living standards and far more poverty reduction. By 2023, China's per capita income was $13,160, close to the top of the range of 'middle-income' countries as defined by the World Bank, while India's was only $2,850. The figures are unflattering to India, in part because the price level in India is out of line with world prices – the country remains a largely closed economy. With the correction to purchasing power parity, the best estimate is $19,160 as against $7,130. China's slower population growth, a product of the one-child policy introduced in 1980, also contributed to higher per capita income growth, though that is now seen as a problem, while India's higher birth rate is being portrayed as a potential 'demographic dividend', of which more below.

13

Much of the divergence between China and India occurred after 1980, when Deng Xiaoping embarked on radical, rapid economic reform in China following the death of Mao. Before that time China had experienced the horrors of the Great Leap Forward, which led to what was probably the worst famine in human history, when as many as 40 million people may have died.[12] This was followed by the upheavals of the Cultural Revolution. These events wiped out much of the rapid advance which occurred in the 'rightist period' of the 1950s. The economic damage is difficult to quantify, not least because, under Mao, statistics were considered to be 'a weapon in the class struggle'.[13] Even when statistics were published and more reliable, China had a different convention for measuring gross national product (GNP) in the form of 'social output'. Fortunately, there was also a set of national income accounts which could be translated into internationally consistent measures to create a time series for the period.[14]

The resulting numbers must be treated cautiously, but they suggest that Chinese growth may have averaged 5% over the period 1950–80 and India's 3.5% (3.6% and 1.2% in per capita terms). This suggest that Mao's China was not entirely a story of disaster. Mass mobilisation for big irrigation projects produced results, while India's agricultural development was held back by legal and political barriers to reforming land tenure. China was also able to force the pace of primitive capital accumulation to generate resources for industrial investment. By contrast, India's considerable achievement was to avoid the famines in years of monsoon failure and drought, which had been seen as inevitable in colonial times. There was also a breakthrough with the adoption of hybrid seeds and multiple cropping from the mid-1960s with the Green Revolution, though its full impact on agricultural production was not felt for over a decade.[15]

Following Deng's reforms, China underwent almost four decades of explosive growth of 9% to 10% per annum (8% to 9% in per capita terms). The growth rates were, in fact, not greatly different from those experienced by other Asian Newly Industrialising Countries such as South Korea and Taiwan when they were at the same level of development, but given China's scale, the impact was much bigger. When the global financial crisis hit in 2008, the Chinese government launched a massive programme of investment – accounting for an estimated 12.5% of GDP over two years – which served to shield the country from the worst effects. But this was followed by a period of tapering growth, averaging just under 8% in the decade 2013–23 and only 4.2% in the last five years of that decade. This latter period includes not only the disruption of the pandemic but growing evidence of economic headwinds caused by serious domestic imbalances and a collapsing property boom. The extent of the damage is difficult to assess, since China is thought to be disguising some key statistics. The Chinese authorities have, however, concluded that the days of spectacular growth are over and that future growth of above 5% is unrealistic. Even that may be optimistic.

India also saw accelerating growth from the 1980s, albeit at lower levels. It was 5% during that decade (3% in per capita terms), following the modest reforms of Prime Minister Indira Gandhi. The tempo quickened following Manmohan Singh's more radical reforms in 1991, leading to 6% annual growth in the 1990s and 7.6% in the 2000s. In the decade 2013–23 growth averaged just under 7%, close to Chinese rates and considerably more than the average of other large developing economies.[16] India slowed sharply because of the pandemic, but it has recovered fast, with an estimated 7% growth in both 2022 and 2023, outpacing China and almost everywhere else. This spurt of growth has potentially changed the narrative of recent decades. But, as in China, growth numbers must be treated with scepticism. In India's case, it has emerged that real growth in the 2011–16 period may have been exaggerated by 2% to 3% a year because of the use of a price deflator (the Wholesale Price Index) which did not properly capture inflation. Moreover, official statistics did not correspond to real-world experience of slow growth in power supplies, road and rail traffic and credit supply.[17]

It is widely believed that China's rapid growth and, to a lesser extent, India's can be primarily explained by high rates of investment. Figure 1.1 shows the importance of rising investment over the last half century. In China's case the share of investment in GNP (gross fixed capital formation) rose from 30% at the beginning of the reform period to peak at around 44–45% in the period around the financial crisis, remaining at over 40% thereafter. These are extraordinary levels by any standard; even South Korea's investment rate has rarely risen above 30%. The high numbers reflect remarkably high savings rates, which are even higher than investment. It was the overriding concern of government to drive economic growth through investment (and exports) rather than consumption. The remarkable investment 'binge' over the 2009–13 period led to rapid infrastructure

	Household consumption			Government consumption			Investment (gross capital formation)			Net exports		
	1970	2000	2023	1970	2000	2023	1970	2000	2023	1970	2000	2023
China	60	51	39	10	15	17	30	31	42	0.2	2.2	2.2
India	74	64	60	9	13	10	17	24	32	−0.1	−0.9	−2.2
USA	60	67	68	18	14	13	21	24	22	0.4	−1.7	−2.9

Source: World Bank Open Data

1.1 Share of demand in GDP (%)

investment and housing construction, prompting the (popular but somewhat improbable) claim that China poured more cement in that short period than the USA did in a century.

However, some researchers have suggested that the role of investment in Chinese growth has been overstated.[18] In the period 1979–94 it was estimated that over half of the growth was explained by total factor productivity (TFP), i.e. not additional investment and labour supply but greater efficiency in their use. The productivity improvements resulted mainly from the radical reforms of the Dengist era: the freeing up of farming from state-controlled collectives; state-owned enterprise (SOE) morphing into a capitalist economy; the movement of vast numbers from low productivity farming to manufacturing; the liberalisation of prices, which created profit-based incentive structures. After 1989 these productivity factors became less important, and productivity growth slowed from 3% or 4% to 1% per annum.[19] It is now clear that much investment was misdirected and wasteful. It has left a legacy of debt, especially with local government and property developers.

India's growth experience has been less extreme, but it also underlines the importance of productivity growth. Investment levels as a share of GDP have been in a range from the low twenties to just under 30%. The economist Arvind Virmani has shown that the contribution of productivity to growth fell in the pre-reform 1950–80 period and that in the 1970s there was little growth, with what there was being mostly due to capital investment.[20] Starting in the 1980s productivity took over from investment as the main driver of growth.[21]

This improvement has been sustained, and it appears that productivity growth (TFP) in India is now consistently higher than in China, by an estimated 1.5% p.a. over the last decade and 0.5% p.a. over the last twenty years.[22] Among the factors sustaining this growth in productivity are big outlays of public investment on infrastructure – albeit on a lesser scale than in China – and the digitisation of government services, issues to which I return in later chapters. Together with other growth factors, such as labour supply, working in India's favour, as well as the Chinese slowdown, these trends suggest that the tortoise is catching up.

Figure 1.2 brings out the contrast. Investment accounts for three-quarters of Chinese growth, though there is continuing productivity growth, at least in relation to developed economies. India, by contrast, derives less than half of its growth from investment and rather more from productivity. It also derives more growth from the growing quantity and quality of its labour force. Labour supply has been and will be crucial to the growth story of both countries. China was able to tap into a vast reserve of underemployed labour and channel it into higher productivity industry. However, with agriculture now providing only 7% of GDP and population growth no longer increasing, and with labour force participation of around 75%, there is no large 'reserve army' of workers.

China's puritanical insistence on work over welfare means that few people drop out of the labour force voluntarily. The country is trying to offset labour shortage by automating as rapidly as possible. Nonetheless there is some unemployment – around 5% – mainly because of a mismatch of skills. This mismatch has become so great among young people that, post-pandemic, China has been shocked to have youth unemployment rising above 20% – so much so that the statistics have been withdrawn from public scrutiny.

	Average growth rate	IT capital	Other capital	Hours worked	Labour quality	TFP
China	7.7	0.6	5.3	0.1	0.5	1.2
India	6.0	0.2	2.7	0.7	0.7	1.6
ASEAN	4.5	0.3	2.6	0.6	0.9	0.1
USA	1.7	0.3	0.6	0.1	0.3	0.4
Japan	0.6	−0.2	0.1	0.3	0.3	0.1

Source: Asian Productivity Organization, Productivity Data Book 2023. Figures derived from Supplementary Table 9

1.2 Sources of growth (2000–22)

In India, however, the job position is much worse. While China is embarrassed by youth unemployment of around 20%, young people in India are estimated by the Centre for Monitoring Indian Economy (CMIE) to have at least 45% unemployment, even excluding those that have dropped out of the labour market.

India's employment story, indeed, is almost the exact opposite of China's: an overall chronic excess supply of labour. According to the International Labour Organization, in the first two decades of this century job growth was around 1% per annum, while the economy grew at over 6%.[23] The official figure for unemployment is around 3.5%, which is absurd to the point of being meaningless (the CMIE produce more credible numbers: around 8%). There is also a vast amount of underemployment among agricultural labourers and in the 'informal sector'. Self-employed informal sector workers were hit hard by the pandemic lockdown and by the government's earlier demonetisation campaign (when it withdrew high denomination notes with the intention of curbing corruption, but hit workers dependent on the cash economy). The clumsy introduction of an otherwise desirable general services tax across India affected the same sector. Yet the informal sector accounts for an estimated 80% of working age Indians who are in the labour force. On top of that, many Indians have been discouraged by the lack of opportunities and have dropped out of the labour force altogether.

There is a particular dearth of labour force participation among women, officially estimated to be around 25% (unofficially, probably in single figures). This is way below the 70% in China. Moreover, the rate has fallen this century, from over 30% to 26%, and is now lower than in Bangladesh and Pakistan. The economist Ashoka Mody regards unemployment as India's biggest failure, and job creation the biggest challenge.[24] It is not currently clear where the demand for labour will come from. Construction is a growth area, but the big infrastructure projects are capital intensive. Manufacturing jobs are being incentivised by a government subsidy scheme, but the projects benefitting – as with chip manufacture – provide few jobs. India is proving to be a successful services exporter, with 300,000 engineers in chip design alone, but the jobs are for highly trained graduates. Business services such as IT and call centres produce an estimated 7% of GDP, a quarter of exports and 1% of jobs. What is happening in India is that for many of the unskilled and uneducated the only work is in peasant agriculture, reversing what seemed to be an inexorable shift towards modernisation and urbanisation. Agriculture is thought to provide 40% of employment but 15% of output and 12% of exports. Why has China succeeded in providing employment when India has failed?

Exports and industrialisation

If there is one factor that can explain India's underperformance relative to China and its problems of massive underemployment, it is the country's failure to adopt the East Asian model of export-led industrialisation.[25] Both countries have espoused industrialisation, but only China recognised the potential for manufactured exports, following the precedents of South Korea, Taiwan and, before that, Japan. Later, China tapped into the potential of global supply chains. The following figures illustrate, rather brutally, the consequences of India's exclusion from world manufacturing trade.

As a share of world manufacturing exports, China's rose from 3% in 1985 to 20% in 2020. India's rose from 0.8% to 2.3%, below the share it enjoyed at the time of independence in 1948.[26] China's share of global manufacturing value added was, on one of several measures, 28.4% in 2020 and India's 3.3%.[27] The share of manufacturing in GDP was an estimated 28% in China in 2022 and 13% in India, with India close to the level of deindustrialised countries like the UK and USA.[28] China was thought to have close to 100 million employed in manufacturing in 2020 and India 35.6 million. China is the world's manufacturing superpower, adding more industrial value than the USA, Japan and Germany combined (Figure 1.3).

The narrative behind these numbers starts with the fact that China's radical 'reform and opening up' under Deng Xiaoping occurred over a decade earlier than the Indian equivalent under Manmohan Singh. The Chinese reforms cut administrative controls around foreign trade, cut the trade barriers and tariffs on imported inputs to manufacturing and liberalised foreign investment.[29] They liberated private, Chinese entrepreneurship through Township and Village Enterprises (TVEs), operating with minimal regulation, and opened China to foreign investment in special economic zones (SEZs). Within a few years, the country had become a global manufacturing hub, specialising in labour-intensive exports, utilising low-cost labour. Firms

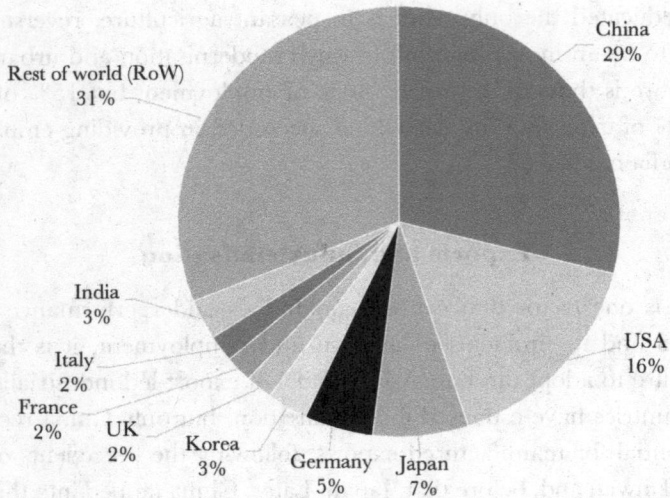

Source: OECD TiVA database 2023

1.3 Share of world manufacturing value added

from the Chinese diaspora poured into the SEZs, and exports surged from $10 billion at the start of the reforms to $70 billion by 1991, overtaking South Korea, with real growth of 15% per annum. Labour-intensive manufactures grew from 31% of exports in 1978 to 57% in 1993, in a classic demonstration of comparative advantage. Crucially, the competitiveness of exports was underpinned by a big – 35% – devaluation in 1994 from 5.8 yuan/renminbi to the dollar to 8.7, and the competitive benefit of devaluation was sustained for a decade.

At first sight, the Indian reforms were similar, with the abolition of industrial licensing, tariff cuts on imports used by exporters and the permitting of majority foreign ownership. There was also a two-stage devaluation – initially small, from 21 to 23 rupees to the dollar, and then to 26 rupees – 19% overall (though the benefit to exporters was quickly offset by inflation). There were positive reactions to the policy changes, which were radical by Indian standards but not by comparison with China. Crucially, foreign direct investment surged in China, especially during the 1990s, from virtually nothing to $40 billion p.a. a decade and a half after the reforms (and to $70 billion after another decade).

Over the same period after liberalisation, India's annual inflows had reached only around $5 billion. It almost doubled its share of world trade, but only to 0.85%. In the area of clothing and footwear, the main sector for early stage labour-intensive exports, India boosted its share of world markets from 1.4% to 3.2%. But the Chinese share had leapt from 1.3% to 37.6%. Belatedly, India has started to make an impact in one area of manufacturing exports: electronics. It has achieved a market share of around 3% of global electronics exports, up from 1% a decade ago, by attracting investors who were hitherto active in China. But production is largely based on imported components, with little value-added, and expensively subsidised.

So, why did Chinese reforms produce stronger outcomes? They were more far-reaching. The scale of the devaluation is illustrative, especially as the competitive advantage of devaluation in India was quickly eroded by inflation. According to the Bank of International Settlements, inflation wiped out any benefits from devaluation, and the currency has appreciated in real terms since 1994.[30] By contrast, Chinese devaluation was bigger, and the benefits sustained. China also had a very permissive regulatory environment in the SEZs, particularly around labour standards, while India had stronger unionisation and protections for workers. Employers in China seem to have been able to obtain skilled workers more easily.

The economist Richard Baldwin also argues that a crucial development occurred in the 1990s, when the nature of globalisation changed and became centred on global supply chains.[31] By that point, China was well-established as a manufacturing exporter, with supporting infrastructure and an increasingly well-trained labour force, and was able to attract multinational companies like Apple to take advantage of low Chinese costs. India participated in global supply chains through IT and other services, but not manufacturing. China further evolved from being part of supply chains to building them, taking advantage of its vast home market. There was supportive industrial policy. Manufacturers developed the complex skills and processes involved in engineering.[32] Chinese exports became more technologically sophisticated and simpler products like garments and shoes shifted to the likes of Bangladesh and Vietnam (but not to India, where costs were found to be uncompetitive because of Indian labour laws affecting overtime and dismissal).

One of the major reasons India missed out on the experience of industrialisation through trade was the size distribution of firms.[33] An extraordinarily high percentage of industrial employment, 84%, has been in small companies (under fifty employees) and, among these, in no fewer than 17 million 'micro' firms (under ten workers, often just one). In China the share is 25%, and large units (over 200 workers) account for 52% as against 10% in India. India had a 'missing middle': 6% as against 23% in China. Small firms have long been protected in India through some products being reserved for their exclusive production. They have not had the scale to invest in the training, marketing and equipment required for globally competitive exports. There are, for example, millions of handloom and handicraft artisans in India producing work of unique and exquisite quality, but it would have required organisation and efficient systems to transform potential into a major export industry. It didn't happen.[34] One sector where it did happen was internationally traded services. India already has around 5% of world exports. Its share is growing rapidly, because of Indian firms' successfully providing software design and other services to international companies and exploiting opportunities in remote services like telemedicine. One of the big questions for the future is whether India's role as a leading traded services exporter will prove better for growth and employment than China's continued dominance in manufacturing.

Social development

Of course, GDP growth provides an incomplete picture. We need to look at a range of human development indicators, though there are serious problems in data collection and in maintaining consistency between countries. Figure 1.4 gives some indicators for which comparable data is available, and these tend to show the higher level which China has reached. The United Nations' Human Development Index provides an approximate composite measure combining a variety of indicators. It suggests that China is well ahead of India in translating economic growth into wider human capital, but is itself a long way from the standards of high-income countries. China is 79th and is part of the upper-middle-income group, with an index of .767 (for comparison, the UK has an index of .929, Thailand of .880 and Brazil .754). In fact, the Chinese underperform on human development relative to what would be expected based on per capita income, where China ranks 64th (market prices) or 72nd (PPP basis). But they are well ahead of India, which ranks 132nd

22

	USA	China	India	Brazil	Indonesia
(a) Per capita PPP GDP (2023)	81,695	24,560	10,175	20,584	15,612
(b) Literacy % (15+)					
M	99	98	82	94	97?
F	99	95	66	94	95?
(c) Life expectancy at birth (2023)					
M	74	75	66	69	66
F	79	78	69	76	70
(d) Under 5 mortality rates per 1,000	6.3	6.6	29.1	14.0	21.3
(e) Access to safe sanitation %	98	70	46	49	–

Sources: a) IMF 2023; b) World Bank; c) WHO (2021); d) UNICEF (2023); e) WHO/UNICEF (2021)

1.4 Social indicators

(out of 191 countries) with an index of .633, which is roughly in line with India's ranking in per capita income. For India, the most invidious contrast is not so much with China, which is a richer country, but with its South Asian neighbour Bangladesh, which is poorer in per capita income terms (PPP) by around 5% but ranks a little ahead in human development. Moreover, India appears to have gone backwards in ranking since 2015.

This broad ranking of human development is reflected in measures for health and education. Based on standardised figures from the World Bank database, a Chinese person now has the same life expectancy from birth as an American – 79 years as against 79.5. India's life expectancy is 72, which is a little lower than Bangladesh's (74). China's child mortality rate is 5 per 1,000 live births, close to developed country levels. India's is 26, close to the world average of 28. India has demonstrated rapid improvement, halving the child mortality rate in fifteen years from 50 deaths (China's rate declined from 20 to 5 over the same period). In terms of health inputs, which partly explain the different outcomes, China has two physicians for every 1,000 people, against 0.9 for India. These figures need to be treated with caution, as there are big differences in professional qualifications, definitions and quality. Both countries have a yawning gap between world-class private clinics and understaffed and resourced public sector facilities with badly paid, overworked, clinical staff. That said, on almost every measure, China has more health inputs than India and has better outcomes.

The same broad conclusion applies to schooling. A young Chinese person currently starting school can expect 14.2 years of schooling, a young Indian

11.9; while the mean figure for schooling completed (based on Pew Research data) is 7.4 years in China (women 6.8 years) and 5.4 in India (4.1 for women). The differential in completed schooling helps to explain differences in basic literacy, which is estimated (World Bank again) to be 97% in China and 75% in India, compared to a world average of 86%.

Education feeds back into better economic performance. It has been argued that China's level of basic education in the Mao era (and before) provided the country with the ability to take advantage of subsequent liberalisation. There were enough people with basic literacy, numeracy and accounting skills to start and run businesses like the Township and Village Enterprises that sprung up in large numbers in rural areas in the 1980s.[35] India was not so well prepared. In 1980 a young Chinese person had, on average, 5.7 years of education, as against 2.5 in India. By the time of the 1990s reform, India had increased average schooling only to 3.6 years.

Looking forwards, however, there are serious concerns in both countries that the levels of education being provided do not meet the standards required of a modern economy. China has some outstanding schools, colleges and universities in the cities, with ferocious competition for places. India too. But, in China, Scott Rozelle and Natalie Hell have argued that of the 800 million rural or migrant workers only 12% have a high school education. Yet 75% of babies are born into this underclass.[36] The underclass is also self-perpetuating, since low educational attainment is reinforced by poor health among rural children, including widespread myopia, affecting reading ability, anaemia and intestinal worms. In India the position is worse. A survey of the three-quarters of Indian children who live in rural areas found that after the end of compulsory education (year 8, around 13 years old), barely 45% could understand basic division and under 70% could read text for 7-year-olds.[37] Worse, standards of reading had declined over a decade and arithmetic skills had stagnated. Teachers are often absent and unpaid (by state governments).

Another way of looking at social development is in terms of poverty levels, though these are exceptionally difficult to measure, since different social groups have different spending patterns and cost levels for the items they buy. One standard measure is 'absolute poverty', calculated by the World Bank in terms of numbers living on $2.15 a day at 2017 prices. On this austere definition, both China and India had around 45% of the population in absolute poverty at the turn of the twenty-first century. Within twenty years China had 'abolished' absolute poverty, amid much fanfare. The initial approach was through broad-brush policies like improving rural healthcare, cutting taxes on farmers and introducing pensions for the rural population. Then a more targeted approach was adopted, with measures to raise the incomes of poor counties and then specific villages. Latterly, under President Xi, an even more precise programme was adopted to move the remaining 90 million over the line. China claims to have crossed this line, but large numbers of Chinese in rural areas are however still very poor by the standards of rich countries or even by the standards of other middle-income countries.

The World Bank estimates that, on its own definition, around 10% of Indians are still in absolute poverty, though the numbers may well have risen because of the pandemic lockdowns. The setback has obscured the improvements in recent years, which had taken India from 22.5% in absolute poverty in 2011 to 10% in 2019.[38] There is a lot of contradictory data, some of which challenges this optimistic picture.[39] But the most recent estimates, which allow for the real value of subsidised food (and other benefits like school uniforms and cooking cylinders for the poorest people), suggest that only 2% of the population are in absolute poverty (though the new methodology has yet to be published and fully scrutinised).[40] In any event, the definition of poverty is extreme, and in India, for example, poverty would normally be regarded as applying also to the 800 million in receipt of subsidised food, for which the qualifying income is $5 a day.

Studied properly, poverty is multidimensional, and there are now comparative figures for levels of multidimensional poverty, vulnerability to it and components of it.[41] The Indian subcontinent in general is particularly susceptible to poor sanitation, unaffordable fuel and substandard housing. India conducts its own multidimensional study, which records a massive improvement over fifteen years from 55% to 16% in the numbers suffering extremes of poverty.[42] Nonetheless, access to basic sanitation coverage is estimated at 96% in China and only 76% in India (the global average is 81%). In India poor sanitation is associated with public defecation, which the government has identified as a particular source of shame (and disease).

Another dimension of poverty is malnutrition, which is approximately estimated at around 13% of the world's population and 15% in India. There

25

is virtually no malnutrition in China, but the significance here depends greatly on annual crop variations, age groups and particular dietary requirements. Little progress appears to have been made on child malnutrition in India, and millions have suffered from stunted growth and lifelong disability as a result. This is also an area where Bangladesh outperforms India, with only around 10% of the population affected. Moreover, the position in India may be deteriorating. The Global Hunger Index has India falling from 97 to 115 out of 157 in world rankings from 2016 to 2019. The Indian National Nutrition Monitoring Bureau in 2016 concluded that 35% of rural men and women were malnourished and 42% of children underweight, and the position appears to be worse than forty years earlier.

These indicators of basic needs and poverty matter enormously, but the tangible feeling of 'progress' in both countries reflects the improved living standards of hundreds of millions of people, often described as 'middle class', enjoying access to basic consumer durables: scooters, televisions, digital devices. Access to mobile phones is almost universal in the West (82% in the USA) and high in China (68%), but also extensive in India, with around 40% coverage. Internet access is thought to be near saturation in some advanced countries like South Korea (98%), and China is not far behind (76%), above the world average of around 66%. The Indian figure is around 33%, but, as with mobile phones, growth is rapid and absolute numbers in China and India dwarf any other market. China, though not India, is also overtaking the USA in the number of cars owned, with 220 cars per 1,000 people as against the US 908 (but with India still behind on 59).

The figures quoted are, in almost all the comparisons, several years out of date and pre-pandemic. The pandemic and associated lockdowns did enormous damage to education and to the health and living standards of many people, much of which is not yet quantified. In India one observer commented, 'where the artistry of a goldsmith was needed, the hammer blow of a blacksmith was used, resulting in an economic collapse and widespread suffering especially amongst the poor'.[43] China received plaudits for the effectiveness of its lockdown in stopping transmission and disease. But the sudden, chaotic lifting of the restrictions may have resulted in as many as 1.5 to 2 million excess deaths.[44] The figure for India may have been between 3 and 5 million, far higher than the official estimate of half a million.[45] For the USA, a more reliable figure of 1.1 million is available.

26

If these are even approximately right, then the US and Indian numbers are roughly the same in per capita terms and China's about half that level. China's authoritarian methods were bitterly disliked and ended badly but, overall, saved many lives.

The broader conclusion, however, is that India has lagged behind China in the wider aspects of human development and not just economic growth. In part the two factors are related. As a poorer country, India had less to spend on social policies. But social development – health and education – was, overall, given lesser priority, and that is evident in the fact that India was out-performed not just by China but also by India's poor neighbour, Bangladesh. Another factor was a function of India's federal, democratic constitution. Health and education were mainly matters for state governments. Some states, such as Kerala, have health, education and anti-poverty indicators well above the national average, while Bihar and Uttar Pradesh lag at the bottom. Mostly this reflects their relative income, though in some cases (West Bengal) the state appears to have outperformed their predicted level.

The level of poverty in India may now be undergoing a steep reduction, with the country rapidly rolling out its Stack, or digital public infrastructure, on top of near-universal banking.[46] There are several elements: a digital, biometric identity system, Aadhar, which has covered 1 billion adults and enables poor people to claim basic entitlements like food rations or vaccination certificates, circumventing corrupt and inefficient distribution networks; transfer payments to individuals in ways that directly combat poverty; and a digital finance architecture that enables all adults to make payments digitally utilising their mobile phones. An estimated 90 billion transactions were made in 2022, from 1.1 billion bank accounts (covering 80% of adults), far more than in any other country, including China (18 billion).

Investment in digital infrastructure, under a scheme first launched under the Manmohan Singh administration, has made it possible to transfer 3% of GDP in transfer payments directly into the bank accounts of the poor (almost all of whom now have bank accounts and can use their mobiles to make transactions). These transfers have been criticised because they only partially compensate for, rather than solve, massive unemployment. And they were introduced alongside a big contraction in the finance allocated to employment subsidies.[47] But the payments have undoubtedly reduced the corruption endemic in earlier programmes. Despite some glitches, India's

27

complex, rapidly installed and efficient digitisation programme is not just – hopefully – reducing poverty and financial exclusion but improving the efficiency of retailing and banking, improving tax collection and providing India with a valuable export industry, helping economic growth.[48]

China's digital revolution is on a different level, however, and the more meaningful comparisons are with the most advanced economies. China now has 1.6 billion mobile users and 1 billion with internet access (around 75% penetration). Some 360 million have access to 5G, and the Chinese middle class now has access to fully integrated payments and social media on the same handset. The focus of policy is not, as in India, financial inclusion and poverty reduction – let alone the creation of a 'decadent' welfare state. The starting point is a perceived need for technological leadership matching and then surpassing the US. Nonetheless, the Chinese digital infrastructure is not without its problems. There is a significant gap between the coastal belt, where the digital economy is as sophisticated as anywhere in the world, and the rural interior, which lags far behind.[49] And the government crackdown on the big internet companies must have affected their long-term expansion and ability to innovate.

On almost every indicator, to the extent that the data is reliable, China outperforms India. But there are two important qualifications. The first is that India is doing better than China when it was at the same level of per capita income. India's development (like its democracy) has been described as 'precocious'.[50] The second is that, in China, work is seen as the key to poverty reduction, and 'welfare' is a despised Western indulgence, while in India there is an embryonic welfare state with payments based on need (also a reflection of democratic priorities).

But there is one set of indicators which touches a sensitive nerve among both sets of rulers: statistical evidence of the gulf between rich and poor.

Inequality

The pandemic exposed some of the harsh effects of inequality, as when millions of migrant workers in India were left to walk hundreds of miles back to their villages. China's migrant underclass was also trapped, unable to move. The bigger picture suggests however that the two countries have both produced a plutocratic class and a rapidly expanding middle class.

In overall terms, both countries have levels of inequality which is higher than in Western Europe – but far from the inegalitarian extremes. If we take – again using the World Bank database – the standard Gini coefficient measure of income inequality, leading Western European countries have an index of around 32/33 while, at the other extreme, South Africa is at 61 and Brazil at 49. The USA is measured at 40 and China comes in at 37, India at 34. The Indian data is flattering and is believed to significantly understate inequality.

There is a richer source of material in the World Inequality Database (2022), rooted in the work of Thomas Piketty and his team at the Paris School of Economics, which gives more detailed and internationally consistent inequality measures for both income and wealth.[51] Across a range of measures, China is less unequal in income, with a bigger middle class but a (slightly) worse distribution of asset wealth (Figure 1.5).

It is possible to isolate the share of the top 1% and the top 10%. As shown in Figure 1.6, China and India are not as unequal as Brazil or South Africa. But despite China being ruled by the Communist Party for seventy-five years and India by a variety of self-proclaimed 'socialists', the two countries have a pattern of income distribution not greatly different from the USA, though with India significantly more unequal than China. In both cases, there have been big changes over time, reflecting historical discontinuities. In China, the top 10% had over 50% of income pre-revolution. Under Communism this roughly halved until after the Deng reforms, when the share rose to 42%. India's income share for the top 10% was thought to be around 50% in late colonial times; it fell gradually to 35% after independence, but over the last three decades has risen again to 57%. Figure 1.7 shows the trend of rising inequality in both countries over the last forty years. The question then is whether relative or absolute levels of income matter more; in India the income share of the bottom 50% appears to have shrunk from 20% to 13% after 1991 to the present, but real incomes are up 180%.

In neither country is progressive taxation doing much to alleviate inequality, despite official rhetoric. Both China and India have a progressive direct tax structure, but few people pay direct tax, which accounts for 6% to 7% of GDP out of around 20% for tax overall. A World Bank study shows, however, that China's spending on education and health makes fiscal policy more redistributive, to levels comparable to other upper-middle-income countries.[52]

29

Share of income (PPP)

	China	India
Bottom 50%	14.4	13.1
Middle 40%	44.0	29.7
Top 10%	41.6	57.1
of which top 1%	14.0	21.7

	China	India
Ratio of top 10% to bottom 50%, income	1 to 14	1 to 22

Share of wealth (PPP)

	China	India
Bottom 50%	6.4	5.9
Middle 40%	25.8	29.5
Top 10%	67.8	64.6
of which top 1%	30.5	33.0

Gender share of income (%)	China	India
Male	67	82
Female	33	18

Source: World Inequality Database (2021)

1.5 Comparative inequality

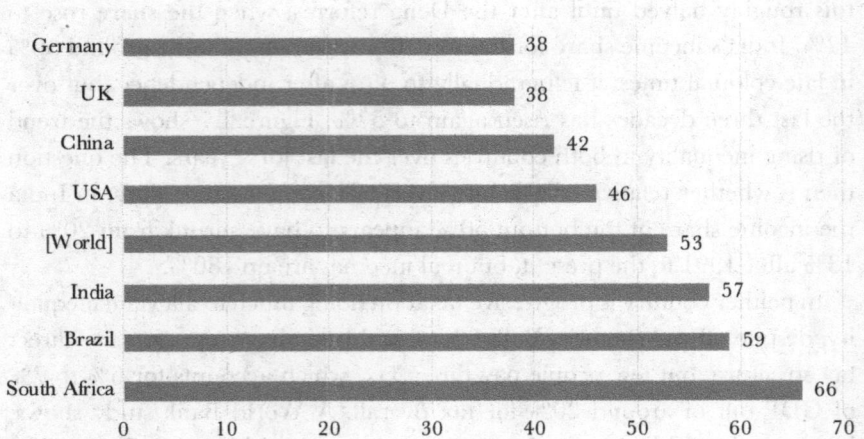

Germany 38
UK 38
China 42
USA 46
[World] 53
India 57
Brazil 59
South Africa 66

Source: World Inequality Database (2021)

1.6 Share of income to top 10% (%)

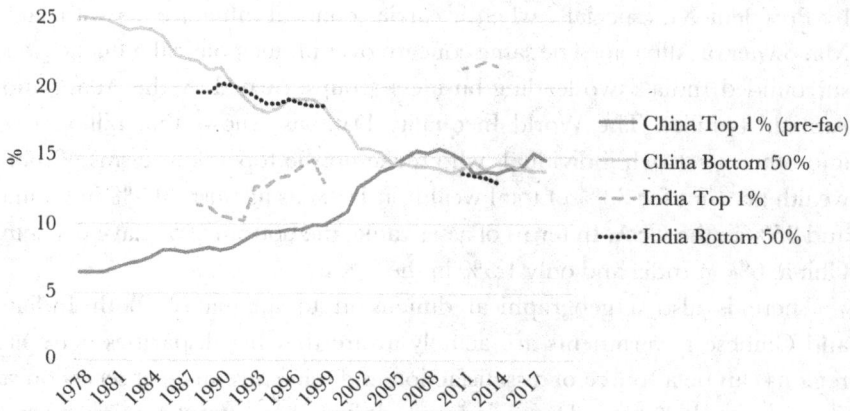

Source: World Inequality Database (2022)

1.7 Trends in income inequality (1978–2019)

One of the most visible aspects of inequality is the proliferation of billionaires: a category based not on their current income but their net worth. There are several different measures, and monetary wealth fluctuates with volatile asset markets and where owners place their wealth. A list compiled from data assembled by Forbes in 2023 suggests that there were 724 billionaires in the USA, 698 in China (plus 71 in Hong Kong) and 237 in India.[53] Another calculation, also using Forbes data, has 735 in the USA collectively worth 4.5 trillion dollars, 539 in China worth $1.7 trillion and 169 in India worth $675 billion. A separate list – the Hurun rich list – has China dominating, with 846 (plus 77 in Hong Kong), the USA with 691 and India with 187.[54] If we look at the somewhat less exclusive category of dollar millionaires in India the estimated number has grown from 34,000 in 2000 to 760,000 in 2019, with the wealth of this group increasing by almost 75% in the same period.

In practice what also matters is how the wealth was accumulated and how it is used. In the USA roughly half of billionaire wealth was inherited, and India also has its family dynasties. Chinese wealth, outside Hong Kong, is by contrast overwhelmingly first generation. In the USA much of the personal wealth comes from owners of tech companies, as in China. But much also comes from inflated property values, especially in Hong Kong. In the USA vast personal wealth is generally celebrated, but in China is being questioned

31

by President Xi, especially when it carries political influence (as with Jack Ma, owner of Alibaba). The same concern over undue political influence has surrounded India's two leading business groups, owned by the Adani and Ambani families. The World Inequality Database shows that billionaires and other asset rich individuals who make up the top 1% in terms of (net) wealth account for 33% of total wealth in India as against 30.5% in China and 35% in the USA. In terms of asset value, the bottom 50% have 6.4% in China, 6% in India and only 1.5% in the USA.

There is also a geographical dimension to inequality. Both Indian and Chinese governments are acutely aware that big disparities between regions can be a source of dissatisfaction and – in extremis – of secessionist movements. In China, Deng's reforms designed to attract foreign investment and to promote manufactured exports were built around the coastal regions and cities. It was assumed at the time that the growth would spread inland. It did, but there was a continuing gap. The authorities countered the trend with a 'go west' – and north-east – campaign. This involved mainly infrastructure development and it was partly successful such that by 2015 GDP per capita in western China had risen from 35% of coastal province levels to 54% and in the north-east from 62% to 71%. More recently, there has been a big push to build up China's 'second tier' cities – Chengdu, Xian, Wuchan, Changsa, Hefei – as a counterpoint to the coastal megacities.

India is also developing a regional dimension to inequality with the states of the south and north-west pulling away from the rest of the country: broadly, the north and east. Over the last decade the seven most southerly states have surged ahead and are now roughly 50% richer in per capita income terms than the average of the rest of India. There are awkward and potentially dangerous consequences. The economically successful states are already preparing to fight difficult battles to prevent 'levelling up' at their expense to benefit the more populous and poorer states which are also the heartland of the divisive Hindutva ideology.

Extreme inequality matters not just for political and moral reasons but because it distorts economies. Michael Pettis, for example, has argued that it is the high level of inequality in China which suppresses consumption and requires an export-led model of growth, which has in turn led to conflict with the USA because of the impact of trade on the American working class.[55]

In India too there is also a structural problem of weak domestic consumption, which undermines employment generation.

Stability and economic sustainability

Another key measure of performance relates to how the two governments have managed financial stability as they have moved to a more open and market-based system. The ability to sustain economic growth and development more widely is closely linked to the ability to manage inflation, government fiscal deficits and debt and, also, the external balance of trade and payments.

Inflation matters, since it can have big distributional effects. For people close to the poverty line, rapid inflation for items which loom large in the household budget can have a serious negative impact on real incomes. It can also have major political repercussions. We have seen in the 2024 elections in India how the BJP failed to appreciate the distress among poor Indians caused in significant part by food inflation eroding living standards. The most dangerous point in the post-1978 reforms in China occurred in 1989, when a surge in inflation caused mass discontent and protest.[56] What was described in the West as a pro-democracy movement was in large measure an expression of public anger over the decontrol of prices. Political discontent can often reach high levels because of inflation affecting one or two sensitive commodities: onions or tomatoes in India, pork in China. Nervousness about the political impact of inflation, including memories of the 1989 protests, goes some way to explain why Chinese policy has had more of a 'anti-inflation' bias than in India.

But management of inflation has been difficult in both China and India. First, food makes up around half of the Consumer Price Index and so, especially in India, supply shocks caused by adverse monsoons feed directly into inflation. Attempts by governments to manage markets through export bans or price controls require speed and skill and can often be counterproductive. Second, both countries have been growing fast and see rapid growth as necessary for poverty reduction and development. The economies are, consequently, hitting up against inflationary supply bottlenecks. And third, both countries are emerging from an era of central planning, involving controlled prices and subsidies. Monetary policy transmission mechanisms have been blunted and there is also an inflationary push when the interventions are removed. Difficult as monetary policy may be, India has moved further than China in building a high degree of de facto independence into the Reserve Bank of India (RBI), while the People's Bank of China is more reactive and subject to political pressure.[57]

The Indian authorities have long accommodated annual consumer inflation above 5%, but have tried to rein in inflation when it reaches double digits. Since 2015, inflation has averaged around 5%, and this reflects a more active approach by the RBI. In 2016, the bank set a medium-term target of 4% inflation and a range of 2% to 6%, the aim being to stabilise expectations. In China, there has been less tolerance of inflation. It was around 1% in the pre-reform period, thanks mainly to price controls. But inflation averaged 8.1% in the 1980s and reached 24% in 1995, after which the Chinese Central Bank adopted a more active anti-inflation policy using interest rates, money supply management and the toolkit of measures available to Western monetary authorities. As a result, inflation settled at a low level, around 2%, for much of this century, despite the bottlenecks which are created by high growth.

Emerging from the pandemic, however, China has a fundamentally different and dangerous monetary problem: deflation caused by chronically weak consumer demand. In 2023 and 2024, China experienced four quarters of falling prices (measured by the GDP deflator). There were several factors involved: the bursting of a property market bubble and falling house prices leading to more cautious spending by homeowners; serious debt problems in the corporate sector leading to retrenchment and reluctance to invest; general nervousness about politics at home and geopolitical conflict with the USA; and the emergence of a deflationary psychology in which consumers stop spending because they expect prices to fall in future. The authorities believe that they cannot risk an aggressive monetary policy response, since a big interest rate differential with the USA risks aggravating a problem of capital flight, dragging down the currency. Forced devaluation not only risks becoming cumulative as currency panic sets in but exposes China to accusations of currency warfare to promote its exports and, thereby, to trade barriers harming exports and manufacturing employment. The obvious alternative policy is an aggressive fiscal expansion, but the Chinese budget position is more precarious than it may seem. The government's tax base is small – around 20% of GDP as against the Organisation for Economic Co-operation and Development (OECD) average of 34%. Revenue including land sales and social security payments was 17% of GDP in 2023, 5% lower than a decade earlier. Very few people pay income tax. Without tax reform, any expansion of public spending means more borrowing.

Chinese budget numbers are difficult to interpret, but IMF figures for net central government borrowing roughly tally with separate estimates of the total budget deficit. The story broadly is that in the first two decades of the century there was little overall government borrowing (2% of GDP on average for the decade up to 2008, 1.3% for the next decade). But, in recent years, the budget position has weakened considerably with a combination of Covid spending and falling revenue because land sales have dried up with the fall of the housing market and cutbacks in new property development. In 2020 net borrowing rose to 9.7% of GDP, and in 2022 it was 7.5%, officially. Public debt, according to the IMF, rose rapidly from 34% of GDP in 2012 to 77% in 2022 and 84% in 2024. The IMF expects the ratio to rise to 120% by 2028. If the economy was growing rapidly, the government could comfortably service growing public debt. But it is now slowing.

It is, moreover, widely believed that the official figures greatly understate the true debt position, which could be closer to 130% of GDP if the liabilities of local government are considered,[58] with an overall fiscal deficit of 13% of GDP in 2024. It is normally considered a strength of the Chinese system that if the fallout from the property crisis were to spread over into the financial sector, a collapse would be avoided by the government bailing out weak banks. If it did so, however, it would add to deficit and debt levels, which already threaten the creditworthiness of public sector institutions.

The Indian government has traditionally borrowed heavily, relying on growth to service the interest. But there is a history of fiscal crises as subsidies and other spending have run ahead of tax revenues. The Manmohan Singh reforms originated in a fiscal and balance of payments crisis in the early 1990s which drew in the IMF. Successive governments have since struggled to keep the overall level of borrowing under control. In the first two decades of the century, net borrowing averaged respectively 4.5% and 6.2% of GDP, which were barely sustainable based on economic growth. Moreover, as in China, borrowing in the last few years rose rapidly with Covid. The government also embarked on a big infrastructure spending spree, with annual net borrowing in the period 2019–22 being 7.7% of GDP, 12.9, 9.6 and 9.2%. In 2022, the debt to GDP ratio was close to 83%. The overall fiscal position is felt to be reasonably comfortable, with revenues boosted by the new, indirect, goods and services tax (GST) whose yields are providing the government with a growth dividend. The government has been reining back planned fiscal deficits to a safer level of around 6% of GDP, though this will be difficult to maintain with growing demands to address chronic under-funding of health and other social provision.

One source of strength for both China and India is to have had virtually no foreign debt. China's external public debt accounts for 13.5% of GDP and India's 17%. Neither country has had cause to worry about a loss of confidence from bond vigilantes. But there are other elements of external financial vulnerability. One of these relates to the financing of external deficits. Typically, developing economies invest more than they save domes-tically and import capital from overseas with the net inflow matched by a deficit on the current account of the balance of payments. Problems arise if capital inflows dry up and foreign reserves are depleted. India has long been a capital importer and has run a matching current account deficit averag-ing 0.3% of GDP in the 1970s, 1.6% in the 1980s and then 0.9%, 1.1% and 1.7% in subsequent decades. Occasional payments crises have been the cause of the IMF programmes which have been the catalyst for Indian economic reform. In recent years, thanks to capital inflows, India's external position has been sufficiently comfortable to build up reserves of around $600 billion, almost a year's import of goods. Furthermore, vulnerability to potential external shocks is cushioned by a floating exchange rate. Still, India has not fully opened its capital account, recognising that short-term capital flows are potentially subject to shifting investor confidence and destabilising.

China, by contrast, has had a structural surplus of domestic savings over investment, leading to large current account surpluses and the accumula-tion of foreign exchange reserves in the form of dollar assets (mainly US government securities). At the end of 2023 foreign exchange reserves were worth 3.2 trillion: by far the world's largest. This may give the impression of invulnerability. But China's vast surplus savings have presented a variety of problems. In the first decade of the century, current account surpluses averaged over 5% of GDP and reached almost 10% of GDP in 2007. They manifested as large trade surpluses, which led to serious friction, especially

	China	India
Inflation (avg 2013–23) (a)	1.75	5.9
Central government debt (% of GDP) (b)	84	83
	(excl. LGFVs)	
(External debt/GDP)	14	19
External current account % of GDP average 2019–24 (c)	+1.8	−1.0
Real effective exchange rate 2005 = 100 (d)	135	115

Source: a) World Bank Open Data; b) IMF; c) IMF; d) IMF and Fidelity International

1.8 Indicators of financial stability

with the USA, which accused China of 'currency manipulation'. Indeed, the devaluation of the Chinese yuan/RMB in 1994 was a factor behind China's remarkable export performance. Under pressure from trade partners, the Chinese allowed their currency to appreciate gradually after 2005, and this was a factor in moderating export growth and the size of the trade, and current account, surpluses (see Figure 1.8).

In 2015 the IMF advised China to open its capital account and let the currency find its market value. Against expectations, there was capital flight. China lost around one trillion dollars of its foreign reserves and the currency weakened. The Chinese response was to reinstate controls and to fix the currency against a basket of currencies. China's economic troubles have since acquired an external dimension. Attempts to stimulate the economy with lower interest rates would open a big differential with the US dollar and lead to a flight of capital along with rich Chinese, unhappy at the direction of the regime, getting their money out. There are an estimated 15,000 millionaires leaving China every year, and there is an industry developing to find ways of evading capital controls. Creating a bigger interest differential would further deplete reserves and drag down the exchange rate, which might provide a welcome boost to exports but would alienate China's trade partners. China is effectively prevented from using interest rates, fiscal policy or the exchange rate to revive weak demand. For the first time in recent decades, India must appear as being in a more enviable place.

Conclusion

A comparison between China and India can be seen as a kind of controlled experiment, in which both countries started from roughly the same place, in terms of development, and at roughly the same time with roughly the same philosophy of development based on industrialisation, 'socialist' state planning and inward-looking 'self-reliance'. On almost all measures of economic and social development China is now some way ahead.

Measurement issues are however a warning against overinterpreting the data. The previous chapter highlighted the large range of difference in crossnational comparisons of GNP as a measure of economic 'size'. In this chapter, it became clear that evidence of the reduction, let alone the elimination, of poverty must be treated with care. China's much-vaunted ending of absolute poverty must be set alongside evidence of serious multidimensional poverty in rural areas. Underinvestment in Indian statistics means that there are wide disparities in evidence on poverty, nutrition and employment. It isn't clear whether the poor are getting richer or poorer. The rich are certainly getting richer in both countries, but much is hidden. Even the fashionable truism that China's economy is dangerously skewed towards investment may be based on measurement anomalies.

To the extent that the data can be trusted, it tells us that a competent but ruthless one-party state was able to embark on a path of 'reform and opening up', embracing capitalism more quickly, radically and successfully than its democratic neighbour. But the past is not necessarily a guide to the future. China finds itself potentially in a 'middle-income trap' – unable to achieve high income status as a consequence of policy failures and growth constraints. India, by comparison, appears to have the potential for rapid and sustained growth.

Lying behind the issues of economic policy, however, is a model of economic development which both countries share: a form of 'state capitalism' with a large state sector and much regulation of business but also a dynamic private sector, including numerous small companies, indigenous big business and some foreign-owned enterprises. China has a much more open economy (or did); India has (at least in theory) a more settled independent system of property rights and commercial practice. But, as the next chapter shows, what is striking is how much the two countries have in common.

2

Two versions of state capitalism

Simple labels do not do justice to complex societies and economies with different histories. But in one key respect, China and India merit the same label. 'State capitalism' is a useful shorthand to describe systems that have a powerful and active state but also a large private sector operating in a market economy. Ideologues in both countries angrily reject the term, but the point is that neither country approximates to the archetypes of a 'capitalist' or 'socialist' system (or a European style 'social democracy'). They are hybrids, with a large, flourishing private sector but extensive regulation and other state intervention; a large amount of state enterprise, often mimicking the private sector; an entrepreneurial state that can also be meddlesome and bureaucratic; and uncertain boundaries between public and private ownership. There are also elements in common with what has been called the 'developmental state', first applied to modern (post-Meiji) Japan and later South Korea.[1]

It is difficult to quantify the public/private split. In both countries, the self-employed and millions of small enterprises operate largely in competitive markets with private ownership. The same is broadly true of residential property and (in China with qualification) agriculture. The statistics covering small and medium-sized enterprises (SMEs) and the informal economy are, however, very poor in both countries and involve hundreds of millions of individuals who collectively account for almost all of employment and probably a majority of GDP. If figures are taken at face value, the Chinese private sector accounts for 60% of GDP, 70% of investment, 90% of employment and 90% of exports.[2] But many 'private' entities are offshoots of national or local state bodies. One study suggests that as many as a million Chinese firms

39

have partial local or national public sector ownership and that, properly defined, the private sector accounts at best for a 50% share of investment.[3] There is also widespread state intervention in product, capital, labour and land markets, and there is pervasive political influence on business large and small. Entrepreneurs are lauded but also expected to observe 'socialist principles'. In recent years getting rich has become less politically acceptable. The political scientist Stein Ringen has suggested that China is a 50/50 economy.[4]

India is more 'private' because it has a higher proportion of agriculture in output and employment and more marginal 'informal' activity. The Indian private sector is estimated to account for 70% of GDP (that is, economic activity other than public investment of 14% of GDP and 15% of GDP in the form of recurrent state spending), roughly 75% of investment and 90% of employment. Stated-owned enterprises (SOEs) account for an estimated 22% of GDP by asset value, 12% of turnover and 2% of value added.[5] But, as in China, there is widespread government regulation of business activity. It is sufficiently onerous to justify the popular Indian saying 'that the economy grows at night when the government goes to sleep'[6] – though recent liberalisation has enabled it to grow by day also.

State capitalism: the corporates

Any economic measurement in China and India must start with a health warning: numbers are imprecise. China's National Bureau of Statistics has done some impressive work, but in the Maoist era and more recently it has acquired a reputation for a lack of transparency in controversial or murky areas, which undoubtedly includes the definitions around 'private' and 'public'. In India, ideology is less of an issue, but there has been a gradual deterioration in economic data, with a lack of investment in survey work and data collection.

Ambiguities abound. There are large numbers of Chinese-owned companies with global presence and supply chains, some private and some state owned, some of each publicly listed in overseas stock markets. The Fortune 500 list of global companies now has more Chinese than American companies. Of the global top 100 by turnover, thirty are Chinese. But of the top thirty Chinese companies only a handful are truly private: the tech companies

40

Alibaba and JD.com and the finance companies CITIC and Ping An. The list is dominated by state-owned oil companies (e.g. Sinopec and China National Offshore Oil), state banks (the Bank of China and Agricultural Bank of China), state utilities (State Grid and China Mobile Communications) and nationalised steel. One of the most valuable private 'Chinese' companies is not mainland Chinese at all: Hon Hai is a Chinese incarnation of the Taiwanese company Foxconn.

The statistics, however, suggest that the proportion of private companies has been rising until very recently.[7] Of the top 100 Chinese companies by revenue, private companies had a minimal share in 2005 and a 4% share in 2011, which rose to 19% by 2021 and subsequently fell a little. If the value of listed companies is the criterion, the private share rose from 8% in 2010 to 50% in 2021, falling since. There are also 'mixed' ownership companies. Furthermore, the aggregate numbers understate the role of Chinese private companies in international markets as opposed to the Chinese domestic market. Leading private global companies include We Chat, owners of TikTok and Huawei, though some critics claim that both companies are subordinate to the Chinese state. Other Chinese private global companies – BYD in motor vehicles, tech companies like Zoom, Shein in fashion, TenCent in online gambling – appear to be growing in importance but take steps to camouflage Chinese ownership.

India has only Reliance – the family company currently owned by Mukesh Ambani – in the global top 100. The large Indian companies that figure in international listings tend, as in China, to be state-owned oil companies (IOC, ONGC, Bharat) or state-owned financial institutions – LIC (life insurance), State Bank of India (SBI: banking). But there is also a clutch of strong private companies, especially from the IT sector – Infosys, Tata Consultancy, Wipro, ICL. Whereas the big private Chinese companies are historically new and products of recent liberalisation, leading Indian companies are often family conglomerates going back generations, such as the Tatas, Birlas and Kirloskars. There are also rapidly multiplying numbers of second-generation businesses (such as the Ambanis) or businesses run by self-made billionaires (Gautam Adani, Ritesh Agarwal). Overall, about 90% of Indian listed firms are family owned, which helps to navigate a world of connections but can lead to bitter and damaging family feuds. Big business is however increasingly managed and led by professionals rather than

41

members of the family, and the share of the top twenty in terms of profits has shrunk from around 80% to under 40% in the five years from 2019 as assertive newcomers have made their mark.

One of the key features of Indian big business has been its close links with the state. In many cases this relationship can be described as 'crony capitalism' and involves close relationships with politicians, leading to allegations of corruption. The country's two richest businessmen, Mukesh Ambani and Gautam Adani, embody this 'crony capitalism'. Adani, who has particularly close links with the BJP leadership, is facing serious bribery charges in the USA. Even when a company has maintained a reputation for scrupulous behaviour, as with the Tata Group, it has close collaborative relationships with government. Tata has, for example, embarked on an ambitious investment programme for making semiconductors in India and, while it is taking big commercial risks, its ambitious new plant in Assam will benefit from government covering 50% of the capital costs and the state government another 20%. One crucial difference, however, between the big Chinese and Indian companies is that, while both often rely on state patronage, Indian businesspeople have less to fear from arbitrary and heavy state intervention of the kind recently experienced by China's tech sector (or, indeed, arrest for 'corruption').

Foreign private investment is essentially private sector activity, though many foreign investors have been required to undertake joint ventures with state-owned companies. Foreign direct investment (FDI) has played a bigger role in China than India. China's approach has been to welcome foreign investors with generous tax and other inducements in sectors where it contributes to exports or the provision of branded consumer goods; to allow FDI in areas like vehicles, chemicals or engineering products subject to technology transfer and joint venture agreements; and to exclude it in sensitive areas especially where 'security' in the widest sense is involved.[8] The trend since the early 1980s has been to liberalise further, latterly to include financial services, though there are growing reports of bad experiences in areas where geopolitics and security issues have intruded. India has a similar hierarchy of preference but has, overall, been less welcoming and more nationalistic though softening in recent years.

These differences are apparent in the data. World Bank measures of net inflows of foreign direct investment into China show that after being close to zero in the 1980s FDI climbed to 1% of GDP in 1990 and reached a maximum of 6% in 1994. Levels remained at 3% to 4% of GDP until 2013, after which they tailed off to 1% in 2022. The contribution of foreign investment was not only to boost capital investment but to integrate China into global supply chains. Apple is the biggest example. Recent analysis by Nicholas Lardy suggests however that multinationals are now withdrawing investment in response to geopolitical trends and Chinese sensitivities around security.[9] India has been less welcoming to FDI, and until recently the protectionism which applied to its trade policy also applied to inward investment. India had negligible net FDI until after the 1990s, gradually rising to around 2% of GDP (with 3.6% of GDP in the peak year of 2008). Despite more welcoming rhetoric, there have been numerous bad experiences with Indian officialdom over tax disputes and politically sensitive matters. Nonetheless, with India now attracting investors who are relocating from China, the historic pattern may be changing.

State capitalist finance

The mix of public and private is especially evident in financial markets. India has a sophisticated and highly entrepreneurial financial infrastructure but powerful state-owned institutions. There are over a hundred banks (as well as over 100,000 cooperatives), of which twelve are public sector, including the largest, the SBI. The state-owned banks account for just under 60% of banking assets by value. Indian state-owned banks were once regarded as dysfunctional to the point of parody and refused for many years to entertain computers. They also had balance sheets weighed down with bad loans which had been mandated by government, or good loans which were arbitrarily written off to placate some politically important interest group. That is now changing rapidly.

Following the arrival of a new RBI governor, Raghuram Rajan, in 2013, there was a concerted attempt to clean up bank and corporate balance sheets. Some twenty-seven state banks were consolidated into twelve. Bad loans were written off. The sector is now more commercial, with state banks operating profitably and with the entry of numerous new private banks, which have helped to ensure that 80% of the population has a bank account (as against barely 20% a decade ago) – in the process reducing the scale of

43

expensive moneylending. The branch network has expanded to 163,000 retail banking outlets, the world's largest, enabling more efficient saving and small-scale lending. And there is now a parallel fintech market, the third biggest in the world: part of a growing 'shadow banking' system meeting credit demand outside the more conservative practices of the traditional banks. There is a similar pattern of commercially driven public and private institutions in insurance, where the largest life insurer (of fifty-seven), by far, is the state-owned LIC, and there are seven state-owned general insurers out of thirty-three together with the sole reinsurer.

Equity markets are expanding rapidly to meet the needs of Indian business, and the largest Indian stock market (Mumbai) has 5,300 listed companies with a combined valuation of just under $5 trillion (early 2024). Until recently the market was dominated by established business houses like Tata and Reliance and by state-owned firms, but new Indian private companies are increasingly traded. There has also been a surge in retail investment in Indian shares – from 7% of the population in 2019 to 20% in 2024 – mostly through asset management companies. There has been a rapid growth of private asset managers but the largest is a subsidiary of the publicly owned SBI and another key player is Unit Trust of India, another public sector body. The new and expanding venture capital market is dominated by private, including foreign, firms, though this market dried up in 2024. And although there have been increasingly diverse equity markets, this is not true of debt markets which are dominated by state-owned banks and insurers which buy up government debt.

China, like India, has a diverse banking sector, but its big banks are among the biggest in the world in terms of assets, with a total valuation of around $40 trillion. There are hundreds of local banks, but the sector is dominated by five banks with over half of banking assets. These are all publicly owned with assets dominated by loans to state enterprises. All have private shareholdings of 10% to 40% derived from listings in Hong Kong. There are also some fully private banks, though they are tightly regulated. And in the last few years, the doors have been opened to Western investment banks. What is remarkable about China is the scale and scope of the 'shadow banking' system. A recent report by the China Banking and Insurance Regulatory Commission (CBIRC) suggested that the sector, widely defined to include all forms of credit outside banking supervision and subject to lower credit standards, had assets of around $13 trillion, just under 30% of all bank assets (and that is after a fall of 16% from a peak in 2017.[10]

Shadow banking took off on a big scale when local authorities wanted to raise money to finance local infrastructure and designed special purpose vehicles, which were snapped up by savings institutions wanting to offer better returns to savers than the official banks. The sector has widened out to meet a wide range of credit demand, especially in the property sector, and with a growing number of credit intermediaries: wealth managers, 'trusts', online lending, peer-to-peer lending.[11] One key feature of Chinese shadow banking is the active participation of the public sector banks which are seeking better returns than on their politically directed loans to state enterprises. They use off-balance sheet accounting techniques, called 'banks' shadow', designed to circumvent onerous regulation.[12] The authorities were, initially, perfectly happy to allow this shadow banking – which facilitated growth – but have recently become alarmed at the level of leverage to the overextended property sector. They have belatedly sought to regulate and rein back lending to reduce systemic risk (but in the process hitting many SMEs for whom this is the main source of credit). To maintain market discipline and to reduce moral hazard, some big institutions have been allowed to go bust using new bankruptcy legislation (another feature in common with India). Although the Chinese shadow banking system superficially resembles shadow banking in Western countries, state-owned institutions provide a large part both of credit demand and supply.

Chinese equity markets are, as with credit, on a bigger scale than in India. The two main domestic stock markets, Shanghai and Shenzhen, had, at the end of 2023, shares trading and capitalised at $7 and $4.4 trillion. President Xi has invested political capital in stock markets as a signal of encouragement to entrepreneurs and instigated new markets for stocks in high tech and in smaller companies. There is apparently an impressive diversity of stock in the two main markets, with total listings of 2,184 and 2,827 respectively. But, to an even greater extent than in India, the market is dominated by state-owned institutions: those which market their shares and the state-owned institutional investors which buy and trade them. Moreover, the markets are actively managed by regulators whenever stability is threatened by market volatility. And the state defines the priority sectors of the future, backing its judgement with investment by state-owned venture capital companies. There is more exposure to genuinely market driven investors in international capital markets via the Hong Kong market (capitalised at $30 trillion) and through listings in overseas markets (though, after Chinese companies raised around $1 trillion on US exchanges, there has been a serious push-back against Chinese companies listing in the USA because of, allegedly, poor audit standards). The Chinese government has also cooled on what it saw as an attempt to evade Chinese regulation.

The ownership structure of Chinese listed companies, as well as that of institutional investors who trade their shares, reflects the blurred boundaries between private and public which is typical of Chinese business. Listed companies typically have one-third state ownership, one-third 'institutional' ownership and the remainder private retail investors (or foreigners). The asset managers who own and trade shares numbered, in one survey, 156, of which 58 were state owned,[13] though the market has, in the last few years, opened to big foreign operators like BlackRock. The Peterson Institute in Washington has estimated that private and mixed ownership companies accounted for 25% of the market capitalisation of the hundred biggest companies on Chinese stock exchanges in 2010, but this had reached almost 70% by 2020 of which fully private companies accounted for 50% of the market.[14] Their popularity with investors owed much to a more investor-friendly approach and to their having less dependence on state bureaucracy. Since 2020, market confidence has drained away, however, and the combined share of mixed and private companies has fallen back to 50% of the market.[15]

The same mixed economy model applies to the venture capital sector. The sector is vast, with 2,250 companies raising money for early stage and growth companies. In some years, the sector raised more equity capital than its US equivalent.[16] International companies like Sequoia are prominent in the market, but it is estimated that 20% of funds are government owned and another 60% have partial state ownership.[17] Indeed, state venture capital is being used as a key driver in the government's industrial policy, filling the gap left by retreating private capital and reflecting strategic priorities rather than market returns.[18]

Property rights and labour protection

Beyond the world of finance, the public/private boundary differs greatly from sector to sector. In both countries, farming is essentially a private activity. In China the land is owned by the state, though farmers are allowed to use it on a seventy-year lease with freedom to hire and fire farm workers. What happens after the seventy-year lease is unclear,[19] and there are many cases reported of local authorities seizing land for development without adequate redress. In India, private ownership is based on legal land rights, but titles are very unclear and there is no meaningful market. Moreover, land policy varies from state to state, and some states intervene to block sales of farmland to business. The Indian government also intervenes to procure grain at fixed prices and offers extensive subsidies to farm inputs, especially fertiliser and irrigated water supplies. There is, as a result, a high level of protection which farmers have mobilised effectively to keep.

One market that is largely free in China is residential property, for which there is an active property market including buy to let, at least in urban areas (in rural areas there are some restrictions on the disposal of homes whose ownership is normally vested in the local community). Urban residential property has become the main store of savings, as well as a place to live. Speculative investment has led to a massive residential property boom which is now bust, leaving chronic oversupply and, in turn, more government regulation. India also has near-universal private ownership and an active market. But the market is seriously distorted by rent controls and the extreme inefficiency of the legal system.

Another ambiguous area is the market for labour. China's economy has benefitted hugely from the movement of rural workers to the cities. But movement is only partially free: controlled by a system of internal passports – hukou – which ties workers to their home areas when it comes to entitlement to services.[20] Workers' rights, while theoretically strong, are also not enforced, and there is widespread abuse (as with non-payment of wages), which leads to serious low-level unrest, as discussed in Chapter 3. India's system of labour market protection, by contrast, has had crippling effects on established firms, preventing rationalisation, particularly in areas where labour unions are strong. But India has long left behind the militant era of the 1960s and 1970s, when aggressive industrial action like the

47

'gerao' (imprisonment of management in their offices) was commonplace. In practice, there is little effective unionisation and labour protection for the millions of workers in 'informal' employment, but there are pockets of protected employment in government and large-scale manufacturing. For example, Apple and its contract manufacturer, Foxconn, recently encountered strong, and effective, resistance to their plans to amend labour legislation to lengthen night shifts in new factories in South India.

To get a sense of the overall 'privatisation' of the economy there is useful information in the World Inequality Database, which, among other measures, calculates the share of private wealth relative to national income (Figure 2.1). There has been a shift to larger holdings of private wealth in most countries, but in China and India it has been extreme. In 1978 the ratio of private wealth to national income was estimated at around 120% in China, but by 2020 had reached 520%. The increase was partly due to the rapid growth of home ownership and the increased share of private corporate ownership, from 0% to 30% of business assets. India is now at roughly the same overall level (560% of national income), but it has increased from a higher base: 290% in 1980. In many countries, as in Europe and the USA, the private share of net assets in national income has grown at the expense of the public share, which is now close to zero in Europe and negative in the USA. But increasing private wealth does not necessarily mean a weakening of the state. In China the state's ratio of net assets in GDP has stayed steady, while private wealth has grown around it. India too.

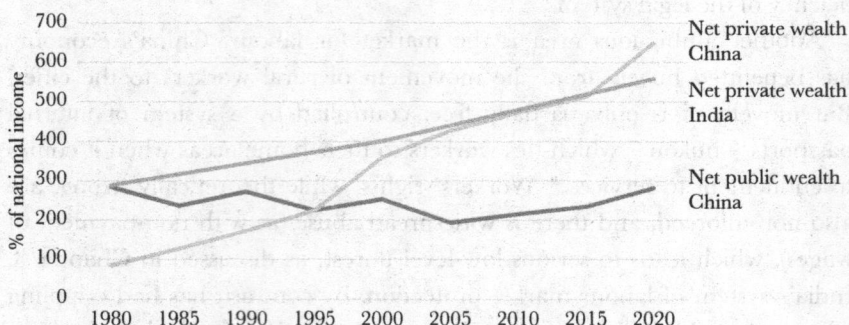

Source: World Inequality Database

2.1 The privatisation of assets

'State capitalism' is a useful shorthand to describe the system in which the state and private sector coexist, compete and complement each other. They are entangled in both countries because of a process by which a system originally based on state planning and public ownership has allowed or encouraged markets and the private sector to operate. Both countries have evolved a market-based system with a thriving private sector and growing private wealth, alongside a strong state as a result of what in China is called 'reform and opening out': the overlapping processes of market liberalisation and globalisation. These processes have shifted the boundary between 'state' and 'capitalism'. I shall now try to unpack them.

Liberalisation

Liberalisation is an umbrella term for the removal or lightening of state regulation and/or the freeing up of markets to allow for more competition. Both are associated with a shift from public to private ownership – though not necessarily so since, as noted earlier, state-owned entities can be highly commercial, and in China often are. Starting with Deng's reforms in the early 1980s, China experienced several decades of far-reaching liberalisation in almost all areas of economic life, though in the last decade the pace has slowed and arguably has gone into reverse, with increased regulation and direction in some sectors. India, by contrast, has pursued a more hesitant and inconsistent process of liberalisation, reflecting the enthusiasms and compulsions of various democratically elected governments. Essentially there have been three phases of liberalisation: Indira Gandhi's Congress government in the early 1980s, the Narasimha Rao/Manmohan Singh Congress administration of the early 1990s and the BJP administration after 2013.

The Deng-era liberalisation in China has been discussed above and does not require further extensive treatment here.[21] But some historical context is necessary. The process began essentially in 1978 with the adoption of the 'Four Modernisations' slogan and a meeting of the 11th Central Committee which cleared the way for ownership and management reforms, decentralisation of economic decision making and price reform, initially to favour agriculture. The trigger for reform was partly political – the defeat of the Maoist Gang of Four – but partly economic – an incipient balance of payments crisis.

There were several striking features of the Chinese reforms. One was a willingness to decentralise power and decision making radically so that most decisions on credit and investment or the formation of new companies could be made at the level of local government. One consequence was an explosion of Township and Village Enterprises (TVEs) – in effect, small firms. Second, and related, the Deng approach involved a willingness to experiment and learn by experience: 'crossing the river by feeling the stones', as Deng put it. Practicality was more important than dogma, with a pragmatic approach to private enterprise and markets: 'It doesn't matter what colour the cat is provided it catches mice.'[22]

Third, the changes involved a political as much as an economic revolution, with China adopting the 'development state' approach familiar in East Asia, and the Communist Party becoming the champion of economic growth. There was some resistance to rapid policy reform, reflected in the arguments between Deng and his more conservative colleague Chen Yun, which came to be known as the 'builders versus balancers' debate. There were also periods of temporary retreat, as when rapid price decontrol led to a spurt of inflation, one of the contributory factors behind the events in Tiananmen Square in 1989. But, for at least three decades, there was little serious resistance to the concept of 'reform and opening up'.

Fourth, the early impact of reforms was in agriculture, where farmers could benefit from the new Household Responsibility System, with freedom to operate land outside of collective farming – de facto private ownership – and to be able to market surpluses. The rapid growth of food production (and consumption) greatly enhanced the popularity of the reforms. Between 1978 and 1990, the share of foodstuffs traded in competitive markets rose from 8% to 80%.[23] And, last, from early in the reform process, Deng and his successors were convinced of the need to learn from abroad through foreign collaboration and investment and to succeed in international trade. Globalisation and liberalisation went hand in hand, as we see below.

The early experience of liberalisation in India was very different. In 1981, India was obliged to turn to the IMF for assistance in managing a balance of payments problem. This event provided an opening for reform-minded officials, businesspeople and external funders of India in the IMF and World Bank. There was a broad consensus on the need to reduce the panoply of controls and regulations that was depressing investment, causing massive inefficiency and fuelling rampant corruption.[24] Businesses required permits to undertake a wide variety of activities, from making new investment to closing branches, carrying out corporate takeovers or mergers and even making an electricity connection. Such a system may have been economically crippling but it enjoyed political support, including from businesses who benefitted and officials whose palms were greased. It required an external force to create change.

As part of IMF conditionality, the government (under Indira Gandhi) accepted the need to liberalise the economy. It did so by lifting some of the controls on business: for example, removing the requirement for government permits to allow investment in new capacity, cutting bureaucratic processes around importing equipment and removing some of the bias against exports. Initially thirty-two industries were delicensed. The beneficiaries were established big businesses who were able to expand and make bigger profits. The liberalisation was limited and provided more rather than less protection against foreign competition, but was seen as pro-business and sufficient to stimulate higher growth and to create some momentum behind further gradual lifting on controls.[25]

The process was accelerated in 1991, when another balance of payments crisis led to another IMF loan and more far-reaching reforms. The official who negotiated the 1981 agreement with the IMF – Manmohan Singh – was made Finance Minister and had a clear view of what was needed to liberalise the system:[26] virtual abandonment of the industrial licensing system, reduction in import barriers and export subsidies, together with rupee devaluation. These reforms were hailed as the end of the 'permit raj'.[27] There was an upsurge in investment from new entrants to the market, while established firms were able to rationalise their operations. But, as the economist Vijay Joshi has pointed out, while there was a lot of new and innovative business activity, competition remained weak, and the established firms were able to entrench their monopoly positions.[28] In addition, there was no willingness to attack the vested interests in labour and land markets or to tackle inefficient state-owned enterprises.

There was liberalisation in both countries but, at least until the last decade, Chinese reforms were fundamentally different in scale and scope, pace and radicalism.[29] An obvious difference is that India's democratic system, with a multiplicity of interests at every level, made rapid movement difficult.

51

By contrast, a key element in Dengist thinking was that economic liberalisation could be kept distinct from political liberalisation. Reformers could open China to free markets, provided that the control of the Communist Party remained intact. Unpopular reforms could be pushed through. Chinese reformers like Zhu Rongji in the 1990s were able to oversee the breaking up of the 'iron rice bowl', whereby vast state enterprises provided, in effect, a welfare state for their employees but at great cost to productivity and the viability of the enterprises. Between 1997 and 2005 the employment in state-owned enterprises fell from 70 to 37 million.[30]

There are political limits to reform even in an authoritarian state, as Deng discovered with his hasty decontrol of prices in 1989. But the Chinese one-party system did not have such inconveniences as elections, noisy opposition parties and painful coalition building and, as a last resort, could use force to push through unpopular change. Nonetheless, the Chinese evolved a spontaneous but effective system where the incentives were for local officials to compete to develop and take risks in raising capital for investment. By contrast, India's 'top down' reforms ran up against institutional inertia, individual decision makers had little incentive to change unless others did and unilateral unpopular decisions had a political cost. Gradually, however, initiatives emerged at state level where local politicians – in Gujarat and Andhra Pradesh, for example – began to innovate and receive political credit for doing so.

Another key difference is that China started liberalisation with agriculture, where a rapid introduction of markets produced more and more varied food, better farm incomes – removing millions from poverty – and a labour supply for manufacturing in the cities as more efficient farming displaced labour. The share of employment in agriculture fell from 70% to 60% in a decade. The first stage of economic reform brought tangible benefit for hundreds of millions of people and genuine popularity for the regime, which encouraged reformers to press on. By contrast, successive Indian governments started by freeing up controls on big business and have been unwilling to tackle the vested interests in agriculture: the subsidised inputs to prosperous farmers and the resistance of landlords to meaningful land reform.

Also worthy of note is that, from early in the reform process, Chinese policy was outward facing, looking to foreign markets, technology and capital and reflecting Deng's belief in learning from abroad. From the mid-1980s development was 'export led', as the experiment with incentives for SEZs brought large inflows of capital from the Chinese diaspora to take advantage of abundant cheap labour. Exploiting a comparative advantage in labour-intensive manufacturing enabled China to ramp up from virtually no competitive exports before the reform period to become the world's largest exporter by value in 2009 and to be the 'workshop of the world'. Nothing comparable took place in India. The liberalisation reforms removed some of the serious disincentives to export, but exports were not seen as a major source of growth. And, while China was using foreign investment to gain access to technology and expertise, India was a slow convert to the idea that foreign investment could benefit the economy. Liberalising ministers had to battle deep political suspicion and vested interests among domestic producers.

Within the last decade, however, there have been signs of the Indian tortoise quickening its pace and the Chinese hare losing its way. Ambivalence about liberalisation in China came to the surface when President Xi assumed leadership. There was a fulsome verbal commitment to markets and some technical improvements to make corporate bond markets more transparent and bankruptcy easier. But there were already signs of liberalisation fatigue in the reluctance to allow big, failing enterprises to close. One big factor in sowing doubts about markets was China's experience of large-scale corruption involving business. Business was often blamed for the use of bribes to speed up decisions and, while Chinese corruption appears to be less damaging to growth than elsewhere, Xi saw it as part of a general loss of discipline with the weakening of party values and state control.[31]

Another key turning point in thinking about liberalisation came in 2015, when China accepted IMF advice to liberalise foreign exchange markets. The policy led to capital flight and a panic in financial markets, which was only stopped by stronger controls. Capital market liberalisation is a big step which requires complete confidence among investors that their property rights will be respected within the framework of the 'rule of law'. And that, in turn, required political liberalisation.[32] This was not the direction in which Xi's China wanted to go (though even in democratic India, the government has retained capital controls for fear of the volatility which free capital movements could bring).

President Xi seems to have retained a residual belief in markets and business, but liberalisation had to be reconciled with a more egalitarian

'Common Prosperity' and state intervention against 'disorderly capital'. There is considerable cognitive dissonance between reassuring words and 'anti-business' deeds. Successful entrepreneurs can expect to be monitored. Zealous officials attack the 'financial elite' and demand cuts to bonuses and curbs on 'high-end taste'. The fierce crackdown on corruption, widely defined, leads to risk-averse behaviour in business. There have been tough and arbitrary regulatory interventions to curb the power of big internet companies, as well as private tutoring, gaming and other activities deemed unwholesome. Furthermore, the growing cold war with the USA has moved priorities away from economics to security and to a Chinese preoccupation with 'self-reliance' in a wide variety of sectors, as dictated by the government. Liberalisation is no longer a key policy objective, and successful private enterprise is suspect. As a result, venture capital and private equity markets have dried up. Unicorns are few.

By contrast, liberalisation has gained momentum in India. Narendra Modi's BJP government launched practical liberalisation initiatives such as the deregulation of real estate transactions and facilitating orderly insolvency and bankruptcy. However, it has avoided many politically sensitive issues in labour and labour markets and has backed off from agricultural reform. The crucial change, however, is what seems to be a genuinely more welcoming approach to trade and foreign investment – globalisation – at a time when China is turning inwards for both geopolitical and ideological reasons. But even here there is plenty of nuance and qualification. For example, the Manmohan Singh reforms had cut the average tariff from 125% in 1991 to 13% in 2014, but over the next decade the average tariff crept back up to 18%, as incumbent firms re-established trade protection.[33] And that, in turn, has a lot to do with resistance to the 'creative destruction' of markets: exit as well as entry.

Free entry, blocked exit

Arvind Subramanian, former Chief Economic Adviser of India, has made an important distinction within a process of liberalisation between entry and exit policies.[34] India and China have both swept away many barriers to entry: allowing private firms into a wide range of sectors; liberalising inflows of imports, capital and technology from abroad; making it easier to set up and expand businesses. What has not happened – more in India than China – is what the economist Joseph Schumpeter called 'creative destruction': closing down 'zombie' enterprises; privatising companies which have no clear rationale for public ownership; ending expensive subsidy programmes. There have been some steps in that direction, in the form of laws facilitating bankruptcy and the clean-up of state banks' balance sheets. But there is still force in Subramanian's aphorism characterising Indian experience with liberalisation as moving from 'socialism with limited entry to capitalism without exit'.

India has long had a substantial list of public sector enterprises which are deemed to be 'sick'. Legislation was introduced in 1983 to identify and designate 'sick' nationalised companies, with the implication, rarely acted on, that something should be done about them. In 2013, sixty-four companies were designated on a more precise definition of 'loss making' (losses more than 50% of net worth). These included Eastern Coalfields (78,000 employees), Bharat Coking Coal (65,000) and Air India (28,000). Seventeen of the sixty-four were designated for closure and a few, like Air India, for privatisation. But others were added, and by 2019 there were fifty-six companies on the list. It has proved difficult, politically, to close big employers. Unions mobilise and politicians rally to protect threatened jobs. And privatisation has proved slow; Air India was eventually sold to Tata in 2022, almost twenty-five years after privatisation was mooted as the best option. Privatised Air India is expanding but still loss-making. There are also genuinely tricky problems: for example, heavily loss-making electricity distribution companies have no likely buyers, nor can they simply be shut down.

In some cases, the government has found it impossible to exit from expensive subsidy schemes of dubious value. Fertiliser subsidies mainly benefit richer farmers on irrigated land. The long-term environmental damage of excessive fertiliser use is considerable, and a substantial part of the subsidy goes to fertiliser plants, which have costs well above international prices. In addition, some food crops enjoy large subsidies through the operation of price support designed to ensure that India has adequate food supplies, even when stocks are well above prudent levels. In some cases the subsidies are seriously perverse, as with water-intensive sugar production in water-scarce states. The fact that the powerful BJP regime was forced to back down from agricultural reform in the face of street protests speaks volumes about the power of farming interests.

There is also a problem of 'sick' enterprises in the private sector which are kept alive by bank credit from state banks. Some firms have been kept alive by bank loans to help them pay interest and stay technically solvent. The banking system has, consequently, accrued a serious level of non-performing loans, much of it hidden.[35] As reported earlier, an attempt has been made in recent years to establish honest estimates of non-performing loans, which turned out to be around three times larger than the RBI had estimated. A balance sheet clean-up, initiated by RBI governor Raghuram Rajan, has greatly improved the position. Nonetheless bad practice persists. Powerful industrialists have been encouraged to borrow heavily from banks for government-favoured projects, mainly infrastructure. State bank managers have been unable to refuse to extend credit or to enforce debt service. When banks have been pressed by the RBI to improve their lending performance, the subsequent credit curbs have mainly affected SMEs and small farmers. Furthermore, the – welcome – introduction of stronger bankruptcy and insolvency law, designed to help creditors pursue defaulters and to force insolvent 'zombie' firms to close, is working mainly against small firms. The big industrialists can stall action in India's inefficient courts indefinitely.

China has its own version of the exit problem, but there have been periods, already described, when a ruthless, uncompromising approach was taken to axing giant state-owned firms through privatisation and rationalisation. One of the legacies of the massive infrastructure boom after 2008 has however been a big increase in loss-making companies with excess capacity, some of which have been kept alive by credit from state-owned banks, which consequently have unhealthy levels of non-performing loans. One of the main concerns of the early days of the Xi presidency was how to manage this legacy. Holding companies under the State-owned Assets Supervision and Administration Commission of the State Council (SASAC) were placed in charge of amalgamating firms on a sector basis and rationalising them. There was a lot of reallocating staff but few closures. The steel industry limped along with serious excess capacity and heavy losses.

One of the government's main methods for strengthening commercial discipline has been to promote the corporate bond market and to improve its transparency through ratings. There were some cases of companies defaulting on their bonds, leading to closure. Initially these defaults were almost entirely confined to the private sector, but in 2020 total defaults exceeded

150 billion RMB, of which half was in state-owned enterprises. The courts are now also giving effect to easier bankruptcy laws introduced in 2014. In 2020, they approved 30,000 cases. Nonetheless, public sector managers have been left confused by contradictory pressures: to be ruthlessly commercial but also to follow the guidance of party committees now embedded in every large firm and whose instincts may be to avoid trouble.

The crisis in the property market is bringing these contradictions to a head, and severely testing the commitment to market discipline. The property sector, widely defined, accounts for over a quarter of the Chinese economy, and the collapse of the sector could do great damage and have global implications. There is an enormous excess supply of apartments: perhaps as much as 20% of the stock is unoccupied, some in vast 'ghost' cities. The developers have built ahead of demand and can no longer raise capital since local authorities, who finance a lot of development, can no longer sell land in a depressed market. The glut is driving down house prices, which in turn seriously affects consumer confidence. Leading developers like Evergrande and Country Garden have failed to honour bond payments and are, in effect, insolvent.

There are no easy ways to exit a collapsing property boom beyond consolidating and then isolating and writing down the bad debts. The government has been trying to manage this process carefully to ensure that house prices do not fall too far. It has also been working to ensure that the honest valuation of bad debt in the banking system does not render major banks insolvent, dragging the country into a financial crisis. A Hong Kong court has declared Evergrande bankrupt, presumably with Beijing approval, which suggests that the regime is (up to a point) willing to let markets work and failing companies go down. One technique available to the Chinese regime, but less accessible in democratic India, is to criminalise commercial failure. Owners of failing property companies, for example, are likely to face trial for 'corruption', leading to long prison sentences or, possibly, a bullet in the back of the head: a Chinese solution to the exit problem.

In other sectors too, the Chinese authorities are following what could be called a Schumpeterian approach, using market discipline to drive out weak companies. The electric vehicle (EV) sector has expanded massively on the back of government subsidy, creating a large amount of overcapacity with many small, unprofitable companies. The Chinese solution, already used in shipbuilding and solar panels, is to allow the weaker, loss-making firms to go bust and to consolidate the industry around a small number of highly competitive firms. These then become national champions, which grow stronger with aggressive exporting and large-scale reinvestment. In sectors where China is developing global leadership such a ruthless approach to exit is being pursued. But it is the state which picks the sectors to receive the 'Schumpeterian treatment' and then how and by how much.

Globalisation

One of the underlying themes of liberalisation in both countries has been an opening up, especially to trade and foreign investment. Globalisation is partly driven by ideas of economic efficiency, competition and lower costs, though these are less relevant for countries with big internal economies like China, India and the USA.[36] Also substantial are the benefits from the flow of technologies and ideas. But opening potentially contradicts the pre-reform belief in self-reliance. The merits of self-reliance and security may now be returning in a world where globalisation is no longer accepted so readily as economically beneficial and the world's leading superpower is no longer committed to it.[37] There is also tension, reflected in the phrase 'state capitalism', between a strong national and ideological agenda and the wider global interest. I will look now at how these contradictions have played out so far in relation to China and India.

One simple metric is the share of trade in GDP. The World Bank measures the exports and imports of goods and services, and data is available for 2022. For comparative purposes, a big continental economy like the USA has a ratio of 25% and a medium-sized trading economy like the UK has a ratio of 70%. India's ratio is 49% and China's 38%. In both cases, the figure is much smaller if PPP figures are used for GDP. The Chinese figure is also somewhat distorted by the large amount of double counting within supply chains and the importance of trade with Hong Kong. The trend for the same metric shows that China's trade ratio rose from 8% in 1978 to 38%, while world trade as a share of world GDP jumped from 3% to 74% – consistent with the idea of China opening in a globalising world. Indian data suggests that the ratio barely changed from 1950 to 1990 (around 17%) and then increased sharply to 49% after the period of opening and liberalisation.

Another number derived from trade data is the share of exports in world trade: a measure of trade competitiveness. China has around 14% of world merchandise exports (with an additional 3.3% from Hong Kong) and is the world's biggest exporter, a massive change from the 1% in pre-reform 1978. The figures are less if we include trade in services and less again if we allow for imported inputs. By contrast, India's share at the beginning of the reform process in 1978 was as low as 0.5% and, while the share has increased to 1.8%, the level is still low for a country of India's size and importance (India is 18th in rank). The story is clear: both countries have opened their economies to trade, but China is far ahead in its share of world trade.

I discussed China's success in manufacturing exports and India's failure in the previous chapter, but some additional points can be made. China's remarkable export performance stems in part from a series of policy reforms at the early stage of the reform process: phasing out of administrative controls, removal of mandatory import and export prices, decentralisation of decision making, tariff cuts, removal of controls on imported inputs and welcoming foreign investment in export sectors. There was also a hefty devaluation of a third in 1994 (and that after a decade in which the real effective exchange rate fell by 60%). The SEZs also provided generous incentives to overseas companies, mainly from the diaspora, to export to world markets. India did some of these things but later, less and slower.

China managed to move rapidly into labour-intensive manufactures and India did not. Between 1980 and 2007, China increased its share of world trade in clothing and garments from 1.3% to 37.6%, while India's share rose from 1.4% to 3.2%. China employed vast numbers in factories at higher productivity than in agriculture. It became integrated into global supply chains, developed the understanding of how to operate high-performance manufacturing systems and acquired foreign exchange to finance big increases in imports without running into balance of payments constraints. India missed out almost completely.

It was only after the reforms of the 1990s that India became serious about trade. Before 1990 the share of exports (goods and services) in GDP had been stuck at around 6% for forty years; India was one of the most closed economies in the world. The Manmohan Singh reforms took the figure to around 22% in 2022. Tariffs were slashed from 145% in 1990 to 10% for manufactures in 2013 and from 134% to 33% for agriculture. Quantitative restriction on manufactures were swept away. India was able to boost exports substantially but, unlike China, it largely missed the boat for manufactures. Instead, export growth was in service sectors like IT.

The two countries' approaches to foreign investment follow a similar pattern. China welcomed, initially, the Chinese diaspora and, later, Western multinationals that met the country's criteria for priority sectors, notably transfer of technology. There was a surge of net FDI after 1990. The flow peaked at 6% of GDP in 1994 but has been steadily trending down to about 1%, reflecting investments overseas by Chinese multinationals and disinvestment by Western companies nervous about the impact of deteriorating US–China relations. India, after the 1991 reforms, switched from a positive to a negative list (that is, no restrictions except for a few sensitive areas like defence industries). FDI took off in this century, reaching 6% of GDP, net, in 2008 and maintaining a level around 2% of GDP since. Another way to assess the degree of openness to foreign investment is to look at the stock of FDI by country, stripping out tax distorted flows.[38] On this measure, the USA is by far the largest host to inward investment (around $10.4 trillion in 2022), followed by China ($3.8 trillion and another $2.1 trillion in Hong Kong). India is a long way behind, with $500 billion.

Trade and investment are not the only indicators of globalisation. People movements in and out for business, study, work and tourism are important for engagement with the world. Before the pandemic China was able to boast that 155 million Chinese people travelled abroad in 2019 (and returned), mainly for tourism, three times the number in 2010. India, by comparison, had few overseas travellers, 20 million a year. Since the pandemic, overseas travel has fallen sharply in both countries, and there has been a rise in domestic tourism (2.8 billion trips in China in 2023 and 1.7 billion in India). There are also diasporas that provide remittances, sources of capital, ideas and – as with the Indian diaspora in the USA and UK – influence. Estimates vary widely, depending on the definition, from 18 to 32 million for overseas Indians and 40 to 60 million overseas Chinese. Both governments devote energy to cultivating them.

Transmission of digital data, information and ideas is at the heart of globalisation, but information also impinges on the role of the state, especially in China, where the Communist Party has a monopoly of power and opinion on many subjects. India is also moving in the direction of internet control for political reasons. At the end of 2023 internet penetration, globally, was around 66%, with most developed economies close to saturation (the USA rate is over 90%). China had achieved 76% and India 53%, each of which in absolute terms represents by far the largest number of internet users.

In both countries, however, the contribution made by the internet to global connectivity and the liberalisation of individual lives has been balanced against the threat it poses to government and the powers of the state. From the outset, a central objective of Chinese policy has been to control access to the internet. Western internet companies have found it almost impossible to operate even when not banned. Commencing in the year 2000, a 'Golden Shield' – later the 'Great Firewall' – was created to identify, intercept and block unwelcome information.[39] Initially the system operated with some subtlety, to discourage access rather than to inhibit it altogether. But after 2015 state controls were tightened in a variety of ways, which I explore further below. The crucial point for now is that these measures have a real cost in inefficiency, demonstrating how security is replacing economic priorities.[40]

India's system of control is far less comprehensive and sophisticated (so far). That may be because India had lagged in internet penetration (it was only 10% in 2010). The main internet companies like Google and Meta operate in India. But there are growing reports of the internet being shut down, sometimes for extended periods. Kashmir, for example, had a 550-day blackout. There have been reports of websites being closed and internet companies being pressed to modify content. India is a long way from creating its own internet, but the direction of travel has been clear, at least when the BJP government had largely untrammelled power. Legislation has been passing through the Indian parliament to establish tighter government control over information, but a more robust opposition and more confidently independent courts could blunt its impact. Both countries are demonstrating that 'state capitalism' is compatible with the internet world, but the state is becoming more intrusive and freedoms more constrained.

Overall, the approach of both China and India to globalisation has become much more ambiguous. Chinese pronouncements extol free trade and globalisation and place China at the centre of them, in contrast with the protectionist and nativist policies attributed to the USA. But even before Donald Trump became President, China had identified greater self-sufficiency as a key objective in many sectors. Trump's protectionism and Joe Biden's subsequent attempts to 'delink' on security grounds have reinforced the security dimension of Chinese policy. Foreign investors are welcomed but also face more difficulties operating in China. Chinese overseas investment is being made unwelcome in Western economies and questioned in China too. Overseas travel has fallen sharply since the pandemic. Information and data flows are restricted more tightly than ever.

In India too, opening out is heavily qualified. Despite a radical cutting of tariffs and controls, protectionism is still strong, and both agriculture and traded services are heavily protected. Foreign investment is welcomed, even courted, but faces many obstacles in practice. India remains reluctant to enter liberalising trade deals where this entails serious competition (especially with China). Nonetheless India is gradually opening, while China appears to be heading in the opposite direction.

Delivering infrastructure

Nowhere in the economy are state and private business, markets and regulation, more entangled than in the creation and maintenance of infrastructure. Until recently the public sector was seen as the natural provider of infrastructure and public investment the main financial vehicle. This changed in the 1980s with privatisation, including the regulation of private natural monopolies, as in the UK. The decision to use the private sector in this way was partly motivated by a desire to avoid accumulating government debt. But there was also a recognition that business had expertise in project management. The two factors came together with the concept of PPP: public private partnership.

PPP has been defined in different ways, and the mix of public and private varies from country to country and project to project, with different combinations in design, construction, operation and financing. China started to use PPP in the early 1980s (while still relying mainly on public sector financing mechanisms like local government land sales) and India a decade later. Both countries now have hundreds of projects at various stages of completion. Of the global total of committed PPP investment in 2022, 33% was in China and 13% in India.[41] China dominates public–private projects outside of the developed world (Figure 2.2).

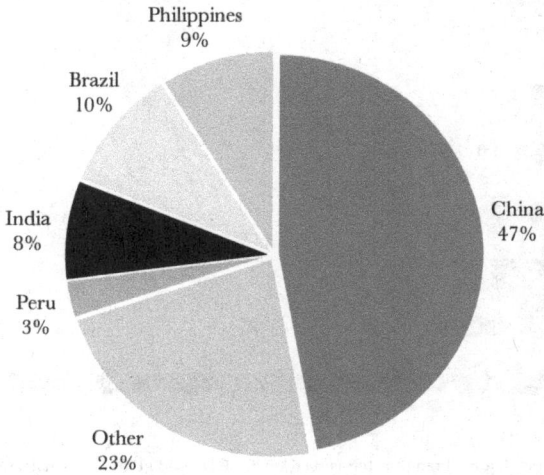

Source: World Bank PPI Database 2023, Chart 3

2.2 Investment commitments in infrastructure projects with private partners (low + middle income)

What is striking is the sheer volume of infrastructure investment. Most countries allocate roughly 2.5% to 4% of GDP to infrastructure investment. China has been investing roughly 8% of GDP (2008), recently declining to 6.5% (2021) but with a peak of around 24% in 2016: 'off the chart' as one observer commented.[42] If we take transport as an example, China has been in a different league from other countries, including India (Figure 2.3). But within the last few years India has also been investing heavily in transport infrastructure.[43]

Investment is the input. What of the output? There are some strikingly visible signs of new infrastructure, such as the Chinese high-speed trains and new airports and motorways, as well as improvements felt tangibly: fewer power cuts, faster telecommunications and drinkable tap water. The current Indian government has also promoted large-scale infrastructure investment, and there are some impressive results, especially for transport projects. But it is difficult to measure the overall quality of infrastructure. One of the more comprehensive measures is the rating of the World Economic Forum, which measures overall performance by a dozen infrastructure metrics, though most are based on qualitative judgements.[44]

USA ▮ 0.5
France ▮ 0.8
UK ▮ 0.9
Japan ▮ 1.1
India ▮ 1.1
Korea ▮ 1.3
China ▮ 5.5

0   1   2   3   4   5   6

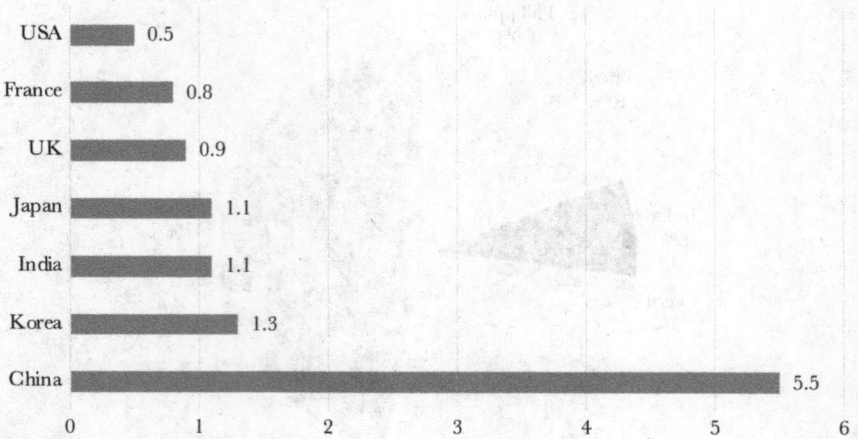

Source: Statistical Brief (Future Transport Infrastructure), OECD and ITF International Transport Forum, June 2024

2.3 Share of GDP invested in transport infrastructure (2018–22 average %)

The results for 2019 suggest that China has matched US levels for air-port connectivity (as has India), electricity supply quality and access, road connectivity and liner shipping access. Otherwise, China ranks ahead of India but behind the USA on six of twelve metrics. It is somewhat ahead of India on almost all remaining measures. India is particularly deficient in access to safe drinking water and China lags on railroad density (its high-speed trains are isolated exceptions in a generally poor network). In terms of overall ranking, the most recent set of indicators, using different weights, puts Switzerland at the top of sixty-three countries, with the USA at five, the UK at sixteen, China at nineteen and India at fifty. That story is consist-ent with what we know of the massive infrastructure investment in China in this century and the fact that the Indian infrastructure boom is currently underway.

The emphasis in both countries has recently shifted from physical to digital infrastructure. As noted above, internet usage is significantly higher in China, but mobile use has taken off to a remarkable degree in India. China currently has an estimated 1.6 billion mobile users and India 1.3 billion. China is far ahead of the rest of world in terms of contactless payments – China is largely a cash-free economy – with 87% of the population using contactless in 2022 as against 43% in the USA and 40% in India. But in terms of the volume of transactions India has far more – 48.6 billion in 2022 as opposed to 17.5 billion – this being on account of the empowerment, by opening bank accounts and welfare payments, of poor individuals and families who spend large numbers of small sums through their phones. It may be that the Indian Stack will soon enable India to match China in digital infrastructure.

Corruption, governance and state capitalism

The process of liberalisation and the exposure to international standards through globalisation should, in principle, have reduced the incidence of corruption caused by attempts to circumvent controls and to meet scarcity. In practice, the murky dividing line between public and private and the continued existence of a large state involved in public procurement and regulation have created new opportunities for corruption. Rapid growth has also generated larger potential gains from graft. In both China and India, in very different political systems, corruption appears to be a massive source of concern.

Corruption comes in different forms, but attempts have been made to provide standard international comparisons.[45] The Transparency International Perception Index gives China a ranking 65 out of 150 countries and India 85, where the lower is better (Denmark and Finland lead, with the UK at 18th). China and India rank above other big 'state capitalist' countries like Brazil, Indonesia and Russia, but well below all developed countries – the nearest in a league table of venality being Italy at 56th. There is another, multivariable index compiled as part of the Global Risk Index, which includes not just corruption perception but also experience of it, legal enforcement and transparency.[46] China does much worse on this index (113 out of 180 countries) and India better (rank 90). Of other comparators, Brazil ranks 85, Indonesia 106 and Russia 127. The ranking of both countries has remained roughly constant in recent years.

The two countries differ enormously, however, in how they approach corruption. Xi has made fighting corruption one of his signature policies and has been extremely active in disciplining party members accused of corruption. Under his predecessor, corruption was widely assumed to be endemic, and one exposé pointed to the corrupt links between business and leading figures, including the prime minister's wife.[47] In the years 2018–23 there are reported to have been around 600,000 annual cases of party members being punished for what is described as corruption, with many imprisoned. A new law in 2022 set out seventy-eight types of white-collar crime that are now being prosecuted. These include forms of non-monetary corruption, such as favouring relatives. The problem with interpreting this crackdown is that corruption is very loosely defined and is known to include many who are being purged because their political loyalty is being questioned. Nor is much distinction made between large-scale corruption and petty misdemeanours. Because there is no free press, and only erratic bursts of revealing information on Chinese blog sites, it is difficult to assess the actual scale of corruption and the effectiveness of the President's anti-corruption offensive.

One big question for China was how large and growing amounts of corruption are compatible with rapid economic development, since economic research suggests that 'rent-seeking' by business is not compatible with market-oriented, entrepreneurial behaviour and is economically inefficient.[48] One answer is that there are different types of corruption with different impacts. The case has been made that Chinese corruption is primarily in the form of facilitative 'speed money', which rewards officials for speeding up decisions.[49] That is not to say 'speed money' is harmless, since there is an incentive to officials to slow development so they can then be bribed to quicken it up.

A contrast is made, however, with 'extractive corruption', involving stealing public assets or threatening those who do not pay bribes with harassment. Yet another abuse is 'collusive corruption', when officials or politicians agree to 'look the other way' to allow theft of public assets or non-compliance with regulation. In fact, what does come to the surface in publicised dismissals or trials is that there is also plenty of 'extractive' or 'collusive' corruption in China. The recent dismissal of the defence minister revealed large-scale 'extractive' corruption from public procurement even in such sensitive areas as nuclear weapons supplies.

In contrast to China, India's inquisitive press has been able to expose and publicise much corrupt behaviour, even if prosecution and conviction are rare. There are some detailed accounts of how development has opened new opportunities for corruption, as in the allocation of spectrum licenses or the granting of permissions for extracting scarce supplies of building materials for the rapidly expanding construction industry or mining.[50] Where complex systems depend on integrity and trust, like higher education examinations marking and grading, corruption can become rampant once trust is lost.[51] Other complex systems involving detailed technical knowledge, like the management of big irrigation schemes and the allocation of water supplies to farmers, can evolve a dense network of corrupt transactions which are difficult to trace.[52]

One particularly pernicious phenomenon in India is the nexus between politicians and organised crime resulting from the financing requirements of democratic elections. There has long been a reciprocal connection between politicians and firms in construction and property development. The mutual interest is obvious. For serious criminals, there is the additional attraction in gaining immunity from criminal prosecution while they are in elected office. And, for politicians, criminals bring not just money but muscle to intimidate opponents. In some states the criminalisation of politics has become embedded, with large numbers of elected members of legislatures facing charges of murder, rape, kidnapping and comparable offences[53] (Figure 2.4). One irony about India is that sitting atop a cesspool of corruption and criminality have been two of the most incorruptible and austere politicians anywhere: Manmohan Singh (the former Congress Prime Minister) and now Narendra Modi.

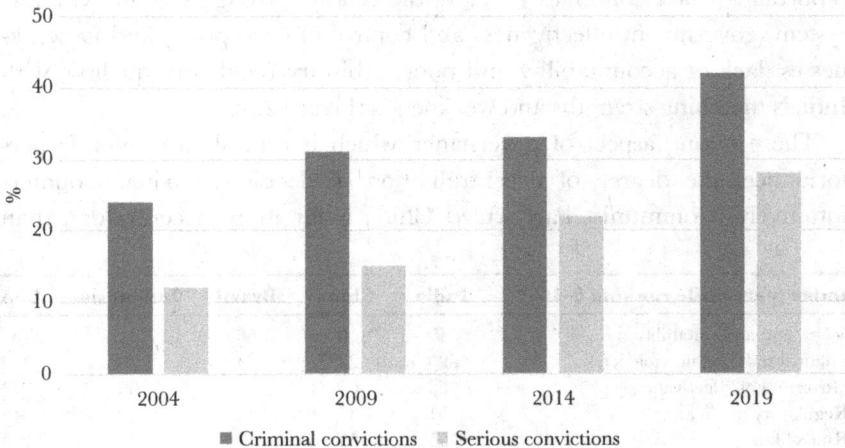

Source: Ashoka Mody, *India is Broken: A People Betrayed, Independence to Today* (Stanford, CA: Stanford University Press, 2023), p. 374

2.4 Share of Indian MPs with criminal convictions

The prevalence of corruption is a symptom of a deeper problem: a poor infrastructure of institutions that are competent, honest, independent of political interference and embedding the rule of law. In short: governance. In the case of China, a one-party state, there may be a strong sense of order and discipline, but institutions and courts are subordinate to the Party. Xi himself has paid a lot of attention to strengthening and professionalising the court system to create 'rule by law', but in any conflict between the Party and the wider national interest the Party will prevail.[54] In India, the principles may be admirable, but the institutions are badly corroded. Sarwar Lateef has pulled together material from Worldwide Governance Indicators and the Rule of Law Index of the World Justice Project to show that, while China ranks best among comparators (India, Brazil, Indonesia, Russia) for 'government effectiveness', stability and absence of violence and control of corruption, it is weakest for 'voice and accountability'.[55] China is weakest for 'rule of law' – ahead only of Russia – but is best of the group for both civil and criminal justice because of the relative efficiency of its courts system. By contrast, India does well in this mini league for 'rule of law' but weakest for 'civil justice', because of the paralytic inefficiency of its legal system. India also scores badly for stability and freedom from violence. Lateef's work on quantifying governance has now become a regular feature of World Bank reporting, which continues to show the relative strengths of the Chinese system (government effectiveness and control of corruption) and its weaknesses (lack of accountability and poor, arbitrary regulatory quality), with India's matching strengths and weaknesses (Figure 2.5).

There is one aspect of governance which is crucial to economic performance: the degree of decentralisation of decision making. Counter-intuitively, Communist Party-ruled China is far more decentralised than

Index (percentile ranking 0–100)	India	China	Brazil	Indonesia	USA
Voice and accountability	49	6	56	53	73
Political stability, no violence	25	28	34	29	45
Government effectiveness	63	65	31	66	87
Regulatory quality	51	37	44	59	91
Rule of law	55	53	43	45	89
Control of corruption	44	55	32	38	82

Source: Daniel Kaufman and Aart Kraay, World Bank Governance Indicators (2023)

2.5 Governance indicators (2022)

democratic and federal India. A key part of the Deng reforms was the encouragement given to local officials to experiment and take initiatives which would benefit their area. Promotion within the Communist Party would depend in part on officials' record of delivery: completing infrastructure projects for example. Xi himself came to attention because of his efforts to develop Zhejiang and Fujian when he held important posts there. Under his rule, other factors weigh heavily in judging the performance of party cadres: adherence to Xi Jinping Thought, honesty, competent financial management. Nonetheless it is almost certainly the case that, other than for big strategic decisions, decisions are still made locally.

A World Bank study showed that in terms of several metrics to measure 'localism', China ranked 21 out of 182 countries, ahead of very centralised developed countries like the UK and far ahead of India (Figure 2.6). The same study brought out the extent to which China is exceptional among both developed and developing countries in the importance attached to local government. Local government is crucial to the Chinese model of development, since it encourages local experimentation and because it encourages competition which forces enterprises, including state-owned enterprises, to confront market forces and adapt to market demand, domestic or foreign.[56] By contrast, Karthik Muralidharan showed that India was the most centralised of eighteen similar countries, with just 3% of public spending decided at a local level as against 51% in China.[57] Devolution to state level does not mean much when, for example, the state of Uttar Pradesh has a bigger population than France and Germany combined. Much of the differential in growth performance between China and India can be explained by the fact that China has highly decentralised economic decision making, trusting local government to make choices, while India is (despite federalism)

	Denmark	USA	UK	China	India
Rank of 182 countries	1	5	30	21	68
Importance of local government (%)	59	24	28	51	5
Administrative decentralisation (%)	90	75	51	71	35
Political decentralisation (%)	59	100	71	25	67
Index of decentralisation	34	14	4	6	1

Source: World Bank Paper (Ivanya and Shen)

2.6 Indicators of decentralisation

very centralised, with minimal power at the local level. However, it may be that this advantage is eroding with Xi's tightening of party discipline and stronger controls on local government finance.

Conclusion

Both India and China have developed versions of 'state capitalism' reflecting their history of state planning and controls followed by a liberalisation and opening to private enterprise. Both have some of the negative consequences of fuzzy boundaries between state and business, including rampant corruption (though Xi's crackdown on corruption has seemingly had a significant impact). There are some major differences: India never nationalised land; China moved faster and more decisively to liberalise its economy. The direction of travel has also recently been different, with the Chinese authorities seemingly moving back to tighter party control over business in the interest of security and the Indian government seemingly freeing up business further (albeit with a strong whiff of 'crony capitalism'). Yet both countries could be crudely characterised as 50:50 economies, reflecting strong residual state ownership and control.

Yet the role of the state in the 'commanding heights' of the economy is not matched by the state assuming wider responsibilities. Both countries have a weak government fiscal footprint, and basic public services like health and education are poor, especially in India. Both countries also struggle with the 'governance' demands of managing a vast superstate. There are two major differences which have emerged. One is that China has superior 'state capacity'. State agencies 'get things done', in large part through the stiffening influence of the monopoly power of the Communist Party (though the pervasive influence of Hindu 'Sangh Parivar' institutions may be moving India in the same direction). The second is that China, perhaps surprisingly, has more effective, decentralised economic decision making. India is a federal state with weak local institutions; China is a unitary state with strong local authorities (though the Xi administration is moving China in a centralising direction to establish tighter financial control). What is clear is that issues of governance cannot be separated from politics.

3

Democracy versus autocracy

A simple caricature of the political difference between China and India is that the former is a highly authoritarian one-party state, while the latter is a pluralistic multiparty parliamentary democracy. While it is a caricature, it captures a fundamental difference between the two countries. And the dichotomy has proved useful in several ways.

First, it provides a convenient explanation for the hare and tortoise parable. Those who – rightly – applaud the survival of democratic India can explain that it has made less progress with economic and social development because of the necessarily cumbersome mechanisms involved in achieving compromise within elected coalitions. Authoritarian governments can cut through political obstacles more easily (even if they also make bigger mistakes). They can ruthlessly prioritise political stability and basic human needs – food, shelter, health, education, personal security – but at the expense of democratic 'freedoms'.

Second, the dichotomy fits neatly into the morality tale at the heart of current geopolitics: a Manichean struggle between the authoritarian forces of evil and the democratic forces of good. In the current geopolitical context that means rejecting the unsavoury 'axis of autocracy' represented by China, Russia, Iran, North Korea and Venezuela, and embracing 'democracies', of which India is the biggest by far. Modi's BJP government has skilfully cultivated Western leaders by presenting India as a democratic counterweight to China.

The problem with framing the politics of the superstates in this way is that it obscures what they have in common. Authoritarian government and 'democracy' are not binary alternatives. There is a matter of degree, and

71

this will change over time. The Economist Democracy Index has a 0 to 10 rating, which has Scandinavian democracies as close to 10 and horror stories like North Korea at 1 or less.[1] India is described as a 'flawed democracy', its index falling over the last decade from 7.8 to 7.0. It is in a similar position to Brazil, South Africa and Indonesia and a little lower than the USA on 7.8 (and that before the return of Trump). Under President Xi, China has moved on this measure from 3.1 to a dismal 2.0, along with Saudi Arabia. Figure 3.1 illustrates the index and its components.

Arguably, the indicator – and the wider debate about 'democracy' – attaches too much weight to political processes rather than outcomes. Ashoka Mody's indictment of Indian democracy, *India is Broken*, makes the point that 'the mechanics of democracy – regular elections and the peaceful transfer of power' – are not 'sufficient indicators of democratic health'. '[T]he shift from the mechanics of democracy to its role in improving lives tells a much gloomier story.'[2] The implication is that with a wider definition of democracy, India is 'worse' (and China 'better') than it initially appears. One international comparative analysis of political institutions does not recognise India as a democracy at all, but as an 'electoral autocracy'.[3] Another concluded that India was 'partially free' (on a par with Hungary) and that Modi was 'driving India towards autocracy'.[4] These judgements, however, predate the 2024 parliamentary elections, which showed Indian democracy – or at least democratic processes – to be more resilient than supposed.

The 2024 Indian election and the fork in the road

As election upsets go, the 2024 general election in India was seismic. The incumbent BJP government, with 303 seats in a 544-seat parliament, expected to win a supermajority of 400 seats, which would enable it to change the constitution and cement its hold on power. Prime Minister Modi appeared immensely popular, or so the polls suggested, and believed that he had a divine mission. One of his campaign messages was 'God sent me for a purpose'. The BJP was well funded by its business backers and had a professional and highly motivated political machine with dominance in both traditional and social media. The opposition had been intimidated and marginalised, its leaders facing arrest on questionable charges. It struggled to put together a last-minute coalition of parties (INDIA) under the seemingly

	Rank (167 countries)	Electoral process	Functioning of government	Political participation	Political culture	Civil liberties
Norway	1	10	9.6	10	10	9.4
UK	18=	9.6	7.5	8.3	6.9	9.1
USA	29	9.2	6.4	8.9	6.2	8.5
India	41=	8.7	7.9	7.2	6.2	5.9
China	148=	0.0	3.6	3.3	3.1	0.6
Saudi Arabia	150	0.0	3.6	2.2	3.1	1.5
North Korea	165	0.0	2.5	1.7	1.2	0.0
Afghanistan	167	0.0	0.1	0.0	1.2	0.0

Source: Economist Intelligence Unit, Democracy Index 2023

3.1 Democracy Index (0–10)

weak leadership of Rahul Gandhi's Congress. In the event, voters defied the pollsters and the governing party. The BJP lost sixty seats, mostly in its supposed heartland, and its overall majority. It remains in power thanks to the support of two regional parties.

There is now a fork in the road. One road leads back to messy but consensual democratic politics. Radical legislative change is slow, but the economy can still grow rapidly under its own momentum, as it did in the years when Manmohan Singh presided over a fractious coalition and before the BJP took power in 2014. Modi is required to change his autocratic – indeed, divine – style of government to accommodate his coalition allies, Nitin Kumar and N. C. Naidu, who represent parties from Bihar and Andhra Pradesh and who have a reputation for political fickleness. And Modi would have to show some humility towards independent-minded leaders of states like Tamil Nadu, West Bengal and Karnataka. The BJP has been in coalition before, operating within the confines of democratic government, and may be able to do so again with or without Modi. Such an outcome would re-establish India's reputation as a functioning democratic country, in sharp contrast to China.

But there is another road, along which the 2024 election is seen by the BJP as merely an annoying bump. Modi and the BJP could double down on their previous flirtation with autocratic government. Their priority is to revive the party base for a fresh assault on secular and democratic institutions, with Modi himself playing the role of 'Emperor of Hindu hearts'. Although the Congress Party has revived, it is still weak (with 99 seats in parliament as against 240 for the BJP) and part of a fragile opposition coalition. It is easy to see how the BJP could put the electoral setback behind it.

Should it do so there will be a continuation of the road Modi and Xi had travelled together in the previous decade. They came to power at approximately the same time, and they both moved towards greater concentration of decision making, more ideological stiffening and less tolerance of dissent, disorder and diverse identities. They both illustrated the attractions of 'strongman' government: stability, security and 'getting things done' and the mistakes and failures that flow from overcentralised political power. Even if Xi and Modi had the almost supernatural powers that are sometimes attributed to them, they would struggle with the responsibility of being 'chairman of everything' and 'micromanager in chief'.[5]

The origins of 'strongman rule'

A concentration of power in both countries has emerged through two over-lapping developments: one-party rule (achieved through revolution and 'the dictatorship of the proletariat' or through the election and re-election of a dominant party) and, within the ruling party, the emergence of a single powerful leader. How did these developments occur?

It was a truly remarkable achievement of independent India to have emerged from colonial rule with a functioning parliamentary democracy in which a vast, diverse and largely illiterate population had the right to vote in free elections. It is even more remarkable that a system of universal suffrage was established and sustained at far lower levels of economic development than the established democracies (Britain did not give women the vote until 1928, and in the USA black Americans were largely denied the vote until 1965).

But, from the outset, a priority of government in India was to maintain cohesion and unity in the face of potentially divisive, centrifugal forces. Although theoretically a federal country, the India that emerged was highly centralised. The country's first Law Minister explained that it was divided into states solely for 'convenience of administration'.[6] Central government controlled key revenue sources. The economy was subject to central planning and control of the 'commanding heights' through public ownership. Troublesome or failing state administrations could be replaced by 'President's Rule' (by central government), as happened seven times under Nehru and many times since. Despite the pull of the centre, there was, however, enough devolved authority for the Communist-led administrations in Kerala and West Bengal to develop distinct models, as with other 'progressive' states, mainly in the South. Those states have continued to provide a degree of diversity.

India had genuinely free elections, but there was a dominant ruling party – Congress – whose popularity derived from its role in the Independence movement. Its political base was an alliance between India's upper-caste voters – Brahmins and landowning groups – and the 'scheduled castes', notably the Dalits ('untouchables'), who had preferential status in government jobs and college entry ('reservation'). A commitment to 'secularism' helped to reassure a quiescent Muslim population. But the authority of

75

central government gradually waned, with unrest in peripheral states, defeat in a short war with China, slow economic growth and growing disaffection among middle-income groups and what were called 'other backward castes' (OBCs). Centrifugal forces were powerful and provided Indira Gandhi with a pretext for imposing an 'Emergency' in 1975: in effect, a dictatorship. Many human rights abuses were committed. But Gandhi overestimated her own popularity. In 1977 she called an election and lost.

The next three decades represented a swing of the pendulum away from strong central rule. There was weaker and less decisive government, with alternating Congress or opposition-based coalitions, sometimes of numerous parties. Identity politics blossomed, with the emergence of state-based parties based on caste, language or other identity markers, in particular, parties representing the middle class and OBCs. In many parts of India there was violence and disorder, often based on religious or caste divisions and fuelled by alienated, angry, unemployed young men. In many ways India prospered, with looser control, especially under the economic reforms of Manmohan Singh. But rampant corruption, widening inequality between states and between classes and high levels of unemployment created widespread dissatisfaction. During the period 2009–14, when Singh was Prime Minister of an unwieldy Congress-led coalition, further economic reform and decision making became difficult.

These conditions were ideal for another swing of the pendulum in the 2014 general election. The swing was to more authoritarian, centralised government under the BJP led by Modi.[7] The election itself was decisive, with a record turnout (66%), and the transfer from Congress to the BJP was magnified by the first-past-the-post electoral system (the BJP won 282 of the 543 seats with 31% of the vote; Congress won 44 seats with 19% of the vote). The 2019 election was a near replica (BJP 303 seats, Congress 52). Against expectations the 2024 election did not deliver the even bigger majority that the BJP was seeking, but it remains the dominant national party.

The BJP is the political wing of an overlapping set of organisations, the Sangh Parivar, originating in the century-old Rashtriya Swayamsevak Sangh (RSS): a cultural movement with beliefs built around a sense of Hindu identity – Hindutva.[8] The BJP broke through politically in the 1991 election and in 1999 was strong enough to lead a coalition government. A key turning point in its fortunes was the 2014 election, for which the party chose as its leader Narendra Modi: a dedicated RSS cadre from a humble background (his father was a tea seller) and whose asceticism marked him out in a political culture seen as steeped in corruption. His reputation was that of an effective Chief Minister of Gujarat, running a competent administration and delivering pro-business development, but his reputation was also marred by his alleged complicity in a massacre of Muslims. The accusations, true or false, did no harm to his political support. For the BJP, he was a brilliant political campaigner with a populist appeal to both rich and poor Hindu voters.

Modi's 2014 victory, repeated in 2019, led to a consolidation of BJP power under his leadership. He oversaw the gradual erosion of independent institutions like the judiciary, the police and the media. Modi's brand of Hindu ethnic nationalism became the dominant ideology. The BJP effectively supplanted Congress as a hegemonic ruling party (albeit still with opposition parties still in power in some states, including five states in the South). And, within the BJP government, Modi was at the centre of everything. He is reported to have run a highly personalised administration. His picture has been the face of government (even on vaccination certificates) and he created a sense that he is personally delivering the largesse of office to the public. He built a powerful 'cult of personality'. It remains to be seen, however, how far he can continue in that vein after the 2024 election when he must compromise with coalition allies who have their own independent power bases.

As to the benefits of his 'strongman' rule, a World Bank assessment of the quality of governance shows an improvement in political stability and government effectiveness between 2014 and 2021.[9] But strongman government also led to bad mistakes, affecting the lives of millions. Modi's seemingly impulsive demonetisation decision in 2016 – where he abolished high denomination rupee notes, 85% by value of currency in circulation – is one example. It was designed to penalise holdings of illegal 'black money' but caused major economic dislocation and hit millions of poor people in the informal economy.[10] Another mistake was the sudden, draconian Covid lockdown, which hit tens of millions of migrant workers who were trapped long distances from their village homes without work, income or transportation.[11] The strongman leader who made these key decisions seemed to have emerged politically unscathed, though the seeds of discontent were sown too.

77

China also knows strongman rule. Since 1949 the country has been ruled by the Communist Party, which has provided the unifying force holding China together after the decades of upheaval and civil war. Its predecessor in power, the nationalist Kuomintang (KMT), also operated, if less successfully, authoritarian single-party rule and, with the partial exception of a short period after the 1912 revolution, China has never experienced democratic government. The CCP has never been anything other than a dictatorial, single-party regime. But China has experienced the same basic political dynamic as India, with periods of uncompromising, centralised power under Mao, and now Xi, alternating with periods of more relaxed rule. As in India, the country is divided into provinces, but these territorial units have no real power. China is a unitary state and other independent power centres do not exist, albeit there is a high degree of day-to-day economic decision making in districts and municipalities. In the case of China, however, the concentration of political power in the CCP is absolute.[12] The Leninist principle of the party as 'the centralised organisation of force' is much less subtle than the periods of de facto one-party rule in India.

The Maoist era saw leadership megalomania, as in the horrific consequences of attempts to force the pace of industrialisation during the so-called Great Leap Forward of 1958 to 1962.[13] Subsequently, Deng Xiaoping recognised that economic modernisation could only happen by decentralising power, allowing local experimentation, and permitting market forces to operate. He was also self-effacing and did not allow himself to be the subject of a cult of personality. He devised a system of succession limiting individual leaders to ten years in office. But he was also clear that stability was the overriding political priority, and that economic liberalisation did not entail political liberalisation, including challenges to CCP rule. He was unapologetic about his role in using force at Tiananmen Square in 1989. His carefully constructed balance involved allowing enough decentralisation to permit local innovation and sufficient central political control to hold the country together. The system he created survived for three and a half decades.

Xi Jinping has reverted to a more centralised, controlling system. He emerged as party leader at a time when the decentralisation of power was seen (at least within the CCP leadership) as having gone too far. The country had become more prosperous and was now a superpower alongside the

78

USA. But the Party, and central government, was losing control. Corruption was rampant, even in the higher echelons of the Party and the armed forces. There were numerous cases of localised riots, strikes and other examples of low-level unrest.[14] The Party no longer seemed to command respect, and its 90 million members lacked a coherent ideological backbone. New, challenging power centres were emerging, in the form of self-confident billionaires and liberal intellectuals utilising websites to publish criticisms. Seen from the centre, there was a threat of 'chaos'. It seems that in choosing Xi, who was known to be a competent, effective administrator and a 'clean' pair of hands, his colleagues wanted someone to stop the rot.[15]

Since taking control in 2013, Xi has demonstrated both the advantages and the problems of centralising power in his hands. By extending his own tenure beyond ten years and ending the succession policy introduced by Deng, he underlined his own authority but created major uncertainty over what will happen when he dies or is incapacitated or forced out. He has demonstrated the ability of strong central authority to crack down hard on corruption (though his appetite for purging 'corruption' seems to be directed at disloyalty as much as venality). He has also shown how strong central leadership can act and mobilise resources decisively, as with the early stages of the pandemic lockdown or the rapid build-up of high-tech industries or rearmament or to deliver the Belt and Road Initiative worldwide.

But the downsides of concentrating power are also apparent in bad decisions. The sudden exit from draconian pandemic restrictions was chaotic and cost many lives. Xi is struggling to navigate the complex challenges of a collapsing property boom and an unbalanced economy while insisting that he alone can manage the steering wheel. He is struggling to get the right balance between using China's dynamic, decentralised system of local economic decision making[16] and strengthening central financial controls to curb wasteful 'overinvestment'.[17] He has been sending contradictory and confusing messages to the private sector while China's vast system of regulation and party management tries to interpret his wishes. A fundamental question he faces is how to reconcile the need for flexibility of an advanced (and semi-capitalist) economy, whose success underpins the popularity of the regime, with the political imperative of party control under his strong, uncompromising leadership. Ideology is an important part of the answer.

Ideology as 'superglue'

What the leaders of China and India have in common, as rulers of vast and complex superstates, is the need for a coherent set of unifying values and ideas. Superstates require an ideological 'superglue'.[18] That is why the Hindutva is a crucial underpinning of the Modi government in India, as is Xi Jinping Thought in China.

Marxist-Leninism, the revolutionary ideology which brought the CCP to power and was adapted and perpetuated by Mao for an agrarian society, no longer has an obvious relevance to an industrialised, mostly urban, society which is on the threshold of becoming a rich country and which craves stability and security. Deng's economic transformation of China was achieved pragmatically, and the big policy changes were driven through with appeals to common sense rather than ideology and the promise of becoming better off and enjoying more personal freedoms. However, the combination of greater economic freedoms with an uncompromising commitment to CCP one-party rule represented a contradiction. But if the Party delivered improving living standards and maintained stability, the contradiction did not matter too much. As Deng put it: it didn't matter if the cat was black or white provided it caught mice.

Deng's successors worried about the lack of an ideological definition of what the Party stood for. Capitalistic Communism, or Leninist Capitalism, however successful in practice, was theoretically unsatisfactory. In 2000, Jiang Zemin came up with The Three Represents: an attempt to reconcile the desirability of an emerging Chinese capitalism with the thought of Marx, Engels, Lenin, Stalin and Mao, as well as Deng. But this left idealistic party insiders feeling confused and disillusioned.[19] Jiang's successor, Hu Jintao, fared no better with his Scientific Outlook on Development – another bit of opaque jargon trying to justify a mixed economy in Marxist-sounding language. Moreover, it divided reformers, who wanted to press on with a more liberalised political system, from conservatives, who worried that the Party was already losing too much power.

Xi inherited this confusion and lack of ideological clarity. He was determined to restore the primacy of the Party and its grip on power: 'government, the military, society and schools, north, south, east and west – the party leads them all'.[20] But the question remained: what did the Party stand for?

The first indication Xi gave was of what he was against: The Seven No's.[21] He was against constitutional democracy, universal values, civil society, neo-liberalism, a 'free' press, historical nihilism (attacking the Party's record) and questioning the role of socialism. What he was for is enshrined in Xi Jinping Thought or, more formally, Xi Jinping Thought on Socialism with Chinese Characteristics for a New Era.[22] It is widely believed in China that this philosophy draws heavily on the ideas of Wang Huning, a party intellectual and theorist who is a member of the Politburo Standing Committee and effectively number four in the Chinese hierarchy.[23] For Chinese officials, many hours of compulsory study are required to understand and internalise Xi Jinping Thought.

When he was first chosen as party leader, Xi made it clear that his ideological beliefs were in the tradition of Marxist-Leninism and Mao Zedong Thought. He distanced himself from those who thought he might be a breath of liberal fresh air by proclaiming 'Socialism with Chinese Characteristics is Socialism, not any other kind of Ism.' He fleshed out his ideas in a speech in 2014, describing the Four Modernisations which would be the focus of his first period in office: building a 'moderately well off society'; deepening economic reform; creating a more structured legal system via the 'rule by law'; and better party governance, involving 'strict discipline'.

It was at the 19th Party Congress in 2017 that what become known as Xi Jinping Thought was fully developed and embedded in China's constitution. The central concept is the 'China Dream of national rejuvenation' (the phrase was mentioned over thirty times in a keynote speech). One interpretation of the China Dream is that of sinologist Kerry Brown: 'it is about building a bourgeois China where the middle classes were king', albeit with the emphasis on collective well-being rather than individual greed, and in an environment of discipline and control rather than chaos and upheaval.[24]

Another interpretation of the China Dream is that the key idea is the 'oneness' of China: 'one country, one people, one ideology, one party and one leader' – 'the greater good of China as interpreted by the Party'. 'Oneness' appears to mean addressing genuine popular concerns like poverty, corruption and the environment, but also eliminating divisive movements. As political scientists Steve Tsang and Olivia Cheung put it: 'whatever is deemed as standing in the way of the effort to forge a common national identity and a common national loyalty will be harmonised or crushed in the process'.[25]

Distinctive ethnic or regional movements, as in Tibet, Xinjiang or Hong Kong are, clearly, not compatible with Xi's 'oneness'.

Xi Jinping Thought is not a settled ideology but is constantly being updated through his speeches. In 2020, Xi introduced a doctrine called 'promoting the comprehensive building of a modern Socialist country', designed to differentiate China modernisation from that of the capitalist West, with a greater emphasis on equitable income distribution and a sustainable environment. In this spirit he embarked on a theme of 'Common Prosperity', which was fleshed out in a speech to the 10th Meeting of the Central Committee for Financial and Economic Affairs. Common Prosperity would 'reasonably regulate excessively high incomes and encourage high income people and enterprise to return more to society'. This was not just rhetoric. He launched an attack on big tech companies, starting with Alibaba, followed up by attacks on the Chinese elite's practices, such as using private tutoring to secure educational advancement for its children. But at the Third Plenum meeting of the Party's Central Committee in 2024, faced with a slowing economy and the need for successful business, Xi emphasised the importance of markets and the private sector, reflecting an essentially pragmatic balancing act between the contradictory elements of state capitalism.

A more controversial element in Xi Jinping Thought has been the co-option of China's pre-revolutionary cultural past: what was called, in party jargon, the 'second integration' (of traditional Chinese thought, in particular Confucius). Xi quoted Confucius in a speech early in his period in office, identifying with a body of thought which emphasised obedience and respect for authority. It was also a neat way to distance Xi from Mao, since Maoists saw Confucius as embodying reactionary, pre-revolutionary values. Xi is for order and discipline and strenuously opposed to Mao's chaotic and violent Cultural Revolution (from which he suffered personally). A party propaganda film, 'When Confucius met Marx', drew the ire of both Maoists and liberals, which probably suited Xi perfectly.[26]

Externally, the China Dream is the 'great rejuvenation of the Chinese nation'. This involves making China respected abroad as a new superpower, expiating the grievances from the 'century of humiliation' and confidently promoting modern China's achievements. In many ways, Xi's approach directly mirrors Trump's Make America Great Again. The China Dream is a more assertive approach to relations with China's neighbours and with the West than the self-effacing style of Deng, whose 'hide your strength; bide your time' had set the tone of Chinese foreign policy for a generation.

Chinese officials frequently try to explain this new assertiveness more sympathetically in terms of 'tianxia' (all under heaven), a Chinese concept which involves a harmonious and peaceful world, albeit with China at its centre. China's vision of the harmonious future is set out in a series of initiatives, launched by Xi, to do with security, development and civilisation. They involve cooperation in a world which has rejected the American-led international order and reasserted the centrality of the nation state. But that world is some way off. In the meantime, there must be 'comprehensive national security', which justifies a forceful assertion of Chinese critical national interests, as over reunification with Taiwan, and increasingly tight, and repressive, rule at home.

While Xi has laboured hard to produce an ideological narrative which explains and justifies the concentration of power in his, and the Party's, hands, he is now struggling with a new problem: how to explain the slowdown in economic growth and the impact on living standards? How to motivate a country which seems to be stuck in a middle-income trap? How to reconcile assertive nationalism and standing up to an increasingly hostile and protectionist USA with continued promotion of globalisation and integration with the Western world on which China depends economically? Part of the answer has been to change priorities. Xi Jinping Thought now emphasises security rather than economics, in what has been called the 'sunset of the economists'.[27] In his opening address to the CPP's 20th Party Congress in October 2022, Xi mentioned security over fifty times. Security has become a dominant ideological theme lying behind many aspects of policy, such as more self-sufficiency alongside globalisation.

India has had a similar ideological challenge: shifting from one narrative of the country to another, albeit, in this case, under a different party. For seventy years, India's dominant ideology was that of the Congress Party, based on an amalgam of ideas: 'secularism', meaning mutual tolerance between different religions; 'socialism', meaning heavy industrialisation, public ownership and planning; 'democracy', meaning competitive elections on the Westminster model; and Indian nationhood, as in the centralisation of political power away from the states. The dilution, or hollowing out, of Congress ideology happened gradually but accelerated under

Nehru's daughter, Indira Gandhi, who Ashoka Mody cuttingly describes as a 'cynical, slogan-peddling politician' who lacked 'any coherent economic or political ideology'.[28]

The ideological underpinnings of Congress rule weakened further as succeeding Congress governments relied heavily on dynastic succession for their legitimacy, first under Indira's son Rajiv, then Rajiv's widow Sonia (as party President) and latterly Rajiv's son, Rahul. An exception should be made for the period of reformist Congress government under Narasimha Rao and his Finance Minister Manmohan Singh from 1991 to 1996, and then with Manmohan Singh as Prime Minister of a Congress-led coalition from 2004 to 2014. Those governments sought to resurrect some of the original spirit of Congress rule, allied to radical, market-based economic reform. But pervasive corruption, and the lingering grip of the Gandhi family and their acolytes on the party machine, prevented political, alongside economic, renewal. But the dynasty has not died yet. In the 2024 election, despite crude attempts by the Modi government to force him out of political life, Rahul led an effective opposition campaign, having rebuilt his reputation by engaging with the voters through long walks across India.

When the Congress Party was driven to the political margins a decade ago, the BJP was waiting with a very different ideological creed and a leader, Modi, able to communicate and apply it: Hindutva. Hindutva was first defined ideologically by Vinayak Damodar Savarkar in 1923. It is rooted in the Hindu religion and a sense of Hindu ethnicity based on historical myths and cultural identity.[29] It has been likened to ideologies elsewhere which are grounded in 'the politics of the soil':[30] a fusion of religion, race and territorial belonging. An added ingredient is a sense of historical victimhood at the hands of Muslim rulers and their descendants and other alien cultures: what wags call 'a persecuted minority of 80% of the population' or 'paranoid triumphalism'. After the establishment of the RSS in 1925, a disciplined movement grew around these ideas involving physical fitness (to counter supposed Western prejudice about Indians being 'puny'), solidarity of Hindus against Muslims and other outsiders and a sense of Hindu Indianness transcending class and caste. In its early years the movement built a cadre structure based on lessons from Mussolini's fascism, and early leaders expressed admiration for Nazism, including the 'final solution'.[31]

The RSS, in turn, spawned a family of organisations, the Sangh Parivar, including the BJP as a political party. A series of campaigning issues gave practical substance to Hindutva: opposition to cow slaughter (by beef-eating Muslims), stopping conversions of Hindus to Islam and Christianity, revision of history books to reflect the achievements of ancient Hindu civilisation and reinstating temples overlaid by mosques. Some of the ideology invited ridicule, notably the claims that ancient Indian civilisation had mastered nuclear and aeronautical technology. But much of it had a visceral appeal.

The BJP enjoyed a big jump in parliamentary support in 1991 by tapping into the discontent of upper and middle castes, who felt disadvantaged by preferences for lower castes. But a defining moment was the demolition by mobs of the Ayodhya Mosque in 1992. The mosque had been built over a temple associated with the birth of Ram, a Hindu deity. The apparently spontaneous mobs were in fact coordinated by an organisation which was part of the Sangh Parivar and supported by BJP activists and leaders. The subsequent sectarian rioting across India may have cost 2,000 lives. But Ayodhya boosted the BJP politically and the party made big advances in national elections in 1996 and 1999. The national leadership under Atal Vajpayee was moderate and worked with other parties in coalition against Congress (Vajpayee became Prime Minister). But the appeal of ethnic nationalism continued to be exploited by grassroots followers of Hindutva like the Bajrang Dal, a movement of angry young men. Then, a wave of Islamist, Pakistan-based terrorist attacks caused many fatalities and united Indians in anti-Muslim and patriotic anti-Pakistan sentiment. Official records show that in the period 2002–17 there was an average of 2,000 riots a year, with an average death toll of around a hundred. Most were communal and many seemingly instigated by Bajrang Dal activists.[32]

A big boost to the BJP and its Hindutva followers came from the success of the party, led by Modi, in Gujarat. His reputation as an uncompromising ethnic nationalist was cemented when, following an attack on a trainload of Hindu pilgrims by Muslims, there were anti-Muslim pogroms in Gujarat, killing thousands. Despite accusations that he allowed the killings to continue and may even have been complicit, as well as widespread international condemnation, he never expressed contrition and was lionised as the 'emperor of Hindu hearts'. As Chief Minister he wove together Hindutva ideology, a populist appeal across classes and castes, together with a reputation for delivering development by embracing business. His political success led to the BJP making him their national leader for the 2014 elections, which he won convincingly, following it up with another victory in 2019.

A decade of BJP rule under Modi demonstrated the power of Hindutva ideology alongside effective government, a focus on development and brilliant campaigning skills adapted to a digital age. RSS cadres have populated state institutions. Education is being 'Indianised'. There have been campaigns against secular, liberal institutions and NGOs. Hindutva vigilantes on the streets and in the digital sphere effectively censor the arts. Others intimidate Muslims accused of 'love jihad' (relationships between Muslim men and Hindu women) or suspected of cow slaughter. The latter has involved lynching at village level. Central government stripped Muslim refugees of citizenship and the only Muslim-dominated state (Kashmir) of its limited autonomy. Discrimination and violence against Muslims have been so widespread that India is listed as of serious concern on Genocide Watch.[33] India is estimated at 8/10 on the genocide scale, just behind China (in Xinjiang) on 9/10. In the run up to the 2024 election Modi made a provocative statement of sectarian belief when he played a starring role in the opening of a new Hindu temple on the site of the demolished Ayodhya Mosque. The gesture backfired politically in the area (the BJP lost the local seat in the 2024 election). But it fired up the activist base of the party.

It has been argued that Hindutva, despite its mass appeal, is essentially for the benefit of upper-caste and upper-class Hindus (who make up a large proportion of BJP MPs). It has not appealed greatly to people in the southern states, who are Hindus but do not share the same history or the same language as those in the populous Hindi belt. And in the 2024 election it was fear of losing statutory job reservation among lower-caste groups which was a factor in the unexpected swing from the BJP. That is why the BJP in government needed a strategy which involved more than simply appealing to religious bigotry. One strand has been to add to the power of good organisation and Hindutva ideology some success in development, providing tangible benefits for the public; to this I return below. But it remains to be seen whether its electoral setback will lead the BJP to intensify its ideological stridency or shift the emphasis onto development.

Although the national ideologies developed by the present Chinese and Indian leadership are very different, one embedded in religion and the other in materialism, they have several features in common. They are strongly nationalistic, promoting pride at home and demanding respect abroad. In the name of 'national security', 'territorial integrity' and 'fighting terrorism', they are accused of bullying neighbouring countries and persecuting 'disloyal' minorities at home. They have built up the idea of a 'civilisation state', embracing a national diaspora abroad. They have both understood that ideology matters to provide a sense of identity: a glue to keep the superstate as strongly united as possible. Chinese one-party rule and India's parliamentary democracy are different political animals. But crucially, what both have in common is an understanding that their ideology and its expression through a strongman ruler is difficult to reconcile with liberal democracy.

The problem of liberal democracy

In any event, there are formidable challenges to superstates in realising the ideal of liberal democracy: a democracy in which individual rights and freedoms are protected and power is limited by the rule of law. The sheer scale of the country means that the mass protests of millions can be difficult to contain, especially in cities, even if the numbers are a small percentage of the population. Also, the scale of the country and the multiple identities of its constituent parts mean that the threat of rebellion or secession is ever present. Governments have the difficult task of reconciling the rule of law and human rights with measures to contain disorder and to prevent centrifugal forces getting out of control. These problems are not unique to India and China but are found in other big, complex, multi-ethnic societies: Turkey, Pakistan, Indonesia, Nigeria, Ethiopia, South Africa, Brazil. Even under a BJP government, with Modi as strongman ruler, India's score in 2023 on the Economist Democracy Index was the highest of any of the list of semi-democracies above: 7.2 – not far short of the USA on 7.8.

The survival of parliamentary democracy in India – and aspects of liberal democracy more broadly – is a remarkable achievement. But the country's endurance as a nation state has frequently involved the use, or at least the threat, of force. India has a violent recent history, beginning with the partition itself and continuing through the seizure of Kashmir and resulting war with Pakistan, the annexation of Goa, a Sikh revolt in Punjab and counter-terrorist actions against over forty designated terrorist organisations, several of them responsible for major atrocities. There have been twenty significant riots since 1967, each resulting in over a hundred deaths.[34] Two prime ministers have been assassinated (as well as the Mahatma Gandhi), and under Indira Gandhi there was a period of rule by decree from 1975 to 1977 that can only be described as a dictatorship. The question addressed here is how far India has regressed to the status of a 'semi-democracy' or 'illiberal democracy'.[35]

One test is how far India has been able to sustain freedom of expression. The answer is that, in recent years, freedom of speech has been severely compromised. Individuals can be classified as terrorists based on offending books and other writings, speeches and social media posts. Numerous civil society organisations have been effectively silenced.[36]

The government has routinely blocked the internet to stop unacceptable social media postings – 2,800 legal orders in 2018 rising to 6,775 in 2022.[37] There have been growing numbers of criminal prosecutions for 'defamation', 'sedition', 'blasphemy' and other charges (including separate and multiple prosecutions by BJP state governments). New data laws, ostensibly intended to protect privacy, minimise online harm and regulate the platform companies, make it much easier for the government to block messages (without approval from judges), to obtain encryption algorithms and to engage in ad hoc rule making.[38] A proposed Broadcasting Bill contains a comprehensive attempt to control all aspects of media (though it has been withdrawn, at least for the moment, following the 2024 election).

Journalists continue to report pressure to censor material and, in extreme cases, physical threats, including aggressive online trolling. Some journalists have been murdered. The most common techniques to intimidate independent-minded news outlets are the use of government advertising to penalise critics, police and tax raids on the homes of critics, the temporary banning of TV channels and pressure on editors to dismiss critical journalists.[39] At first sight, India has remarkable media plurality, with 100,000 newspapers and 380 news channels. But plurality is limited by the fact that the powerful billionaire Mukesh Ambani owns seventy of the more lucrative channels, while another favoured billionaire, Gautam Adani, took over the previously influential and independent NDTV channel. Reporters without Borders World Press Freedom Index has ranked India 160 out of 180 counties and as against 105th in 2009. India now ranks below Singapore,

Pakistan and even Zimbabwe and Afghanistan, and is only slightly better than Russia, with the situation is described as 'very serious'.[40] After the 2024 election, a reinvigorated opposition is now able to push back, but to what extent is still unclear.

One of the few countries even more repressive of free speech is China (179th) – exceeded in repressiveness only by North Korea. But China makes no claims to be anything else. Press freedom was one of Xi's Seven No's. He has also shown himself to be hypersensitive to any criticism, however oblique.[41] Over time, the regime has gradually tightened its grip, using sophisticated technology to reduce the risk of critical material being aired through the internet while still allowing access to useful data and comment. Long before Xi, Deng Xiaoping was concerned about 'flies getting in through the open window'. But the fly problem became serious with the emergence of the internet. The first fly trap was the Golden Shield, invented in 2000 and later upgraded to the Great Firewall. The initial approach was subtle, involving 'friction, not fear',[42] using techniques of distraction, such as 'flooding' or creating inconvenience, to keep the curious away from sensitive material. For those who needed access to foreign data, such as business or scientists, there was the option of a virtual private network (VPN), but these were costly, awkward and discouraged. The Great Firewall provided protection for the emerging Chinese internet companies, and there was enough flexibility for users. Those who wanted to let off steam could use microblogs on Sino Weibo.

But since Xi has emerged, this more relaxed approach has changed.[43] A more sophisticated filter was launched: the Great Cannon. Microblogging became more restricted, with the authorities quick to take down anything deemed subversive and requiring users to identify themselves. VPNs became punishable. AI has given the regime new technologies to improve censorship and there is a large army of monitors helping censorship to operate quicker, more effectively and less intrusively. The US–China Economic and Security Review Commission reports that under Xi, 'the Party has significantly expanded the scope and stringency of its censorship apparatus' while 'allowing limited discussion of sensitive topics that do not threaten its hold on power'.[44] It notes that self-censorship has been intensified by assigning legal liability to internet service providers, but also notes attempts to be flexible by boosting positive propaganda, while using the blocking or deletion of posts as a last resort.

All these controls on freedom of speech are on a higher level of severity and harshness than anything yet attempted in India. But there is sufficient overlap to blur the boundaries between autocracy and democracy.

Controlling opposition

That conclusion is also true of the treatment of organised but non-violent opposition: the active suppression of opposition parties and independent political organisations. In India, in the run-up to the 2024 election, opposition parties and outspoken opposition figures faced criminal charges or legal and tax investigations. The opposition and Congress leader, Rahul Gandhi, was charged with and convicted of defamation. He was subsequently embroiled in a long and expensive campaign against a prison sentence and eviction from parliament. Leaders of another opposition party, the Aam Aadmi Party (AAP), which has a seat-sharing pact with Congress, were charged with excise fraud. An outspoken female opposition MP was subject to accusations of 'immoral and indecent' behaviour and expelled from parliament after she asked awkward questions about Modi's links to the Adani business conglomerate. Opposition MPs were routinely suspended from parliament after seeking accountability for government actions. Despite this, there was some vigorous public debate, and in the 2024 election an alliance of regionally based opposition figures with a strong local base were able to defend their political turf from the BJP.

Indeed, the most important power struggle taking place in India is not in Delhi but between the centre and the states. India was never as federated as the United States or Canada, but the states retained important responsibilities for health, education (in part), agriculture and law and order. Central government has long encroached on the power of the states, and with Modi's BJP an additional centralising feature has been the use of the state governors – a mostly ornamental role – to intervene directly to undermine or control state administrations. Nonetheless, some states have used their independence to progress economically and socially further than the Hindi-speaking BJP heartland in the north. These states are the drivers of Indian growth. And they generate disproportionate tax revenue. A potential conflict is coming to a head when a parliamentary boundary redrawing will cut the representation of these states, since their population is growing less rapidly than in the big, poor – and BJP-dominated – states. So far, the dispute has been successfully contained.

Much of the vigour of Indian democracy and society comes from the proliferation of NGOs, which operate at local level, taking up grievances and injustices as well as performing charity work and the provision of basic services that state administrations fail to deliver. There are believed to be (based on registration) around 3.3 million NGOs[45] – more than the number of schools. However, an estimated 18,000 civil society organisations have been effectively disabled by being refused registration or their overseas funding curbed.[46] Some NGOs have been subject to tax raids or other intimidation: Care India (which specialises in public health education for women and girls), Oxfam, Amnesty International and the Centre for Policy Research, which has devised numerous anti-poverty programmes. Others have faced anti-terrorism charges. These attacks on the sector stem in part from criticism of the regime (as with Amnesty International) or a suspicion that they are aligned with the Congress Party. Others, with Christian or Muslim connections, have been closed or harassed and have been accused of plotting to convert Hindus. But the NGO sector remains a formidable force.

Moreover, the suppression of critical political opposition in China is on a different level from India. Western-style multiparty democracy does not exist and is another of Xi's Seven No's. Apart from a brief flowering of partial democracy in the 1920s, before it was snuffed out by regional warlords, China has never experienced this form of democratic politics. That is not to say that there is no competitive politics in China; it is just very opaque. But one exception was the law enacted in 1998 to allow competitive elections at village level. An estimated three million such 'democratic' events took place and, in theory, continue.[47] But Kerry Brown judges that 'these initiatives have largely ceased ... the Party is now about unity and discipline'.[48]

During the decade of President Hu (2004–14) there was some discussion of more transparent 'intra-party' debate to hold office bearers to account, but little more has been heard of the idea. Instead, there have been many rumours of faction fighting behind closed doors. One distinction is between party officials associated with Shanghai and others in Beijing (or elsewhere). Before Xi there was a semi-public debate between the Shanghai faction, associated with market reforms, and Hu Jintao's Youth League, with a more egalitarian approach.[49] Under Xi, starting with the imprisonment of his

91

main rival for power – Bo Xilai – there has been no public dissent from official policy, although there is a cottage industry of commentators in academic think tanks in China offering carefully coded and nuanced views.

What is much closer to Indian experience has been the proliferation of NGOs and the state's attempts to manage them. There are an estimated 675,000 registered NGOs in China and perhaps as many as three million altogether.[50] Such bodies grew rapidly alongside the liberalisation of the economy. In 2016, however, moves were made to bring the NGOs within a more controlled system. Those with foreign links (around 7,000) were registered and subjected to the stringent disciplines applied to foreign bodies in China. The Chinese NGOs were required to observe such principles as 'national security' and 'social morality', which are potentially all-encompassing.

An obvious question is how independent NGOs can operate in a highly authoritarian country. Many work with national or local government or are in a subcontracting relationship, providing services such as lunch clubs for the elderly or children's playgroups. The vast majority are operating in fields which do not clash with the objectives of the CCP, and even campaigning groups may well be pursuing the same objectives, at least in principle: gender equality, environmental and consumer protection, workers' rights. But some NGOs have been actively involved in protest at the activities of local authorities.

Indeed, and surprisingly, there is a long tradition of popular protest, and it has continued even in periods of serious political repression.[51] It is widely believed in the West that protest is rare. On the contrary, there are reported to be tens of thousands of protests a year: mostly localised and centring on abuses by local officials or employers, but some more widespread and advertised on social media.[52] The period 1993–2002 saw a major upsurge, but protest continued in the Xi era.[53] Much protest is crushed, with exemplary prison sentences given to 'ringleaders', but some takes place with the tolerance and perhaps even encouragement of the authorities, as in the case of office occupations by homebuyers across China furious at the non-completion of homes by failing property companies. The Covid lockdown produced protest at the harshness of the restrictions, and the internationally publicised protests in Shanghai and elsewhere were a key factor in persuading Xi to abandon the restrictions. There were riots in Urumqi after a fire trapped and killed a dozen or so locked down residents in flats. After the lockdown there were protests by pensioners in several cities over the impact of changes in health funding, to which the authorities seemed to have listened.

There is now a substantial literature on protest movements and how the Chinese authorities respond to them, with varying degrees of accommodation, concession and repression.[54] Anything overtly political, attacking the CCP, will be dealt with harshly, but local officials will not want to make themselves unpopular by suppressing protests, even riots, which enjoy wide sympathy.[55] In some cases, the authorities genuinely try to get to the root cause of discontent by, for example, channelling resources to aggrieved districts in what has been called 'innovative social governance'.[56] In other cases, there are attempts to diffuse anger by negotiation and attrition, including channelling anger into legal routes through petition and court action.[57] A good example of the sophisticated approach of some authorities was the response to violent protests by taxi drivers against the Chinese Uber (Didi). Protests resulted in prison sentences for assailants, but local councils brought in regulations sought by protestors.[58]

An example of constructive engagement with the authorities is the role played by environmental NGOs locally and nationally, for example Friends of Nature. They have had considerable success in forcing prosecution of polluting firms and getting agencies to adopt tougher air and water quality standards and enforce them.[59] Prolonged protests in the so-called 'cancer villages' in Hubei eventually forced the authorities and polluting firms to act.[60] And, while protestors run the risk of being identified as 'troublemakers' and monitored under China's increasingly pervasive surveillance system, the same system is being used to identify genuine grievances and to address them.[61] The Party goes to great trouble to monitor public opinion and satisfaction levels, as part of what is called 'whole process democracy'. But sceptics believe that such a carefully managed equilibrium between control and protest can only be sustained under tranquil conditions, when the economy is delivering constant improvements.[62]

Labour protests and strikes are a good indicator of how well this equilibrium is being maintained. Unlike in India, which has a legal, well-organised and often militant trades union movement, China's has been effectively neutered. But independent labour NGOs mushroomed with China's admission to the World Trade Organization (WTO), and with the many cases of bad labour standards and conditions in the burgeoning export sector.[63] In the Hu period, NGOs supported trades unions with legal and organisational advice, making use of courts, but also using strike action, which was sometimes effective. Legislation was introduced in 2008 giving workers the right to a contract and to severance pay with redundancy. Gradually, the state has clamped down on labour activism.[64] Nonetheless, there were strikes caused by non-payment of wages after the Covid lockdown and the abuses of zero-hours contracts by food delivery workers. The China Labour Bulletin, a worker advocacy group, has noted that in 2023 there was a doubling of labour-related incidents, mostly in the construction sector, where the property crisis has led to bankruptcies and non-payment of wages.[65] Much of the protest appears to be spontaneous and angry and not channelled through organised NGO activity.

NGOs in China flourish when they work with and alongside the state, as with environmental monitoring, or when they act, in effect, as subcontractors for the state, as with emergency services in disasters or welfare suppliers. They are likely to be suppressed if they threaten widespread disorder or the authority of the CPP (as in the Hong Kong crackdown), if they seem to be making a major criticism of state agencies (as in the case of the victims of contaminated blood) or if they seem to be challenging the current conservative social mores advocated by the Party (gay rights activists, radical feminists, AIDS sufferers). But what the NGOs have demonstrated is the scope, in China, for using the law. And that raises the whole issue of what the 'rule of law' means.[66]

Erosion of the rule of law

The rule of law is fundamental to liberal democracy. The World Justice Project has sought to monitor how effectively this principle is observed by different countries on eight criteria. The overall ranking has India at 79 out of 142 countries and China at 97.[67] The gap is narrower than one might expect, given that India is a democracy that embraces the rule of law and China rejects the whole concept in favour of 'rule by law'. India also ranks behind China on five of the eight metrics that make up the index. India is far ahead of China in respect of legal constraints on government powers (India 58; China 134), fundamental legal rights (India 99; China 139) and open government (42 as against 108). China, however, ranks higher on access to justice in respect of civil law (India 111; China 73) and criminal law (India 93; China 74), order and security (India 105; China 39), freedom from corruption – including of the police and the courts (India 96; China 52) and regulatory enforcement (India 83; China 74). In essence, India's legal principles are stronger, but China is more efficient in providing legal remedies.

There are two respects in which the legal system in both countries is currently in a state of flux and the rule of law under threat. India has long valued its independent judiciary. But when it came to power nationally in 2014, Modi's administration was determined to ensure that the judiciary was brought under political control. Shortly after being elected, it refused to approve a nominee from the Collegium of most senior judges, Gopal Subramanian.[68] Subramanian was an independent-minded judge who had an earlier involvement in a case involving a Muslim gangster, Sahrabuddin Sheikh, who was gunned down in what was believed to be a fake encounter by Gujarati police. Modi was Chief Minister at the time and his current deputy, Amit Shah, was allegedly involved in the killing. The police officers were acquitted amid accusations of judicial interference. The details are murky and have spawned conspiracy theories, but they fed a narrative that BJP leaders would play fast and loose with the law.

Within a few weeks of taking office the BJP government put forward legislation to scrap the Collegium system and replace it with a mechanism which the Supreme Court believed would jeopardise its independence. There was a long war of attrition over implementation of the new system, during which time no judges were appointed, despite an estimated need for an additional 50,000 to clear a backlog of millions of cases. But, by 2017, a more pliable Chief Justice ushered in a period of what the political scientist Christophe Jaffrelot calls 'nonconfrontation' by a combination of 'government pressure, ideological affinities and blackmailing'.[69] New judges were appointed who were known to be members of the RSS.

To this, it can be objected that the politicisation of the judiciary happens in Western democracies too, the USA especially. There are also recent cases in India of independent court rulings which went against the government's interests. For example, the Supreme Court ruled against the use of bonds to finance elections (a device introduced by the BJP government to hide the identity of BJP donors) and greatly limiting the government's plans for mandatory use of the new (Andhar) ID cards. In both these cases, however, the findings were sufficiently nuanced to be interpreted positively by both the government and its critics.

China, by contrast, has no claim to judicial independence. Judges are the servants of the state and the Party and do their bidding on any matter deemed political. But there have been developments, especially under Xi, which give real substance to rule by law. The Chinese legal system has traditionally operated on broad principles and rules, as set out originally by the Emperor and latterly by the Party. The role of the courts has been to implement the rules efficiently. But in the Maoist era, implementation was arbitrary, leading to an abuse of power by party officials. Subsequently, a constitution was introduced defining an individual's rights, but the court system remained arbitrary and often corrupt. Xi has undertaken major reforms in the name of rule by law, designed to systematise the law and to train and appoint professional judges.[70] Consequently, it is now possible for citizens to enjoy a degree of legal protection and certainty in property, neighbour and family disputes, and for NGOs, as well as individuals, to pursue claims involving consumer or environmental protection. Property rights and other non-political rights now enjoy reasonable protection under the law, though anything in the field of 'human rights' which challenges the Party's authority is subject to politically expedient decisions. That is especially bad news for minorities which depend upon respect for human rights.

Rejection of minority rights and self-determination

Liberal democracy protects the rights of ethnic and other minorities. Superstates present a particular problem because of their enormous demographic diversity. China has an estimated fifty-five different ethnicities, together with the dominant Han (with 90% of the population), each with a distinctive language and cultural identity. Additionally, there are an estimated 300 languages, 275 of them indigenous, in eight to ten language groups and with numerous dialects within each language. Even after major efforts under the Communist regime, 20% of the population in 2020 did not speak Mandarin. And superimposed on that rich tapestry is religious diversity. Even in an officially atheist country, a majority self-identify with indigenous folk religions, Buddhism, Christianity or Islam.[71] Yet, even by Chinese standards, India is remarkably diverse. There are an estimated 2,000 eth-nicities, four major language groups with numerous subgroups, hundreds of castes and sub-castes and a big dividing line between the (80%) Hindu majority and the Muslims (14%), with significant numbers of Christians, Buddhists, Sikhs, Jains and Parsees.

The politics of running superstates of such diversity are profoundly dif-ficult: accommodating the diversity while creating sufficient of a sense of China-ness or India-ness for the nation to function as a state. The two main perceived threats are: first, the existence of a distinctive, large minority which does not identify with the country or is rejected by it – the Muslim minority in India; second, the existence of geographically concentrated minorities which can plausibly secede to form their own country: the Chinese regions of Tibet and Xinjiang and Indian states in the north-east, as well as Kashmir. The response to these issues has become increasingly repressive in both countries under Xi in China and Modi in India. Both have treated minority problems as an existential threat and have rejected the multi-ethnic model of their predecessors.

The Chinese approach to its ethnic minorities has been heavily influenced by the fact that they may constitute a small proportion of the Chinese popu-lation but have occupied a large part of the surface area. Martin Jacques has written about Chinese 'cultural racism' over a 3,000-year history.[72] But Bill Hayton has argued that the concept of China as we know it today is histori-cally recent and originated in the early twentieth century, when the Qing dynasty was overthrown.[73] The Chinese Nationalists believed in the concept of a Chinese 'race' – they were influenced by European ideas of race – and were advocates of assimilation for minorities. Their approach was to resist attempts to assert independence in peripheral areas like Xinjiang (then Turkestan), as happened in the chaotic and violent interwar period of the warlords, Japanese invasion and civil war. There was then a real possibility of China breaking up.

When the Communists came to power, by contrast, they had a well-defined commitment to a multi-ethnic China as the best way to hold the country together. The existence and rights of ethnic minorities were recog-nised and valued and regional autonomy promised, albeit within the 'Chinese nation'. These principles were written into the constitution in 1954 and again in 1982, and were accompanied by policies of positive discrimination, such as exempting minorities from the one-child rule and giving preference in university admission. Autonomous regions and districts were designated to provide for a degree of administrative independence. Such good intentions did not apply in Tibet, where distinctive Tibetan culture, language and religion formed the basis of an independence movement which the regime has suppressed violently and sometimes brutally.

Under Xi there has been a big shift of policy away from the earlier multi-ethnic principles. A party paper in 2017 emphasised the 'Chinese nation' and 'oneness'. Subsequent policy declarations have talked about 'blending': an explicit commitment to a policy of assimilation or 'Sinicisation'.[74] In areas like Inner Mongolia, use of the local (Mongol) language has been suppressed in favour of Mandarin. The most severe manifestation of this new policy has been in Xinjiang, where Uyghur culture overlaps with the Islamic religion. Much has been written about the repressive policies employed in Xinjiang, but a definitive statement was that of the UN Human Rights Commissioner, Michelle Bachelet, in 2022 whose report concluded that the treatment of ethnic minorities 'constituted international crimes, in particular crimes against humanity'.[75] There is a debate over the extent to which mass preventive detention was precipitated by Uyghur terrorist groups and whether it is right to describe the abuses as 'genocide'.[76] But the human rights issue has badly affected China's international reputation and has blown away any illusions that China will tolerate multi-ethnicity whenever it is seen by the Party as undermining Chinese unity and 'oneness'.

India has arrived at a similar place by a different route. Post-independence India relied on two approaches to reconcile unity and nation building with minority rights and identity. The first was secularism: religions coexisting within a secular state and with freedom to worship. The second was federalism: the creation of states with devolved powers which broadly reflected ethnic identity. In several cases states have been split or reconfigured to ensure that a minority religion or language had its own territory (Tamil Nadu for the Tamils, Punjab for the Sikhs, Maharashtra for the Maharathas, Telegana for the Telugu speakers, Oriya for Oriya speakers). As a 'secular' state, India could be represented by minorities (a Sikh Prime Minister, Manmohan Singh; a Muslim President, Abdul Kalam). The emergence of the BJP as part of the Hindu Sangh Parivar and champion of the Hindu religion has, however, changed the position of minorities, and for the worse.

I have already described above the different ways in which the rise of the BJP has been built on ethnic identity and stigmatising minorities, especially Muslims. India has seen the promotion of Hindu religion and history at the expense of Islam; localised physical violence, in the form of urban riots and rural lynching, often endorsed by national leaders; political campaigns targeted at Muslims; discrimination in political representation and in policing. Two major pieces of legislation were sectarian in nature. The Citizenship Amendment Act explicitly stated that immigrants entering India before the end of 2014 were entitled to claim citizenship, but not Muslims. Public protests led to riots in Delhi which degenerated into communal violence with many Muslim victims. Also, in 2019, the government revoked the constitutional provisions which gave Kashmir, India's only Muslim-majority state, devolved powers. The ensuing violence in Kashmir led to army intervention, with many reports of human rights abuse, including torture and disappearances. As for the future, BJP activists are pressing to adopt nationally the civil code of the BJP-ruled state of Uttarakhand, which explicitly discriminates against Muslims. The UN Human Rights Commissioner has written, as she did for Xinjiang, on human rights abuses in India, and while they are not as extensive, systematic or pitiless as in China, they bear comparison.

Minorities and minority rights matter, but majorities matter more when it comes to the popularity of regimes and their ability to survive. So, how is popularity sustained?

Regime popularity and trust

Repression can go a long way to sustain governments in power, but it is difficult to see how countries of 1.4 billion people can be ruled for long periods without public support. What is remarkable about China and India is that despite major departures from the norms of liberal democracy and major failings of governance, they enjoy remarkably high levels of public support and trust. The Edelman Trust indicators measure trust in government and other institutions.[77] Of the twenty-seven countries surveyed by Edelman, China has the consistently highest trust level in its government (and other institutions like business and the media). India ranks fourth. There appear to be much higher trust levels in autocracies (as also in Saudi Arabia, the Emirates and semi-democratic Singapore) than in democracies like Argentina, South Africa, the USA and the UK. Their societies are also much less polarised in opinions. Sceptics might argue that surveys in authoritarian countries are unlikely to yield totally honest answers, but much effort goes into correcting biases.

In the case of India, the underlying legitimacy of the political system is underlined by high turnouts in national elections despite the enormous logistical challenges. In the parliamentary elections in 2019 there was a voter turnout of 67%, slightly up on the 66% of 2014. In 2024 the turnout fell to 64% – still remarkably high given an extreme heatwave in which many died. By contrast, the US presidential elections in 2020 had a turnout of 66%, which was the highest since 1900, while the last mid-term Congressional elections had a turnout of 49%, the highest since 1914. However, the use of a first-past-the-post voting system in both India and the USA (and the UK) means that the government's legitimacy is somewhat weaker. In 2019, at the peak of its popularity, BJP candidates received 37% of the votes, from only 25% of the electorate (31% and 20% in 2014). That said, the underlying level of support, or at least consent, has been as strong or stronger than in Western democracies.

China does not have contested national elections, so there is no validation of that kind. But independent surveys suggest that the regime is regarded positively. The Ash Center at Harvard University produces the largest academic study of Chinese public opinion by an independent body outside China. It shows high levels of satisfaction with central government (95% as against 38% in the USA).[78] But there is strong dissatisfaction with local government (11% are 'very satisfied', against 70% in the USA). Systemic issues like corruption were blamed on local party officials rather than 'the system'. Indeed, one of the biproducts of China's highly successful model of empowering local government is that it has also decentralised dissatisfaction.

Observers with recent inside knowledge of the CCP summarise the situation as being one in which the regime 'enjoys general, though not 100%, support from its population' based on 'economic growth and social stability' among younger people and memories of more chaotic and poorer times among older people.[79] But the Party is obsessively worried about its popularity: 'the ruling party is worried that it will be driven out just like the last Emperor in 1911 and the Nationalists in 1949 if the party cannot live up to the high expectations of the population'. Much of the sophisticated system of surveillance is geared to identifying problems before they become serious, as with crime blackspots or traffic bottlenecks, thereby enhancing the popularity of the authorities.[80] As noted above, localised protest is tolerated if it can be seen as a way of heading off wider discontent.

The Ash Center study identifies inequality as a source of dissatisfaction. Recent research by Scott Rozelle and Martin King Whyte has monitored growing resentment of a self-perpetuating elite and the lack of social mobility.[81] This explains, in part, Xi's preoccupation with corruption and his Common Prosperity programme, which incorporated crackdowns on private tutoring to gain access to top universities and gig practices by the tech platform companies. But the biggest source of vulnerability is disenchantment among the educated, young, urban middle class, for whom the implicit social contract was to deliver improving quality of life (including freedom to travel abroad) in return for accepting the constraints of one-party rule. That is why a crucial ingredient in regime survival is successful economic policy and rising living standards and why China's recent economic difficulties are so dangerous. That is true not only in authoritarian China but also in democratic India – indeed, the poor performance of the BJP campaign in 2024 had much to do with its failure to translate impressive economic growth into jobs and improved living standards and jobs for large numbers of voters.

Development men

Both the Indian and Chinese governments promise and depend upon economic success, since this is a means to maintain domestic support and to project power and influence abroad. Indian politicians have the bigger challenge, since survival in office depends on showing quick results or persuading voters that better times are on the way. Empty populism – like Indira Gandhi's promise to 'abolish poverty' – may win one election but not a second or third. Technocratic governments, such as the Congress administrations that oversaw Manmohan Singh's reforms, also struggled to sustain support. That is the context for trying to understand the success of Modi's BJP in three successive general elections and many state elections, where they managed to combine brilliant campaigning techniques and the ideological appeal of Hindutva with visible economic results.[82]

As Chief Minister of Gujarat, Modi coined the phrase 'Vikas Purush' or Development Man. Development Man set about building what was called the Gujarat Model.[83] It was based on investment by big business, facilitated by efficient administration with minimum red tape and delay. Some of India's leading economists endorsed it.[84] There were pro-business policies such as reduced labour and environment regulation and the creation of special economic zones making land available and offering generous financial inducements (some of them secret and subject to a lot of criticism). Some of the leading Indian, and Gujarati-owned, companies – Mukesh Ambani's Reliance Group, the Adanis, the Essar Group of the Ruias – invested heavily in capital intensive heavy industries like oil refineries. More investment led to rapid growth and Gujarat's burgeoning reputation. An important symbol of success was when the Tata group – not Gujarati and with a reputation for probity – built a car plant, having been exasperated by delays in West Bengal. Critics argue that the Gujarat Model involved 'growth without development', with minimal attention to social welfare, little job creation and poor wages.[85] But economic growth and the hype around it helped to strengthen the image of Vikas Purush.

Once in national office, Modi was able to reproduce the Gujarat Model on a bigger scale. The BJP government unleashed a big programme of infrastructure investment: roads, railways, airports, power plants, telecoms networks. The formula has been, as in Gujarat: quick decisions, cutting through red tape, government financial backing and heavy investment by favoured business groups, notably the Adanis. In fact, a lot of the groundwork for infrastructure projects was laid in the Manmohan Singh era. But skilful PR by the BJP also reflected measurable progress on the ground.[86]

The fact that much of this development was driven by 'crony capitalism', with a growing concentration of ownership, was easier to overlook in a rapidly growing economy.[87] A deeper problem, which only became apparent in the 2024 election, was that an impressive development story had failed to translate into new jobs. The BJP had abandoned one of the best targeted programmes of the Manmohan Singh era designed to alleviate poverty: the rural employment guarantee, which provided minimum wage work for 50 million of the poorest Indians.[88] Nor was there much sign of progress in the provision of public goods such as health and education. Dalits saw their job reservation protections diluted. Evidence suggests that the rich were getting richer while poverty grew.[89] And that was before the pandemic, which greatly set back the progress in poverty reduction.[90]

To set against these negatives, Modi had three programmes specifically targeted at the poorest. The first was a campaign against public defecation, long a source of national embarrassment, infection in polluted water courses and personal humiliation, especially for girls, who are often deterred from going to school by the absence of toilets. Sceptics have pointed out that many of the newly installed toilets do not work and are not maintained. But the existence of the programme shows that the government cared about the poor: not so much in terms of their income as their dignity. A second initiative has been to spread energetically the availability of private goods, which must be paid for but are now more easily available: gas cylinders for cooking, bank accounts, mobile phones and broadband connections, electricity and water connections. A third has been the use of direct payments through the Stack system, ensuring that recipients receive what they are entitled to without the intervention of corrupt intermediaries (and that women have their own, independent access to bank accounts and benefits). Not much of this activity involved redistribution from the BJP's middle- and upper-class supporters, but a lot of it enhanced the dignity and agency of poor Indians. In the event, the 2024 election proved the limits of such appeal, when large numbers of poor Indians in one of the poorest states did not see enough real material benefit to stay with the BJP.

China's Xi does not have to worry about how to get the votes of the poor, or anyone else. But his China Dream was, and is, about cementing China's place as an economically successful middle-income country and ensuring it is not stuck in a middle-income trap. He is all too aware that the Party is not universally loved and that its legitimacy, if not survival, depends on the continuing support or acquiescence of the educated middle class, for whom the social contract involves trading political freedom for good and rising living standards. Xi's difficulty is that it is his predecessors, notably Deng, who have earned the credit for the transformation in Chinese living standards. The problems he now faces are deep-rooted and difficult and may be leading to slow growth, even economic stagnation. Their resolution requires action to boost private investment and consumption which is at odds with what he has been trying to do to create a coherent ideology on Marxist-Leninist lines and to put the Party back in a central role.

Xi had a clear understanding of how to work with the private sector and incentivise it based on his career as a successful Party official in states – Fujian and Zhejiang – which were among the pioneers of economic reform and rapid development. When he came into national office his early speeches emphasised markets and private enterprise. He associated himself with reforms designed to engender more 'creative destruction' – through bankruptcy laws and more effective commercial bond markets – and rationalisation of the state enterprise sector. His interventionist instincts were channelled into curbing financial excesses, in the form of high leverage and undisciplined bank lending. But it became clear that strengthening the role of the Party took precedence over markets, albeit that markets have been partially rehabilitated to help re-energise the economy after the property sector crash. And the Party was 'extractive' rather than wealth creating.[91] Entrepreneurs were tolerated rather than encouraged and cut down to size if, like Jack Ma, they seemed to be becoming separate power centres. The Common Prosperity programme was perceived as anti-business not because of the curbs on tech companies, which continue and are profitable, but because the government's actions were arbitrary and not subject to the processes of consultation and rules-based regulation. Disappearances of prominent businesspeople for no obvious reason have added to uncertainty. While many lucrative opportunities exist, who makes money is heavily influenced by the government (and the Party).

Politics and economics are now working against each other. The economy is being held back by lack of consumption. Low public morale, caused in part by more intrusive and restrictive government, is leading people to hoard rather than spend. Entrepreneurs lack 'animal spirits' because of arbitrary government, attacks on tech companies and other unfashionable sectors and party interference. Migrant workers face lower wage growth and the restrictions and frustrations of the hukou system. University graduates face unemployment or the need to adjust their expectations sharply downwards. The middle class has been hit by falling property prices, which represent family savings. The sense that the social contract has broken down and that the CCP, and Xi personally, are failing to deliver is not directly threatening to the regime. Rather it is inducing among young people a sense of hopelessness (called 'lying flat'). The regime cannot risk large-scale unrest and so will avoid difficult decisions (as with radical restructuring and closure of failing state enterprises) or introducing effective property taxes or freeing up avenues for protest. The disruption to trade and investment caused by a cold war with the USA potentially makes the economic problems worse by scaring off investors. Until recently, economic success was a key to the legitimacy of the regime. Now that economic success is elusive, the regime faces the issue of how to contain threats to its legitimacy. It has pivoted to security as the main concern, while economic issues and economic advisers have been relegated in importance.

Both Modi and Xi have lost their aura as Development Men: Modi at the ballot box, Xi through the many signs of economic stress. In Modi's case it is clearer what must be done to recapture earlier popularity: to focus on job creation and poverty reduction in an otherwise healthily growing economy. With Xi, the problems are serious and the solutions less obvious.

Conclusion

Politically, present day China and India have more in common than is comfortable for those who believe that liberal democracy or democratic capitalism is not merely the best model of governance but also the only one that works in the long run. India's commitment to liberal democracy compares well with other big, complex, multi-ethnic countries. But under Modi and the BJP India has come close to embracing the idea of rule by one man and one party, with shrinking areas of dissent. Democracy has survived and been vindicated for the moment, but there will continue to be a debate as to whether democracy or autocracy is best for development.

One fashionable way of reconciling these opposing views is to argue that autocratic rule is a necessary but temporary evil until countries reach 'developed' standards of living. The public accepts a kind of social contract in which political freedoms are surrendered in return for rising living standards for a generation or two – and then, political freedoms follow. This is the South Korea and Taiwan story (and Singapore, with its idiosyncratic democratic one-party state). China seemed to be travelling along this road, though Xi's rule shows no sign of evolving in that way, even to be a gigantic Singapore. And India is now being offered a sectarian, Hindutva philosophy which in no way resembles the non-ideological approach of the development states of East Asia.

Democrats will argue that bad authoritarian politics will lead to bad economics. Guha notes that 'the principal source of India's survival as a democratic country and of its recent economic success has been its political and cultural pluralism, precisely those qualities which the Prime Minister and his party now work to extinguish'.[92] Democracy has never been part of the China story, but as Martin Wolf argues in his book *The Crisis of Democratic Capitalism*, 'it is hard to believe that China can indefinitely combine a sophisticated information economy and educated population with today's political system. The idea that a bureaucracy dominated by one man will control everything in such a vast and sophisticated country forever seems implausible.'[93] Politics and economics are inextricably linked.

4

Economic growth: the great reversal?

The metaphor of the Indian tortoise and the Chinese hare is a questionable approximation to reality. But, to the extent that it is illuminating, the tortoise seems to be scuttling along at a brisk pace while the hare is limping. Looking at the future, there appears to be a consensus that the Indian tortoise, still a long way behind, will keep scuttling. But the views about China are mixed. Does the present pause represent a hiatus or a fundamental slowing in the hare's athletic capacity? The hare could be tired, injured or crippled by a serious disability. In this chapter I review the different assessments representing their respective growth potential.

We cannot confidently predict the long-term economic future because of big uncertainties around technology, policy choices and politics, internal and external. There are no real precedents for such vast and complex countries continuing along a particular growth path for generations. The experience of the East Asian Newly Industrialising Countries is useful, but countries like South Korea and Singapore are much smaller. There is a broad view about economic development that poorer countries will tend to catch up with wealthy nations as they take advantage of known technology and realise the productivity benefits of a rural to urban migration, while developed countries have the more demanding task of pushing outward the 'production frontier'.[1] Another, opposite, rule of thumb is that of growth rates reverting to the mean. But these generalisations do not necessarily apply to individual countries, and there is some evidence of divergence rather than convergence in recent years.[2] In any event, China and India are unique in scale and scope. What we can try to do is to break down the main components of economic growth and to look at various scenarios as to how these could evolve.

107

Long-term growth

The long-term view of growth matters, since it affects the future relative size of what are likely to be the three biggest economies in the world: China, India and the USA. A crucial starting point is to ask what measuring stick we are using when measuring levels of, and changes in, GDP. I discussed earlier the difference between purchasing power parity and market exchange rate measures. On a PPP basis China already has the largest economy in the world by some distance, and this tells us the country's relative position in terms of how much is produced, earned and consumed. On this basis, India has the third biggest economy. But at market exchange rates, China is number two and India number five.

Measurement of future growth is partly about growth in the domestic economy but also about how far price levels converge. Thus, if India or China were not to grow their economy at all they would grow in market exchange rate terms if their currency appreciated in real terms (that is, if the price level rose, relatively, as it should as they become part of the world economy, and/or if their exchange rate appreciated relative to the dollar). The mechanism by which this occurs was first described by economists Béla Balassa and Paul Samuelson in the 1960s and has been demonstrated empirically for many developing economies.[3] India, especially, could benefit from such an adjustment, since its relative price level is so much lower (according to the World Bank Indian prices are around 30% of US prices; for China the figure is 60%).

Even putting aside this complexity, differences in growth rates can have spectacular effects due to long-term compounding. The Lowy Institute illustrate this point with a simple thought experiment:

> in terms of market exchange rates, China's economy is three-quarters the size of America's. However, the IMF forecasts that the figure will be 90% by 2026 and if that trend continued would overtake the USA before 2030. If China remained on a commensurate trajectory over the following decades, its economy could be more than twice the size of America's by mid-century when measured in US dollars. Some extrapolations show that China has the potential to grow even faster in which case its economy could reach a staggering 4–5 times America's by 2050.[4]

But others have extrapolated from China's current economic difficulties and the current, dynamic, post-pandemic recovery of the USA to argue that

108

'China is no longer sure to become the largest economy'.[5] Linked to this recent pessimism about China is the – contested – idea of a middle-income trap which has prevented several countries once predicted to become 'developed' from making the final step to 'high-income' status.[6] Others talk of 'Peak China'.[7] The difference between the optimistic and pessimistic view is very large.

Unsurprisingly, there is a wide range of long-term growth predictions for the period to 2050 from serious researchers using different models or techniques or different theoretical frameworks (Figure 4.1). At the optimistic end, for China, is Justin Lin, formerly of the World Bank, who believes a growth rate of 7 to 8% p.a. could be sustained for decades based on East Asian experience of countries which were once at a Chinese average level of per capita income and development but have grown far past it.[8] A more pessimistic study by economists Lant Pritchard and Larry Summers in 2014 made the then unfashionable prediction that long-term growth would be at most 4% p.a. and as low as 2%.[9] The most recent studies are at the pessimistic end of the spectrum and contradict the consensus forecast as summarised by the Lowy Institute: 'overall, among 20 recent studies, the majority suggest that China's economic growth could average around 5% a year or higher to 2030 and about 3.5–4% from 2020–2050'.[10] These numbers lead to China

Source and date	Growth trend (%)
Lin (2019)	7–8 (East Asia growth)
Lardy (2019)	6–7 (with reform)
Wang (2020)	5.1 (median)
Lu and Cai (2016)	4.2
Bai and Zhang (2017)	4.0
Bloomberg (2021)	3.7 (median)
Lee (2017)	3.6
International Energy Agency (2021)	3.6
Barro (2016)	3.5 (range 3% to 4%)
World Bank (Innovative China) (2019)	3.4 (median)
Pritchett and Summers (2014)	3.0 (range 2% to 4%)
PwC (2017)	3.0
OECD (2018)	2.6
Rajah and Leng (2022)	2.5

Source: Roland Rajah and Alyssa Leng, 'Revising Down the Rise of China', Lowy Institute Analysis, 14 March 2022, Technical Appendix

4.1 China long-term growth projections (2020–50)

having an economy two to three times bigger than the USA by mid-century. But with a growing awareness of China's deep structural problems, arising from lack of demand to absorb the country's large accumulation of savings, the consensus at the time of writing was that long-term growth would do well to exceed 2% to 3% p.a.

By contrast, the long-term projections about India are fewer but involve a high degree of consensus and optimism about growth (Figure 4.2). The long-term growth rate is taken to be in the range 5% to 7% for the next decade but with subsequent slowing over time to a 3% to 4% range in later decades: faster than China but without the spectacular double-digit growth at the same stage of development. One might question why India is thought to be capable of only around 6% growth when other countries, including China, have managed close to 10% for prolonged periods. One explanation, given by Karthik Muralidharan, is that India lacks 'state capacity'.[11] The public sector, in his view, is currently incapable of delivering the necessary supporting infrastructure and services. But he also points out that the reforms needed are perfectly feasible. Even on a more modest growth assumption, a major long-term growth study by the OECD has India overtaking the USA in economic size before 2050 but is still 60% of the size of China. The OECD study is based on a standard growth model in which investment drives growth but is subject to declining marginal productivity.[12] The model also assumes a falling contribution of technological progress which is particularly contentious given the growing importance of AI and the scope for innovation in the 'green transition'. Suffice it to say that there is a great deal of debate and uncertainty around the deep determinants of

	2023–30	2030–50
OECD (2018)	7.0	5.4
Bloomberg (2022)	8.4	8.0
Morgan Stanley (2022)	6.5	–
Australian Treasury (2022)	6.0 (to 2035)	–
Ernst & Young (2023)	6.4	6.0
FT (Wolf) (2023)	⟶	6.0
Standard and Poor (2023)	6.3	–
IMF (2023)	5.6	–

Source: Ernst & Young, *India@100: Realizing the Potential of a US$26 Trillion Economy* (Kolkata: Ernst & Young, 2023)

4.2 Annual growth projections for India (%)

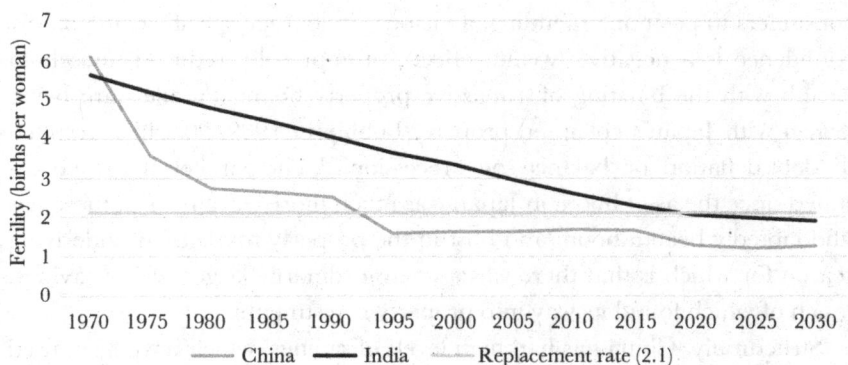

Source: United Nations, World Population Prospects 2022

4.3 Population and fertility trends in China and India

long-run growth. For that reason, it is useful to start with the shorter-term constraints.

China's crisis of confidence

It is China rather than India whose immediate growth outlook is relatively poor and whose difficulties may imperil longer-term growth. Growth had been gradually slowing from double digit figures to around 7% p.a. in the run up to the pandemic. Since the end of the pandemic, the recovery has been modest by Chinese standards. In 2023 growth was thought by some to be below the government's claim of 5%.[13] The IMF, however, has cautiously endorsed the official prediction of 5% growth in 2024, slowing slightly to 4.5% in 2025. Among the real world manifestations of this slowdown is a surge in youth employment to over 20%. There are also indicators of a loss of consumer confidence including poor sales figures for cars and luxury goods after people's sense of job and income security was dented by the pandemic, though Chinese official data suggests that consumption has been rising faster than income. Evidence of weak investor confidence ranges from depressed stock exchanges to outflows of foreign investment.

There are deeper problems. At the heart of those is weak demand, reflected in very low inflation and, on some measures, deflation. Lack of spending pushes down prices and the expectation that prices will fall causes

111

consumers to postpone spending: a vicious circle. One specific cause of low confidence is a negative 'wealth effect', prompted by reduced household wealth with the bursting of a massive property boom. Parallels are being drawn with Japan's collapsed property bubble in 1989/90 which resulted in 'debt deflation' or 'balance sheet recession'.[14] The parallels may be overstated since the asset boom in Japan was much more extreme. But there has undoubtedly been a boom and bust in the property market, an underlying reason for which is that there was an extraordinarily large level of savings, much of which found its way into property investment.

Structurally, China has had high levels of savings, which have been used to finance investment in infrastructure or property while the excess of savings over investment has manifested itself as a current account and trade surplus. The high savings (and weak consumption) is partly down to Chinese precautionary savings – for health bills and for retirement – in the absence of a generous welfare state. Another factor is forced saving in the form of retained profits by (mostly state-owned) business at the expense of low wages. Michael Pettis has built a theory of Chinese growth weakness based on a very unequal distribution of national income with a low proportion of income coming back to workers to consume.[15] But Chinese official data excludes from consumption a lot of 'social transfers in kind' like subsidised food and medicines, worker canteens and cheap cultural facilities. If they are included the share of consumption in GDP may be closer to 45% than the 37% recorded in 2022.[16] By international standards, however, this is still low.

Pessimism about China's short-term growth is based in part on the difficulties of managing the burst property boom; the reluctance of the government to indulge in a large-scale consumer stimulus and income redistribution through welfare or public services spending; and the creation of barriers to Chinese exports in the USA. These problems are amenable to policy change in China, but that requires a radical change of economic direction that the regime finds it difficult to make. Some critics believe that the regime has an ideological obsession with investment over consumption and manufacturing over services. Others can point to genuine problems limiting the government's freedom of manoeuvre, such as growing public debt worries, especially in local government. At the end of 2024 the government appeared to have listened to the critics, responding with an ambitious stimulus involving incentives for consumer spending, recapitalising banks and refinancing indebted local government. Reviving consumption was put as top economic priority. Time will tell if this is sufficient to revive consumer and private sector confidence.

There is also a strong counterargument against even short-term pessimism. Lardy reminds us that 'China is still rising',[17] and that China's apparently weak relative growth in market exchange rates has been partly a statistical phenomenon created by a strong dollar, boosted by a big interest rate swing against China: a 5% rise in the USA as against a 0.25% cut in China. In inflation adjusted and Chinese currency terms, 'crisis-hit' China has been growing at 5% p.a. (if we believe the numbers) and 'booming' USA by 2.5% p.a.

Looking further ahead, there are some growth problems that are potentially very serious, and that do not have quick, easy solutions: a falling labour force and an ageing population. India, by comparison, may have a 'demographic dividend'.

Demographic dividends and deficits

An expanding population is one contributory factor in economic growth, increasing the numbers of both workers and consumers. It was striking that, in 2023, India's population overtook China's at around 1.42 billion, but with the two countries on very different trajectories. Census data is not wholly reliable and up to date (India's last census was in 2011). United Nations projections in 2018 had the Chinese population peaking in 2025, but Chinese data at the end of 2022 suggest that China's population has already peaked – indeed, it started to decline in 2022. China's population could now decline to around 1 billion by 2075, at the latest, while India's continues to expand to a peak of 1.65 billion at around 2060. There is an enormous range of possible outcomes as fertility and death rates change over time. The UN forecasts have India's population at the end of this century anywhere between 1 and 2.2 billion with China's in the range 0.5 to 1.2 billion.

The different population trends of the two countries can be explained largely by different trajectories for fertility (Figure 4.3). In China, the forecasts of severe population decline stem from abrupt changes in levels of fertility which far outweigh the gradual improvements in life expectancy. Fertility fell from 6 children per woman in the 1950s and 1960s to an average of 1.7 in the first two decades of this century. Fertility rates have been an estimated 1.2 in the last few years, slightly below Japanese levels. Crucially, fertility is well below the replacement rate of around 2.1, which means that the population must fall. The initial, sharp fall in fertility was partly due to the one-child policy, which was introduced shortly after the death of Mao in 1976. The new policy was motivated by development reasons – to raise incomes per head. The policy was sometimes applied coercively by zealous officials, with pressure to have abortion and sterilisation, but, nonetheless, it appears to have been broadly supported. In recent years the cost of having children, especially for urban and educated women, has also been a further deterrent to having big families – so much so that the government has reversed policy, which is now to encourage births (without any observable impact).

India is heading in the same direction, but more gradually. From a fertility rate of 6 per woman in the 1950s and 1960s, followed by a short period of coercive birth control during Indira Gandhi's Emergency, fertility rates have fallen steadily to the current – replacement – level of around 2.0. Development has been both a cause and effect of this trend, with falling child mortality, greater female education, and the availability of contraception. Levels of fertility are roughly twice as high in the poorer, less-developed northern states, Uttar Pradesh and Bihar, as in Tamil Nadu and Kerala, but are falling almost everywhere in India.

The different demographic trends have already made a big difference to the structure of the population of China and India. The average age in China is 38 and in India 29, with both those figures set to rise. The UN median projections suggest that by 2050 the Chinese over-65s will rise from 13% to 30% of the population, while the number of Indian over-65s will rise from 7% to 17%. There is a growing issue, especially in China, of a smaller number of workers paying for increasing numbers of elderly dependants making demands on China's pay-as-you-go pensions system and healthcare. These problems are familiar in the developed world, but China is 'getting old before getting rich'. Another feature of both countries is the big gap between the numbers of males and females – 30 million in China, 45 million in India – as a result of widespread infanticide of female babies.

What is most relevant for future growth is the size of the working-age population. For both China and India, in the period 1960–80, the share of the population of working age, between 16 and 65, was around 55%. China

114

then enjoyed four decades in which – thanks mainly to the rapidly declining number of children – it enjoyed a demographic dividend in which the share of the working-age population rose to a peak of 73% around 2010: from 550 million people to 1 billion. This increase was a factor behind the rapid economic growth of that time. India's working-age population share grew more slowly and was 62% in 2010. It has been estimated, however, that by 2030 the growing Indian working-age share will overtake the – falling – Chinese share at close to 70%.[18] This process is illustrated in Figure 4.4. Rates will diverge thereafter with China's working-age proportion falling back to 57% in 2050 as the population ages rapidly while India's remains at 67%. India is now said to be enjoying the demographic dividend that China enjoyed before 2010.

The demographic dividend has two components. One is a rise in the 'support ratio' as the number of people in the labour force grows faster than those – children or elderly – who depend on support, permitting more resources to be invested in development. The second is the impact on savings and investment. The traditional life cycle approach tells us that retired people run down their savings, and so in an ageing population the saving ratio should come down. But in a country like China, with poor pension, care and health provision and a slowing economy, the middle aged may collectively save more for retirement, by choice or through tax, which can be deployed in productivity raising investment.[19] The economic effects are, however, complex. A potential shortfall in the labour force manifests itself in

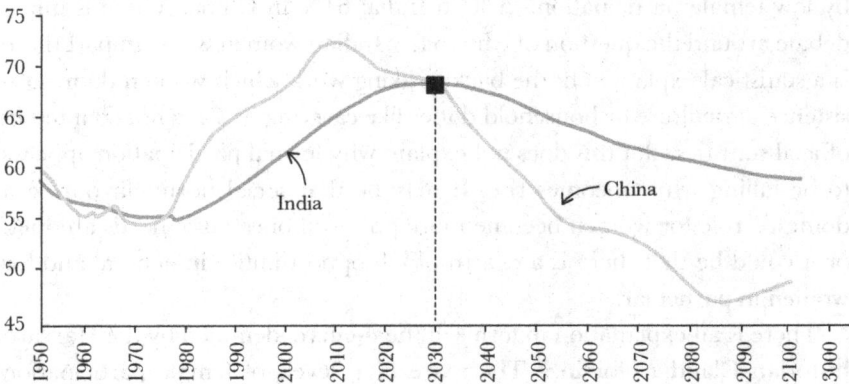

Source: India@100. Ernst and Young

4.4 Labour force in India and China (% of population)

115

rising wage costs and higher living standards, with more disposable income and higher spending. There could then be an increase in investment as capital replaces labour. And with China's rather frugal pensions, older people may well work longer and spend more carefully in retirement.

The demographic dividend is, consequently, a slippery concept and potentially misleading.[20] In addition, the dividend will be affected by what share of the working-age population works and how skilled, educated and productive workers are. As to the first issue, participation rates are affected by levels of un- or underemployment, by sickness and disability and by the numbers enjoying higher education or early retirement. Female participation can vary greatly depending on custom and tradition, education levels and childcare availability. A study by Xin Meng, an economist at the Australian National University, has shown that a significant part of the Chinese demographic dividend was cancelled out by a fall in labour force participation from 85% to around 70%.[21] This was due to compulsory retirement for most of the urban population (at age 60 for men, 55 for white collar women and 50 for women factory workers), growing numbers of post-school students and women dropping out of work because of childcare costs.

Different participation rates may also eliminate much of the supposed advantage which India has over China from having a younger population. Based on World Bank data, even though the Chinese participation rate has fallen and is estimated at 67% at the end of 2022, it is far higher than the Indian participation rate of 49%. The disparity is explained almost entirely by low female participation: 29% in India; 61% in China. There is much debate around the question of why so few Indian women work. In part there is a statistical explanation: the backbreaking work which women do in subsistence agriculture or household duties like carrying water is not counted in official statistics. But this does not explain why formal participation appears to be falling while incomes rise. It may be that social norms favouring a domestic role for women become more powerful once basic needs are met; or it could be that there is a dearth of job opportunities in general and for women in particular.

There is an explanation in terms of the u-curve identified by the Harvard historian Claudia Goldin.[22] There are high levels of female participation in very poor, subsistence economies, much of it in arduous, dangerous and dirty work. As incomes rise, women drop out of this unappealing work until safer, more attractive and better paid work in offices and factories leads again to higher participation. With half of enrolment in universities now of women there is potentially an educated female workforce. But, as of now, India is stuck at the bottom of the Goldin u-curve and will remain there without a big expansion of work opportunities, especially for educated women, in labour-intensive goods and services.

What do these past trends tell us about the future? UN projections suggest that the working-age population in China will shrink by around 60 million by 2030 (from 2020 levels) and 220 million by 2050. It is unlikely that this trend can be reversed by natalist policies. In early 2025, the government proposed an increase to the retirement age for men to 63, white collar women to 58 and women factory workers to 55. But this would be very unpopular, since much of the labour force has already experienced decades of toil in tough working conditions and expects to retire. China may be authoritarian, but the CCP is nervous of antagonising its working-class base. There are widely varying estimates of how much additional labour supply this policy would realise, from over 50 million down to the low teens by 2030.[23] We may also see more older workers continuing to work after retirement age, but there is an offsetting fall from more older workers dropping out of the workforce before the new retirement age.

A more promising source of labour supply is the continuing transfer from low-productivity farming. An estimated 180 million currently work full time on the land, and there are around 300 million who are migrant workers: working in cities but registered in the countryside to which they are tied by the hukou system of internal passports. These restrict entitlement to public services and benefits to where citizens are registered which means, in practice, that migrant workers are required to use the inferior services of rural areas. The government has repeatedly trailed the idea of abolishing hukou which would free migrants to move permanently to employment in the cities. But that is not a straight-forward matter. Because of low levels of education among the rural population, many are ill-equipped for a modern workforce, especially older workers in their fifties.[24] Without investment in education and skills, the rural migrants could simply end up in the cities as unemployed or as precarious informal sector workers (as they already are in India). The mismatch of skills and education levels with the needs of the labour market also explains rising youth unemployment, for 16- to 24-year-olds, for which

117

the embarrassed authorities no longer publish statistics (but when last published were over 20%, including many university graduates).

Overall it is possible to see how the labour force problem might be kept at bay for a decade or so by policy reform but, beyond that, the constraint becomes increasingly serious. The response in many Western countries has been to relax restrictions around immigration and, while this may meet the short- and medium-term needs of the labour market, there is considerable political resistance. In East Asia this resistance is even stronger though, in decades to come, we may see acceptance of 'guest workers', including in China. But that is not an option in the foreseeable future. To counter adverse demography, there will also have to be a sustained growth in labour productivity, as through more intensive use of robots and AI. Suffice it to say that there are different views in China about how easily demographic constraints can be overcome. Some see an inevitable decline in long-term economic growth rates to 4% in the 2030s.[25] Meanwhile, optimists believe that a healthier population can work longer and more flexibly, and that better education will make for higher productivity, largely removing the demographic constraint.[26]

For India, the issue is quite different: how to realise the potential demographic dividend, much of which is currently wasted in unemployment and underemployment. Ashoka Mody estimates that there is currently a shortfall of at least 80 million jobs.[27] Estimates based on labour force and household surveys suggest that around 8% of the labour force – 40 million people of working age able and willing to search for jobs – cannot find employment. Among young people aged 15 to 24 the rate is closer to 30%. And, beyond that, there is the vast underemployment in rural India and the poor female workforce participation. I referred above to the low female participation rate which is probably far worse than the officially recorded numbers. India's Population and Labour Force Surveys show a sharp improvement from 21% to 32% over the five (financial) year period 2017–22.[28] But, nonetheless, these numbers are worse than for any other significant economy, even including Saudi Arabia where, until recently, women were actively stopped from working. Unless India can find ways to absorb its underemployed workforce, the idea of a demographic dividend will be a fantasy.[29]

By contrast, the consensus view of Chinese demographic problems is that they are very real and will act as a drag on growth (subtracting perhaps 0.5%

to 1% from annual growth), reversing the demographic dividend of the previous four or more decades. But one should not discount the optimistic view
that policy innovation and better health and education will ease the problem. That raises the question of how far long-term growth in both countries
can be supported by another factor of production: capital investment.

Savings, capital investment and debt

Simple models of economic growth make growth dependent on capital formation: investment. The discussion of past growth performance in
Chapter 2 shows that high rates of investment, originating in even higher
rates of domestic saving, were a key factor in China's explosive, double digit
economic growth. In the last decade, investment has been sustained at very
high levels – over 40% of GDP – but growth rates have been falling, suggesting that investment is increasingly inefficient, with more and more required
for the same increase in output. Much of this unproductive investment is in
property, and an oversupply of housing has led to a financial crisis in the
property sector. Nonetheless, China's extraordinary savings rate of over
40% of GDP – the result of precautionary savings by an ageing population,
together with a low household share of national income – means that there
are, for the foreseeable future, abundant domestic savings to invest. Whether
that contributes to growth depends on the success of business, including
state-owned business, in absorbing the savings in productive investment in
consumer goods industries and services, high-technology sectors and exports.
The first of these is crucial since the second is of limited scale and the third
assumes continued openness of international markets to Chinese products.

India, by contrast, has the usual profile of a developing economy in which
domestic savings lag investment – by 2% to 3% of GDP, typically – requiring
inward investment offsetting current account deficits. There was also a big
jump in investment (gross capital formation) from 20%–23% of GDP in the
decade 1991–2001 to around 30%–35% in the period after 2008. As in China,
the aggregate investment figures are less important than where the investment
goes and who does it. As already noted in Chapter 2, India has a history, in
the period of state-led investment within a system of planning and controls,
of inefficient capital formation in heavy industry and slow growth. The more
recent upsurge in investment has however been in the private sector alongside

public investment and has been used to drive a boom in growth-enhancing infrastructure. Future growth hinges on that process continuing.

The high savings rates in both countries should ensure a rapid expansion of investment, albeit constrained by demand. But, in the case of China, there is a serious legacy problem in the form of corporate and local government indebtedness which, while the debt is almost entirely internal to China, will require major balance sheet restructuring. And that affects the ability and willingness of companies and indebted agencies to invest.

So, why is debt potentially a problem? In Chapter 1 I discussed why the seriousness of debt problems in China is more serious than might appear. Foreign public sector debt is among the world's lowest (14% of GDP for China; a similarly low 18% for India) and so there is currently no issue of external credit worthiness. Public sector debt is also apparently not exceptional – 77% of GNP for China; 82% for India – which should be comfortably serviced even at reduced real economic growth rates of 5%. But, in China, these figures exclude roughly the same amount again in hidden local government debt. In China, with its decentralised fiscal system, local government has borrowed heavily, both directly from banks or the public or indirectly through the issuance of LGFVs (local government financing vehicles), an opaque form of investment that provides the basis for a lot of shadow banking. With slump conditions in the property market, councils now find it more difficult to sell land to raise cash to service their debts and finance new development.[30] A central government bailout of local government is acknowledged to be required, and that process has started. But until it is completed, the more indebted parts of local government will be inhibited in investing more.

There is another dimension to the problem of indebtedness of Chinese institutions. Non-financial corporates have leveraged their balance sheets to the extent of 136% of GDP as against 52% in India. The culprits are mainly property development companies which gambled on prices and sales continuing to rise, bringing in more cash to finance construction. Many are now insolvent. They survive only by forbearance (by state-owned banks) and now face major restructuring or bankruptcy. In practical terms, this means that the institutions driving Chinese growth face several years of consolidation rather than expansion. India has had a milder version of the same disease in the form of non-performing loans constricting bank lending but with a recent clean-up of bank balance sheets and with the widening and deepening of financial markets, that is not a serious constraint on growth at present.

Housing investment: boom, bust and after

These different experiences help to frame any analysis of the different sources of demand for future investment, starting with housing. In recent years Chinese housing investment has absorbed a large proportion of savings: around 14% of GDP.[31] The wider property sector including commercial real estate and supporting infrastructure accounts for around 30% of GDP, according to economists Kenneth Rogoff and Yuanchen Yang.[32] There are alternative, lower, estimates which eliminate double counting and the IMF uses a figure of 20%. What can be said with confidence is that there will be serious repercussions for future investment in housing from the property market crisis, at least until the current cycle has run its course. The market crash has bankrupted overleveraged property companies. And, faced with a drastic fall in the number of sales, developers are no longer investing in new developments. Housing investment is thought to have fallen to around 50% of peak levels, although the government is providing modest support for the market by buying up unsold property.

There are significant impediments to new housing investment. There are currently around 80 to 100 million vacant or incomplete properties: about 15% to 20% of the housing stock. These are visible in the form of large numbers of unoccupied or incomplete blocks of flats in many Chinese cities. In addition to this large inventory overhanging the market, underlying demand is set to fall as the population falls. In a market economy, prices should fall, expanding demand by making property more affordable. But while prices have fallen by around 20% since the peak, they are still far above affordability levels for low-income families. Prices are also being artificially supported by the government to avoid a disastrous wealth loss among homeowners, many of whom invested in property as an investment rather than for occupation. There is still some demand to be created by the demolition of substandard slum housing, but much of that has already largely happened (66 million homes were demolished in the 2013–18 period).

In the longer term, once the stock of unsold property has cleared, the market will find a new balance at levels of fundamental market demand.

There will also be a need for low-cost social housing. One estimate is that demand will bottom out at around 45% of pre-crash levels.[33] Based on that assumption, future housing investment could be half of levels in the last decade. But that may be pessimistic as China still has large numbers living in rural areas and who will move to the cities once the (hukou) restrictions are removed; maybe as many as 200 million people in the next two decades.

India has almost a mirror image of the Chinese property market. There is enormous unmet demand and restricted supply. The real estate sector is also far smaller than in China: an estimated 7% of GDP. Indian forecasters believe its share of a rapidly expanding GDP could double by 2050.[34] Housing is only one of four components of the real estate sector, but growth is prodigious, recently close to 50% per annum. Yet, as noted above, demand far exceeds supply. The supply of new homes for middle- and high-income households in the seven biggest cities in the period 2016–20 was around one million, but that demand from a growing and increasingly affluent middle class grew by 4 million, resulting in rapid house price inflation. Demand for better and affordable housing for the wider, low-income population in rural areas is vast. Indian official sources state that 19 million urban families and 43 million rural families 'need' affordable housing to replace substandard accommodation.[35] (Definitions are fuzzy; 'need' takes in the 5% of people in officially designated 'slums', but also those living in much of the 40% of the housing stock currently deemed 'liveable' but substandard). And demand is growing rapidly. India's urban population is currently around 36% of the total and is expected to exceed 50% by 2050 due to a mix of population growth and rural–urban migration.

The potential for new housing investment in India is therefore very large. There are, however, serious supply constraints. Developers' access to scarce urban land depends on opaque and often corrupt dealings at local level and may be at the expense of public housing. The restrictions of the 'permit raj' have eased but are still a major drag on development with complicated and corruptly enforced regulations over the height of buildings and other planning requirements. India's cities, unlike China's, are expanding in an unplanned way with poor infrastructure. Private developers have large margins but precarious financing resulting in many stalled housing projects. Indian local government does not have the resources to drive development. And while national government has ambitious plans (for new 'smart' cities for example) it lacks the Chinese capacity for delivery (and overdelivery), Nonetheless, there is every reason to expect a big increase in housing investment, unlike in China.

Infrastructure limits

There is a similar contrast in infrastructure: shortage rather than oversupply in relation to demand. In the three years after the global financial crisis, when China opted for a massive fiscal stimulus based on infrastructure, it is claimed that more cement was poured than in a century of such investment in the USA (though this is perhaps apocryphal). China's commitment has been remarkable: IMF figures suggest it has been making an average of around 16% of GDP in public investment (largely infrastructure), far more than other East Asian countries. OECD figures suggest that, with 5% of GDP in transport infrastructure alone, China is in a league of its own.[36] Despite a big programme, India has been investing only around 1% of GDP in transport infrastructure (and South Korea, the nearest in scale, has investment under 2% of GDP). For the future, the key issue for China is whether there is sufficient demand for productive infrastructure to justify the large-scale investment which the Chinese authorities have relied on to sustain economic growth, along with housing.

China's massive infrastructure investment has left both a positive and negative legacy. As for the positive, China now has physical infrastructure of the standard of many developed countries. The World Bank Logistics Index has China on the same level as the UK and slightly behind the USA and Japan. The IMD World Competitiveness Index has China ranking 21 of 64 countries in terms of infrastructure, ahead of the UK and Japan but well behind the USA. The World Economic Forum has China ranked first or second for airport and shipping connectivity and electricity access and tenth for road connectivity. The negative legacy is in the form of the serious indebtedness of local government which finances much of the local infrastructure work. There are reports that a new body has been established to discipline local financing and to stop wasteful investments which are often vanity projects designed to boost the prestige of local officials.[37] The *Financial Times* has reported seeing documents which show that the central government has been trying to stop infrastructure projects, barring ten provinces and two big cities from new investment and demanding debt reduction plans elsewhere.[38]

For the future, infrastructure investment is subject to the law of diminishing returns, and this is particularly true of interior provinces where population densities are low and the engineering challenges, and costs, can be forbidding. In extreme cases there are 'roads to nowhere'. Central government has acted to curb infrastructure investment in some of the interior provinces, but this goes against other, levelling up, objectives. There is considerable debate as to how much more productive investment in infrastructure can usefully be absorbed. But the arguments are not clear-cut. China's high speed train network covers over 45,000 kilometres, more than the rest of the world put together, and is sometimes cited as an example of 'wasteful' investment, but World Bank research has shown it to be producing strong economic benefits as well as being financially viable.[39] There are moreover ambitious plans for large-scale infrastructure projects: improving urban infrastructure – including metros and other public transport systems; extending the high-speed rail and highway systems; renewable power generation, high-voltage transmission systems and district energy systems; water supply, including the south–north water transfer scheme; flood defences; and the digital and telecoms infrastructure required for the next stage of data technologies. Nonetheless, it seems implausible that China could in future invest close to the 16% of GDP experienced in recent years.

The Indian infrastructure story starts from a much lower base level of investment and provision. Alongside China's commitment to overall public investment in infrastructure of 16% of GDP of which transport is 5.5%, India plans to raise its commitment to 3.3% in the next financial year (of which 1.7% of GDP is for transport, which will be a record). Investment projects are expanding fast and represent a key element in the Indian government's claims to rapid development. It is difficult to make direct comparisons since there are, for example, different levels and quality of roads, but some indication of scale can be derived from the fact that China invests roughly 2.5% of a much larger GDP in highways, while India in 2023/4 was expected to invest around 0.8% of GDP, and that was more than a doubling in five years. The BJP government claims to have added around 5,000 km of national highway a year since it came to power as against half that in a comparable period under the previous administration.[40] China added around

10,000 km a year throughout this period on expressways which are broadly comparable to Indian national highways.

There is a similar story in relation to railways: China investing more, earlier, but with India accelerating its network expansion. India is now investing just under 1% of GDP on rail electrification projects, having increased the network from 22,000 km to 61,000 km in the decade from 2014. China has been investing a smaller part of its transport infrastructure spend on rail (0.7% of GDP) but has 100,000 km already electrified, including the 45,000 km used by high-speed train (which India is just embarking on, with a Japanese-assisted link between Mumbai and Ahmedabad). India is also creating fast rail corridors to reverse a long decline in rail freight, while the country's notoriously accident-prone system is also now much safer. Both countries are investing heavily in urban metro rail systems, with India increasing the number from 5 in 2014 to 20. China already has an estimated 49 in 47 cities, including 9 of the 10 biggest networks in the world. There has been substantial investment in airports too. India has doubled the number of civilian airports from 74 in 2014 to 149; China has 249. Infrastructure investment in energy and digital systems are sufficiently important to deal with separately below, but China and India are progressing rapidly in both areas.

In this comparison, China has continuing advantages, including high levels of expertise in technically complex areas like tunnelling, train design and construction and the software systems around transport systems. India struggles with issues around land acquisition because of its inefficient system of registering and litigating land rights, while the Chinese authorities are often able to ride roughshod over localised opposition. It is premature to say that India is catching up with China in terms of infrastructure investment and capacity, which is at a far higher level in China. But it is enjoying increasing economic returns from higher levels of investment while China is now experiencing diminishing returns from falling levels of investment. This disparity will be reflected in future relative growth performance.

'New productive forces' to the rescue

For China, faced with a sharp fall in housing investment and seeking to make itself less reliant for growth on investment infrastructure, where else could investment demand come from? The Lowy Institute envisages, by 2030, a drastic cut in the share of GDP allocated to investment in infrastructure and housing from 30% to 12.5%, while investment overall falls from 43% of GDP to 30%.[41] When so much investment is directly financed by state institutions or subject to state intervention, it is feasible to contemplate a big switch of investment. An obvious step would be to channel resources into human rather than physical capital: health and education, concentrating on poorer, rural areas where levels are low. In India such a shift is also desirable but constrained by the powers and responsibilities of the states. China's reticence is less easily explained.

Xi has, instead, come up with the concept of 'new productive forces' to fill the gap in investment demand. Essentially, this means advanced manufacturing industry: a mixture of 'chokehold' technologies, as in the production of advanced semiconductors which are vulnerable to US export controls, and futuristic industries where China hopes to be ahead of the rest of the world. The development of new productive forces is however not a commercial proposition and requires lavish state support of the kind which helped to launch China's successful new industries like EVs and solar panels. Preliminary evidence is that the state is already subsidising or directing investment though its industrial policy to the tune of 1.75% of GDP as opposed to 0.5% of GDP in the USA and 0.5% in Japan.[42]

As a result, much investment is taking place in consolidating China's growing role in advanced manufacturing: robotics and automation, high-precision machine tools, integration of computer systems into manufacturing processes and biomanufacturing. Dan Wang of Yale Law School has argued that the West has overlooked China's development of 'process knowledge', using 'a large and highly experienced skilled workforce which can be adapted as needed for most tech-intensive industries whether in the supply chains for electronics manufacture or in heavy engineering'.[43] After years of failure, for example, China has now started producing its own aircraft for the civil aviation industry. China now dominates world shipbuilding manufacture[44] and, increasingly, car manufacture and their supply chains.

A particular focus of industrial investment has been in support of companies developing green technology where China is already a world leader in EVs and batteries, solar panels, wind turbines and (arguably) nuclear power. What is remarkable is the speed with which China emerged from having a small car industry at the turn of the century to being the world's largest producer by 2009; then, as an exporter, from 1 million cars in 2020 to 5 million in 2023 (overtaking Japan); and, from 2020 to 2023, emerging as the world's dominant EV and hybrid maker with 10 million cars in 2023 (with Chinese BYD overtaking Tesla in revenue terms in 2024). The speed is less surprising bearing in mind that fifteen years ago EVs were designated a 'strategic emerging industry' and allocated heavy subsidies. The new productive forces are the industries that will dominate global markets in fifteen years time.

The EV industry represents a remarkable achievement for China, but also illustrates the limitations of China's strategy. Rapid expansion of production in China has resulted in considerable excess capacity leading to cut-throat competition and the emergence of strong 'national champions' to take on the world, like BYD. But global car sales, overall, have not yet reached pre-pandemic levels and there is considerable excess capacity. Although there are parts of the world – the Gulf states; Australia – happy to absorb Chinese EVs, those countries with indigenous car industries prefer to give domestic producers time and help to make the green transition. The USA is now largely closed to Chinese EVs. The EU has imposed 45% tariffs. The EU is conflicted. With 14 million people and 7% of GDP in the car industry, countries like Germany, France and Italy faced an enormous challenge adapting the industry to EV technology, even without Chinese competition in the form of 30% lower costs. China also provides EU car producers with a big, profitable if declining market for up-market brands. Collaborative solutions may be found with Chinese companies producing EVs in Europe and capturing the value added in battery production. But there are serious limits to export growth.

The car industry is emblematic of a wider problem. The solar power industry, where China is also a world leader, has also faced the same issues with excess capacity in the production of photovoltaic equipment. The authorities' response is to rationalise the sector by forcing cut-throat competition. Such remedies, however, deal with the symptoms rather than the underlying problem which is lack of demand. There is a large home market, but home demand is now growing slowly, and so rapid industrial expansion relies on exports. But many overseas markets are saturated or resistant to Chinese dominance. China starts from a position where it already has over 30% of world manufacturing, which raises the issue of which countries will contract their manufacturing to accommodate more exports from China.[45] The USA and the European Commission have already invoked trade remedies of various kind, and there are escalating disputes around Chinese industrial products in Brazil, Vietnam and Mexico. Not just Western governments and commentators but also Chinese economists have warned that intensifying an export-based strategy for manufactures is not sustainable.[46] China must boost domestic demand.

One way of reducing the risk of overseas protectionism is to be at the production frontier with technological leadership. Opportunities are opening in, for example, driverless vehicles or flying taxis where Chinese development is currently thought to be roughly on a par with the USA. But the sensitivities around security potentially loom large in a sector where machine learning and sensor-based systems are a high proportion of value. And that takes us into how far Chinese growth will be inhibited by security issues: an issue pursued in the next chapter. Nor does China yet have the chip-making capacity or the software, which is where the value lies in these frontier industries.

India has missed out on the manufacturing export route to development, as explained in Chapter 1. In any event this would be the worst possible time to embark on it with markets closing and trade warfare escalating. In a few specialist areas there are signs that the country's traditional weaknesses in manufacturing are now being overcome, in part by attracting elements of what were Chinese supply chains but are now in search of other low-cost locations. India's Production Linked Incentives have already attracted investors into the market for mobile phone handsets, for which India has a large domestic market, as well as export competitiveness. India already has the second largest mobile manufacturing industry in the world (with growth from $11.3 billion of production in 2016/7 to $34.4 billion in 2021/22). The incentive scheme is also being used to attract investment into EVs and the associated supply chain (but this is essentially for the Indian domestic market). In any event, India does not have a demand problem exporting in those areas where it has an established comparative advantage, as in traded services.

But there is also another sense in which India may have a growth advantage over China: India's – seemingly – higher productivity growth.

The productivity puzzle

If China is to offset the forces leading to much slower growth, and if India is to sustain its growth potential, a key factor will be productivity: the efficiency with which the economy uses its resources of labour and capital investment. A common measure is total factor productivity (TFP) growth. There are however serious issues in calculating TFP, and there are different theories as to why it varies over time and between countries. One relates to technological change and the impact of innovation, as with digitisation and the spread of AI. Another emphasises improvements in the business environment, including private sector confidence, the intensity of competition, access to finance and the quality of governance. Yet another emphasises improvements in 'human capital' ranging from education levels to skill-specific training. Since TFP is a residual from the deduction of other factors, it can be used to justify a range of theories and prejudices. But it is the best overall measure of productivity that we have.

The pioneering work on TFP suggested that it could continue to grow exponentially because of new knowledge.[47] But others have shown that TFP is growing in a linear fashion with slowing progression, as when Western economies run out of steam and poorer countries converge on the richer: 'conditional convergence'.[48] There could also be a link to the so-called middle-income trap, in that some middle-income countries seem unable to move from crude capital accumulation to more productive systems.[49] The last theory may well apply to China.[50]

Figure 1.2, based on data from the Asian Productivity Organization (APO), showed that TFP has played an important part in the recent growth of China and India, especially India, and much less in the USA and Japan: a finding consistent with ideas of 'convergence'. The same database also shows that, over a thirty-year period, the USA averages around 0.5% annual growth of TFP while emerging economies committed to economic reform average well over 1% (China 2.3%; India 2.2%; Taiwan 2.0%; South Korea 1.3% growth). There is, however, a decline in TFP growth in China after the global financial crisis when investment capital was deployed with falling returns, alongside steady improvement in India. Other studies suggest that, in China, TFP growth may have become negative.[51] But TFP is notoriously difficult to measure and interpret. For what it is worth, the World Bank has estimated that, since 2008, TFP in China has grown at 1.1% p.a., less than a third of the rate of the three previous decades but, still, twice the US rate.[52]

Figure 4.5 uses the same APO database to show how the contributions to growth of capital investment and TFP have varied over time. The China story is the familiar one of investment-driven growth and, in the last decade, a sharp fall in growth with a reduced labour input and declining TFP growth. The increasing tempo of Indian growth (until the slowing in the

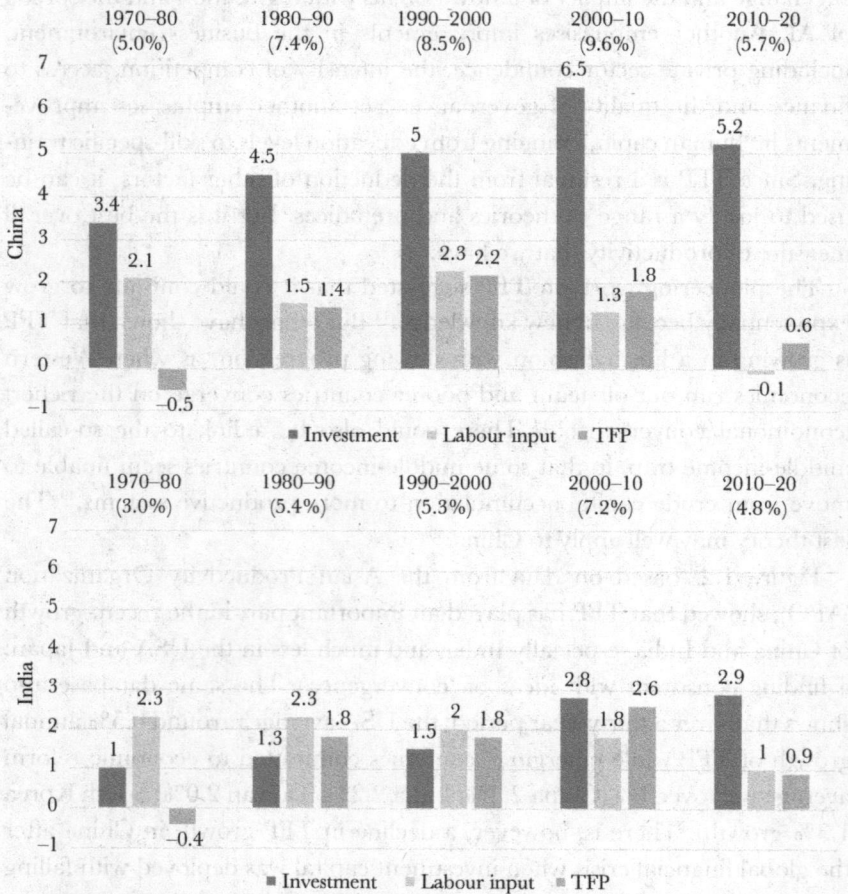

Source: Asian Productivity Organization, Productivity Data Book 2023.
Figures derived from Supplementary Table 9.

4.5 Contributions to growth (%)

2010–20 period) is explained both by increased investment and productivity growth.

Measures of productivity growth have been used to show that India is now in a better place than China. Surjit Bhalla and Karan Bhasin note that 'over the last 20 years Indian TFP growth exceeded that of China by 0.5% per annum. Over the last ten years, excess TFP growth was 1.5%',[53] though those figures are not consistent with the APO database, which suggests a smaller differential. But using the Bhalla and Bhasin numbers, and extrapolating forwards with their estimated productivity growth differential, they argue that there could be a 3.5% differential in growth rates, which would lead to full convergence in living standards between China and India in twenty-two years – more conservatively, thirty years. India would also then have a larger economy.

But that is to fantasise. These numbers are approximate and subject to several key assumptions. But it seems plausible to accept that to achieve long-term 5% growth China, given other constraints, would need 2% p.a. TFP growth, which is well beyond recent rates. If China maintained 1% p.a. TFP growth it would produce 3% GDP growth.[54] India could enjoy a differential above that level of TFP growth in addition to bigger contributions from labour supply.

Policy reform and productivity improvements

Productivity growth is subject to policy change. And, while India has recently experienced relatively healthy growth compared to China, the level of productivity remains much lower. China's quality of infrastructure, ease of logistics, competitiveness of business taxation and stock of skilled and educated people are all higher than in India. Policy reform is necessary for India to move to higher productivity levels.

The Indian government can claim credit for some policy reforms, such as the introduction of the national goods and services tax (GST), strengthening the national single market; a limited degree of privatisation (Air India); and simplified bankruptcy procedures. But the sluggish legal system causes long delays in resolving contractual disputes (four years on average). Red tape is a big impediment to quick decision making. India still has high protectionist tariffs (overall, much higher than in China). Competition is blunted

131

by preferential support for 'crony' businesses. Labour laws are more rigid than in China (though there has been some liberalisation). Above all, India produces a third by value of China's agricultural produce on a third more land under cultivation, yet the government is unable to advance agricultural reform, having backed down after protests. All these points underline the low level of factor productivity but also the scope for productivity growth.

Because of its ageing and shrinking labour force and overinvestment in housing and infrastructure, China now has the greater reliance on productivity improvements to achieve growth. Much depends on the meaning and practical significance of President Xi's Common Prosperity agenda. It has often been interpreted as anti-business and undermining of entrepreneurship. The public criticism and regulatory intervention against some big tech companies has had a severe impact on their valuations. Seemingly random regulatory moves against certain activities – private tutoring, gaming, gig employment – suggest a wider hostility to private business. Those who attribute China's current difficulties to Xi's 'anti-business' agenda would argue that he is to blame for the decline in the private sector's share of investment from around 60% in 2014 to 50% in 2023. But almost all this decline is due to the contraction in the private-dominated property sector. Otherwise, the private sector's share remains largely unchanged.

Indeed, a more generous interpretation of Xi's agenda is that the regime is now seeking to address some underlying problems such as high levels of inequality, low consumption and worker insecurity. A key test of whether the government is serious about the kind of reforms which could encourage growth is the hukou system. At present, hukou prevents migrant workers from enjoying public services in big cities. The system is not only unfair, entrenching inequalities, but condemns migrant workers to an inferior education. It discourages both consumption – since the migrants have insecure work – and permanent moves to cities in search of high-productivity work. The resistance to reform comes from the reluctance of city local authorities to take on extra costs, as well from a general fear of big, destabilising population movements.[55] Here, as elsewhere, the President can demand change, but local bureaucrats can still stifle it.

Linked to the moving of many of China's remaining rural population into more productive cities are ideas for making cities themselves more efficient. There are plans for city clusters of which the top five would each

have populations of over 100 million. The city clusters would unite neighbouring cities through fast inter-city rail links and more carefully managed traffic systems on new motorways, and thereby create regional labour
markets sustaining new, high-productivity industries. This vision, however,
requires innovative private companies to take advantage of the infrastructure improvements. There is plenty of evidence that manufacturers have
invested heavily in robots and in digitisation, but sustained improvements
depend on maintaining business confidence.

Yet the government is seen as anti-business, especially by foreign investors.
Direct foreign investment recorded the first decline in twenty-five years in
2023, and there has been a substantial outflow of portfolio capital. This
downturn follows a record level of FDI ($189 billion) in 2022. A lot of
this recent decline has to do with geopolitics and the de-risking of supply
chains, of which more below, and some also results from pessimism about
growth prospects in the wake of the property market crisis. There has also
been an adverse reaction to actions taken on security grounds, including
raids on leading Western consultancy companies – Capvision, Bain and
Mintz – for alleged breaches of data security and possible espionage as they
conduct due diligence searches. The government from Xi down broadcasts
messages encouraging business in general and foreign investors in particular.
But the reality is often different. What is clear is that technology development and innovation is becoming more state directed to correct what has
been seen as 'the disorderly allocation of capital'. It is however premature
to judge whether China has found a fundamentally different, but successful,
model of development, utilising but directing the private sector, or whether
it is sacrificing the productivity-raising potential of business for other priorities: security and party control.

One area of policy reform that applies to both countries, but is acute for
China, is taxation. Both countries have a low tax base, which has implications
for inequality – there is a heavy reliance on regressive indirect taxation, with
few paying income tax and little taxation of assets, notably property. One of
the criticisms of current Chinese economic policy is that the government is
failing to give a fiscal stimulus to support consumption. And, therefore, it has
become overreliant on exports to sustain demand. The government's reluctance to use more expansive fiscal policy is partly because its fiscal position is
so weak on account of weak tax revenue: with a ratio of around 12% tax to

GDP (though the World Bank has even lower estimates). To create a bigger base for active fiscal policy and to finance investment in human capital, the IMF has proposed raising the tax ratio by 5% to 6% by increasing income tax and introducing a national property tax together with a carbon tax.[56]

India's budget is similarly overdependent on indirect taxes, especially the new goods and services tax (GST), with the tax ratio, as in China, of only around 12%. Income tax in India is steeply progressive, but few pay it. In both countries, radical tax reform would bring improved economic and social outcomes, but both governments worry about a political backlash, democratically expressed or not.

Technology and innovation

Wide-ranging policy reform could make a big difference to productivity growth in both countries. But at the heart of productivity growth is something more specific: the productive use of new technology. Technology is also at the heart of the geopolitical competition between China and the USA and, eventually, India and others. Technology is crucial for several reasons: it is a key factor in growth and increasing living standards; it has a major bearing on military strength (as abundantly demonstrated in the Ukraine War, and in the spread of cyberwarfare technologies); it is key to regime survival (as in the development of surveillance systems and control of information); and it provides important public goods (as in the development of vaccines or renewable energy).[57]

Both China and India have been, until recently, technology followers, though they could reasonably claim to have been technology leaders in ancient times and are now becoming so again in particular sectors. Their recent development has however involved being largely technology acquirers, following a pattern established originally by the USA and, more recently, Japan, South Korea and Taiwan.[58] This has involved getting access to foreign technology through imports, scientific exchanges, joint ventures and partnership arrangements, inward investment and, in some cases, theft of intellectual property (IP). Many headlines have been generated, in relation to China in particular, by the issue of intellectual property theft. In fact, there is an established and predictable pattern whereby technology followers favour weak intellectual property rights and exploit weaknesses in it until they become sufficiently developed and start to protect their own IP.[59]

Both India and China have already started patenting their own IP, and China is accepted to be at the technological frontier in several sectors: e-commerce, fintech, high-speed trains, renewable energy, electric vehicles and batteries, 5G and 6G telecommunications. The list is expanding rapidly and may now include biomanufacturing, nanomanufacturing, additive manufacturing, drones, radar, robotics and sonar, as well as post-quantum cryptography.[60] In aggregate terms, China accounts for almost half of all patents globally.

Underpinning technology advances is science. China is now unambiguously a science superpower. One metric is the share of science and engineering published articles, where China is quantitatively the leader, with 27% of articles as against 14% from the USA (2022).[61] India's share is rapidly increasing: 6.2% from 3.7% in 2012. In terms of the top high-impact papers with most citations, China has overtaken both the USA and the EU, having had only a twentieth of the number twenty years ago and a quarter of the number ten years ago. China also now tops the list of published articles in the most prestigious journals, such as *Nature*. And on these measures China leads the world in physical sciences, chemistry, earth and environmental sciences (but not yet biology and medical sciences).

Strong science comes from people and resources. In terms of scientific and technological development both China and India are producing large numbers of graduates and expanding fast. The Center for Security and Emerging Technology in the USA estimates that, in 2020, China produced 3.6 million STEM (science, technology, engineering and mathematics) graduates; India 2.6 million; the USA 820,000. At STEM PhD level China is graduating around 77,000 a year; the USA 40,000; India 24,000. There are obvious issues in comparing quality, but large numbers of these Chinese and Indian graduates have studied abroad in Western universities – an estimated 6 million Chinese in the two decades of this century – and are now finding employment in internationally competitive job markets.

A recognised measure of scientific and technological investment is R&D (research and development) investment as a share of the economy. The World Bank estimates, taking private and public spend together, that the USA invests 3.46% (2021) as against 2.43% in China and a mere 0.65% in India (the world's technological leader on this metric is South Korea on 4.93%). In both the USA and China most of the R&D is carried out by business (albeit that much of business is state owned in China) with both around

75%. In India the share is 37%, with government conducting most of the R&D and providing most of the money. China and the USA are clearly locked in a competition to be globally dominant in science and technology and India is, so far, behind, at least in these terms.

Research and development spending is a measure of inputs; it tells us nothing about outputs. The World Intellectual Property Organization (WIPO) Global Innovation Index combines no fewer than eighty-one different indicators, including the above, but also number of patents, quality of universities, digital competitiveness, market and business sophistication and other measures of a country's capacity to innovate, to absorb and disseminate new technologies.[62] The WIPO produces a global ranking of 132 countries, but also measures capacity in relation to the level of development recognising that many of the indicators depend on how much is available to spend. In global terms, Switzerland comes out as Number 1 with the USA 2nd. China is 11th, ahead of France and Japan and far ahead of other upper middle-income countries. India is 40th, again, far ahead of other lower middle-income countries and advancing rapidly (its rank was 80th in 2015). The broad conclusion from this multidimensional analysis is that, in terms of innovation, both countries are way ahead of their peers in terms of income levels and have both scale and time on their side.

Digitisation and AI

Much future innovation will occur through digitisation: making use of existing digital infrastructure and developing it. China is somewhat further advanced. The big difference between the two countries is that China is trying to strike a balance between rapid economic development through digital development and control of content through surveillance and censorship. India, by contrast, has an open system with no firewall (at least, so far – the cutting of internet links to censor material from Kashmir suggests that there is a wish for more control). That difference might widen if security concerns and sanctions from the USA lead to China diverging even further in digital technology, and if India becomes more tightly integrated into Western markets and supply chains.

India's internet penetration was just over 50% of the population in 2023 – 750 million people, as against 76% in China (1,100 million) – and there is rapid growth in both countries, strongly promoted by government. The global average is 67%. Both countries rely mainly on mobile telephony for broadband. In China there are 108 mobile broadband subscribers per hundred inhabitants and 41 fixed broadband as against 56 and 2 in India, according to data from the International Telecommunications Union at the end of 2023. Ericsson figures (also at the end of 2023) suggest that there is now 95% 5G coverage in China – one of the world's highest, along with South Korea – while India's 5G penetration is 25%.[63] Other data shows that the cost of subscription is two to three times higher in India, though costs of internet connectivity are falling rapidly.

A consequence of the rapid spread of internet access is that both China and India are in the process of creating the world's largest digital economies: in the private sector in the form of e-commerce, banking and entertainment; in the public sector in the form of benefit payments, health and education services. One rather dated (2021) estimate is that the Chinese digital economy was worth $7 trillion, second only to the USA ($15.5 trillion), with India under $1 trillion and the eighth biggest, though Indian sources have estimated that India is now the third in size.[64] China's e-commerce market is now the world's biggest by far: $3 trillion in 2023,[65] accounting for almost half of all retail sales, as against $1.2 trillion in the USA and $119 billion in India. India has the sixth largest market and one of the world's largest growth rates, and with the potential to grow faster than China.

Both countries have also pioneered the use of the internet for public service provision with India bringing the poorest people within the digital economy. India's Stack is a set of open APIs (application programming interfaces) and has become one of the big success stories in development. The Chinese and Indian programmes have different motivation, but also have a lot in common. One of the key building blocks is the establishment of identity in digitised form for everyone. India's Aadhar is based on biometric data which then gives unique access to welfare payments, bank accounts, tax accounts and medical records. The Chinese system uses facial recognition, which has attracted Western criticism because of the wider potential for surveillance.[66] In both cases, however, there is the considerable merit that no one must appear in person more than once to authenticate their identity, greatly improving efficiency and reducing access barriers to public services.

The second building block is a united payments interface to provide a secure link to bank accounts and payments networks. In China, migrant workers have been able to use a social security card to collect payments. In India, cash entitlements can be paid straight into bank accounts. In China, 90% of all payments are now by mobile phone – 45% in India (2021), a similar level to the USA.

The third element in the system is that there is a mechanism for the secure sharing of data, which is important for presenting proof of ownership documents in legal disputes or for health data. Much of the data collection and transfer may well be benign and improve the efficiency of business and everyday life. But there is, especially in relation to China, worry that the data will be used to bolster the monitoring capability of the proposed Social Credit system under which all citizens can, in theory, be monitored for compliant behaviour.[67] There are reports from China of widespread complaints about excessive data collection and data leaks.[68]

What does this experience tell us about the future capacity of both countries for growth-enhancing productivity improvements? China's internet system controls content and makes individuals and companies subject to greater control from the state. But, contrary to the expectation of many Western observers, such a system does not appear to have blunted innovation. There is no lack of innovative companies. Arguably, the most successful and creative of the big internet companies operating internationally in recent years has been Chinese: TikTok. Another, the Instagram-like platform Xiaohongshou, is growing rapidly inside China, as are many other innovative products and systems. Western scepticism about China's capacity for innovation has been shattered by the emergence of DeepSeek, China's low-cost, open access AI language model, the more so as it emerged from a private hedge fund and Chinese-educated technologists. But in general, Chinese innovators must contend with a stream of new laws and regulations governing data security. Even where the regime's intentions are benign there are costs of compliance and continuing uncertainty over when regulators will intervene.

By contrast, Indian innovators face much less friction. Indeed, India is demonstrating an ability to provide digital services on a competitive basis for the world economy – not just domestically. India's share of traded services by value has grown from 1% in 2000 to 3% in 2010, and in 2023 was above 5%. Almost all this expansion has come from IT services and business process outsourcing (BPO), for which growth has been driven by global (and Indian) IT companies. The big growth area is in Global Capability Centres which involve outsourcing from big companies of high-value services, including digital engineering, semiconductor design and R&D. India has 1,500 of these centres employing 5 million people:[69] almost half of the global total. These centres developed largely on the back of low labour costs, but are now marketing their quality and efficiency internationally with India developing centres of excellence for cloud computing, data analytics and AI. In rapidly expanding areas like the use of AI to improve software programming, India has the largest pool of programmers after the USA, and will soon surpass it. And the salaries of software programmers are far below those of its competitors.

A widely held view is that AI will be the main source of innovation in future (though there are sceptics).[70] China has some advantages in becoming the leading player in AI. It generates vast amounts of data, which is important for creating algorithms for big regenerative AI models, where China has had some success. On some estimates, China has the largest pool of data in the world on account of the scale of internet use. Its internet companies have thereby been able to gain early adoption for their AI products. The AI Ernie Bot reached a million users in nineteen hours, while the US equivalent, Chat GPT, took five days to reach the same level. But Chinese controls on data flows in and out of China are potentially a serious limitation, as is the fact that most of the world's data is in English, not Chinese.[71] One big advantage enjoyed by China is a pool of high-level postdoctoral students, many trained overseas (especially in the USA) and many also with a history of entrepreneurial activity. The Thousand Talents programme was designed to maximise this group (though China has become a less attractive place to migrate to).[72] Another plus is the size and variety of venture capital firms in China, a lot of them state-owned, providing a deep pool of risk capital (though privately owned American companies are thought to have generated over twice as much risk capital than their Chinese equivalents over the last decade).

Until the emergence of DeepSeek, it was assumed that the USA was some way ahead. The Harvard Business Review TRAIN index, which measures a combination of innovation, human and financial capital, rulemaking for data accessibility and data consumption, has (as of the end of 2023) the USA on an index of 90.7, China on 68.5 and the UK third on 58.8.[73] But there is rapid change, and the industry is now developing a complex ecosystem around the infrastructural building blocks – chips and cloud computing – foundation models and a wide variety of applications. India ranks only fifteenth on the TRAIN measure, but the study acknowledges that it is catching up fast. It will have the biggest data pool by 2028, and already has the third largest stock of scientific talent.

China has two major disadvantages in the longer term. The first is internal politics. The massive efforts to control offending content through the firewall will be needed even more in the case of AI. What if a language model produced answers which were critical of the ruling party? In fact, the problem is not just censorship. Since 2021, China has adopted legislation with tight data protection rules similar to the European General Data Protection Regulation (GDPR). Although there is no sign that the entrepreneurial spirit of Chinese companies has been dampened so far, common sense suggests that a less regulated environment – as in the USA and India – is likely to be more successful at incentivising innovation.

The other disadvantage is external. The 'chip wars', designed to deprive China of access to the most advanced Nvidia and TSMC (Taiwan Semiconductor Manufacturing Company) semiconductors and the machines to make them, will slow down progress in AI, though pragmatism, ingenuity and a vast amount of government support may minimise the damage. There is evidence, furthermore, that China is now pursuing a different strategy from the USA, one that recognises the US lead on ground-breaking AI innovations, and instead concentrates on applications based on smaller language models that have practical applications in areas like EVs and autonomous vehicles. WIPO data suggests that, in the decade to 2023, Chinese firms filed over six times the number of AI patents as the USA, seemingly with this in mind. DeepSeek has also shown that it is possible to achieve work-arounds using inferior chips that are much more efficient in the demands on computing power.

Even if China succeeds in plugging gaps, as with advanced chips and innovation breakthroughs such as DeepSeek, restrictions will continue to reduce its access to the latest technology and inhibit innovation through cross-border collaboration.[74] An IMF study suggests that technological spillovers have contributed 0.3% p.a. to China's productivity growth, much of which could now be lost.[75]

What is clear is that internal and external forces are pushing China to develop its own capability across a range of technologies: advanced semiconductors, the internet of things, big data, AI, blockchain, quantum computing, drugs. It is doing so through heavy investment led by the state. There are greatly contrasting views on Chinese capacity and potential. Chinese commentary tends to stress the level of ambition, but acknowledges that China is some way behind.[76] Western comment ranges from the awe-struck to the dismissive. As to the former, a senior Pentagon figure regarded China as a 'near peer adversary' in AI.[77] In the crucial area of advanced semiconductors, however, Douglas Fuller has described the long history of failure, scandal and waste working through state-backed enterprises.[78]

But Chinese companies, with heavy investment and state support, have also shown a capacity to learn from mistakes. In November 2023, for example, Huawei unveiled the Kirin 9000S processor, incorporating a new advanced chip produced by the hitherto derided state company SMIC.[79] A few months later it unveiled an even more advanced – 5 nanometer – chip in collaboration with an unnamed Chinese company.[80] The outcome of these endeavours will be determined by the interplay of economics, technology and geopolitics – a subject I will examine in the next chapter.

Conclusion

We cannot predict the future, but current consensus forecasts for both China and India tend towards pessimism. The assumed Indian growth of 6% to 6.5% p.a. is well below the growth achieved by East Asian countries, including China, at comparable stages of development or, indeed, by India itself earlier in the century. However, India is tackling some of the most important structural impediments to growth, notably physical infrastructure. There is a broad political consensus, at least in general terms, welcoming domestic and foreign private investment. And India enjoys a following wind in international investor sentiment.

China has experienced a substantial slowdown, halving the officially expected growth rate from the double-digit levels of recent decades. Many Western critics argue that even 5% growth is well beyond the capability of an economy with a serious structural imbalance favouring wasteful investment and disfavouring private and public consumption. But Western critics have been wrong before about China's ability to adapt, and about the strengths as well as the weaknesses of China's state-directed development

141

and 'Communist capitalism'. And the regime has made a massive commitment to restructure away from infrastructure and housing towards advanced manufacturing and 'new productive forces' (and, more cautiously, towards private and public consumption).

The main question about the future may not be about whether these superstates can grow more rapidly and catch up with the USA (and the EU) by the mid-century, at least in economic size. They almost certainly can. The key question is whether they will be allowed to. China now risks hitting a wall of opposition, and not just from the United States. The mass production of high-value manufactures is intended, in part, for export. The European and Japanese as well as US car manufacturers are directly threatened by Chinese EVs. Brazil's Embraer as well as Boeing and Airbus will be threatened by the new Chinese civil airliner. Countries in the Gulf, India and others aspire to make semiconductors of the type that will pour out of Chinese foundries. India has many other anti-dumping cases against Chinese firms in steel, laser machines, among others. Protectionism will be a growing barrier. Then, the massive subsidies being poured into the new productive forces will represent, for others, unfair trade and attract countervailing duties, or worse. These forces put China on a collision course with the USA and potentially the EU – and even erstwhile allies.[81]

India may sidestep these forces in two ways. One is by concentrating on traded services – becoming the 'back office of the world' as opposed to China's 'advanced manufacturing workshop of the world'. The second is to follow what has been China's playbook so far: for Indian companies to insert themselves into the supply chains of multinational companies (including those that are trying to 'friend shore' from China). But India is, so far, a small player in international trade. And as it becomes a bigger player, angry competitors will emerge who run to their governments for help and demand trade barriers. And services trade is not exempt from protectionism, since it usually involves people moving from country to country, to study, work and interact – in other words, immigration, an aspect of globalisation that is even more controversial than trade in goods. With this in mind, I turn now to the issue of how the rest of the world sees the economic rise of the superstates: China today, India tomorrow.

PART II

Two traps and three global public goods

5

Geopolitics and geoeconomics

Long before China became a major economic power, its relations with the West were defined by geopolitics. The 'Nixon in China' moment, the meeting of President Nixon and Chairman Mao in 1972, orchestrated by Henry Kissinger, was inspired by the idea that China could be a counterweight to the USSR in the Cold War. And there were other motives for engagement. Mao saw an opportunity to relaunch China on the world stage. It was no longer promoting and exporting world revolution. Nixon also had a long-term vision: 'we do not want 800 million people living in angry isolation. We want contact. … In fifty years' time we shall be adversaries and we shall need to be able to talk to them.'[1] Economics didn't figure. Kissinger, when preparing the Shanghai Communiqué, advised that the Chinese should not waste time on commerce 'which can only be infinitesimal in terms of our total economy'.[2] He was to be proved embarrassingly wrong.

Relations with India may be embarking on a similar trajectory. After over half a century of being largely ignored as a closed and marginal economy, politically irrelevant and annoyingly non-aligned, India has been cultivated by the West – the USA in particular – for geopolitical reasons: to act as a counterweight to China in a new cold war. But the fact that India is on track, within a generation, to become another China in its weight in the world economy seems to have been largely ignored. Moreover, India is emerging as a major economic force in a very different economic policy context than when Deng Xiaoping launched China on the world economy. Open trading systems and enthusiasm for globalisation more generally has given way to more protectionism, as with President Trump's 'tariff wars', and a preoccupation with security. The China–US relationship is at the centre of this emerging world of security-based and transactional, zero-sum economic policy, and this chapter will focus on that relationship. But India's role in the world economy will be shaped by what may become a trade war between the US and China and more widely.

The decline of the old economic paradigm

In 1979, less than a decade after the Nixon meeting, Deng visited the USA. The purpose was partly optical: to improve China's image, showing the country was no longer hostile, threatening and ideologically driven. But Deng's main purpose, as with an earlier visit to Japan, was to lay the foundation for Chinese modernisation by gaining access to technology, investment and trade opportunities. He raised the issue of most-favoured-nation (MFN) – non-discriminatory trade arrangements – to which the Americans apparently made no objections.[3] Deng's visit, together with the burgeoning commercial relationship that followed, disarmed even those who had deep suspicion of the CCP. Reagan, shortly to become President, noted that Deng 'didn't seem like a Communist'.[4] The lifting of barriers to business dealings, and trade in particular, also fitted the mood of the time: what came to be called 'neo-liberalism'.

The first big setback to relations were the events that took place in Tiananmen Square in 1989. China was seen as brutally suppressing a bid for political freedom at a time when other Communist regimes were falling like ninepins. There was widespread demand in the Western world for sanctions. Crucially, President George H. W. Bush saw the bigger, longer-term picture. He traded on his personal relationship with Deng to tone down the call for sanctions in return for the release of some political prisoners.[5] Bush accepted, as would future US administrations, the underlying formula that Deng had laid out: radical economic liberalisation in the interests of Chinese modernisation and growth – 'reform and opening up' – but no liberalisation of the political system. After a short hiatus, double digit Chinese growth resumed with the spectacular success of Deng's policies and those of his successors.

The next potential setback was the arrival of President Clinton, whose supporters wanted more of a focus on human rights in US foreign policy and wished to make annual approval of China's MFN status conditional on political change, including on Tibet and political prisoners. There was a backlash from American business and unions, which were experiencing the benefits of working with China. Companies like Boeing and farmers who were profiting from the Chinese appetite for animal feedstock were powerful spokespeople for maintaining economic links. Clinton invoked his mantra 'It's the economy, stupid' and dropped MFN conditionality.[6]

That became the established paradigm for the next quarter of a century. China was granted full MFN status through the WTO. The underlying assumption was that positive engagement was not just good for China but good for the world. The world would benefit from the disinflationary effect of cheap Chinese manufactures and the market opportunities generated by Chinese growth. And China would be locked into the multilateral trading system which had underpinned the world's remarkable postwar economic success and was a cornerstone of the international order. Indeed, China was seen as a 'responsible stakeholder'.[7] Some also believed that an economically successful China would evolve into a more politically liberal society, or even a democracy in the manner of South Korea, though the Chinese themselves never gave any indication that this would be allowed to happen.

In recent years, that consensus for both political and economic engagement has come close to collapse. Why? There are several reasons, coming from different actors in different countries at different stages. The first was in the form of Trump and Trumponomics:[8] trade protectionism and the use of tariffs. I argued in *Money and Power* that Trump could be credited with being one of the few politicians in history to have changed the economic policy orthodoxy of his time. And his MAGA (Make America Great Again) movement has largely untrammelled power to have these ideas embedded in policy. Within Trump's protectionism, there are several strands to the arguments for a more aggressive approach to China on trade. First, Trump regards all bilateral trade imbalances as 'unfair' to the United States. China had and has the biggest, and was therefore Trump's main adversary, though he has been no more kindly disposed to Germany, Mexico, Canada or Vietnam, among others. In his first term as President, his plan was to use tariffs as part of a negotiating strategy to land what he perceived as good deals.[9] Trump Mark II is even more aggressive in tariff-driven dealmaking. Economists dismiss, even ridicule, this narrowly mercantilist view of international trade, with its echo of eighteenth-century, pre-Adam Smith economic thinking. But his world view has prevailed, with tariff warfare unleashed.

Some members of Trump's circle, notably Peter Navarro, see in China a much bigger economic threat than that represented by trade imbalances, one that involves wider issues around national security (as with Huawei in Trump's first term).[10] In addition, there has been a domestic political motive for ramping up the hostility. There was some – contested – evidence of the damage caused by Chinese imports in Trump-voting areas with a strong base of traditional manufacturing.[11] But four years of threats, tariffs and other restrictions (as on Huawei) and tit-for-tat retaliation did not produce a deal. Trump's answer has been to threaten even bigger – 60% – tariffs on Chinese goods during the 2024 presidential campaign. Now re-elected, his threats appear to be serious if not literal.

What was once seen as a Trump aberration has become US political consensus. The succession from Trump to Biden did not seriously change the growing negative feeling about China and, specifically, the Trump tariffs were left in place, despite the negative effect on American consumers.[12] Biden brought in new tariffs on Chinese manufactures, particularly EVs. But the issues have become more fundamental than tariffs. China's success had made it comparable to the USA in terms of economic size and potentially much bigger, along with comparable equality or dominance in technology and the things that more Chinese wealth could buy, like weapons and global influence. President Biden made it clear that the USA would no longer accept not being Number 1.[13] A Democratic president's determination not to be seen surrendering America's leadership role chimed with the long-standing warnings of some China 'hawks' that China's leaders had been planning to displace the United States.[14]

The arrival of a Democratic president also reinforced the differences with China over human rights, an issue that did not loom large in Trump's transactional administration. One of Biden's first acts was to accuse China publicly of a 'genocide' in Xinjiang, building on an initiative by the outgoing Secretary of State, Mike Pompeo, and then to impose sanctions over the security clamp down in Hong Kong. These human rights campaigns had the effect of cementing a cross-party critical narrative on China in the USA, uniting liberal Democrats with those in the Republican Party who harboured deep hostility to China based on ideological grounds. The campaign also created a bond with America's democratic allies in Asia as well as Europe. Increasingly, governments in Europe and Asia, particularly Japan, have come under pressure to align themselves with the USA on trade and political issues affecting China.

Third, under Xi, Chinese behaviour changed in a way that made the country seem more 'assertive' and threatening. There has been a change in tone and substance from Deng's injunction: 'Observe carefully. Secure our priorities. Cope with affairs calmly. Hide our capacities and bide our time. Be good at maintaining a low profile. And never claim leadership.'[15] Diplomacy was increasingly couched in the aggressive language of 'wolf warriors' determined to respond to insult with insult and not to tolerate perceived slights. Countries whose governments had caused anger were subject to disproportionate sanctions, as when Lithuania appeared to be recognising a Taiwanese entity. Australia was subjected to trade sanctions because of a public demand to investigate the origins of Covid. Relations with Australia have since improved, but there remain long-standing disputes on China's frontiers, some subject to more aggressive moves, as with the South China Sea and the Philippines. On the economic front, China's publication of *Made in China 2025* was seen as proof that the country intended to establish global dominance in key advanced goods and services.[16] Other sources have claimed, in vain, that the document had no official status and made no economic sense anyway.[17] But the damage was done (and the 2025 ambitions are being realised). With the return of Trump, who also uses economic coercion and disruption to achieve his objectives, China is having to revise its approach both to avoid damage from US actions and to cultivate good relations with victims of Trump's coercion.

Fourth, there is no longer a strong, united business lobby pushing for engagement with China. There has been a mounting list of disillusioned businesses and others with bad experiences of trading with or investing in China or being excluded from the Chinese market. These companies argue that the benefits of integrating China into the world economy are offset by the negatives and that, anyway, China is not a normal country and does not play by the rules. Recent action against Western companies performing due diligence in China and tougher data-sharing laws have alarmed companies otherwise keen to do business there. Powerful business voices such as the big internet companies – Google, Meta, Amazon and Microsoft – are no friends of China, having been largely excluded by data restrictions created by the Great Firewall (though Apple had and has a massive and lucrative involvement with the country).

149

In fact, the reality is much more nuanced: trade barriers in China are lower than in most emerging markets, especially India. Many Western companies have had highly successful experiences doing business there, and those that haven't have often failed because of commercial, marketing failures in a difficult and highly competitive market. Even the USA has ceased to claim that the exchange rate is being used for currency manipulation, not least because it makes little sense in a world of complex supply chains.[18] Elon Musk has recently defied fashionably negative opinion by obtaining special treatment for Tesla manufacture and committing to develop his 'full self-drive' Teslas in China. But he is a maverick, though a highly influential one, given his close relationship with President Trump.

That said, there clearly are pressing and genuine concerns over the levels of subsidy and support for new high-tech industries, even by comparison with those now available in the West. There are still issues around theft of intellectual property, though China's legal protections have been strengthened. And, crucially, the reluctance of the Chinese authorities to address macroeconomic imbalances by boosting domestic consumption is creating structural, manufacturing export surpluses. By virtue of their volume, these surpluses have created a sense of threat and foreboding in the USA, Japan and Europe in industries like automobiles and seem to threaten their future existence.[19]

These are not the only factors that have fuelled distrust. The Covid pandemic largely severed human contact for a period, over and above the blaming of China for the outbreak. The Ukraine War, in which China has claimed neutrality while giving moral, political and practical support to Russia as part of its 'friendship without limits', has alienated Western Europe, which was hitherto more inclined to engagement with China than the USA. Episodes such as the floating of a Chinese 'weather' balloon across the USA in January 2023 added to suspicion. The upshot is that the old paradigm, based largely on the mutual benefits of trade and investment flows and the overriding importance of economic growth and living standards, has been replaced, at least in the USA and increasingly in Europe, by the priority of security: economic as well as military. And China's approach too is dominated by security concerns – perhaps more so.

A vicious circle has developed, where actions designed to reduce mutual dependence are treated as hostile acts leading to retaliatory reaction, which in turn reinforces the narrative of 'threats' and the need for greater self-sufficiency. The Trump tariffs and controls were a reaction not just to Chinese imports but to Chinese trade and technology ambitions, as in the *Made in China 2025* document. The Trump measures in turn led to Chinese suspicions that the USA was trying 'to prevent its rise', and contributed to greater emphasis on security and self-sufficiency. Further measures to 'contain' China and the isolation of Covid have engendered a more paranoid mindset in China, with stronger counter-espionage laws and other restrictions. And so on in a downward spiral, with Chinese activities in the West characterised as spying or economic sabotage: the sense that China is an enemy. And the logical outcome is trade – and, perhaps, wider – war, which Trump's return to office makes more likely.

The new paradigm of security and 'geo-economics'

The old paradigm was based on the idea that there is mutual advantage in trade and economic integration more widely. The phrase 'win–win', much used in Chinese speeches about the world economy, captures the sense of it. The new paradigm is based on another cliché: the zero-sum game. If one party gains it can only be at the expense of another. Trump popularised this pessimistic view of the US–China relationship, but it has become part of a cross-party consensus, despite his promise of a big deal.

The Biden administration most clearly defined its approach to the international economy in a series of speeches and comments by National Security Adviser Jake Sullivan. He set out a New Washington Consensus in which security concerns should take precedence: 'ever greater global interdependence is no longer desirable'.[20] The new doctrine was not exclusive to China and gained traction from those who had become disillusioned by globalisation and free trade largely because they appeared to be at the expense of important domestic interests.[21] But China was at the heart of it.

Relations with China would be characterised by 'de-risking and diversifying, not decoupling' and would involve a 'small yard and high wall' erected around technologies with sensitive security concerns. Other influential members of the administration, notably Janet Yellen, the Treasury Secretary, endorsed the primacy of national security while arguing more positively for a 'healthy economic relationship with China'.[22] America's European allies had been moving in the same direction, albeit they maintain more confidence in the benefits of globalisation.[23] The Japanese too. A 'strategy for economic security' has however emerged, with more boundaries around trade, investment and research, implicitly if not explicitly directed at China.[24] The battery of measures is now extensive and formidable: export controls, tariffs, inward and outward investment screening, controls over data flows, restrictions on collaborative research and exchanges of scholars. Trump has inherited this strategy and policy toolkit, and while his overall approach may be transactional, his overall framing of the relationship with China is less nuanced and couched in zero-sum terms.

The Chinese have hardened their approach in parallel. National security concerns have never been absent from Chinese thinking about integration with the world economy, but have now been given a new emphasis. The concept of 'comprehensive national security' was formulated in 2014 and encompassed all aspects of national life, including the economic. Sixteen types of security concern were identified, including international economic threats from Western-led campaigns to contain China. In what has been characterised as the 'securitisation of everything', Xi 'has turned national security from a policy goal into a mode of governance'.[25] He has made it clear that there may have to be economic costs resulting from the prioritisation of security. Those costs are growing.

Ideas of economic security did not begin with the current geopolitical differences between the USA and China. The oil shocks in the 1970s made economic prosperity vulnerable to the politics of the Middle East and elevated the energy sector to a matter of national and collective security. And a generation ago, America felt there was a threat to its Number 1 status from another Asian source: Japan. The political scientist Samuel Huntington, writing about why US primacy matters, said: 'Japanese strategy, behaviour and declarations all point to the existence of a cold war between Japan and the United States.'[26] Writing in the same vein, historian Edward Luttwak coined the word 'geo-economics' to describe a zero-sum world in which the gaining of primacy by one country (in this case, Japan) necessarily involved defeat for another (the USA).[27] In the geo-economics of the time, as with Trumponomics today, the bone of contention was the bilateral trade deficit between the two countries. There was a spate of commentaries and political speeches about Japan, invariably talking about battles and war.[28] In a distant

152

echo of the arguments used today about China, the fear was that the USA would become dependent on imports of goods and money from Japan and vulnerable to Japanese threats. In the event, the collapse of the Japanese property market and stock market asset bubble led to three decades of economic difficulties: deflation and slow growth. No one now talks about Japan threatening US primacy.

Although the Japan problem has largely gone away – and an economically diminished Japan is now regarded as a key ally against China – economic security has become a central part of government decision making. This entails some long-standing concerns, but also some that are new. One is the nature of Chinese 'state capitalism' within a 'party state'. The boundaries between public and private are not clear. As the Chinese state has come to be perceived as an adversary (and China perceives the West, and especially the USA, as an adversary), security concerns are potentially all embracing. The boundaries between private and public sectors in 'Japan Inc' were also fuzzy, but there was no wider sense of Japan as a potential military adversary. The other big difference is that the process of globalisation has become much deeper through overseas investment flows and the development of multinational supply chains. There have been big benefits, but there are more points of dependency and of potential conflict. And, not least, China is a far bigger presence in the world economy than was Japan, especially when it is seen, as some do, as part of a bloc including Russia, Iran and others.

It is possible to identify several distinct areas of concern under the general framework of 'economic security' and tariff warfare that now relate to the rise of China but also predate it.[29] One of these is *military technology*. Few would dispute the general proposition that governments will, and should, seek to control trade or investment involving equipment or IP that relate directly to national defence.[30] The rules of the WTO do not cover armaments for this reason. Instead, there is a more limited, informal agreement between US allies – the Coordinating Committee for Multilateral Export Controls (CoCom) – which tries to police arms exports to China and other potential adversaries. The problem lies in grey areas. Governments change or they change policy. Britain suffered in the Falklands War from having supplied weapons to once-friendly Argentina. Then there is the fraught area of 'dual use': items that have a benign use but could possibly be used to help a military and political adversary. Examples from my own experience of administrating arms export controls include protective equipment for an overseas (Communist) dictator, cleaning fluids featuring elements that could be extracted and used to make poison gas, equipment to rescue trapped submariners in the navy of an unfriendly country and advanced optical equipment needed for medical purposes which could also be part of a nuclear weapons supply chain. The list is endless.

Another dimension to military technology relates to cyberwarfare, including attempts to cripple companies or infrastructure or to obtain their secrets. China's capabilities and activities figure prominently in official analysis of the China threat. Much of this activity is also 'grey', with the boundaries between state and non-state actors and between offence and defence being unclear. In the case of China, the grey area, 'dual use' concerns centre on advanced semiconductors to be used for developing AI, which has some military applications, and other core technologies like quantum computing. The Chinese are known to have invested heavily in quantum computing and quantum networks, which have many useful applications but potentially could get to the point where all non-quantum communications can no longer be protected through encryption. Drones, a technology where China excels, have many innocuous applications but are also a crucial part of the modern battlefield, as the Ukraine War has demonstrated.

Security of supply has become a concern as a result of the disruptions in supply from China following the Covid pandemic, the alarm created by the dependence of European countries on Russian pipeline gas and the interruption of oil and other supplies caused by conflict in the Middle East and hazards in the Red Sea and Suez Canal. Trump Mark II has added alleged Chinese threats to the Panama Canal. Security of supply issues arise because of accidental disruption (war, revolution, pandemics, accidents) or overseas suppliers acquiring a degree of control to leverage better returns or political change. Or a mixture.

To a degree, this is a market economy problem, and firms can use stocks, diversification and hedging instruments to minimise the effects of supply disruption. But there may be a public policy issue if the impacts are potentially widespread and serious. Moreover, the security of supply issue is not new to policy. The EU Common Agricultural Policy had, as part of its original rationale, and continued protection, arguments about the need to safeguard food supplies.[31] And, as already noted above, the oil shocks of the 1970s and

154

the early 1980s provoked much debate about security of oil supplies in the face of the OPEC cartel: the role of strategic reserves; cooperative versus unilateral action; the respective roles, in weakening dependence, of fuel import substitution, fuel substitution and energy demand reduction.[32] With the return of President Trump, domestic oil and gas are being given a big boost in any event, and in China we can expect to see a boost for coal as part of a 'securitisation' of policy. Moreover, concerns over supply disruption have not been limited to energy. There has also long been a worry over 'strategic' metals and minerals for the same reason.[33] One sector that has exercised US Congresspeople is pharmaceuticals, where Chinese companies carry out clinical trials in the USA and supply what is considered to be a worrying share of drugs. Another is foreign ownership of shipping.

One recurring question is this: what are the industries, technologies, and products for which security of supply is essential? Many producers can and do argue that what they make is both essential and potentially subject to supply disruption: all manner of foodstuffs, steel, shipbuilding, clothing and shoes (we need uniforms and boots for soldiers) and much else. As the economist DeAnne Julius has observed: 'taken to its logical extreme, the quest for economic security implies minimising trade relations with all but one's closest allies and seeking economic self-sufficiency wherever possible'.[34]

But that in turn raises the question of costs and benefits: how much security is needed by society and what is the cost of providing it? In the case of China, there is a perceived threat to supply security because of entangled supply chains and China's dominance of rare metal processing. On the Chinese side there is (chronic) insecurity over imported technology, especially in the semiconductor supply chain, energy and food. There were reports in 2024 of China accumulating large stocks of food (wheat, maize and soya beans), crude oil, natural gas and metals (copper, nickel), in several cases on a scale to move commodity markets substantially. It might seem prudent to have strategic stocks in the event of future conflict. But there is a cost, which raises the question of what is the price of more supply security and who pays it?

Strategic technologies have become a central part of the arguments around economic security, partly because of military applications and partly because of vulnerability to supply disruption, but mainly because they are seen as crucial to 'national competitiveness' in a zero-sum world of nations being winners or losers. Economists frequently dismiss this way of looking at the world as misconceived. But a branch of economic thinking – strategic trade theory – has been used to justify the protection of 'strategic' technologies or industries where there are only a few competitors and the 'winner' has the potential to exploit the terms of trade.[35] The Clinton administration used such arguments to support the 'strategic' high-tech industries of the time, which included microelectronics, biotechnology, new materials, telecommunications, civil airliners, machine tools and computer hardware and software.[36]

Economists were critical. Paul Krugman argued that 'the focus on the supposedly competitive nature of international economic relations greases the rails for those who seek frankly protectionist policies'.[37] A further criticism was that 'techno-nationalism ... does not work anymore', because of the poor history of 'picking winners'.[38] China did not feature in those debates, but is now central to them, the argument being that the country is already well advanced down the techno-nationalist road and that there is a strategic case for not ceding a monopoly of these technologies and, indeed, for maintaining a lead in them through controls over technology exports. Today these concerns centre on advanced semiconductors, green technologies, AI and quantum and involve trade, inward and outward investment, cybersecurity and leakage from shared research. In the closing days of the Biden administration connected and autonomous vehicles were added to the list.

Critical infrastructure has become an issue in countries like the UK and the USA where there is a relatively free market in the ownership of utilities and foreign investment is generally welcome. Many countries have nationalised utilities or imposed bars on foreign ownership based in part on the idea that energy supplies, water supplies, transport networks, telecommunications systems, ports and airports should be owned nationally. In the more open economies, by contrast, it is now common for utilities to be owned in whole or part by foreign firms, portfolio investors such as pension funds and sovereign wealth funds. Or, alternatively, there are collaborative arrangements involving overseas operators. And there are fears of dependence on hostile powers for equipment used in infrastructure. The US has recently had a panic over the cranes used in US ports, almost all of which are made in China.

Even before China emerged as a significant economic force, there was much debate in the USA as to the limits on foreign ownership in 'critical infrastructure'.[39] The latter is widely defined in legislation (the US Patriot Act): water, public health, emergency services, telecommunications, energy, transportation, banking and finance, postal services, shipping. In these sectors, screening of investment was carried out by a review committee, FIRRMA – formerly CFIUS.[40] A landmark case was Dubai Ports World, which in 2006 tried to buy US ports but backed off in the face of Congressional hostility, despite presidential approval. In the five-year period to 2022, 70% of CFIUS cases leading to intervention involved Chinese companies, and semiconductors was the most affected sector.

The American screening process has now been adopted in the UK. The UK has generally been more open to foreign investors, which has attracted broad criticism as inappropriate in a security-conscious world.[41] But there is now a specific issue of critical infrastructure. Where the overseas owners and operators are from potentially hostile countries, as with China, the issue has arisen as to whether this exposes the host country to security risks from politically inspired disruption. That in turn raises the issue of what the points of vulnerability are – such as kill switches – what share of ownership commands control of operations and how critical to economic security is the utility in question. In practice, the main battleground has been telecommunications, and specifically the role of Huawei. Minority ownership of nuclear power generators has been another controversial issue. In addition to national utilities there is shared infrastructure in the form of cross-border pipelines and electricity grids, undersea cables, satellites and services operated collectively like air traffic control. Undersea cables in particular have become a major concern.

One emerging area of concern is control over *media and communications*. Freedom of speech and a free press has long been a key part of the offer of Western democracies, and the Cold War era was characterised by restrictions on information in the Soviet bloc and attempts to escape them. The internet opened the potential for universal, free dissemination of information everywhere: part of the idealistic vision of 'the end of history'. The vision did not long survive Chinese attempts, increasingly sophisticated and effective, to create a parallel internet inside the Great Firewall. The emergence of social media has created a new dimension to the problem in more open societies, in the form of large-scale disinformation. Alleged Russian involvement in the 2016 US presidential election and the UK Brexit referendum has created a security issue in the form of bad overseas actors. More recent concerns have centred on Chinese-owned social media companies, TikTok in particular. It is far from clear that there is a genuine problem with TikTok, but attempts in India and the USA to have it barred have been justified in security terms.

An aspect of economic security that has been live for several decades, but which has recently acquired a new dimension, is *currency*. The dollar has long been seen as the global currency for most international transactions and as a store of value. When China, with Japan, Germany and others, ran sustained current account surpluses with the USA, it acquired dollar assets in the form of US Treasuries in return. There was mutual benefit in the arrangement: China grew with the help of exports to become the world's largest market, while the USA was able to finance its budget deficit and deficit in domestic savings. There was also a mutual dependency in the form of a 'balance of financial terror', since a large-scale sell-off of dollar assets would drive down their value.[42] The symbiotic relationship was characterised as 'Chinamerica' or 'Chimerica'.[43] Neither the USA nor China has sought to destabilise this mutual dependency. But a new element of instability has arisen with the introduction of international sanctions against Russia following the invasion of Ukraine, utilising the dollar-based payments system. China has been directly affected by the Office of Foreign Assets and Control, which restricts access to dollars for specified acquisitions. These actions in turn have given impetus to moves, long favoured by China but largely ignored, to separate from the dollar-based system. China, India and other emerging economies have been exploring the potential of the BRICS group of countries to pursue this agenda, but President Trump has likened the loss of dollar hegemony to defeat in war. I pursue this issue in detail in Chapter 7.

The above list is a simplification and excludes other activities which could be regarded as aspects of national security. The smuggling of highly addictive drugs like fentanyl and the capacity to assemble them has become a source of friction between the USA, Mexico and China, whose companies are heavily involved. Belarus has sought to weaponise migrant flows. Each of these areas is potentially problematic, but taken together they represent a major potential source of conflict, hot or cold. Third parties like India are also affected, both as beneficiaries from attempts to diversify supply and as losers from lower global growth and from weaker international economic institutions and rules.

The new paradigm is unsettled and unstable, with government intervention and security-based restrictions in some sectors but open and unrestricted trade and investment in others. While economic security is now widely used to justify intervention, as in the areas described above, it is a profoundly unsatisfactory guide to policy: a slogan rather than a solution. It is virtually impossible to quantify and difficult to define. That hasn't stopped its spread, and I review below the different ways in which economic security is playing out.

The chip wars

It has been understood for at least half a century that semiconductor chips represent the world's most critical technology. The failure of the USSR to keep up with the USA in chip making and applications meant that they fell behind in computing and the myriad uses of semiconductors in advanced weapon systems.[44] The Cold War was won on the back of chips.

Electronic systems based on semiconductors are now at the heart of our daily lives: computers, cars and traffic management, phones, household gadgets, train and aircraft infrastructure, electricity supply and distribution systems, hospital equipment, robotics and much else. Production of chips is distributed in global supply chains. Production of the most advanced chips used for training AI models depends, however, on a division of labour within a more exclusive set of relationships:[45] advanced chip design, mainly in the USA, with Nvidia, Intel and ARM; equipment manufacture for the most advanced chips, which is concentrated in a handful of companies in Holland and Japan, as well as the USA; and the actual manufacture in foundries, among which those owned by TSMC in Taiwan account for around 85% of the highest specification chips and a third of all chips.

It was inevitable that the cooling of relations between the USA and China would lead to a focus on the world's most critical technology. The emergence of AI as a new, frontier technology with military applications has intensified the importance of competition in this area. Until recently it was clear that American companies were well ahead, the main vulnerability being that much of the country's advanced chip supply is manufactured in Taiwan – potentially in the middle of a battlefield should the Taiwan issue explode. Early Chinese efforts to create companies capable of designing and

159

making complex, sophisticated chips were characterised by failure, scandal and waste.[46] In 2022, around 3,500 Chinese companies in the sector closed, despite many of them having enjoyed government subsidies. China was, and still is, heavily dependent on imports. It is the world's largest market for semiconductors (variously measured at 25% to 35% of world sales), with only about a third of Chinese demand being domestically produced. These chips are China's main import by value, eclipsing crude oil. Indeed, China accounts for over a third of the American industry's overseas sales and profits, making it a key market.

The journey from China being a market to a deadly rival had a key inflection point in October 2022, when the USA introduced a set of export controls covering all semiconductors, not just those with military applications. The controls were seemingly designed not just to maintain the US lead but to degrade China's capacity. There followed, in March 2023, agreement from Japan and Holland to complement the sanctions. The controls are severe and comprehensive, covering design and design software, fabrication, the chemicals and metals used in production and, crucially, the equipment for etching, lithography, metrology and other processes. One assessment was that China would not be able to produce advanced chips without a complete set of capabilities and that the restrictions were potentially crippling.[47] The same sources however noted that China had anticipated the crackdown at least five years earlier, when Huawei was effectively banned from the USA and another telecoms company, ZTE, faced severe restrictions on access to American chips. China has since been identifying 'chokepoints' and building domestic capacity. An example is Electronic Design Automation, a market which is heavily dominated by US producers, involving highly sophisticated software involved in design and testing. Chinese producers are rapidly filling the gap. Across the piece, Chinese companies are investing heavily in import substitution, stockpiling chip-making equipment and developing a strategy to retaliate effectively. Crucially, with DeepSeek – a startup emerging from a laboratory in a private hedge fund – China seems to have found a way to develop an open source AI language model – R1 – without reliance on high-specification chips and, because of economies in computing resource, at much lower cost. DeepSeek is not a one-off. Chinese tech companies are matching their US peers in capability with greater cost efficiency.[48]

It will take some years to see who is winning the new chip war. Some commentators believe that the sheer scale and ingenuity of the Chinese effort, the unlimited budgets and the many potential cracks in the sanctions will in time erode the American (and allied) advantage.[49] China has already surprised the industry with demonstrations of high-specification chips, though the most advanced 5 nanometer chip advertised by Huawei, Kirin 9006C, may have originated in Taiwan.[50] Who wins the war will depend on several factors. The first is whether the US-led alliance will hold when there are complex, cross-cutting commercial interests. South Korean semiconductor and equipment firms, for example, have a big market in China, and the US authorities have had to agree to allow South Korean firms to sell China all but the most advanced chips. Similarly, the Taiwanese TSMC has a complex trade and investment relationship with China and is also investing heavily in the USA under the Biden programme for US self-reliance. There are reports that TSMC has stopped making advanced chips for the Chinese market for fear of American sanctions. American pressure on the Dutch government stopped ASML selling 3 and 5 nanometer chip-making machines, though China managed to order and secure many machines before controls were formally introduced.

A second factor is how successful the Chinese have been in evading controls. There are reports of technological know-how being smuggled into China through cloud computing operations in the UAE and Saudi Arabia, via entities with close links to China. Vital skills have been poached from Taiwan using financial inducements. There is plenty of espionage, too. And skilful use of chips falling fractionally on the side of legality produces a good second best, as for example when the leading Chinese internet companies placed large orders for an Nvidia chip which fell just within the rules. Nvidia regards the Chinese market as crucial to its own profitability and was happy to supply, though US authorities have moved to close the loophole, leading the Chinese authorities, in turn, to investigate Nvidia. And, crucially, there is the question of how far the Chinese government has been able to improve the efficiency of its industrial support and to get Chinese companies fully aligned with the goal of self-sufficiency. The 2023 trade data suggests that China now imports many fewer chips but is massively increasing the amount of machinery to make them. What is clear, however, is that, for all its efforts, China is still somewhat behind in the most advanced technologies. What is unclear is whether, after facing this battery of export controls, it is falling further behind or catching up (or, even, overtaking).

A third factor is that the nature of the security problem may have changed or expanded. Some are now arguing that the issue is not only the physical production of chips but what happens to the AI technology which the chips help to generate and which is being developed in data centres. The vast agglomerations of data in these centres are managed through cloud computing. There is now an international race to build data centres, which require access to large amounts of electricity, and to control the data which flows through them. The 'cloud war' involves competition to build capacity and establish control, via ownership or regulation of data flows, in the overseas locations of data centres.[51] But DeepSeek may have greatly reduced the demand for such energy-intensive centres.

Recognising that there is an existential battle ahead, China has also been trying to strengthen its bargaining power and ability to retaliate. The American company Micron was subjected to harassment in China in the form of cybersecurity investigations and is being cut out of supply chains. China has built up a dependent customer base with its supplies of low-specification legacy chips, around 10% of world supply, needed for the car industry especially. There have been fears that China will flood the world market with cheap chips to gain a monopoly position.[52]

China's retaliatory weapon: scarce minerals

The most striking retaliatory Chinese actions in the chip wars have involved exploiting the country's control over the supply of critical and rare minerals. When the USA pressed ahead with a tightening of controls over advanced Nvidia chips, China retaliated by introducing an export permit scheme for graphite, an important component in batteries. No actual curbs were announced, but there is now an explicit threat to use export controls over synthetic graphite, for which China has 70% of the world supply, and natural graphite in processed form, for which it has a comfortable majority.

Several other minerals are thought to be good potential 'weapons'. One is gallium, which is not only used in chips but has separate military uses. China is thought to make 98% of current world production and has 90% of processing capacity. Germanium is used in solar panels and optical fibres,

162

and China is thought to control about 60% of supply, including imports by the US chip industry. China also dominates the market in antimony, used in precision optics and armour-piercing weapons.

The issue of strategic minerals is, however, not new and long predated the rise of China. As many as forty-two raw materials were stockpiled from the beginning of the Cold War. The OPEC cartel was also a reminder of the power of producers who could corner a market and helped to stimulate a flurry of reports, including by the British parliament, warning of potential vulnerabilities.[53] These lessons were not heeded in the West, and US strategic stocks shrunk to very little. China, by contrast, took the problem seriously, whether for offensive or defensive reasons is not clear. It invested heavily in both raw materials and in messy and costly processing, acquiring near-monopoly positions which it reinforced by driving down prices to keep competitors at bay: a popular move with China's industrial consumers in the West.

The significance of the Chinese dominance became apparent in 2010, when it cut off supplies of rare earths to Japan as 'punishment' for a territorial incident around some disputed islands. Rare earths are a subset of seventeen metals with important applications in magnets, for example, with nine of the seventeen having military applications. The action against Japan did not last long, and the Japanese quickly reduced their vulnerability by investing with Australian partners in a rare earth processing plant. But China continued to dominate the market, with almost half of the world's rare earth exports over the decade 2008–18.[54] Their dominance stemmed from the high barriers to entry, in the form of large capital costs in highly polluting plants required to extract tiny amounts of material from large amounts of ores containing other metals. The geopolitical potential was obvious.[55] In 2019, there were threats to use the rare earth weapon again – also in 2021, specifically against two US companies which had been involved in arms supplies to Taiwan.

Rare earths have now assumed greater importance, along with other critical minerals, because of the rapid growth in demand for raw materials used in batteries for electric vehicles.[56] China has emerged as the world's leading EV producer, with 60% of world sales in 2023 and over 50% of global battery production. It now also has a dominant role in the production of battery materials. China 'dominates the midstream and downstream but not the upstream'.[57] Lithium, the key raw material in the dominant lithium-ion batteries, is mainly mined in Australia and Chile, but Chinese companies do two-thirds of the processing and are responsible for half of investment in future production. China accounts for perhaps 60% of battery-grade lithium. Almost half the world's nickel comes from mines in Indonesia, but Chinese smelters produce three-quarters of the refined product. The Congo accounts for 75% of the world's cobalt, but Chinese companies dominate Congolese mining such that China controls almost 50% of world supply, despite having virtually no domestic raw material.

Of the thirteen materials now regarded as critical, including rare earths collectively as one, China accounts for over 50% of production of eight (rare earths – with over 90% of global supply of rare earth metals like neodymium, gallium, tungsten, vanadium, germanium, indium, titanium, antimony). It indirectly has substantial leverage over the cobalt market through Chinese companies in the Congo and over niobium as the main customer for Brazilian exporters. China's position is potentially powerful, and we have already seen critical minerals being used as a weapon. But the weapon is double-edged. If it is used, this will accelerate moves to diversify away from China, as we saw with Japan in 2010. The United States has already set in train plans to process rare earths in Texas in 2025. China's interest lies in being indispensable to global supply chains, which means continuing to supply at low cost. Once it uses the critical material weapon, by withholding supplies, it sets in train measures to make itself dispensable, albeit at considerable cost and after a delay. But, in 2025, it used the weapon.

Rounding up the Trojan Horses

The geopoliticisation of commercial relations with China has centred on several Chinese companies which have been highly successful abroad as competitive providers of advanced technology. The privately owned Huawei and, to a lesser extent, the state-owned telecommunications company ZTE, have been seen by their Western critics as the embodiment of the modern Trojan Horse. They gain access to a protected citadel by posing as an innocuous and well-intentioned offering, but there are lethal warriors hiding inside, waiting to attack sleeping defenders. In the case of Huawei the allegation is that the company has taken advantage of open tendering processes in Western countries and liberal rules on foreign investment to get its equipment embedded. This can then be used for spying, cyberwarfare and what is called its 'backdoor potential'.[58] Since Huawei reached the point of dominating global telecommunications technology, with 100,000 patents, its standards were becoming global standards and a Chinese company was set to dominate one of the technologies critical to emerging fields like AI, Big Data and the Internet of Things. The USA decided to act by excluding Huawei from the USA – as part of the Trump trade war in 2018 – and pressing allies to do the same.

The case made against Huawei was that its founder, Ren Zhengfei, is a former military man who has acted on behalf of the Chinese state as a 'national champion', with a long-term mission to carry out espionage and to exercise political control over a technology which is fundamental to the modern information economy. Critics argue that Huawei muscled its way into becoming the leading company in the sector by questionable business practices, including IP theft and 'low-level piracy', with Chinese government financial backing.[59] Moreover, even if the company now wishes to be commercially independent, it will be obliged by Chinese legislation and practice to act for the Chinese state. A somewhat opaque ownership structure, theoretically based on worker ownership, adds to suspicions. The United States acted in 2018 to prevent Huawei operating by depriving it of access to American semiconductors necessary for its operation.

The defenders of Huawei would say that the above account is a travesty. Huawei emerged in China after fierce competition with state-backed rivals.[60] It built up its business globally by being long term in its outlook rather than opportunistically chasing short-term profit.[61] It invested heavily in parts of the world other investors shunned (Africa) and in parts of the network other providers ignored (rural America). It ploughed back profits into R&D and provided an attractive working environment for talented young scientists (including 10,000 PhDs). Despite numerous legal actions and investigations in the USA, none of the charges stuck. No evidence has ever been found that Huawei misused its business overseas to exploit its backdoor potential. The economist Stephen Roach describes the anti-Huawei campaign as based on 'exaggerated threats' and 'competitive insecurity and anti-Chinese vengeance'.[62]

Whoever is right, the United States has been effective in its campaign to exclude Huawei from its own networks and those of allied countries, who have imposed bans on Huawei and its equipment or restrictions on future contracts. Huawei has effectively been banned from the USA, the Five Eyes Anglosphere countries, almost all of Western Europe, Japan, Singapore and India. Some European countries have been ambiguous: France is committed to phasing out Huawei, but has left some wiggle room; Germany has tried to maintain a Huawei collaboration with Deutsche Telekom while imposing more severe security checks. The UK attempted to strike a compromise, backed by British telecoms companies (BT and Vodafone), having been satisfied that Huawei's role in 4G technology could be managed. It decided that Huawei would be allowed to participate only in the peripheral functions of 5G. The US government, however, made it clear that American chips were banned for Huawei, leaving the UK dependent on insecure components. The British government folded, agreeing to remove even Huawei legacy equipment entirely from its telecoms system. British 5G telecoms has since fallen behind.

But in the Global South many governments have asserted their independence and continue to work with Huawei in much of Africa, Brazil and other parts of Latin America, the Middle East, including Saudi and the UAE, Southeast Asia, as in Thailand and Indonesia, Russia and parts of non-EU Eastern Europe and Hungary. Huawei can offer them efficiently delivered, advanced, proprietary technology, as against the more uncertain and complex process of using open networks.

The effect, and probably the intention, of US sanctions was to damage Huawei severely in two ways. First, Huawei was denied, under US export controls, access to the semiconductors that are necessary to make its smartphones and other gadgets. Second, by excluding Huawei from important markets for its telecoms equipment, a big source of revenue was hit. There is little doubt that the actions against Huawei did a lot of damage, and for some time the company's future was in jeopardy. But it has proved to be resilient, albeit with government help. It has replaced the chips used in smartphones, acquired technology from foreign and Chinese firms to eliminate its dependence on overseas components, diversified into other business lines – notably the manufacture of semiconductors and the provision of cloud services – and invested heavily in telecoms technology to maintain its leadership role in 5G and 6G. It has even developed its own operating system – Harmony – for use in its smartphones. Far from being crippled by sanctions, Huawei is now bigger and stronger than ever and leading in 6G innovation.

Another alleged Trojan Horse has been TikTok, a popular video app owned by the Chinese company ByteDance. In this case, the security threat is less obvious, and the product is popular with an estimated 170 million (mainly) young people. TikTok annoyed President Trump when it was used in a social media campaign to boycott one of his rallies, and this may have been a factor behind his decision to issue an executive order to force the Chinese owners to sell TikTok in the USA (the order was blocked in the courts). TikTok later annoyed pro-Israel groups when pro-Palestinian videos appeared to predominate. Neither of these two incidents could be considered breaches of national security. But TikTok had also clashed with the commercial interests of its US competitors, notably Meta, and appeared to cross the established, if partially observed, principle that foreigners should not own media companies. After all, the competitors argue, we are restricted in China. A Congressional investigation into TikTok pursued national security arguments and, while nothing was produced in evidence to suggest any malpractice, the issue, as with Huawei, was the potential.[63]

There were two concerns. One was that ByteDance could, hypothetically, hand over data on US citizens to the Chinese government. For that reason, the Five Eyes Anglosphere countries, as well as the US, have excluded TikTok from government devices. But wider anxieties are more difficult to understand. All social media companies collect vast amounts of data and ByteDance offered plausible safeguards against data leaks. A more decisive argument was that the algorithm, powered by advanced AI, could in theory be manipulated in China to influence opinion in the USA. Since other social media companies have spread disinformation with a political motive, Elon Musk's X being a prime example, presumably the Chinese also could?[64] If Chinese ownership of TikTok were to be banned in the USA and elsewhere, the mechanism would be a forced sale. But ByteDance might then be required by the Chinese authorities to close the app down, which would annoy many young consumers. TikTok lost a long legal battle but found an improbable saviour, and late convert, in Donald Trump, who has been seeking a sale in the form of a compromise 50/50 joint venture.

Another sector that has attracted the attention of Congress as a potential Trojan Horse is healthcare. Chinese companies such as WuXi and MGI

167

Tech carry out drug research, make complex drug products and supply gene sequencing machines to the American healthcare system. The products and services are cheaper and, in some cases, make essential inputs for clinical trials. A draft BIOSECURE law could however potentially impose considerable costs on the sector, as well as damaging the Chinese companies involved.

The hunt for other Trojan Horses is producing many suspects. Politicians, including President Trump, opposed the takeover of US Steel by Nippon, from friendly Japan, for reasons that have nothing to do with national security. But national security was invoked on the basis that Nippon has a substantial presence in the Chinese steel industry. Politicians in several states have also sought to legislate against Chinese land purchases, allegedly acquired near military bases. Investigation has shown that Chinese-owned land amounted to 1% of foreign-owned land and 0.03% of total land. The share was shrinking and not connected with military bases.[65] Nonetheless, one Chinese-owned company, a crypto miner, was found to have land near a nuclear base and has been ordered to sell it.

A more pervasive and worrying concern is the questioning of collaborative scientific research conducted between China and the USA and its allies, on the grounds that it might conceivably have some military value, or expose national secrets to 'spies', or simply, in a zero-sum world, involve giving away knowledge. Silicon Valley companies have tightened vetting of staff for fear of espionage and IP theft, and, while Chinese ethnicity is not a bar to employment, there have been cases in the courts of illegitimate racial profiling. Specific accusations stem from a US rule that bars Chinese postgraduate students with links to China's 'military – civil fusion strategy' in the hundred or so Chinese universities which are alleged to have links to the military.[66] In Britain, too, Imperial College scientists have been exposed to public criticism for tenuous links to Chinese colleagues and institutions which might, conceivably, have military links. Tighter restrictions on research and researchers have followed. Scientific journals have however looked at the many joint projects whose work they have published and concluded that restrictions on research were disproportionate and damaging to Western economies.[67]

None of the above should imply that the Trojan Horses are all Chinese. The Chinese authorities have demonstrated considerable paranoia about Western 'spies' in their midst – targeting foreign investors, researchers and others. Data theft is a particular fear. Even Tesla, which is doing so much to develop EV technology in China, found its vehicles banned from the vicinity of military installations on the basis that their sensors might pick up classified information. On a more prosaic level, Chinese women with Western boyfriends are publicly warned of the dangers of consorting with spies. Paranoia has become a contagious disease.

Fighting over the plumbing

An inevitable casualty of the breakdown of trust between China and the USA and its allies is that there is less confidence in shared infrastructure. In the internet era this mostly means the undersea optic fibre cables which carry almost all the data between continents. In a rational, win–win world – the old paradigm – there would be shared cables, and it would not greatly matter who owned and maintained them, provided they were built and repaired. Just as it would be considered rather foolish to have competing railway tracks side by side, it would be expensive and unnecessary to compete with duplicate telecommunications networks across the globe.

Yet that is what is beginning to happen. There are two main reasons, both connected with the new cold war between China and the USA. The first is China's long-standing policy of censorship, to protect its internal communications through the Great Firewall (or the upgraded and more powerful Great Cannon). In practical terms, this means international networks cannot be piped straight into the Chinese system. Instead, data is routed through tightly controlled entry points. There is a considerable cost to Chinese users, in the form of slow speeds and high fees. The second source of fragmentation is American attempts to block Chinese companies from laying or maintaining undersea cables, which also serve US consumers.

For the best part of 150 years, intercontinental cables had been laid by – initially British – companies, mainly state-owned, to create a global network of telephone connections and, more recently, digital messaging through optic fibre cable. There are around 900 active cables, stretching over an estimated 1.4 million kilometres under the ocean. Data-hungry services like AI are creating an explosion of demand which is estimated to require almost 500,000 km of new cable over five years. Much of this is now being provided by the big tech companies, which have replaced the consortium of telecom utilities who previously dominated the business.

But there is a geopolitical dimension. In 2009 a Chinese company, Huawei Marine, partnered with a British company, entered the market for laying cables and gained a significant market share. But the expulsion of Huawei from the United States prompted its withdrawal from the cable market also. Another, exclusively Chinese, company, HMN, entered the market and is thought to have laid around 100,000 km of cable in over 130 projects.[68] The US response was a Clean Cable Initiative, the upshot of which was the freezing out of HMN from international consortia, as with a cable from Singapore to France, and sanctions against HMN. The American authorities went so far as to cancel a transatlantic cable linking the US west coast with Hong Kong which had already been laid. The reasoning has been that hostile powers could gain access to sensitive data and redirect flows of data to serve subversive, non-commercial purposes.[69]

The consequence of these geopolitical moves is that the Chinese have developed their own comprehensive expertise in the subsea cable business, from cable manufacturing to laying and operating separate networks. Chinese projects service China exclusively or involve partners, mainly in the Global South, who are attracted by competitive pricing and speed of completion. Among the recent projects are a Latin America to Africa cable which bypasses Western connections and a PEACE cable from Pakistan to France via Kenya. A Chinese-built cable from France to China via Singapore, Pakistan and Egypt will compete directly with the cable project from which Chinese companies were excluded. The infrastructure is being created for a parallel and separate internet, designed to avoid direct US–China interaction. But this is by no means a simple operation, not least because there are fourteen trans-oceanic cables which have joint US–China ownership. Over and above peaceful, if costly, competition there are worries about sabotage, though at present these concern Russia rather than China.

The 'plumbing' does not just involve undersea cables. There are overland cables, data centres and internet exchange points: the physical underpinnings of the internet. Taken in combination with data management laws and telecoms ownership these factors provide a comprehensive infrastructure for digital services. China has been providing that comprehensive service through its Digital Silk Road and many countries in the Global South have signed up to it, India being one of the exceptions.

The costs and contortions of 'decoupling'

The mixture of competition and cooperation at the bottom of the oceans could serve as a metaphor for the confusing story of trade and investment flows on the surface. As described above, the new paradigm of relations between China and the US and its allies was set out most explicitly by former US National Security Adviser Jake Sullivan in his Brookings Address in March 2023. But ambiguity abounds. The formula 'de-risking, not decoupling' – a phrase of the President of the European Commission – is an attempt to clarify a strategy which involves diversifying corporate exposure from China and prioritising economic security but not 'decoupling', which according to the then Treasury Secretary Janet Yellen would be 'disastrous' and 'destabilising'.[70] Such ambiguity may not long survive the Trump presidency.

Concretely, the US policies have involved export controls on security-related applications, screening of inward investment and active industrial policy based on import substitution. There is a steadily widening 'entity list' of hundreds of Chinese companies with whom it is forbidden to trade. Tariffs have been imposed specifically on Chinese EVs, solar cells and EV batteries, and the EU has followed suit with higher tariffs on EVs. Less concretely, the expectation is that business will diversify from China through 'friend-shoring'. For their part, the Chinese have added to the ambiguity by loudly proclaiming their support for globalisation and for inward investment, while simultaneously indulging economic nationalism involving retaliatory export controls, penalties on companies which observe overseas sanctions, consumer boycotts, counter-espionage activities, stronger but vaguer cyber security laws, raids on advocacy firms, exit bans on some foreigners and arbitrary intervention by regulators.

What is the actual and potential economic cost of all this de-risking? We are still at an early stage of seeing what the rhetoric means in practice, and then assessing its consequences. Also, China and the USA are not the only actors; the EU is a major player in international trade, and one study has shown the potentially major costs of the EU putting into practice its rhetoric around 'strategic autonomy'.[71] Of more immediate relevance is an IMF study that looks at the potential costs of geopolitical fragmentation using a multi-country model. In one simulation it looks at full decoupling between an EU-USA bloc and a China-Russia bloc. The costs to the world economy would be big: at least 2% to 3% of GDP annually, which would be more damaging than, for example, the Covid pandemic.[72] The biggest casualties would be low-income countries (with costs over 4% of GDP), because of the subsequent fall in commodity earnings. That study predates the threat of re-elected president Trump to impose a 60% tariff on Chinese products and 20% tariffs on the rest of the world. The 'tariff war' began with threats of 20% tariffs on Mexico and Canada and higher on China. The Chinese tariffs went ahead, prompting Chinese retaliation.

In terms of what has happened, as opposed to what might happen, the story is one of actual decline in US–China trade. A detailed study of US exports to China shows a clear decline below the trend that would have been expected before the Trump tariff dispute.[73] An apparent surge in 2022 can be largely explained by improved commodity prices. The study relates only to US exports to China, but US imports from China tell a similar story, with 7% growth by value in the five years from 2023 as against 38% from the rest of the world. Several factors could have been involved, including Covid disruptions and price movements. But there is some wider statistical evidence of trade delinking. In 2023 global trade actually fell (by 1%) while global GDP grew 3% (though emerging market exports grew by 15%). If we look at the ratio of trade in goods to global industrial production, it appears to have declined in the last few years and this is due in part to a higher proportion of Chinese production being absorbed at home.

The data suggesting delinking is, however, misleading. There is growing evidence that Chinese exporters are circumventing US tariffs by transshipment through Mexico, which has a free trade agreement with the USA. Other ingenious techniques are also being employed. One is exploitation of the 'de minimis' rule, whereby tariffs are not payable on small packages. Companies on the Mexican side of the border split shipments of goods into packages worth less than the dutiable $800 threshold. Chinese producers, US consumers and Mexican packagers all benefit; the US Treasury and American producers lose out. Another example is 'nearshoring', where Chinese companies outsource to subsidiaries in Vietnam, Cambodia or other Asian countries, which then export to the USA or Europe. There is evidence that imports to the USA from low-cost producers in Asia have been surging at the same time as Chinese exports to those countries have been rising fast.[74] Studies by the World Bank and IMF confirm that while the USA decoupled from China between 2017 and 2022 by reducing China's share in its imports from 22% to 16%, the difference was made up by other Asian countries which were themselves deeply embedded in Chinese supply chains.[75]

This process of creating phoney supply chains was most advanced in those 'strategic' sectors where the USA was most anxious to displace Chinese companies. Furthermore, the Chinese had expected for some years to be caught by trade barriers in the USA and the EU and have been lining up bilateral trade deals or regional deals as in the fifteen-country Southeast Asian trade group, RCEP (Regional Comprehensive Economic Partnership). One estimate is that around 40% of China's exports are now covered by bilateral trade agreements, and others are planned in Africa and the Middle East.[76] What may be happening is not the exclusion of China from US global supply chains but the creation of more complex supply chains which still have China at their heart. President Trump has made it clear that such backdoor routes will be closed. And it is difficult to believe that having the 'leader of the free world' as a long-standing opponent of globalisation will not have some impact on the real world.

Declaring tariff warfare on Chinese imports has had other knock-on effects. The EU tariffs on Chinese EVs have affected European companies who make EVs in China for export. European companies are also vulnerable to retaliation in China. Furthermore, Chinese EV exporters are adept at changing their price points to remain competitive on price even with tariffs in place. Most significantly, Chinese car makers are already drawing up plans to establish factories in Europe for the European market but with Chinese supply chains, including batteries or battery components. The US tariffs on EVs and lithium-ion batteries may well lead to the same pattern of behaviour. There will be a cost to consumers, and the introduction of EVs will be delayed, with an environmental cost. But the Chinese dominance of EV and battery technology means that their industry will probably prevail. That is, unless a new competitor emerges with a mass market and low costs. India?

India's role in the new, security-based international economic order

As the content of this chapter suggests, developments in geopolitics have been essentially about China and the USA. And the new paradigm of international economic relations, heavily influenced by security concerns, is also largely driven by the US–China relationship. India has so far had little influence on these trends, but that may change, radically. The one big reason why India has been marginal up to now stems from its inward-looking, protectionist approach to trade, which, as we have seen in earlier chapters, prevailed until recently, in contrast to China's 'reform and open-ing up'. India's share of world trade in goods was 2.3% in 2023 (average of exports and imports), which is a vast improvement on the 0.5% at the nadir of India's postwar economic isolation, but far below that of China (12% excluding Hong Kong). Indian tariffs remain among the world's highest, despite recent liberalisation. But in the services industry, India's share of world trade is close to 6%, which hints at a growing importance in a world where data flows and the movement of skilled people matter more. And India's economic size and rapid growth has, for the first time in the coun-try's postwar history, turned it into a major driver of global growth. For this reason, it has to be taken seriously.

The USA and its allies have recently 'discovered' India and now see it as a counterweight to China. It is doubtful whether Indian policymakers see India primarily as a counterweight rather than a serious weight in its own right. Foreign Minister Subrahmanyam Jaishankar, in a recent book, makes it clear that a more powerful and self-confident India is not going to be con-scripted into someone else's cold war but will stick to the traditional mantra of non-alignment in a multipolar world.[77] There are some deep divides, as between two nuclear-armed adversaries – China and India. But, in some contexts, India and China are in the same camp – as members of the BRICS and Shanghai Groups – with some common goals, such as reducing depend-ence on the US dollar, while both have a warm and lucrative relationship with Russia. Being courted by the United States, however, has advantages, in terms of the supply of advanced weaponry for the armed forces and trade and investment opportunities.

In one key respect, de-risking and decoupling from China, India and Western economies have a common goal, though the motivation is some-what different. In the twenty years since China and India started engaging in bilateral trade on some scale, Chinese imports into India have built up rapidly: a mixture of consumer goods such as toys, laptops and cameras, and inputs into high-tech industries such as memory chips and pharmaceutical ingredients. By contrast, there has been little that China wants to buy from India. As a result, trade is heavily unbalanced, with Indian imports from China in 2022 of over $100 billion and Indian exports of $15 billion. The commercial relationship offends the mercantilist Indian approach to trade and underlines the fact that the countries' economies are competitive rather than complementary. India also declined to join RCEP, because of fears that lowering regional trade barriers would expose Indian producers to even more Chinese competition. That said, China supplies technology that Indian companies need and goods which Indian consumers want to buy. Chinese investors potentially create manufacturing jobs. These factors seem to have tempered some of India's protectionist instincts.

Those negative instincts have been reinforced by security concerns over Trojan Horses. The border clashes in 2020 have provided a powerful motivation to reinforce the already sceptical attitude to Chinese foreign investors, especially in the data-based industries. India led the way in banning TikTok, as well as hundreds of other Chinese apps. Huawei and ZTE hardware is not allowed into the Indian system. Data protection reasons are given, though lobbying by India's big and powerful telecoms companies probably also played a part. Chinese EV makers and smartphone companies have become ensnared in Indian investigatory bureaucracy. There is now a special screening mechanism for investments from countries with adjacent borders (which just happens to include China) and, reportedly, few companies pass the test. Many Western companies have, over the years, struggled to fight through Indian red tape, which is world-beating in ingenuity, but for Chinese investors there is now the additional barrier of national security, which will put off all but the most adaptable.

By contrast, there is a welcome for Western and other multinationals seeking to diversify their supply chains from China. The highest visibility attraction has been Apple and its Taiwanese partner Foxconn. Apple is heavily invested in China, and the Foxconn operation alone employs 700,000 to a million people. But it has begun to diversify out of China, and at the end of 2023 had 70,000 workers in southern India. It is proving difficult to transplant the China employment model to India, where there are trades unions and no tradition of women working in dormitories with strict shift patterns. Nonetheless, there are growing numbers of supply chain manufacturers operating mainly in South India.

The chips war also has implications for India. India is not – yet – in contention for making the most advanced semiconductors, but big, subsidised chip-making complexes are being launched by the Tata group in Gujarat and Assam, the first in association with a Taiwanese group. It can be argued that rather than join a subsidy race for the manufacture of commoditised chips – the market for which could soon be flooded by cheap Chinese products – India might do better to deploy its army of brainy science graduates in chip design. But political ambitions are of India as a chip superpower, which includes manufacture.

Another area where India has been late to join the scramble for insecure supplies is for critical minerals. Indian companies are seeking lithium mining contracts in South America and elsewhere for a nascent EV industry, and there is a search in India for native deposits. India has joined a US-led Minerals Security Partnership. But, as with chips, the country is a late entrant. And in relation to the internet plumbing, the leading Indian telecoms companies have joined consortia investing in ambitious new subsea cabling to Asia and the West, in competition with Chinese-backed groups serving the same markets.

India is also part of a push to reduce dependence on the dollar as a global currency. But it has no wish to be part of a China-dominated currency system either, or party to rather half-baked ideas for a BRICS currency. Rather it is part of a move to have more currencies, including the rupee, used for invoicing and payments. This is happening on a modest scale for oil transactions with the Gulf. But as for wider ambitions, India has all the disadvantages of the Chinese RMB – non-convertibility on capital account – but without China's trade volumes.

There is one respect in which India already has a strategic and growing role in the world economy: oil and energy markets. Together with China, India is the world's biggest influence on oil markets on the demand side, and the International Energy Agency (IEA) has estimated that the country will account for a third of additional world demand to 2030. India has been able to use its position as a major purchaser to secure supplies of Russian oil at generous discounts and establish its independent position in geopolitics. But the important long-term significance of India's role as the world's third largest consumer of energy and carbon emitter is its potential role in dealing with the global challenge of climate change, the issue to which I turn in the next chapter.

India's importance in world markets is also a measure of its vulnerability – in the important area of military equipment. India is the world's largest arms importer, with around 10% of global imports over the period 2019–23. Efforts are being made to develop Indian fighter jets, with the help of various foreign collaborators. But as long as the country depends on Russian supplies or Western technology it will depend on the goodwill of others in the event of serious conlict with its neighbours.

Conclusion

With an economic system increasingly built around national security rather than free and open markets there should be consequences in the real world. Short-term trends have been ambiguous. In 2023 global trade actually fell (by 1%), while global GDP grew 3%. But these crude numbers are part of the mixed picture that has emerged since the pandemic. Emerging market exports grew by 15%. If we look at the ratio of trade in goods to global industrial production, it appears to have declined in the last few years. This is due in part to a higher proportion of Chinese production being absorbed at home, albeit offset by growing trade in the rest of the world.

The focus on trade relationships is, however, merely one dimension of a deep and complex process of international economic integration that could unravel with far-reaching consequences. There is already a move to curb the activities of Chinese-owned enterprises in the USA and vica versa. Curbs on foreign investment are no longer limited to direct foreign investment but to portfolio investment through institutional investors. The use of the dollar as a global currency is coming into question. The symbiotic relationship whereby China finances US savings deficits by acquiring US Treasury assets has, so far, remained largely intact, but that may change. Trust in shared infrastructure is breaking down. In many of these areas of weakening bilateral cooperation there are impacts on third parties. The idea of shared global commons is coming into question.

6

Global public good no. 1: the climate

The world described in the previous chapter is zero-sum. Security concerns and trade imbalances between China and the USA dominate international relations. One of these superpowers may gain an advantage at the expense of the other, but there is little scope for cooperation and a real risk of escalating conflict: the Thucydides Trap. Competition and conflict between the established superpower and today's rising superpower is essentially technological, economic and political, but it could become military.

There is also another kind of trap to consider: the Kindleberger Trap. Named after Charles P. Kindleberger, who played a major role in the reconstruction of Europe after the Second World War, this describes a situation where the declining power ceases to be able to shoulder responsibility for providing global public goods, while the rising power refuses to do so.[1] Both 'traps' are simple constructs, and in the vastly more complicated world of the twenty-first century there are other powers of importance – the EU, Russia, Japan and India – and a dense network of international cooperative institutions. Nonetheless, we must ask: is the Kindleberger Trap real?

What are global public goods?

At their most basic, global public goods provide economic prosperity, peace and security, while ensuring the habitability of the planet. In the interwar period, the mechanisms for providing the first two failed catastrophically, leading to global depression and the Second World War. In the postwar era, by contrast, the US-led international order has, with important qualifications, delivered a remarkable period of rising living standards in a globalised economy and – despite localised conflicts and a cold war – maintained global peace. But the global financial crisis, the emergence of China as a competing superpower, the retreat of Trump's America from global responsibilities, and war in Europe have cast doubt on who, in future, will ensure the provision of global public goods.

A pithy description of public goods has it that they are 'non-excludable' and 'non-rival'.[2] Typical private goods, such as food or clothes or houses, are 'rival' (if we buy them then someone else cannot enjoy them) and 'excludable' (they can be isolated and charged for). There are also some goods that can be isolated and charged for (excludable) but are not rival, at the expense of others, such as toll roads or the internet. And there are goods that are rival but non-excludable: many natural resources. But there are also public goods that cannot be isolated and charged for and can be enjoyed collectively: anti-pollution measures to secure clean air or rivers; public health measures preventing the spread of diseases; planting woodland, which protects species or stops soil erosion; knowledge acquired in public libraries.

Public goods are difficult to manage, since they must be paid for indirectly, either through general taxation or regulations affecting all users. There will be 'free riders' who will try to enjoy the benefits but dodge the regulations or the tax. Often the provision of public goods involves taking a long-term view, while the public and politicians think short term. There can be costly 'spillovers', as when polluted air leads to disease. A major responsibility of governments is to ensure that public goods are provided. But governments vary greatly in their ability to provide them.

International public goods are an extension of the same principle.[3] To be more concrete, Joseph Stiglitz identifies five global public goods: international security, global environmental goods, global standards, international economic stability and knowledge.[4] They are much more difficult to manage than domestic public goods. States value their sovereignty and may reject international taxation or regulation. 'Free riders' are difficult to penalise, as in the case of rogue states, or may be weak or failed states that are unable to meet collective obligations. Governments may be concerned with short-term survival rather than long-term welfare. Ideally, cooperation between countries, backed by strong multilateral institutions, will overcome these problems. But there are a lot of countries to coordinate and many divergent interests. Even when there are overlapping interests, cooperation may

179

be difficult to secure because of lack of trust or the constraints of national politics. That is why the periods of modern history that have seen the most effective delivery of international public goods have been those when there has been a hegemonic power to persuade and to police common action.[5] For almost a century that power was the USA. But that world seems to be disappearing.

In this chapter and the two that follow I look at three areas where China and India are central to the provision of international public goods: the environment, the international economic architecture and security. It should be noted that both countries were largely absent from the creation of the postwar order, whose institutions and rules have provided the framework for managing these public goods. Indeed both contest it, to varying degrees. Hence there are problems of governance as well as substance.

The global environmental commons and climate

There is a particular challenge with environmental public goods. They degrade. They are subject to the 'tragedy of the commons' whereby, in the absence of a system for excluding self-interested users, common resources like watersheds or grazing land become depleted, permanently.[6] A classic example of a public good being undermined in this way is fishing stocks when overfishing leads to the depletion of stocks.[7] That problem applies both locally and globally. Concern over oceanic depletion was one of the factors that led to the Law of the Sea, with its provision of 200-mile exclusive economic zones (EEZs), protected by national governments. But the regime does not protect deep-sea fisheries outside the EEZs, which depend on voluntary international agreements. And weak states find it difficult to protect their EEZs. The superstates, meanwhile, have a chequered history. China is often singled out for failure to respect other countries' EEZs and for aggressive exploitation of the deep seas.[8] Indian fishing is also becoming an issue in the region. And the United States has never signed up to the Law of the Sea.

Another global public good in danger of being destroyed by uncontrolled use is Antarctica. The 1961 Antarctic Treaty allowed scientific research but sought to exclude military activity, banned mining and created a framework for more detailed agreements to protect the fragile ecosystem in the surrounding oceans and on land. The treaty was initially successful but has recently been undermined by new powers. China, Russia, India, South Africa and Saudi Arabia have all expressed an interest in Antarctica, having previously not participated or having been excluded from decision making. China has established a network of research centres which are said to have military potential and has engaged in mining exploration. China and Russia together have blocked agreements on environmental protection, including measures to protect penguins.[9]

Climate change is a far more demanding test of states' ability to manage a key environmental part of the global commons: the atmosphere.[10] Climate is a public good; greenhouse gases (GHGs) are a 'bad'. The science is now largely undisputed. The threat is recognised to be existential – as with the risks of nuclear weapon proliferation. But there are serious governance issues, since the costs and benefits of the status quo or policy action vary greatly between countries. The benefits of action to curb GHG emissions are long term, and the costs of curbing economic growth based on fossil fuels are immediate, which can make 'free riding' a popular option for some countries.

There is an established forum for cooperation through the United Nations Intergovernmental Panel on Climate Change (IPCC) and the biennial Conference of the Parties (COP), but participation is voluntary and collective action requires unanimity. There is also a successful precedent for binding multilateral cooperation, in the Montreal Protocol on protection of the ozone layer. Both China and India are central to the issue, as major generators of GHGs and in terms of the impact of climate change.

It is possible that universal bodies built around the United Nations – COP in the case of climate change – will advance through cooperation, consensus and collective action. We can hope. But experience suggests that without the active support and leadership of the major powers not much will happen. The withdrawal of Trump's America is a major problem, but provides scope for the EU and/or China to play a leadership role. China and India's role will, in any event, become more significant because of the importance of coal in both economies, and because both countries aspire to grow their economies rapidly to achieve something approaching the living standards of the developed world. They are leaders in the deployment of renewable technology required to reduce emissions, while also contributing disproportionately to emissions through economic growth. They are also two of the countries most vulnerable to the impact of climate change.

181

The impact of climate change on China and India

Governments are less likely to be motivated by abstract, impersonal concepts like international public goods than by the impact on their own citizens. There has been mounting evidence that China and India are already being substantially affected by climate change, and the risks and impacts are growing. A German survey of climate vulnerability has India as one of the ten countries most affected in terms of fatalities and material damage in recent years.[11] Neither China nor India has the extreme vulnerability of some sub-Saharan countries, but simply by virtue of their scale, their vulnerability affects large numbers of people. On one estimate of the fifty regions of the world most vulnerable to climate change, twenty-six are in China and nine in India.[12]

There has been a good deal of research on and analysis of the potential consequences of sea level rise. Climate change studies by the IPCC have warned of sea flooding risk, mainly in the form of greater frequency and seriousness of storm surges as the sea level rises due to thermal expansion and the melting of glaciers and polar ice.[13] Clearly, the estimated consequences of sea level rise will depend on what assumptions are made about the level and speed of the rise, the time horizon and the effectiveness of defences against it. In terms of sheer numbers of people, China is most exposed, since over 30,000 square kilometres of the coastal provinces in eastern China are close to sea level. By the end of the century, 50 million people (in a range of 36 to 62 million) could be affected: 4% of the total population. For India, the figures are 12 million and 1% (on the same assumptions, 26% of the population of Vietnam and 47% of the population of the Netherlands could be affected).[14] Especially at risk are low-lying major cities, and of the top twenty cities in the world at risk, the two most exposed are Kolkata and Mumbai, with 4.7 million people likely to be affected, potentially rising to 25 million by 2070. Four more are Chinese: Guangzhou, Shanghai, Tianjin and Ningbo.[15]

Another indicator of vulnerability to climate change is temperature extremes. In 2023, a combination of long-term global warming augmented by the El Niño effect produced the highest global temperatures on record. China recorded its highest temperatures in 2023, with over 52°C in the north-west of the country. Beijing had twenty-seven consecutive days over 35°C. At the other extreme, Heilongjiang recorded minus 53°C in winter.

Analysis by the IPCC suggests that what could have been regarded as a 1-in-250-year temperature event before the rise of modern GHG emissions has become a 1-in-5-year event in China.[16] One NGO, World Weather Attribution, estimates that extreme heatwaves are now thirty times more likely in India because of climate change.[17] An estimated 300 million people could be at risk in India in 2050. And that is on top of an estimated 24,000 dead over the last twenty years from extreme heat.[18] But fatal heatstroke is just one consequence of extreme temperatures. There is also a greater likelihood of drought affecting water supplies, destruction of crops and overall economic damage.

Although urban air pollution is only indirectly related to climate change, and connected more to airborne particulates produced by vehicles, coal and waste burning, there is some overlap. Air pollution has also had a disproportionate impact on public opinion, galvanising political action. The global Air Quality Database shows India to be the third most polluting country out of 134, and China the seventeenth – the latter after a decade of falling levels.[19] Delhi is by far the most polluted capital city in the world (Beijing is fifteenth), with levels regarded as 'drastically poor'. China has demonstrated the importance of coal burning to both climate change and urban air pollution, and its action to clean up air in the big cities has mitigated the damage, albeit inconsistently.

Both countries, but especially India, have water stress, aggravated by climate change and specifically by drought, which is linked to increasingly erratic and extreme storms and monsoonal rainfall.[20] Water stress matters, since it is linked to other aspects of development such as the availability of clean drinking water, sanitation and hygiene. Some twenty-five countries are said to have 'extreme stress', including India.[21] China has 'medium high' stress. Around 40% of China's population in the north live in areas classified by the UN as subject to 'water scarcity', which is why the regime has invested billions to transfer water from the south in a massive water diversion project. The Indian position is measured by the fact that annual availability of water is 1,500 cubic meters per capita per annum, whereas it was 5,000 cubic meters half a century ago.[22] The World Resources Institute estimates that India has 18% of the global population but only 4% of water supplies.[23] Only some of this water stress is climate-related; the main factors are population rise, industrialisation and political reluctance to charge for water use.

But climate change is aggravating the stress levels. Moreover, the fact that both China and India utilise the same headwaters is adding another dimension to stress in the form of conflict over water supplies. China is planning a mega-dam on the Brahmaputra, which also serves India. China's harsh approach to security in Tibet is also explained in part by a need to protect its main source of fresh water.

Both China and India are big countries, and the incidence of these climate impacts will vary from one region to another, between urban and rural dwellers and between groups of people defined by class or age. These distributional effects add to the complexity and to the political difficulties of the problem. Taken together, all these factors have motivated the Chinese and Indian governments to treat climate change as part of a collective global problem for which they support collective action. President Xi's Global Civilisation Initiative explicitly recognises the centrality of 'environmental responsibility'. Crucially, it was an initiative between the Obama administration and the Chinese which led to the Paris Agreement in 2015, on which subsequent action has been based. Continued dialogue on methane emissions, for example, albeit rather stilted, is one of the few areas to have survived the recent freeze in relations.

Emissions from economic growth

China and India are central both to the causes of and remedies for global warming. They both embody the fundamental dilemma at the heart of policy: the need for economic growth to achieve higher living standards and poverty reduction, but also the need to curb the emission of GHGs that economic growth brings in its wake. Both countries also have a structural reliance on coal, which heightens the policy dilemmas. The most recent data suggests that China produces annually almost 31% of the world's GHGs in terms of CO_2 equivalents – over twice the US share of 14%, which in turn is just under twice the Indian share (8%) and just over twice the share of the EU-27.[24] The data is approximate and changes a little if we allow for trade (around 10% of Chinese and Indian emissions are 'exported' and around 10% of US emissions are 'imported'). It also excludes agriculture. These figures are used to argue that China now has overwhelmingly the greater share of responsibility for curbing global emissions.

However, both China and India are now industrialising and modernising at lower levels of income than the developed world has achieved, and they are clearly not responsible for the legacy of emissions, still in the atmosphere, from the Industrial Revolution. Figure 6.1 shows the difference between present and cumulative emissions. In per capita terms, the USA leads the field at present, with around 18 tonnes of CO_2 equivalent, as against 11 tonnes for China and 3 tonnes for India. In legacy terms, the share of cumulative emissions since 1700 is approximately 13% for China, 23% for the USA, 13% for the EU and 3% for India (less than the UK, which accounts for around 4%).

Arguments over who is to blame for the damage already done are unlikely to produce conclusive outcomes or meaningful action. If action on emission reduction is to happen, it will only be on the basis that all share some responsibility, but there should be allowance taken for the level of development. The poorest countries, which face major adjustment costs, should receive financial help. That is, broadly, how negotiations within a multilateral COP framework now proceed, though commitment varies between parties (the USA withdrew from the process altogether under President Trump in 2017–20 and he will very likely do the same in his second term).

The various parties to the United Nations COP 28 in Dubai in 2023 reached agreement. But analysis by the IPCC suggests that, based on current trends and declared government objectives, it will now be very difficult to meet the target of keeping warming to 1.5°C above pre-industrial levels without intensified efforts by member states. The core commitment of the major participating countries is to achieve net zero emissions as soon as

	GHG (bn tonnes CO_2 eq 2022)	Share of world	Cumulative emissions (bn tonnes)	Per capita emissions 2022
World	53.8	100	N/A	6.8
EU	3.6	6.7	296.0	8.1
China	15.7	29.2	260.0	11.0
India	3.6	7.3	60.0	2.6
USA	6.0	11.2	427.0	17.9
UK	0.4	0.8	79.0	6.3

Source: International Energy Agency, Energy Data Explorer, 2024

6.1 Greenhouse gas emissions by country

possible. So far, 140 countries have set targets covering about 90% of emissions, though they vary from vague aspirations to carefully designed plans. The main developed economies – the USA, the EU, the UK, Canada, Australia and Japan – have set the net zero objective for 2050, as have Brazil, South Africa and South Korea. Sweden and Germany have set the more ambitious target of 2045. China has a 2060 date, shared with Indonesia, Russia and Saudi Arabia, and India is aiming for 2070. This staggering of objectives reflects the fact that some countries are already well advanced in emission reduction: the UK, France and Germany reached peak energy-related CO_2 emissions in the 1970s, the USA around 2000, Japan in 2013, Brazil in 2014 and South Korea in 2018. China has a target date of 2030 to reduce emissions in absolute terms but may have already reached peak emissions. India is likely to reach the same point in 2030–35.

Targets are only targets, but they give some measure of how individual countries plan to contribute to the global goals. The Climate Action Tracker (CAT)[25] uses sophisticated modelling to provide an independent assessment of how current policies, actions and targets match the overriding objectives of temperature stabilisation, allowing for 'fair shares' between rich and poor countries.[26] Even after Biden's ambitious Inflation Reduction Act, which mandated and financed ambitious climate objectives, the CAT judges US efforts to be 'insufficient'. The 2030 objectives are likely to fall short by 23–37%. The USA has also moved in the wrong direction by increasing oil and gas drilling and pipeline capacity. And despite a promise to help poorer countries with 'loss and damage' funding, the amounts being approved by Congress are deemed 'critically insufficient'. Moreover, the rating does not take into account policy regression under President Trump.

The CAT also gives a sobering and critical assessment of China's performance and prospects: 'highly insufficient'. Although the country reached peak emissions well ahead of its 2030 target, emissions then plateaued rather than fell. China's targets are now compatible only with global warming of up to 4°C, which is way beyond what is regarded as safe. This is because fossil fuel use and expansion is deemed necessary for reasons of geopolitics and energy security. Coal and imported gas offset the considerable gains from rapid expansion in renewable energy. Despite the gloomy assessment, during the Biden administration the USA and China agreed to work together. They also made a joint commitment on methane emissions, which have

186

a dangerously accelerating effect on global warming, although the commitment is vague on detail. Any assessment of China's performance must also take account of the fact that fossil fuels, mainly coal, have historically not only been central to power generation and heating but also to heavy industry, for instance steel and cement, which accounted for 35% of the CO_2 emissions from the energy sector in 2020 (power and heating accounted for 50%). China's future performance will clearly benefit from strong and clear political direction from the top and a commitment to pursue 'high quality' economic growth, but the current trajectory involves contradictory objectives.

The CAT assessment for India is equally bleak, even making allowances for the country's lower level of development. The rating is 'highly insufficient', such that past performance and future plans are consistent only with global warming up to 4°C (or 3°C on a 'fair shares' basis). As with China, the government's published plans start from recognising the reality of high dependence on coal (and imported gas). India's carbon intensity overall is 52% above the global average (China is 30% above average, the USA 10% below and the EU 36% below). This carbon dependency will undoubtedly continue for some time because of population and economic growth. India is expected to be responsible for a quarter of the world's increased energy consumption by 2040. A positive trend in the opposite direction is that in recent years India has outperformed its own plans for decarbonisation. There was a 2016 target under India's commitments to the Paris COP for a non-fossil fuel capacity increase for electricity generation of 40% by 2030. It was reached by 2022. A commitment to reduce emissions intensity relative to 2005 levels by 30–35% in 2030 was met in 2021. A commitment to renewable capacity of 175 GW in 2022 was almost met. If India and China continue to outperform expectations in renewables development that will go some way to addressing the CAT scepticism.

Good and bad news: renewables and coal both have priority

Coal is the biggest source of GHGs, making up around 40% of carbon emissions globally. This is because coal is almost pure carbon and because of associated emissions like methane gas from coal mines. Coal mining is also a major source of methane emissions. The IEA estimates that coal

187

consumption needs to fall by 11% a year to be consistent with a 1.5°C warming maximum above pre-industrial levels. In fact, global consumption in 2022 was almost identical to the level a decade ago, during the previous peak in 2013: 8 billion tonnes.[27] Since 2013 the USA has almost halved its coal consumption (from 840 million to 465 million tonnes), and the EU has also curbed demand (677 to 478 million tonnes). But these cuts have been largely offset by China and India (respectively 4,037 million increasing to 4,250 million tonnes and 806 million increasing to 1,103 million tonnes), together with rapid growth in Indonesia among others. China alone accounts for over half of world demand, and India is second with just over 10%.

Figure 6.2 shows the continuing dominance of coal in power generation in both countries. Both China and India (along with Indonesia) are also expecting domestic coal demand to increase and are working through a programme of building coal-powered power stations. China has a long pipeline of new coal-fired power stations – some to replace inefficient old ones, some to add capacity. China committed in 2021 to 'strictly control' the amount of coal-powered electricity but is thought, nonetheless, to have added 95% of the world's additional capacity in 2023.[28] This change of emphasis back to coal is partly the result of a spate of blackouts and partly because of the disruption in supplies and gas market volatility caused by the Ukraine War.

For China and to a degree India (and other big players such as the EU and USA), energy security has come to dominate policy. Coal-based power stations can run for twenty-four hours a day and use domestic raw materials. China has also shown reluctance to become too dependent on energy supplies from the Gulf or Russia, and is heavily influenced by a deteriorating geopolitical outlook. Both China and India have, however, reduced their dependence on coal relative to other fuels (China from 70% to under half of energy demand within a decade, India from 57% to 48% within five years). But in a growing economy, coal demand will continue to rise. That may be less of an issue in China, where the economy has slowed because of the collapse in the property market and cutbacks in infrastructure investment (which directly reduces demand for coal-intensive cement and steel). India's coal demand is expected to rise from 1 to 1.5 billion tonnes in 2030, when coal will still be responsible for half of electricity generated. The government has authorised a big expansion of underground mining to augment its mainly open-cast industry.[29]

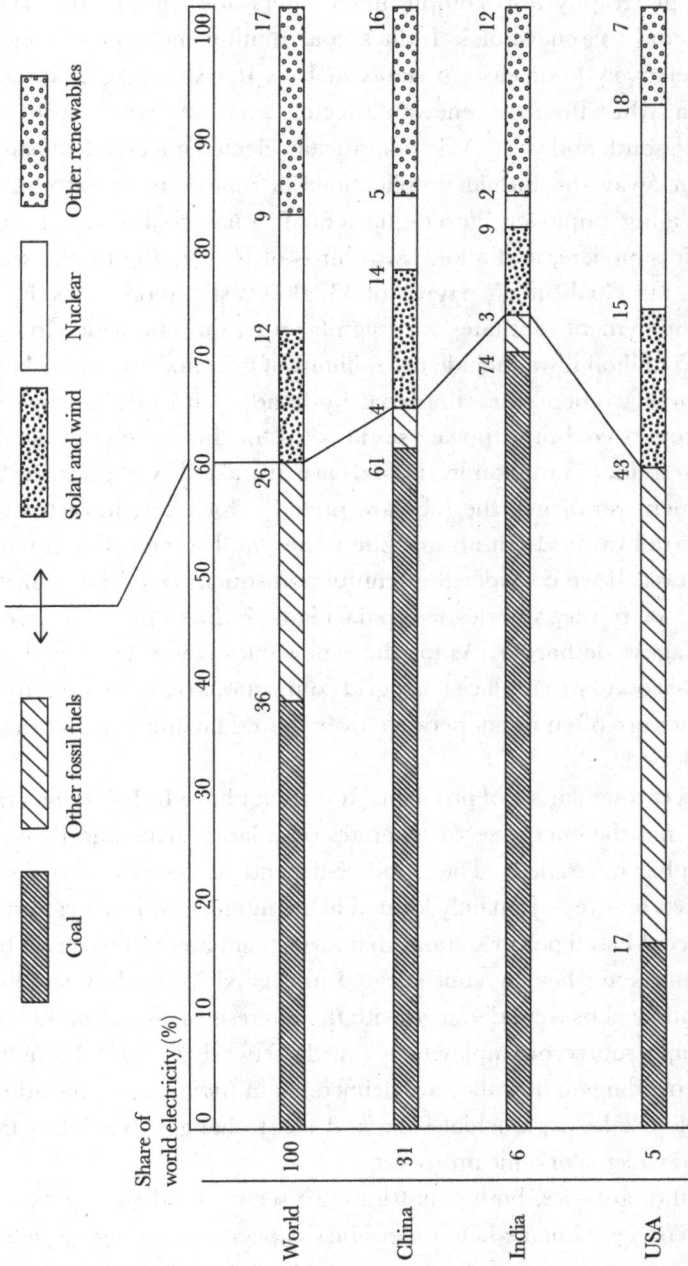

Share of world electricity (%)

Legend: Coal · Other fossil fuels · Solar and wind · Nuclear · Other renewables

Source: International Energy Agency, Energy Data Explorer, 2024

6.2 Electricity generation by fuel, 2022 (%)

Internal geography also complicates matters and inhibits the transition from coal to renewables. India's coal mining industry is concentrated in relatively poor eastern states such as Jharkhand, Chhattisgarh and Odisha, while the new renewable sector, solar and wind, is concentrated in the south and west. A democratically elected government cannot simply wish away the human implications of major structural change, and coal is a big employer. Three-quarters of Indian coal demand is met by domestic suppliers, and about two-thirds of that by the public sector Coal India, but Coal India's payroll of 337,000 vastly understates the job impact. Employment estimates vary significantly, but one widely quoted number is 5 million if we include the millions of informal sector workers – many of them women extracting coal by hand – and others employed in work around coal-fired power stations.[30] One Indian energy analyst has estimated that 25 million livelihoods are at stake.[31] And given India's unemployment problems, the jobs are prized. Moreover, infrastructure such as the railways is built around the mines, and so adjustment would be a huge task. If we consider the painful adjustment required of British coal mining or in the American Appalachians, India's challenges are an order of magnitude harder. As for the renewables being developed elsewhere in the country to replace coal, grid connections between regions are patchy, states are often uncooperative over shared facilities and storage is underdeveloped.

China faces a similar set of problems. It may not have India's democratic constraints, but the energy sector operates on a larger scale and there are big geographic differences. The weather-dependent renewables sector – including hydropower – is mainly located in the interior, while cities and the traditional coal-based power stations that serve them are in the coastal belt. The coal mines are heavily concentrated in Shanxi in north-west China. The grid connections were designed with the interests of coal in mind. Coal is also a major source of employment – with between 1.5 and 2.5 million workers, depending on how they are defined. As in India, provincial administrations often take a parochial view and resist changes that affect their revenue and wider economic prospects.

Despite the obstacles, both countries have seen a prodigious growth in renewable energy. China's new renewables capacity is far bigger than in other major economies, with a large renewables sector which is arguably

	Renewable capacity	O/W Wind	Solar
China	1,202	366	393
USA	373	142	114
India	168	42	63
Germany	155	66	85
Brazil	177	24	Negligible

Source: International Renewable Energy Agency (IRENA) 2024

6.3 Renewable energy generation capacity, 2022 ('000 MW)

bigger than the rest of the world put together. One estimate suggested that in 2023 China had 65% of global solar capacity and 60% for wind.[32] It was estimated that renewables (with hydro) had reached 50% of China's electricity generating capacity from 29% a decade earlier in 2013.[33] However, to put the achievement in perspective, and as shown in Figure 6.2, coal still accounted for 60% of electricity generated – as opposed to capacity – while renewables accounted for around a third. In relation to solar power, China installed more capacity in 2022 than the rest of the world combined. The IEA estimates that China is investing over $3 in renewables for every $1 in fossil fuels, as against a world average of $1.80 and a US figure of $1.23.

Two factors are helping to drive the rapid expansion in renewables. The first is a falling cost curve as economies of scale reinforce the benefits of leading-edge technology in the components of solar panel and wind turbine production. Large-scale, sustained investment by state-owned enterprises – less fickle than Western capital markets – has made this expansion possible. A second factor is that falling costs increase the competitiveness of green industries based on decarbonised electricity, notably electric vehicles and the batteries that power them, which in turn increases the demand for 'green' electricity. To the alarm of European, Japanese and American car makers, China now dominates the global market for electric vehicles as well as new renewable technology and manufacture. China now has a powerful self-interested economic reason for promoting the green transition globally, which it will dominate.

The rapid expansion of renewable energy in China has however run into problems familiar to Western economies. There is insufficient grid capacity to make use of the green energy, and supplies are having to be curtailed. The grid system still depends on central planning rather than markets, which favours coal use over renewables. There is an ambitious programme to increase grid transmission and storage capacity, but it is inevitable that the investment in renewable energy will have to slow – one of the sources of the pessimism in the Climate Tracker's assessment.

India's expansion of renewables is less spectacular, but it is now the world's third biggest renewable power generator. The sector is increasing rapidly, with hopes to expand capacity of non-fossil fuel power to 500 GW by 2030 from 170 GW at the end of 2023, when renewables accounted for 40% of installed generating capacity. Analysts looking at the totality of policy have argued that India's 'smart' auctioning system for electricity is one of the best in the world for sustained support of the renewable sector.[34]

China and India also lead the world in expanding a more traditional – and more expensive – form of renewable power: nuclear. According to the IEA, in 2024, when there were around 400 reactors worldwide, China had twenty-two nuclear power plants under construction to add to its existing fifty-five, with aspirations to add another six to eight a year, while India had seven under construction to add to its twenty. By contrast, in developed economies construction has largely stalled, with the USA adding just one to its ninety-three. Russia was adding six to its thirty-seven. The long time horizons involved in nuclear power construction require a consistent approach to policy and a strong, centrally driven commitment, which is also necessary for the wider coal to renewables transition. China, and to a lesser degree India, has that capacity; Western countries, it appears, no longer do.

Both China and India have demonstrated a commitment to delivering their extremely important contributions towards the global public good of managing climate change. It could be argued that most of the actions taken would have been done anyway for long-term, self-interested reasons and are not primarily in response to international obligations. China's dominance of electric vehicles, battery and new renewable technologies gives a powerful economic motive for promoting a green transition. However, both countries have development plans that are environmentally ambitious but still not consistent with slowing global warming to moderate levels. A major contributory factor is the large coal sector which, particularly in China, is supported because of geopolitical conflict and insecurity. A cold war with China almost guarantees that security concerns – and coal – will dominate.

A more positive story, however, is the fact that working through a United Nations (IPCC) process has made it possible to create a global, multilateral, framework for negotiation on climate that encompasses countries big and small, rich and poor. Both China and India are part of that process and accept its overarching goals. But the failure of the 2024 COP29 conference in Azerbaijan to produce a consensus compatible with the Paris Agreement of 2015 (to limit global temperature increases to 1.5°C) underlined the political limitations of multilateral cooperation to protect the global commons. And that was before the second Trump presidency, committed to disengage from the process. If the public good of managing climate change is to be realised it will depend on China, and to a growing degree India, assuming global leadership.

7

Global public good no. 2: the liberal international economic order

The Kindleberger Trap is being most seriously tested in the field of international economics. The postwar success story of improving living standards almost everywhere and rapid economic development in Asia was based in significant part on having a process of globalisation, supported by what has been called (rather portentously) a rules-based international order (the RBIO). That system in now under attack.

China and India – China especially – have been major beneficiaries of globalisation. They have also long been critics of the RBIO and advocates of reforms to global governance arrangements to better reflect the growing weight of developing countries in the Global South. India championed multilateral institutions from its independence, and in the 1960s pressed for the establishment of the UN Trade and Development organisation (UNCTAD) and the New International Economic Order, based on principles of global redistributive justice. The Non-Aligned Movement (NAM) and the G77 bloc acted as a collective voice for newly independent countries, with India taking a major role in both. And India was a prominent part of the shift from G7 to G20 deliberations on the global economy. But India's negative approach to liberalisation in the GATT/WTO (General Agreement on Tariffs and Trade/World Trade Organization) earned it the reputation of 'the India that cannot say yes'.[1] It justified its negativity by arguing that it could not be expected to provide global public goods at its current stage of development.[2] The Modi government has continued India's role as champion of global governance reform while remaining, as far as possible, 'non-aligned'.[3]

China has shared many of the same political positions as India and operates in many of the same forums, notably the BRICS group. In the Maoist period it stood apart from the main multilateral institutions and even from the NAM, but with Deng's reforms there was an abrupt shift to enthusiastic membership of important multilateral bodies – the IMF, World Bank, GATT, the WIPO (World Intellectual Property Organization) and the Asian Development Bank. Just as India has been accused of negativity, China has been accused of being obstructive by pressing for special treatment for developing economies while insisting that it is still a developing country itself. A Brookings Institution report observed that 'China has generally lived up to obligations in these institutions but has been reluctant to take on responsibilities which fall on developed countries ... insisting on being treated as a developing country.'[4] But under President Xi there is a more assertive approach: 'to lead the reform of the global governance system with the concept of fairness and justice'.[5] To understand the implications of this, I look at different aspects of global economic governance.

The IMF and money

A central part of the global international economic architecture after the Second World War was the creation of the Bretton Woods institutions and in particular the IMF. Its mandate was to establish a global currency regime which would facilitate global commerce and avoid the beggar-my-neighbour behaviour, using aggressively competitive exchange rates or trade protectionism, of the interwar years. In practice the system that evolved did not incorporate a new global currency, as John Maynard Keynes had urged, and the dollar assumed that role. But the IMF provided an important function as lender of last resort for countries with large external imbalances in the form of current account deficits.

Until this century, China and India (and especially India) saw the IMF primarily in terms of its lending facilities and policy support. China used its standby facilities in 1986 in support of its economic reforms, paid off the loan without difficulty and leaned on the IMF for policy advice. The IMF (with the World Bank) played a major role in building up institutional capacity in fields like monetary policy, and China in turn was regarded as a star pupil. The same was broadly true of India, which resorted to IMF loans in response to crises in 1957, 1965 (in support of a devaluation and trade liberalisation package), 1981 (in support of Indira Gandhi's first attempt at reform) and 1991 (the Manmohan Singh reforms). In India, the IMF did not attract the opprobrium it experienced in Latin America and Africa because of unpopular adjustment measures. And it appeared comfortable dealing with competent Indian economic officials and would claim some credit for having acted as midwife to the reforms that have helped to stimulate India's current growth. China and India have arguably been the IMF's biggest success stories. They now want to own more of it.

As China and India have become more substantial economies, a constant refrain, shared with the rest of the Global South, has been that they should be more effectively represented in the Bretton Woods institutions. Voting shares still largely reflect the balance of the world economy when the IMF and World Bank were established. The arithmetic is set out in Figure 7.1. On a PPP basis China has 18.6% of the world economy and India 7.7%, but their respective vote shares are 6.1% and 2.7%. By contrast, the USA has 15.3% of the world economy but a 16.5% vote share, Japan 4.0% of the world economy but 6.4% voting share, both the UK and France 2.3% of the world economy but 4.0% of the votes. The disproportions are less obvious if GDP at market prices is used as a measurement, and the current voting shares represent a recent slight improvement. But the USA has strongly resisted any attempt to push its share below 15%, since an 85% vote

	Share of GDP – PPP (nominal)		IMF voting	World Bank voting	ADB voting	AIIB voting	UN annual contributions (permanent*)
China*	18.6	(17.5)	6.1	5.6	5.4	27	12.0
USA*	15.3	(25.1)	16.5	15.8	12.8	–	27.0
India	7.7	(3.1)	2.7	3.1	5.3	7.6	0.8
Japan	4.0	(6.0)	6.4	7.6	12.8	–	8.5
Germany	3.3	(4.6)	5.3	4.3	3.7	4.1	6.0
Russia	2.9	(1.8)	2.6	2.9	–	5.9	3.0
Indonesia	2.6	(1.3)	1.0	1.0	4.6	3.2	0.5
Brazil	2.5	(1.7)	2.2	1.9	–	0.2	2.9
France*	2.3	(3.2)	4.0	3.9	2.1	3.2	5.6
UK*	2.3	(3.2)	4.0	3.9	1.9	2.9	4.6
Saudi Arabia	1.2	(0.8)	2.1	2.5	–	2.4	1.1

Source: World Bank Voting Powers, IMF Member Quota and Voting Powers, Asian Development Bank Members Capital Stock and Voting Power, Asian Infrastructure Investment Bank (AIIB) Members and Prospective Members of the Bank, United Nations funding by country, World Population Review

7.1 Decision making in international bodies (% 2024)

is required for major decisions. And the other developed economies have clung to their inflated representation.[6]

The fact that the IMF is still a US-dominated institution, and the dollar remains the global currency, is being questioned in a world where the country's share of the world economy is now below 20% (15% in PPP terms) and its share of world trade is being overtaken by China. There is also a long-standing deep fault line in the current international monetary arrangements. The problem is how to deal with major imbalances in payments which involve both deficit and surplus economies accepting responsibility for adjustment. In the 1980s large current account surpluses in Japan and Germany existed alongside big US deficits, but US domestic policy involving large fiscal deficits and tight money policies was pushing up the dollar, which in turn contributed to a widening current account deficit. The coordination problem was resolved through the Plaza Accord negotiated among the G7 countries, and the subsequent Louvre Accord, under which the dollar was able to devalue by around 40%. This had positive results for US trade and defused a potential crisis.[7]

The coordination problem was difficult enough when the USA was clearly the dominant party and was dealing with political allies. But China now has rough parity and is a geopolitical rival. Even before the geopolitical rivalry, there had been serious adjustment problems as China developed a highly competitive and growing export sector. In 1994, China devalued and pegged the RMB to the dollar at what it saw as a 'competitive' rate, helping its 'reform and opening up'. The USA, meanwhile, saw this as currency manipulation.[8] The peg was, however, sustained for a decade. At one point, China had a current account surplus of around 10% of GDP. Chinese savings were financing US deficits and Chinese exporters were feeding the appetite of US consumers for cheap imported goods. This was the era of Chimerica: the symbiotic if uncomfortable mutual dependence of the US and Chinese economies.[9] Chinese resistance to pressure to revalue led to some friction with the IMF as well as with US politicians. In the event, the Chinese currency was allowed to appreciate – by 60% in real terms – some rebalancing occurred and complaints about 'currency manipulation' largely disappeared (for a while).

The problem of imbalances was overtaken by the 2008 global financial crisis. China emerged as a constructive player, and its massive investment

197

stimulus helped to save the world economy from depression. It used its enhanced credibility to become the champion of IMF reform in the shape of a proposed New Bretton Woods, with a large distribution of SDRs (Special Drawing Rights) to grow liquidity in the world economy, but particularly to help distressed developing economies. China was committed to reforming the system from within, working with Western politicians such as Gordon Brown.[10] In the event, nothing fundamentally changed – indeed, the US 'tightened its grip on global finance',[11] though China (together with India and others) was rewarded with a small change in quota shares.

The Covid crisis seemed to provide a new rationale for the IMF. Even before the pandemic there had been a build-up of debt servicing problems in developing economies, and these problems were then aggravated by disruption of production during lockdowns, a fall in commodity prices and a strong dollar, hardening dollar liabilities. The IMF mobilised around a trillion dollars for emergency lending to distressed countries. Little has however been used, and the problems of debtors have grown.

On this occasion, China was the villain rather than the hero. China has been accused by its critics of undermining the global initiative. First, it launched its own bailout funding operation (in the form of credit swap lines), which has been large in scale – an estimated $240 billion, equivalent to 20% of all bailout lending in the last decade – but opaque, at high interest rates and channelled only towards countries in receipt of China's own Belt and Road funding.[12] Second, China has been obstructing multilateral efforts by dealing with debtor countries separately from other creditors in the Paris Club of official – government – lenders. That matters, since the IMF cannot proceed with its loans in the absence of prior agreement on debt. China did initially cooperate in a joint G20 initiative, the DSSI (Debt Service Suspension Initiative) scheme, in 2020/21 by deferring around $8 billion in debt service from Angola, Pakistan, Kenya and Congo.[13] But outside that scheme Chinese bank lenders, which are together the largest single source of developing country debt, have refused to give debt relief in the form of debt write-downs (a 'haircut'), and will not go beyond rollovers and rescheduling. The debtors are insolvent rather than illiquid and require debt cancellation, which China will not concede. The practical effect has been prolonged negotiation between creditors over parity of treatment and delay in IMF agreements – three years for Zambia – during which economic conditions have deteriorated. There have been few signs of greater flexibility.[14] The intransigence of Chinese creditors led the head of the IMF to issue a rebuke: 'we have worked hard to get the Chinese leadership to recognise that with more wealth comes more responsibility'.[15] For better or worse – worse in this instance – China has been increasingly calling the shots in international finance.[16]

The IMF remains in limbo: unreformed but functioning in effect as a development agency overlapping with the work of the World Bank, providing limited amounts of last resort lending to distressed poor countries. Moreover, it has become absorbed in arguments as to whether its objectives include climate change mitigation and how to manage environmental projects – very far from the original aims of Bretton Woods. I review below how China's (and increasingly India's) participation is changing the whole outlook for development aid.

In another respect, however, the old problems of the international monetary system have returned in a new form. There is again an issue of serious payments imbalances, in the case of China aggravated by trade surpluses which reflect weak domestic consumption, and which are politically combustible in the USA. For its part, the USA has been running a large fiscal deficit of around 7% of GDP, taking levels of debt to GDP well above 100%. But in a dollar-dominated system the US authorities can sustain growing deficits and debt simply by creating more dollars, which the rest of the world, including China, hold as assets. A combination of raised interest rates to head off inflation and a loose fiscal policy has, as in the 1990s, led to a strong dollar, causing distress to emerging economies whose debts are fixed in dollars. China, like Japan, is experiencing a forced devaluation, widening the trade deficit with the USA and aggravating tensions. Chinese options are limited. Ideally the authorities would boost consumption through fiscal deficit financing, but the government is reluctant to take serious fiscal risks. Revaluation would be difficult to engineer, since the currency is already threatened by capital flight, and the prospect of negotiating a Plaza-type agreement is remote. Trade conflict is a more likely outcome, and America has a president who relishes the idea.

Challenge to dollar hegemony

One aspect of the world economy where the USA is still largely unchallenged is through the power of the dollar as a global currency. But in a world of trade conflict and geopolitical competition that can no longer be taken for granted.

The dollar has long been accepted, among fiat currencies, as the best international medium of exchange and the best store of value for other countries' reserves. The dollar prevails because of America's size, deep and broad financial markets and reliability in observing the rule of law. Its role is an example of Kindleberger's 'global public good'.[17] In return for the benefits of economic efficiency and having access to a liquid and reliable global currency, the rest of the world surrenders to the United States what has been called an 'exorbitant privilege'.[18] The USA can, in principle, finance potentially limitless fiscal and current account deficits by having foreigners hold its debt as their assets (though some writers have argued that this 'exorbitant privilege' is in fact a burden, since it encourages the US to pursue self-harming economic policies which lead to dangerous asset bubbles).[19]

Other major countries, starting with France but since then mainly emerging economies, have long questioned their dependence on the national currency of a country whose wider interests may not coincide with their own. But the sheer convenience of having the dollar as a global currency, and the success of the dollar-based system in underpinning decades of globalisation and economic growth, has sustained its role. The rise of China represents a serious challenge. The first manifestation of discomfort was the period of 'mutually assured destruction' starting in the mid-1980s, when China's large current account surpluses were, in effect, financing US deficits and led to a large accumulation of dollars in the form of US Treasury debt. If China had offloaded the dollars, it could have forced a major, destabilising dollar devaluation, but at the cost of depreciating the value of its own reserves. What the historian Niall Ferguson calls 'Chimerica' was in fact beneficial to the economic objectives of both sides.[20] As discussed earlier, the system held in any event, and then survived the 2008 financial crisis. To the extent to which other countries diversified their reserve holdings away from the dollar it was to hold currencies from other developed countries with open economies and liquid markets.[21] Or gold.

China's emergence as a strategic rival to the USA has focused attention on the extent of the 'exorbitant privilege' in geopolitical terms. The USA has been able, for example, to operate and pay for a global network of hundreds of military bases, much of it designed to protect against China, but financed by Chinese savers. The Chinese signalled an ambition to end this monetary dependence on the USA, but its own currency was not an attractive alternative proposition because of a lack of exchange convertibility and a perceived weakness in the rule of law. The experience of 2015, when China's partial relaxation of exchange controls contributed to capital flight, killed off any premature talk of the RMB as a global currency.

What has radically changed the picture is the use of financial sanctions against Russia following the invasion of Ukraine. Russian dollar foreign exchange reserves have in effect been frozen, and there has been talk of expropriating them. In addition, selected Russian banks have been prevented from using the Europe-based SWIFT system for settling transactions (which take place mostly in dollars). The precise workings of the sanctions is complex, but the bigger signal it sent to China and other countries is that they are vulnerable to similar sanctions on a larger scale.[22] Financial sanctions could be invoked in the event of a major escalation in a bilateral dispute with the USA (as with China and Taiwan) or if the country incurs secondary sanctions because of a failure to implement primary sanctions. For example, a country may not have a quarrel with the USA but may wish to retain its trade links with Russia or Iran, and thereby risk secondary sanctions.

This situation has accelerated efforts to diversify out of dollar reserves and to devise means of financing transactions outside dollar-based settlement arrangements. For China, that has meant improving the efficiency of the Chinese CIPS (Cross-border Interbank Payment System) trading system and internationalising its Central Bank digital currency, e-CNY, for rapid settlement. The e-CNY is not fully operational internally, let alone internationally, but the potential is there.[23] China is also seeking to insulate itself from future sanctions in a variety of ways. It has agreed swap lines with forty countries worth $550 billion. Trade with Russia has been moved rapidly onto an RMB basis, from 10% of Chinese exports to Russia in 2016 to 66% in 2022, and from a share of overall Sino-Russia trade of 3% in 2021 to 33% in 2023.[24] China can now potentially settle half or more of China–Russia cross-border trade and investment in RMB.

There is anecdotal evidence that a variety of countries, not just China, are seeking to trade without recourse to the dollar.[25] Saudi Arabia is invoicing oil in RMB, in acknowledgement of the fact that China is its leading customer (a symbolically important move, since it was Saudi's decision to use dollar invoicing fifty years ago that gave credibility to the dollar as a global currency). Brazil is using RMB to settle bills with China. French companies financed a gas deal using the currency, and Bangladesh and Russia have both used it for settlement of a debt. Argentina paid off IMF debt in part using RMB. The proliferation of RMB deals has led to an offshore RMB market, and the availability of liquidity is a further incentive to use the currency.

But the Chinese currency is not the only option. A group of Southeast Asian countries (Indonesia, Malaysia, Thailand, Philippines) are looking to expand trade in their own currencies without recourse to either the dollar or the RMB. India is using the rupee to settle business with the UAE and transactions within the SAARC (South Asian Association for Regional Cooperation) group. India has no wish to be part of a China-dominated currency system or to be party to half-baked ideas for a BRICS currency. Rather it is encouraging a move for more currencies, including the rupee, to be used for invoicing and payments. This has been happening on a modest scale for oil transactions with the Gulf. But, as for wider ambitions to make the rupee a global currency, it has the same disadvantages as the Chinese RMB – nonconvertibility on capital account – without China's trade volumes.

At the BRICS summit in Russia in 2024 a clear plan emerged called the BRICS Bridge, which will enable cross-border trade to be settled digitally using platforms run by central banks. This proposal is significant because it is not based on other-worldly concepts such as a BRICS currency but on a model that already works. A grouping of China, Thailand and the UAE, latterly joined by Saudi Arabia, and backed by the Bank for International Settlements – mBridge – is experimenting with digital settlement and is already providing immediate costless settlement between its members. China is also believed to be working on the software and code to create a settlement scheme exclusive to BRICS members. There are still problems, for example in settling transactions where trade is seriously unbalanced. But there is now potentially a way forward which sidesteps Western-controlled settlement arrangements.

As of 2025 there is little sign of any change in the dominance of the dollar for reserve holdings or transactions (Figure 7.2). IMF figures suggest that

US dollar 44%

RMB 12%

Sterling 7%

Yen 8%

Euro 29%

Source: IMF Special Drawing Rights based on weights after 2022 review

US dollar 58%

Other 15%

RMB 3%

Sterling 5%

Yen 6%

Euro 13%

Source: Society of Worldwide International Financial Transactions

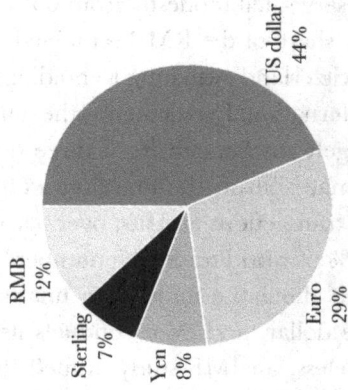

US dollar 58%

Other 9%

RMB 2%

Sterling 5%

Yen 6%

Euro 20%

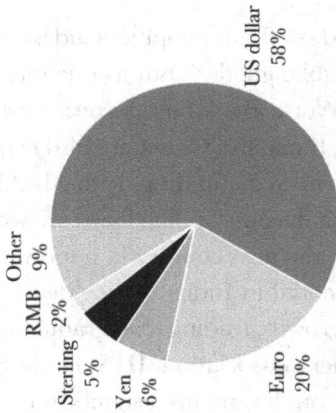

Source: IMF Currency Composition of Official Foreign Exchange Reserves 2024

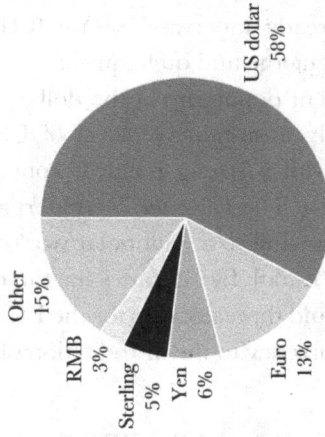

7.2 Currency shares

the dollar's role in foreign reserves fell modestly from 65% in 2016 to 58% at the end of 2023, while the share of the RMB remained at 2.3%. Almost all the decline was due to Switzerland switching to holdings of more euros. According to the Bank for International Settlements, the dollar still accounts for 88% of transactions, largely unchanged from three decades ago. It is however possible to see a small shift at the margins, with the RMB now accounting for almost 5% of transactions and just over 5% of trade finance. Since China accounts for 15% of world trade, the numbers are surely going to rise. But China is realistic about the underlying unattractiveness of its own currency relative to the dollar, and even conducts its Belt and Road Initiative in dollars. Nonetheless, an IMF study argued that 'the international monetary system transition from a bipolar system (US and Euro) to a tripolar – with the RMB – is already underway'.[26] If the BRICS Bridge takes off, a multipolar system could emerge and quite quickly.

Notwithstanding the persistent popularity of the dollar, sentiment could change rapidly. The seemingly unsustainable level of US public debt is one vulnerability, combined with a strong political appetite for tax cuts, along with more public spending. The *Financial Times* journalist Gillian Tett, among others, sees an inevitable shift to a multipolar world.[27] It may simply be a matter of time. After all, it took five decades for the dollar to replace sterling as the global currency and three decades for the EU to progress from talk of a common European currency to the introduction of the Euro.[28]

The World Bank, aid and the BRI challenge

There is a vigorous debate as to how far development aid is necessary for, and contributes to, international public goods.[29] But as one of the pillars of the postwar economic order, the World Bank merits consideration here as the leading multilateral aid donor. India and China are also central to its story. India is by far the main recipient of its funding, with $102 billion over the seventy years from 1945 to 2015. Its outstanding loans are worth $40 billion, twice the amount of Indonesia, the next country in importance. The World Bank has been massively influential in Indian policy development and has contributed to its accelerating growth, leading to a 'graduation' from concessional International Development Association (IDA) lending in 2014. India has now become an aid donor, but it remains a significant borrower.

China has made the same journey in a compressed time frame. It started borrowing in 1980 and made some use of the concessional IDA facility until it graduated in 1999. It now has the fifth largest outstanding stock of World Bank debt ($16 billion). But, as in India, the main influence has been on policy in support of the reforms that China first embraced in the 1980s. China became an aid donor in 2007 and is now arguably the biggest official lender, though it remains a recipient of World Bank loans and is a major beneficiary of procurement through World Bank loans (which has caused some annoyance in the USA).[30] China has its own development agency, China International Development Cooperation Agency (CIDCA), which provides zero-interest loans, though it has also supported the concessional lending of the World Bank as the sixth largest contributor to the replenishment of IDA. Furthermore, President Xi's Global Development Initiative sets out China's ambitions to lead the debate on development through its bilateral lending and concessional aid as well as its participation in the World Bank's multilateral aid. China's distinctive contribution is the scale and reach of the bilateral Belt and Road Initiative: the problems, as well as the development benefits, that have come from it. Significantly, India has launched its own version of the Belt and Road Initiative (BRI).

China and India have both had a positive experience with the World Bank and remain supportive (as with China's support for IDA replenishment). But there is a bone of contention: their share of voting rights does not come close to reflecting their importance as economies. The position is very like that in the IMF. China has a voting share of 5.6% in the World Bank and India 3.1%, as against 15.8% for the USA, 7.6% for Japan and 3.9% for each of France and the UK. There are similar issues for regional banks. The Asian Development Bank is especially important for China and India. Voting shares are respectively: United States 12.8%, China 5.4%, India 5.3% and Japan 12.8%. The disproportions in voting reflect the fact that richer countries have provided higher levels of funding (though that is changing). But voting shares unsurprisingly give a bigger say on policy, and that is increasingly resented.

To counter developed country dominance, China and India and other emerging economies have moved to establish parallel institutions where they have a bigger say. China was the moving force behind the Asian Infrastructure Investment Bank (AIIB), based in Beijing, which is backed by the UK but not the USA. The AIIB has so far earned a reputation for professionalism and for collaborative work with other multilateral lenders, and has retained a high credit rating. India is the main beneficiary of its loans. India and China were also among the five BRICS countries that established the BRICS Bank, now the New Development Bank, located in Shanghai.

The main controversy centres on the Chinese Belt and Road Initiative, which celebrated, in some style, its tenth anniversary in 2023. The BRI has invested around $1 trillion in 3,000 infrastructure projects in 152 countries – mainly energy and transport. Debate around the Belt and Road has become highly polarised between uncritical eulogies from official Chinese sources to damning, and often politically motivated, verdicts from Western politicians and commentators. In fact, there are good and bad, and many nuances amid the vast scale and complexity of the programme.[31] There is also a process of learning and evolution and some fundamental rethinking on how the BRI operates.[32]

From China's standpoint, there is a clear geopolitical and economic rationale.[33] By contributing to global development on a massive scale, especially with the withdrawal of the USA from humanitarian aid as well as development assistance, it can acquire influence and prestige in beneficiary countries. China can provide what Western donors and investors cannot or will not: large-scale, rapidly completed infrastructure projects. In turn, this creates a demand stimulus to the Chinese economy, helping to use up spare capacity in steel and other sectors, while simultaneously improving security of supply through better access to raw materials. The BRI opens up new markets for manufactured goods while reducing dependence on specific raw material and energy suppliers. The initiative was sufficiently important for President Xi to have it enshrined in the Chinese constitution in 2017.

One of the main criticisms of the BRI has been that the quality of the projects is poor, with many failures, costly environmental and other side effects and inadequate safeguards against corruption and other bad practice. Part of the problem is that procedures for project evaluation and procurement are somewhat opaque, and there is not the rigorous monitoring expected of Western lending agencies.[34] China is not, for example, a member of the OECD's Development Advisory Committee (DAC). The response from the Chinese side and from many recipients is that the procedures employed by Western agencies (and bodies like the World Bank) are slow and cumbersome, and result in prohibitive barriers to infrastructure projects and endless delays. Attempts to evaluate the portfolio have suggested that only a smallish percentage, around 10%, are 'troubled'.[35] Where BRI has acquired a bad reputation for producing 'white elephants', as reportedly in Pakistan, the cause may be that otherwise perfectly good infrastructure projects have not generated the expected private investment to use them, for example because of security concerns.[36]

The other major criticism of BRI projects is that they have left a legacy of unsustainable debt. The BRI was never presented as 'free money' but as large-scale funding by Chinese state banks which could not be raised from conservative lenders in international private capital markets or Western development agencies. Loans would be free of difficult conditionality or the need for US-style trade and investment agreements to safeguard property rights. However, global economic conditions have proved to be difficult for borrowers. Many developing countries – both low and middle income – have been unable to service their external debt in the toxic conditions created by the Covid pandemic, the Ukraine War and monetary tightening in the USA (BRI loans are dollar-denominated).

The Chinese have also offered BRI funding to countries with a poor record of economic management and debt service, notably Argentina, Venezuela, Zimbabwe, Sudan and Pakistan. One study showed that of sixty-eight countries in receipt of funding, twenty-three were in 'debt distress' even before the pandemic-related economic deterioration.[37] But accusations that the BRI is a 'debt trap', designed to ensnare unwary borrowers into surrendering valuable collateral, have been dismissed by independent Western analysts, despite some bad instances, as with Sri Lanka.[38] Well-organised recipients, such as Indonesia, have been able to negotiate relatively favourable terms with the Chinese.

Western criticism of the BRI has little traction in the absence of a better alternative. In 2021 the Biden administration launched Build Back a Better World, or B3W, backed by the G7. General principles have been enunciated and the initiative has been rebranded as the Partnership for Global Infrastructure, but there is little evidence of much delivery on the ground. The Chinese have also rethought the purpose and operation of the BRI. China's own domestic economic difficulties have focused attention on Chinese banks' balance sheets, which are having to absorb losses in the property market as well as bad loans under the BRI. Painful debt negotiations at intergovernmental level have soured relations with countries whose goodwill was one of the objectives of the BRI. The initiative has been scaled back radically, with a new emphasis on 'small and elegant' projects and 'fine brushstrokes'. Moreover, projects are being realigned to track changing geopolitics with, for example, more emphasis in Europe on Hungary, Serbia and Belarus, while Italy and Greece cool. In Asia, Vietnam is a new target of interest, while Malaysia and the Philippines have cooled on the BRI.

Western critics have portrayed the downsizing and redesign of the BRI as evidence of failure.[39] But this almost certainly misses the point. Less capital-intensive projects concentrating on digital technology are effective in embedding Chinese technology.[40] The cornerstone of the new approach is the Digital Silk Road, launched in 2017 and designed to promote Chinese companies in 5G, the Internet of Things, AI, big data, cloud computing, surveillance technology, underground and undersea cables and other technologies. The DSR provides an opportunity to embed Chinese standards in BRI countries, with long-term benefits for China in terms of trade and investment opportunities.

A key negative influence on international thinking about the BRI has been India, whose government has been a relentless critic, based on the BRI's prominent role among India's neighbours: Pakistan and Sri Lanka and, to a lesser degree, Nepal and Bangladesh. Arguably India was one of the earliest countries to launch a comprehensive critique and warning of the risks in BRI.[41] The Indian press has been a rich source of negative stories. The Modi government has however drawn positive as well as negative lessons from BRI, and has crafted its own version, which takes advantage of India's success in harnessing digital technology for social purposes. This is being used to roll out an ambitious programme, which was given pride of place during India's Chairmanship of the G20 in 2023. The Aadhar system of digitised payments has been adapted for overseas use through a modular open-source identity platform (MOSIP) and has been taken up by the Philippines and Sri Lanka as well as several countries in Africa.[42] Like China's BRI, it could prove a lucrative source of exports (in this case software engineering) and a source of influence and prestige. Indian initiatives are seemingly less divisive than those from the USA or China. India is also one of the few countries other than China to have developed a competence in big, rapidly completed infrastructure projects.

It is clear from the history of the BRI that China has been trying to create its own global system outside the framework of Western aid (the OECD DAC), the Bretton Woods institutions (IMF and World Bank) and debt negotiations (the Paris Club). But there are elements of convergence: agreement for emergency debt relief – the G20's DSSI – and the attempts by the Chinese-led development bank, the AIIB, to work cooperatively with the World Bank and Asian Development Bank. The inability or unwillingness of Western governments to compete with sizeable resources suggests that China will continue to have a major role in setting the development agenda, albeit with growing competition from India.

The slow death of the open world trading system

The cornerstone of the postwar global economy was a largely open and liberalising trading system. Global institutions such as GATT, later the WTO, together with regional agreements, as in the EU, oversaw the dismantling of trade barriers – a process that contributed much to postwar growth and provided an opportunity for emerging economies to grow and prosper. China has been a major beneficiary, as have, more recently, Bangladesh and Vietnam. India's recent moves toward liberalisation are predicated, in part at least, on the assumption that it will enjoy a benign trade policy environment. A crucial test of the strength of the multilateral, rules-based framework is whether it can accommodate both China and India. It was difficult enough to absorb Japan and South Korea, which had highly competitive exports and highly protectionist import regimes. Now there is a challenge on a much bigger scale.

India was a founding member of GATT and then of the WTO and a prominent participant in WTO negotiations, despite its small share in world trade. There have been several consistent features of India's trade negotiating stance. First, it has always insisted that developing economies – itself included – merit special treatment and should not be expected to open their markets in the same way as developed economies. For this reason it has opposed any attempt by developed countries to bring issues like environment and gender into trade negotiations. Second, India has been fiercely protective of sensitive sectors in its own economy, notably agriculture (in the interests of 'food security') and fisheries. And third, India has earned a reputation for a fiercely uncompromising defence of its position and as a voice for the Global South. India was widely blamed for the failure of the Doha round of negotiations in 2008 – its minister earned the soubriquet of 'Dr No' – and has become a champion of those opposed to market liberalisation.[43]

It has become increasingly apparent that there is a glaring contradiction between India's domestic policy – its more liberal and open approach to business and markets, and its welcome to foreign investors – and its negotiating stance in relation to trade, which has scarcely budged in decades. The same outward-facing protectionism has prevailed in relation to potential bilateral, regional and multilateral trade negotiations. India has, for example, declined to participate in the regional RCEP trade agreement, whose dominant member will therefore be China, though India has struck bilateral trade agreements with RCEP members. More recently, the Indian government has come under attack for being a supporter in principle of multilateralism in trade while doing everything it can to obstruct it.[44] With the USA also trying to stymie the WTO by refusing to appoint judges to the appellate dispute settlement panel, there has emerged an unlikely champion of the rules-based order and the WTO: China.

China applied to join GATT in 1986 and it took fifteen years of difficult negotiation to secure admission in 2001. It agreed to slash tariffs, quotas, distorting subsidies and non-tariff barriers. There was also an agreement that China would make its system of subsidising state enterprises more transparent and reform intellectual property rights. In return, China was given MFN status, which ensured that there would be no discrimination against it by member states. Specifically, it was protected from the risk of the US Congress cancelling MFN rights in the USA every year in its annual review. It was recognised from the outset that it would be difficult to integrate China's system of state capitalism into the more transparent and market-based regime demanded by the WTO. But, to China's great benefit, and arguably the world's, China was admitted.[45] In 2001 China was the world's sixth largest exporter; by 2014 it was Number 1.

In the USA and to a lesser degree in Europe, there was growing regret about giving China MFN status. There were complaints that China had dragged its feet in respect of treatment of foreign investors and technology transfer, and about delays in opening the China market for banking, telecommunications and payments systems, a reversal of tariff cuts on cars and an increase in subsidisation.[46] That said, China had been promised that it could achieve market economy status (MES) in 2015, which would give it protection from anti-dumping action (since it could then claim prices are set in the market, not by government). But developed country members of the WTO refused to accept that China merited that status, since it was not behaving like a market economy and seemed to be retreating from whatever liberalisation had been achieved. China is not the only country to have run into this obstacle; Vietnam has also been refused MES status for similar reasons.

One question has become increasingly pressing: how to pursue complaints against China within the multilateral rules of the WTO. The Obama administration successfully used the WTO in a dispute over tyres, resulting in a fine for China for infraction of the rules. And there are established remedies within the WTO for dealing with Chinese subsidised, 'unfair' competition using countervailing duties. The EU has understood the options and used the WTO to pursue a variety of complaints. There have also been other proposals to reform the WTO in such a way as to recognise the reality of 'state capitalist' economies like China – also India, Brazil and Vietnam – while binding them to global rules.[47]

However, with the arrival of President Trump there was no longer any interest in such 'globalist' solutions; the United States was going to act unilaterally and strongly. According to Trump, it had been subjected to 'the greatest theft in the history of the world' and 'raped' by China (and indeed by many other countries which had accumulated bilateral trade surpluses with the USA). His solution was, and is, higher tariffs. The story of the bilateral negotiations with China during the first Trump administration has been told at length elsewhere and does not need repetition here.[48] Suffice it to say that action was taken to raise tariffs on Chinese goods (the main costs of which fell on American consumers) using US legislation (the dormant Section 301 of the 1974 Trade Act). The Chinese retaliated, but a pause in hostilities was agreed in 2019. The Biden administration made no effort to row back from the Trump measures and added the security-based trade restrictions discussed in the previous chapter. With Trump now into a second term with fewer restraints, there has been recourse to historically high tariffs on the rest of the world. China has faced prohibitive tariffs. Whether the Trump administration will use tariffs as a negotiating lever with China or as part of a sustained trade war remains to be seen.

Two other US actions, not directly related to China, have taken the world even further from the rules-based trading order the USA once championed. First, Trump effectively sabotaged the workings of the WTO by refusing to appoint judges to the settlement panels that handle trade disputes. The Biden administration continued this policy. As a result, disputes involving China, or any other country, simply cannot be dealt with through multilateral channels. Second, there has been a distinct bipartisan shift in US politics away from free trade towards protectionism, making it extremely difficult to negotiate regional or even bilateral trade agreements with anyone. For example, the Obama administration launched the TPP (Trans-Pacific Partnership) with eleven countries in the Asia-Pacific – a form of 'open regionalism' which would bind the USA to the region, promote American technical standards and, by implication, exclude the Chinese. But the Trump administration killed it. Under Japanese leadership, it has reformed as the CPTPP (Comprehensive and Progressive Agreement for Trans-Pacific Partnership) without American participation but with the Chinese applying to join. The USA is making it clear to partners in Asia and Africa that partnership cannot involve improved access to the American market. In the meantime China is busily negotiating free trade agreements, covering around 40% of its exports at the end of 2023 and rising, and actively promoting trade liberalisation in groups like RCEP in Southeast Asia.[49]

Thus an extraordinary situation has been reached whereby China is now able to present itself as a champion of free trade, open markets and multilateral rules in the face of American protectionism and unilateralism – and to do this while posing as a leader of the Global South. The story is sufficiently implausible that it may not last. But while it does, the Chinese are able to act on the insight that prompted President Obama to launch the TPP: that countries that lead a trade liberalising agenda can set the common standards which govern future international business.

Standard setting as the invisible battleground

The reality of globalised trade and investment is less likely to be found in high-profile international conferences and political speeches than in mundane meetings of engineers and corporate managers in Geneva hotels, as they try to thrash out a consensus on whether a new technical standard for a wire or widget can be certified for international use.

The process of standard setting has long been dominated by standards bodies and businesses in the developed world. And there has been a recognition that the most important step to dismantling barriers to trade and cross-border fixed investment lies in reconciling different, incompatible national standards: standards for engineering and design, food quality and safety, aviation and shipping specifications. Something as simple as three- versus two-pin electric plugs or as complex as internet architecture. The most advanced process of economic integration – the EU single market – has been built around patient and prolonged negotiation to reconcile different national standards.

Around the turn of the century, according to analyst Alex He, the Chinese started to wake up to the fact that the technical aspects of their participation in world trade were being decided in bodies in which they had no say. If China was to become a high-tech, innovative economy, Chinese companies would have to be part of shaping global standards, and preferably set them.[50] It became a mantra in Chinese business that 'first tier companies make standards; second tier companies make technology; and third tier companies make products'. A national plan, formulated in 2015, set out Chinese ambitions to be a 'standards power'. South Korea has also been down this road, and more recently India has started to recognise the importance of the issue.[51] Standards have become geopolitical.

The key bodies involved in technology standard setting are ISO (an NGO bringing together national standards bodies), the IEC (an NGO dealing with 'electro-mechanical' industries which has expanded to all things digital) and the ITU (a United Nations agency responsible for telecommunications). The Chinese approach to this world was to develop Chinese standards, initially using the large-scale platform provided by the Chinese home market, augmented by overseas linkages through the BRI and other bilateral agreements. The next step was to put them forward for international acceptance. The aim was to have stronger representation in the apex standards bodies – Chinese leadership of both the IEC and ITU followed – and then on technical committees, including chairing those committees.

Alex He's evaluation of the Chinese contribution notes two achievements to date. First, Chinese participation has been through companies, including state-owned companies, and not through government directly. These companies have often pursued their own commercial objectives, such as market growth and profit, rather than China's geopolitical objectives, sometimes collaborating with Western partners. But it is clear that the Chinese activities are coordinated and supported by government. Second, there are some areas where Chinese standards have been adopted on their merits: 5G and the 3rd Generation Partnership Project (3GPP) thanks to Huawei, UHV (ultra-high voltage transmission) and the Internet of Things. But in general Chinese companies are still far from being dominant in most areas in which there is an active Chinese presence – including AI, big data, data centres, cloud computing. What Chinese companies have learned is 'how to play the game' in a crucial area of the global economic system otherwise dominated by European and American companies.[52] So far at least, India and other emerging economies have yet to show the same degree of involvement in standard setting, though critics have pointed out that if India is to become a serious player in data-based services, it will have to move out of a protectionist mindset and help set global standards.[53]

Is the rules-based international order breaking down?

There is a popular narrative in the Western world that the postwar rules-based system that provided stability and prosperity is now breaking down, largely because China and its allies are trying to undermine or overthrow it. The re-election of President Trump brings into a leadership role someone who is happy to jettison the old system. The pessimistic view of the Thucydides Trap is that we are headed towards inevitable conflict between declining and rising superpowers, within which the crumbling international order will be collateral damage. In this world, security dominates economics and cooperation gives way to competition, containment and conflict.

The view that emerges from this chapter is much more complex and nuanced. Some bits of the existing system work well; others do not. Alignments and alliances are multidimensional, reflecting the influence of other key players, such as India and the EU. Global goods continue to be provided, and in relation to the existential challenge of climate change

214

the three biggest emitters of GHGs (China, the USA and India) have continued to work together, however uneasily, within a global framework. The global trading system based on the WTO is in serious trouble, largely because of the actions of the United States in disengaging from it (with unhelpful contributions from India), but world trade continues to expand, and the practical day-to-day work around technical standards continues uninterrupted. There has even been agreement in principle on a common approach to tax, though progress has ceased and is disowned by President Trump.[54] The Bretton Woods financial institutions are being marginalised, in part because China is not cooperating in key areas like debt rescheduling, but China supports the work of the World Bank in other ways. American financial sanctions are prompting a move in the Global South to look for alternatives to the dollar. But, so far, the public good of a global currency remains intact, and big payments imbalances continue to adjust.

An example of potential cooperation is the tentative progress on creating binding international law to prevent the abuse of AI and to manage AI risks. There is already a lot of 'soft law', including a UN General Assembly resolution proposed by the USA and co-sponsored by China. And there are some pioneering 'hard' laws, such as the EU AI Act, which are too strong for the USA and have yet to be reconciled with China's particular concerns, or India. The fact that China and the USA have maintained a dialogue on the subject, as on climate, despite other areas of hostility, suggests a continuing recognition that there is an important international public good involved that requires a common approach.

An important – perhaps the most important – test of the rules-based order is whether it can preserve the peace: common security. At the time of writing, there are two wars taking place in Ukraine and Gaza, with one involving the threat of nuclear weapons. There are civil wars in Sudan and Burma and several major 'frozen' conflicts: a combination of factors contributing to a level of danger unsurpassed since the end of the Cold War. Arguably the most dangerous development is the escalation of armouries of nuclear weapons after years of disarmament since the Cold War. The USA and Russia appear to have lost the appetite for further disarmament. Partly in response, China is known to be expanding its arsenal from around 500 warheads to as many as 1,000 by 2030.[55] That in turn is prompting increases in India's arsenal (now 170) and Pakistan's (now 170). These numbers are not remotely on the scale of the USA (1,670 deployed) or Russia (1,710), but momentum is in the direction of expansion.

Apart from checking nuclear proliferation, there is a variety of global commons related to common security: access to space, dismantling criminal networks, countering violent extremists, peacekeeping operations, protecting air and maritime routes.[56] There have been some areas of limited cooperation. The USA and China have agreed to cooperate to curb fentanyl, which is manufactured in China, smuggled into the USA through Mexico and then used as the base for opioids, which are feeding a lethal drug epidemic. But Chinese commitment to the agreement has been questioned by President Trump, leading to threats of trade sanctions. There is a degree of cooperation over the space exploration being conducted by China, the USA, India and Russia by extending offers of scientific collaboration to other countries. There has been common action to curb piracy on sea lanes. The Indian Navy has been active in a crossnational effort to deal with piracy in the Western Indian Ocean. Both China and India have been zealous supporters of UN peacekeeping, with India contributing 195,000 troops over forty-eight missions and China 50,000 over twenty-five missions, while the developed world contributes money. Cooperation isn't dead, but badly wounded.

But there have been serious obstacles to deeper engagement across a wide range of security-related issues where there is potential for common action. The Convention on the Law of the Sea was one of the most significant extensions of international law to protect global commons, but the USA did not ratify it, and as a result it has diminished authority in maritime territorial issues.[57] China has agreed to the Convention but declined to honour rulings against itself, most egregiously in the South China Sea, when an international tribunal ruled in favour of the Philippines but China pointedly refused to accept the outcome. By contrast, and much to its credit, India accepted a ruling against it in favour of Bangladesh.

Elsewhere the story is more bleak. To take another pillar of the international order – basic legal checks on the use of violence – the International Criminal Court exists to prosecute individuals who perpetrate genocide, crimes against humanity and war crimes. But the USA, China, India, Russia, Israel and other countries have declined to join the court. More generally, the ability of the United Nations to intervene to take common

216

action is paralysed by the power of veto. In this century, China has used its veto powers seventeen times and the USA eighteen (Russia thirty-six). India does not have that power, though countries of less economic and political significance, such as the UK and France, do. Overall, the rules-based order is fractured – perhaps broken beyond repair – and can no longer rely on the USA to defend and promote it. Instead, new alignments are emerging.

8

Global public good no. 3: security; alliances and alignments

If the global international order is crumbling, or at least being reshaped, the question is: what is going to replace it? The USA and its allies – a group that may be called the Global West – still dominates economically and politically, but it is being challenged by China and those countries that see themselves as part of the Global South. And Trump's second term has called into question the whole idea of a cohesive West, as opposed to America First and various transactional alliances. The Asia-Pacific is becoming the world centre of economic gravity, with India as well as China transforming into major players – but Asia is being integrated, and divided, by an alphabet soup of new regional groupings (Figure 8.1). The old structures – institutions and alignments – no longer fit. There is, instead, a variety of overlapping groups, reflecting different combinations of countries and interests.

From NAM to BRICS+: non-alignment to multi-alignment

There is a popular view in the USA and much of the Western world that we are now in a new cold war. An axis of authoritarian and aggressive powers – China, Iran, Russia and their allies – pose a danger to democracy everywhere, but are directly threatening free societies in Ukraine, Israel and Taiwan. Trump's MAGA movement has somewhat diluted the cohesion and ideological basis of the West, however. Moreover, the polarised view is not shared in much of the Global South – and, of particular importance, in India. India is crucial to the argument, as it is the world's largest democracy by far, as well as an economic power of substance. In India there is a more complex view which draws on the experience of colonialism and a perceived

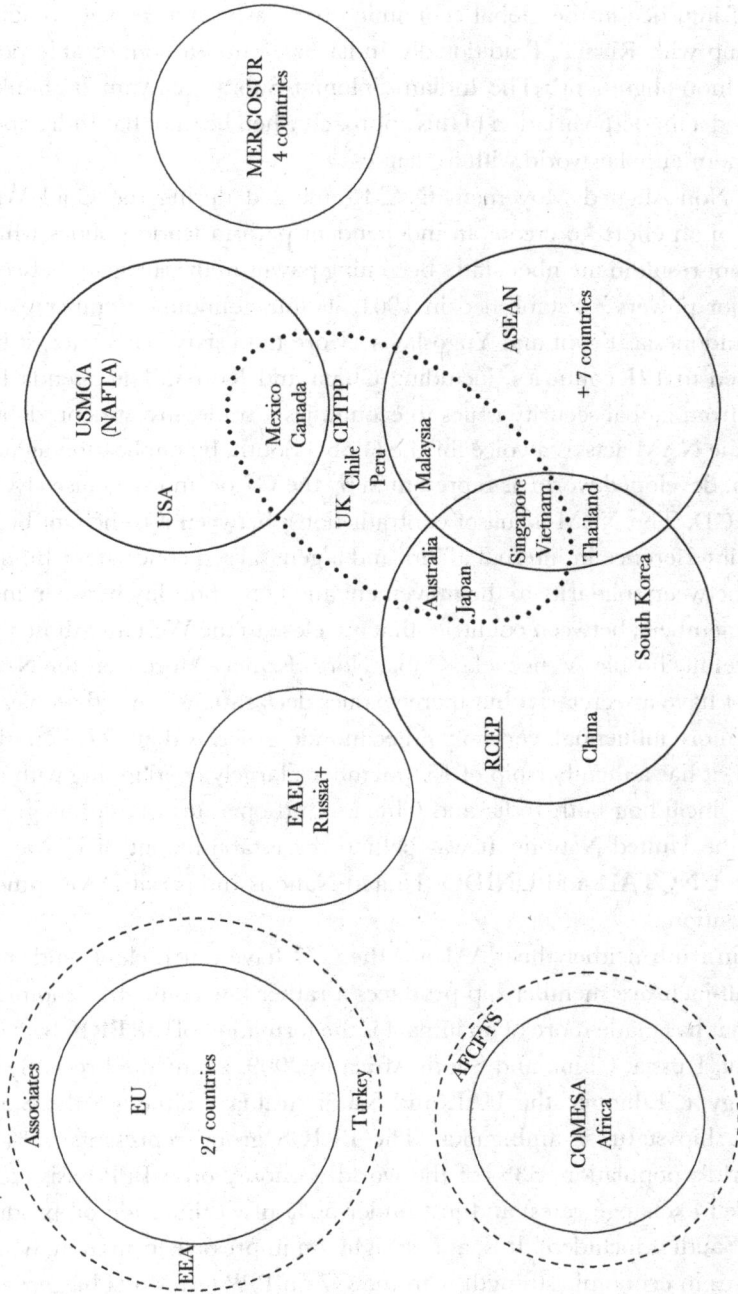

8.1 Regional blocs

MERCOSUR
4 countries

USMCA
(NAFTA)

USA

Mexico
Canada

UK Chile CPTPP
Peru

Malaysia

ASEAN
+ 7 countries

Singapore
Vietnam
Thailand

Australia
Japan

South Korea

RCEP

China

EAEU
Russia+

Associates

EU

27 countries

Turkey

EEA

AfCFTS

COMESA
Africa

sense of injustice in the global economic order, as well as a long-standing friendship with Russia. Traditionally India has found a comfortable position in 'non-alignment'. The Indian diplomat Subrahmanyam Jaishankar expressed a modern variation of this approach when he said that India operates in a 'multipolar world with frenemies'.[1]

The Non-Aligned Movement (NAM) emerged during the Cold War, as part of an effort 'to create an independent path in world politics which would not result in member states becoming pawns in the struggles between the major powers'.[2] Established in 1961, its four founding members were India, Indonesia, Egypt and Yugoslavia. More than sixty years later, it has expanded to 121 countries, including China and Russia. The agenda has shifted from global security issues to economics – trade, investment, debt – where the NAM acts as a voice for the Global South, by implication against the rich, developed world as represented by the G7 or, more inclusively, by the OECD. The NAM is full of contradictions: between a trenchant belief in non-interference in internal affairs and a generalised concern for human rights; between solidarity to the movement and fierce hostility between individual members; between countries that are close to the West and those that are viscerally hostile (Venezuela, Cuba, North Korea). Moreover, the NAM does not have a secretariat but merely issues declarations every three years. A little more influential, certainly on economic issues, is the G77. Founded in 1964, it has a membership of 134 members, largely overlapping with the NAM – including both India and China – and operates as a lobby group within the United Nations. It was behind the establishment of UN agencies like UNCTAD and UNIDO (United Nations Industrial Development Organization).

But in truth neither the NAM nor the G77 have much clout, and their large, all-inclusive membership produces a rather low common denominator. What has made more of an impact is the formation of the BRICS group of Brazil, Russia, China and South Africa in 2009, augmented recently by Iran, Egypt, Ethiopia, the UAE and Saudi Arabia – although the Saudi membership status is ambiguous. The BRICS group represents 45% of the world's population, 33% of the world economy on a PPP basis (28% at market exchange rates) and just under 50% of world crude oil production (if Saudi is included). It is, at first sight, an impressive formation, which compares in economic strength with the G7 (in PPP terms it is bigger) and has ambitious goals: 'to restructure global political, economic and financial architecture'.[3]

But the August 2023 BRICS Summit, which saw the expansion to incorporate new members, also exposed an underlying weakness. Saudi Arabia backed off from membership and is still considering the issue. Argentina, under a new president – Javier Milei – decided to pull out. Indonesia, which should be a member if size and importance are the key criteria, declined to apply, worrying that its membership would be seen as anti-West and an endorsement of Chinese leadership.[4] There were also barely concealed differences between China and India. China was pushing for more members and, with Russia and Iran, keen to use the BRICS for promoting an anti-Western agenda, while India wanted a more focused approach, geared to the reform of international economic institutions. India also attached more value to strengthening the G20 forum, which it chaired in 2023.[5] For its part, China has no wish to see its influence diluted by India becoming a permanent member of the UN Security Council with a veto. Lord Jim O'Neill, who originally coined the acronym BRIC, has expressed extreme scepticism as to whether the group is now of more than symbolic importance, especially given its haphazard and politically inspired membership criteria, which exclude such obvious major emerging market members as Indonesia, Mexico and Nigeria.[6]

Although there is justified scepticism, this must be tempered by acknowledgement of what the BRICS have done so far, and their potential. One concrete result has been the establishment of the New Development Bank, with an initial capitalisation of $100 billion, 70% of which is committed to – mainly – infrastructure projects. Headquartered in Shanghai, it is designed to complement the other China-based and inspired institution, the AIIB, which is focused more on Asian lending and has some developed country shareholders, such as the UK and Australia. The two banks highlight the unrepresentative nature of the traditional, Western-dominated multilateral banks like the World Bank, where the BRICS' combined shareholding is only 15%. Sceptics point to heavy Chinese involvement and the BRICS-style emphasis on big infrastructure projects, but both banks have so far been seen as professionally run.

The BRICS also have, at first sight, a high level of trade interdependence. One estimate is that intra-BRICS trade is 40% of their total trade, up from 20% a decade ago.[7] UNCTAD concludes that 'the growth rate of intra-BRICS trade is above the global average and that there has been a rapid growth of intra-BRICS investment, from 1.3% of their collective stock of inward FDI in 2010 to 4.7% in 2020'.[8] However, this has little to do with the formal structures of BRICS but largely reflects the trade and investment priorities of Chinese companies, the changing pattern of commodity trade and the diversion of trade after sanctions on Russia.

The BRICS group has one serious shared project, with major long-term implications: to advance the objective of de-dollarisation. The most ambitious version of monetary cooperation is to create a common currency.[9] The most fanciful version of this idea is to replace the existing BRICS national currencies and introduce a common monetary policy along the lines of the Eurozone. Sceptical Western commentators have enjoyed pointing out that the BRICS group does not remotely approximate to an optimum currency area (OCA), which requires free movement of capital, labour and goods and assumes a much higher level of economic integration. In an OCA, the costs of adjustment through wages and prices and movement of labour and capital would be less than the costs of adjustment through exchange rates. But the BRICS economies are far removed from that possibility.[10] Lord O'Neill called the idea 'ridiculous'.[11]

However, what may be emerging is more modest and practical: to gradually replace the use of the dollar as a store of value (to hold as reserves) and for transactions. One proposal for a BRICS currency is that it could be held as a reserve currency in the same way as the IMF-created SDRs (Special Drawing Rights) currently are. It would provide security with 100% backing from gold (or some other commodity-based asset). And BRICS countries would agree to use it as backing for their own settlements instead of dollar reserves. At present it is not obvious why it would be attractive other than for political reasons – why not just use gold? But if, in future, the dollar loses its appeal because of political upheaval, debt mismanagement and inflation in the USA, there may be an appetite for a new currency, if it can be made secure as a store of value.

A more immediate need is to find ways of carrying out transactions without using the dollar, to avoid the risk of being caught in US sanctions: an issue discussed at length in the previous chapter. The motivation is strong for Russia, which has seen half of its foreign reserves frozen and suffered exclusion from the European SWIFT settlement system. China is trying to sanction-proof its exposure to world trade and investment should its relations with the USA deteriorate further. And other members, such as India and the Gulf states, worry about being caught in 'secondary' sanctions or otherwise antagonising the USA. BRICS countries are already encouraging the use of national currencies to make transactions. The BRICS group is promoting this process through the creation of a Contingent Reserve Arrangement to help countries with severe balance of payments problems. It has created a payments app (BRICSpay), and it is advocating the use of national currencies, as with RMB lending by the New Development Bank.

As noted earlier, however, the barriers to extensive use of non-dollar transactions are formidable, and there is an efficiency cost involved.[12] Recent data suggest that for 97% of rupee trade dollars are involved on one side of the transaction, 94% for the Brazilian real and even 88% for the Chinese RMB. There is no liquid market for assets originating in non-dollar pairs of countries. Most commodity trade is priced in dollars. And none of the BRICS countries have the infrastructure for smooth and cheap settlement outside dollars (the so-called PvP – Payment versus Payment – commercial contracts). But it would be foolish to ignore the many small ways in which BRICS national currencies are gaining a foothold in cross-border BRICS settlements. Through swap lines with other central banks, the new CIPS payments mechanism and RMB clearing banks, use of the RMB is spreading for SWIFT transactions, growing from 1.9% in 2016 to 4.7% in mid-2024. India is also promoting use of the rupee. As long as national currencies remain non-convertible the process is halting. But de-dollarisation is an objective that unites the otherwise diverse and divided BRICS group, albeit that enthusiasm ranges from the urgent (Russia and China) to the lukewarm (India). And at the 2024 annual BRICS meeting in Russia there was endorsement of a 'bridge' system of digital settlements through central banks developed by the Bank for International Settlements.

Beyond the BRICS, India's approach to non-alignment involves membership of a wide variety of organisations. Some are regional, such as the SAARC group for South Asia. SAARC is an attempt to soften, through practical cooperation, the sharp divisions which are the legacy of Partition, notably with Pakistan. It also gives a status to the small countries of the subcontinent, which otherwise fear domination by India. That said, trade connectivity is derisory – 5% of the region's trade – compared to trade within the Asia-Pacific region including China (around 50%) and within Africa (22%). It is far below its potential.[13] That failure reflects India's historic and continuing trade protectionism. India does however participate actively in a variety of regional groupings, including the Indian Ocean Rim Association for Regional Cooperation (IOR-ARC) and, crucially, a defence cooperation agreement, the Quad, bringing together India, Japan, Australia and the USA – explicitly designed to deter China.

Despite the adversarial military relationship with China, there is overlapping membership of the Shanghai Cooperation Organisation (SCO), as well as the BRICS. SCO provides a forum for discussing security issues. China and India share a deep hostility to separatist movements, especially those involving terrorism. The SCO comprises mainly authoritarian states, but in the complex multipolar world that is evolving it is possible for India to be a member of the SCO but also of the Warsaw-based Community of Democracies. India values membership of South–South groupings like the BRICS and the NAM, but also of North–South groups like the G20 and even the Commonwealth. It can work with China in the BRICS, the SCO, the Chinese-led AIIB and NDB, but simultaneously participate in groups designed to counter China such as the Quad. There is what Europeans call 'variable geometry' – illustrated in Figure 8.2. There are also informal subsets of bigger structures like IBSA (the South–South alliance of India, Brazil and South Africa) or BASIC (the partnership of Brazil, South Africa, India and China in climate change talks). These cross-cutting groups, in which India is the common denominator, demonstrate flexibility. There has, however, been pressure on India from the West to take sides, and it is not clear that the 'multipolar world' sought by India and other non-aligned or 'multi-aligned' nations can survive growing polarisation and the pressures of economic and actual war.

War and taking sides

Russia's attack on Ukraine made it more difficult to be 'non-aligned' or to sustain the multipolar, rather than bipolar, view of the world. In the West there was a clear and consistent narrative that Russia should be condemned

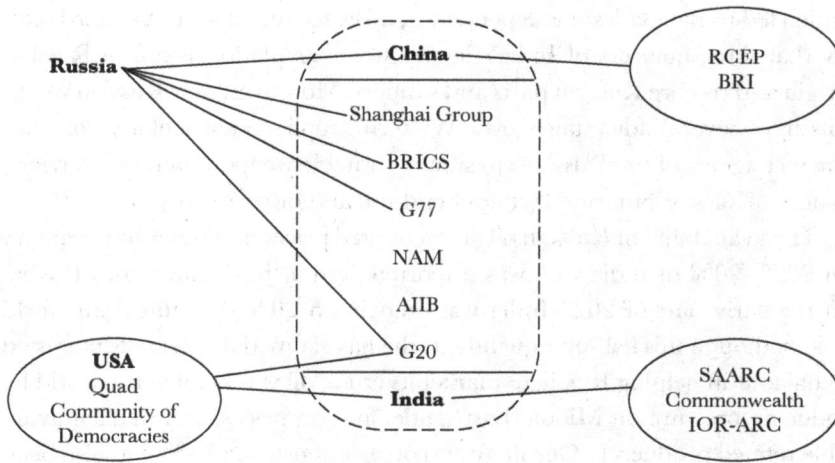

8.2 Multi-alignments

for an unjustified act of aggression against a sovereign country, violating its
territorial integrity and threatening its democratic government. Yet democratic India, as well as China, has rejected this narrative. Both countries
have refused to condemn Russia in various forums in the United Nations.
Both have continued to trade with Russia. Both have greatly increased
purchases of Russian oil, helping to pay for the Russian war machine. Both
have continued to participate in groups like the BRICS and SCO, in which
President Putin is a prominent member.

The motivation of each is, however, very different. In the case of India,
the 'strategic ambiguity' is driven by a careful balance of interests, prominent among them being an effort to prevent a long-standing friend and ally –
Russia – becoming too dependent on a current rival and emerging enemy,
China.[14] For India, the geopolitics of the subcontinent are the dominant
concerns, with the threat of two hostile nuclear-armed states on its borders.
India has been concerned about Russian attempts to befriend Pakistan as
well as Russia's growing dependence on China. India's relations with China
are characterised by deep distrust and that is unlikely to change. This has
to be balanced against the fact that India has an established friendship with
Russia from both Soviet and post-Soviet times. However, sentiment, including appreciation of Russian backing in key conflicts, notably the 1971 war

225

which led to Bangladeshi independence, takes second place to the hard reality that three-quarters of India's legacy weapons platforms are of Russian origin and require Russian parts and support. Moreover, new Russian weapons have several advantages over Western suppliers: particularly cost and the willingness of the Russians to supply strategic weapons (aircraft carriers, cruise missiles, submarines) without end-use and other restrictions.

The availability of Russian oil at discounted prices is another inducement. In 2023, 90% of India's oil was imported, and a third came from Russia. In the early part of 2023 India was enjoying a 20% discount from world prices, though this fell subsequently. India has claimed that its self-interested behaviour in helping Russia to market its crude oil was helping the world by reducing pressure on Middle East crude, and on prices, and making available refined products to Germany and other importers.[15] India has also been able to take advantage of Russia's bargaining weakness to make payments in rupees, with large amounts of unusable Indian currency piling up in the Russian Central Bank. Beyond the short-term economic gains to India from its stance in the war, there is a deeper motivation for keeping a distance from the Western position. There are mixed feelings about the growing commercial, political and military influence of the USA in India – that this could lead to entrapment in a relationship which reduces India's options, including the freedom to operate in a multipolar world. The souring of relations with the USA (as well as Canada) over India's extraterritorial pursuit of Sikh separatists has confirmed the wisdom of India not putting all its eggs in the American basket.[16]

All of that said, there are some clear disadvantages from maintaining neutrality in the Ukraine War. The first is that India's position has virtually no impact on the China–Russia 'no limits' partnership. That partnership has its own strategic rationale, and there is nothing India can do to prevent Russia becoming economically and politically more dependent on China. By implication, Russia would be of little help in any future military clash that India might have with China. The underlying reality, it could be argued, is that India needs the USA and the USA needs India from a wider Asia-Pacific perspective, and that wise American heads should not be influenced by India's continued cultivation of Russia.[17] Furthermore, the benefits of military links to Russia are being eroded by Putin's war. There is some scepticism that Russia will be able to maintain the quantity and quality of its arms exports to

India after the depletion of its capacity. And there is friction with Russia over how India pays for its arms – and oil – since India wants to pay in rupees.

While these transactional concerns are important, what really matters for India is to avoid being dragged into what it regards as a phoney ideological conflict based on 'democracy versus autocracy'. Any discomfort at having an entirely values-free, interest-driven foreign policy based on 'realpolitik' has been eased by the Gaza conflict, which has dislodged the West from the moral high ground it has occupied over the Ukraine War. The Trump administration attaches little importance to values, in any event. India appears to have broadly achieved its objective of keeping its non-aligned status intact while also protecting its long-term defence interests through membership of the Quad, as well as its strengthening economic links to Western (and Israeli) markets and investors. Lest these interests be compromised, Prime Minister Modi paid a visit to Ukraine in August 2024 to demonstrate that India was not too close to Russia.

Like India, China has been faced with a difficult balancing of interests. It has chosen to build on a partnership with Russia to strengthen its position vis-à-vis the USA and its allies, while avoiding economically damaging sanctions from the West – what has been called a 'strategic straddle'.[18] Most analysts concur that the Chinese leadership had little or no foreknowledge of the Russian invasion of Ukraine, was wrong-footed by it and is genuinely concerned about the dilemmas it created. China has claimed neutrality but has in practice adopted and promoted the Russian narrative. It emphasised the provocation of NATO enlargement, seeing parallels with the strengthening of defence alliances against itself in the Asia-Pacific. And it built on the pre-war statement of friendship which 'has no limits. There are no forbidden areas of cooperation.' The relationship falls short of a military alliance but is nonetheless close and appears to have become closer during the war. The 'friendship' between Xi and Putin is measured by the fact that in the period 2013–24 the two had forty-three meetings, albeit often in the context of multilateral settings like the BRICS and SCO, where Chinese and Russian membership overlapped. By contrast, Xi had nineteen meetings with Modi, seventeen with US presidents, fifteen with the German Chancellor and twelve with the French President.

China has recently played down the language about 'friendship without limits', and a senior official called the phrase 'nothing but rhetoric'.[19]

The 'friendship' related to the Ukraine War has however gone beyond rhetoric to material help for Russia, notably through importing large amounts of oil (like India). Russia has replaced Saudi Arabia as China's biggest crude supplier. China also imports Russian gas, which can no longer be sold in Europe. Crucially, China has supplied Russia with large quantities of so-called 'dual-use' goods, which are regarded as crucial to sustaining the Russian war machine: microelectronics and chip-making equipment (albeit of dated technology), ball bearings, machine tools. China has been at pains, however, not to cross American red lines, which involve the supply of military equipment.

There are several possible reasons behind China's tilt towards Russia – what has been called its 'hybrid support'. China has every reason to be fearful of Russia losing the war and of Putin being overthrown. A more pro-Western replacement would likely be less friendly to China. The war in Ukraine is also a welcome distraction from a confrontation with the USA in East Asia over Taiwan and the South China Sea, and the build-up of US military presence and alliances there. There are many reports of joint exercises between Russian and Chinese forces, including joint air patrols near Alaska, which reinforce the fact that China's tacit support for Russia potentially cements any reciprocal support from Russia should conflict break out in the Asia-Pacific.[20] If it was ever likely that China would attempt a full-frontal invasion of Taiwan, Russia's experience in Ukraine has surely discouraged it. But the risk remains that 'grey zone' intimidation and encroachment could result in escalation, when Russian support may prove important. While the Russian 'friendship' is a useful insurance policy in the case of conflict with the USA, the greater likelihood is that China will continue to play a long game on Taiwan, hoping to achieve its goals without recourse to war.[21]

At a minimum, the 'friendship' with Russia ensures that China has secure access to energy beyond the reach of any potential sanctions. There are also tangible economic benefits in the form of booming exports to Russia, which have doubled since the war began. They receive discounted prices on energy supplies – in 2023, the volume of oil imports from Russia rose by 26% but the value only by 4%.[22] Russia now has a high level of dependence on China economically, which will be difficult to reverse. It is believed that one of the reasons why China has not committed to supporting the Power of Siberia 2 gas pipeline, which is crucial to Russia's future export earnings in the Far East, is that a more dependent Russia can be forced to accept tougher terms.

Also among the real economic benefits is the opening of Arctic shipping to Chinese vessels and access to Russian natural resources in Siberia; indeed, an under-reported aspect of the competition between China and the USA is a race to develop the latest technology in ice-cutting vessels.[23] But the economic advantages should not be exaggerated. War is bad for business, overall.[24] It has damaged China's extensive economic ties with Ukraine, including food imports from the Black Sea. And Chinese banks are now heavily exposed to Russian debt. Russia is China's biggest debtor, and it is not a good one.[25]

There are real limits to the 'friendship', which reflect an awareness of the risks China is running by throwing its weight behind Russia. China has been careful not to arm Russia, which would immediately trigger US sanctions, and Chinese banks have avoided dealing with sanctioned Russian entities. Although Chinese analysts have argued that Russia cannot be defeated by Western sanctions, the Chinese are anxious not to see these sanctions extended, since China remains vulnerable in the absence of an alternative to the dollar-based monetary and settlement system.[26] There are also political reasons for caution. China, after all, is a voluble defender of 'territorial integrity', which Russia has blatantly breached in Ukraine. So China has not supported the invasion (though it has sought to explain and excuse it) and does not recognise Russian occupation in Crimea or the Donbass. Xi appears to have discouraged Putin from the use of tactical nuclear weapons and has insisted on not taking risks with the safety of nuclear power stations.

China has also sought to keep alive the idea of acting as a peace negotiator by putting forward a succession of plans, and participating in Ukrainian reconstruction. Nonetheless, the Chinese are painfully aware that the war has seriously undermined their political and commercial position in Western Europe, which has not been restored by a Xi visit to France and a German Chancellor's visit to Beijing. The philosophy of 'engagement' with China which was widely held in Europe before the Ukraine War has been undermined by Chinese support for the Putin regime, which is seen as a direct threat to European security. China's export dependence on Western markets is a powerful reason why it continues to hedge around the risks created by the war and to keep at least some distance from Russia.

The damage to China's reputation in the democratic, Western world is evidenced by surveys of public opinion. A Cambridge University study of opinion in seventy-five countries since the Russian invasion of Ukraine shows that in 'liberal democracies' 75% had a negative view of China and 87% a negative view of Russia. By contrast, in the rest of the world, 70% had a positive view of China and 66% a positive view of Russia.[27] Crucially, however, the shared reluctance of both China and India to condemn Russia reflected a wider view in the Global South that was much more sympathetic to the Russian position than the West expected, with a popular belief that the USA and Western Europe were being hypocritical in denouncing Russia while indulging in their own military interventions in the rest of the world. And Western sanctions, rather than Russian aggression, were blamed for the increase in food and energy bills at the start of the war. Moreover, vast sums have been committed to Ukraine, which were not made available to low-income countries when in dire need, as in the Covid pandemic. The idea that the world would split to separate Russia and China from the rest hasn't been borne out. Opinions are more complex.

This interpretation of shifts in public opinion in different countries is broadly confirmed by the Pew Trust, which has carried out detailed tracking over time, including a study of twenty-four countries published in November 2023.[28] This showed that, in the countries of the Western world, together with Japan, South Korea and India, there was a clear majority looking favourably at the USA but unfavourably at China, while in other countries in the sample (Nigeria, Kenya, South Africa, Mexico, Brazil, Indonesia) a majority had a favourable view of both the USA and China. Pew surveys have shown how attitudes to China in the West and in East Asia have nosedived over the last decade, with the most extreme negative views in Japan and South Korea. In the USA perceptions of China have gone from a positive rating a decade ago to 82% unfavourable. In general, the surveys show that China enjoys respect for its technological prowess and its economic strength (until very recently) but – relative to the USA – it is not much liked. But on almost all metrics covered by the surveys, it is judged more favourably in the Global South.

If China and India are to be judged by likeability they are in very different places. A Pew survey suggested that India has a broadly favourable rating internationally: 46% favourable and 34% unfavourable across twenty-three countries.[29] India's approval is as high in the West as among other middle- or low-income countries. The belief that India is a growing influence in the world is clearly recognised in Canada, South Korea, the UK, Japan and the USA (in that order), though the belief is strongest by far in India itself. India is also one of the few countries where Russia is seen favourably (by 57% as against 14% in twenty-two other countries). By contrast, India is the only middle- to low-income country to have a very negative view of China. The sense that India and China are, at best, rivals and competitors rather than allies is an issue I explore in detail below, but it is becoming apparent too in the competition for influence in the Global South.

Different kinds of non-alignment

The big picture that emerges from the polarisation created by the Ukraine War is that both China and India are driven by interests rather than values. Both claim neutrality but otherwise their positioning is very different. China sees its 'non-aligned' allies in the Global South as allies in the bigger geopolitical contest with the USA. The advent of the Trump administration has made life more difficult for China in the short term, because of the costs of trade warfare and pressure on weaker countries to take sides with the USA. But in the longer term the CCP hopes to benefit from building ties to countries alienated or damaged by Trump's behaviour. China is also heavily motivated by achieving a position as the world's leading high-tech manufacturing country. India, by contrast, is trying hard to stay genuinely non-aligned between the West and Ukraine on one hand and Russia on the other: part of the Global South, as in the BRICS, but also fully engaged with bodies that include the West, like the G20, and maintaining a deepening economic and military relationship with the USA. This difference of approach is being noticed more widely.

The Middle East is testing these different strategies under near-war conditions, with the conflict in Gaza. China's apparent success in its objectives was pithily summarised by the Indian Foreign Minister: 'the USA has been fighting and losing in the Middle East; China has not been fighting and winning'.[30] The fact that almost all the countries in the region have non-democratic authoritarian governments – except for Israel and, to a degree, Turkey – plays to China's advantage; unlike the USA and its European allies, it does not lecture on human rights or promote destabilising democratic movements like the Arab spring. The Gulf states find the Chinese competitive presence useful in helping them to squeeze economic and political concessions from

231

their traditional security guarantor and economic partner, the USA. Saudi Arabi and the UAE, especially, are eager to be seen as influential 'middle powers' with independent views and interests.

China concentrates on trade and business dealings. In 2023, for example, its trade with Saudi Arabia was over $100 billion, just shy of the combined total of its trade with the US, the UK and the EU. China has been able to deliver big infrastructure and energy projects, including a joint refinery with Saudi Arabia, and has helped to make real Crown Prince Mohammed's rather unreal Neom project in the desert. Chinese firms have been more willing than those from the USA and European countries to offer technology transfer (for example agreeing to establish a big EV production plant). Cooperation has expanded to supplying Saudi Arabia with missiles (and allegedly nuclear technology) unavailable from the USA. Playing the China card has also enabled the Saudis to extract more from its security agreements with the USA than would otherwise be forthcoming. The UAE has cooperated on defence with China too, and has gone so far as to conduct joint naval exercises.

Underpinning China's relationships in the Middle East is the simple fact that it is the world's biggest oil importer. In the case of Iran, it has been able to provide a market in breach of US sanctions and has leveraged the relationship by getting Iran into the BRICS group. It has also advanced defence collaboration, including joint exercises featuring Russia. China was given credit – perhaps too much – for brokering a rapprochement between Iran and Saudi Arabia in 2022. Before the Gaza conflict, it was one of the few countries in the world to have good, businesslike relations with Iran, Saudi Arabia and Israel (the last based on technology deals).

But China is also discovering that the region is violent and politically risky. Its distant but opportunistic pro-Palestinian stance will have undermined its economically productive relationship with Israel. The Iran-supported Houthi attacks on shipping have damaged Chinese trade. The ambitious 'strategic partnership' with Iran has a costly price tag of $400 billion. And political capital is being spent keeping Middle Eastern Islamists from asking awkward questions about the treatment of Muslims in Xinjiang. Overall, however, the Indian Foreign Minister's judgement holds: the USA has been sucked into another politically damaging conflict, albeit indirectly, in Gaza, while China sits on the sidelines and bides its time.

India's interests in the region are, like China's, mainly economic. Prime Minister Modi has made repeated visits to the Gulf and especially the UAE to cement commercial relations. These centre on protecting supplies of oil – 80% of India's crude oil consumption is imported, over half from the Gulf, despite recent increases in oil from Russia. Another concern is to sustain remittances from 8.8 million Indian workers, of whom 3.5 million are in the UAE, dwarfing the indigenous population.[31] India is also attracting large amounts of inward investment from the Gulf states and has been given pledges of large-scale infrastructure investment from Saudi and UAE sovereign wealth funds.

By contrast, conflict in the region is exposing the fragility of India's attempt to pursue non-alignment while remaining linked into US-led security arrangements. India has (or had) plans to participate in an embryonic I2U2 group (India, Israel, USA, UAE) and a Middle East Corridor to rival the Chinese BRI. The former project may have been one of the casualties of the Gaza war, while the latter remains largely theoretical. For the time being the main tangible gain from the association is a series of military exercises and joint training, and the – far from trivial – gain of good, close relations with the UAE, which is important economically.

A close association with Israel is toxic in much of the Global South, though in the long run India may be well rewarded, especially by the USA, for defending Israel politically and refusing to join condemnations in the United Nations. Modi has identified the Israeli leadership as 'fellow religious nationalists threatened by Islamic extremism'.[32] In terms of concrete actions, India has shared intelligence on Islamic terrorists. A tangible benefit from the Israeli relationship is that Israel is one of India's top arms suppliers and sources of technology investment. A tangible loss has been the formerly close relationship with Iran. India took the decision, unlike China, to comply with US oil sanctions and to abandon joint projects in Iran.[33] Iran and other Middle Eastern states such as Turkey are potentially receptive to Pakistan's appeal for Islamic solidarity, invoking Kashmir as an issue to embarrass and potentially threaten India. Multi-alignment is proving a difficult sell in the Middle East, and it is hard to avoid the conclusion that in this China is somewhat better placed than India.

The same is true in sub-Saharan Africa. China has three main sources of strength relative to the USA, let alone India. First, China has invested over two decades of concentrated effort into building up commercial and political ties with Africa, at a time when the Western world was largely disengaging.[34] The Chinese took a strategic view that Africa would be a rising force, in part because of demographic trends – a growing labour force and urban market. And its decision makers could see that African governments were seeking greater independence from Western donors (and former colonial powers). Second, there has been massive investment in infrastructure. In the period 2007–20, an estimated $23 billion was invested by Chinese banks, as against $9 billion from all other sources. China became regarded as 'the lender of first resort'.[35] The BRI was the template, but Africa has also accounted for almost half of China's aid programme. Third, China's approach of not imposing policy conditionality around human rights, environmental standards and corruption has resonated with many African countries, especially those with authoritarian governments.

China's commitment to Africa has not been without missteps and problems. From the outset there were complaints about exploitative behaviour.[36] The large Chinese presence on the ground – 250,000 at its peak in 2015 – attracted some resentment. Some of the projects have proved to be 'white elephants' or of little development value. The bank lending has resulted in serious debt problems for some recipients, such as Zambia, Ghana and Angola. And, as discussed in the previous chapter, China has not dealt sympathetically with pleas for debt forgiveness or expeditiously with rescheduling, leaving ill feeling in some African countries. Chinese banks have also been left with large bad debts, latterly with Sudan. The flow of new finance and new projects has now largely dried up. But despite the negatives, Africa is one part of the world where public opinion has been largely positive towards China, as shown by surveys in Kenya, Nigeria and South Africa.[37]

China has also gained much from its investment in Africa. It has secured a military base in Djibouti, giving the Chinese navy a base in the Indian Ocean, and it is reported to be negotiating for another on Africa's Atlantic coast. China has become a major arms supplier to Africa, with no fewer than twenty-one countries in receipt of major deliveries in the 2019–23 period, and is now the region's largest arms supplier, displacing Russia.[38] Most of Africa aligns with China on north–south geopolitical issues. China's Forum on China–Africa Cooperation (FOCAC) involves fifty African countries, with regular high-level visits and initiatives. Only one small African country – Eswatini – is left that recognises Taiwan.[39] Around 10,000 Chinese firms do business in Africa. Huawei dominates basic telecoms infrastructure. China is now Africa's largest trade partner, with a significant Chinese surplus. Chinese companies have acquired ownership or valuable contracts with raw material producers, including the metals critical to the green economy like cobalt and copper. China is now well placed to be Africa's dominant economic partner in years to come, investing in African manufacturing to supply growing urban markets, processing African raw materials while maintaining control of supply and providing the technology for renewable energy and telecommunication systems.

In the face of this formidable competition, India has started to create a commercial and political presence in Africa. India's current penetration is low, with around 6% of Africa's imports as against 18% for China. And the historic connection through diaspora communities in East and South Africa is a mixed blessing reputationally. Nonetheless, there have been two major forward steps. First, at the India-hosted meeting of the G20 in 2023, the Indian government pushed to include the African Union as full members. Important countries like Ethiopia, Nigeria and Kenya now have a voice in the most significant north–south forum.

Second, India is launching its own version of the Chinese Digital Silk Road, based around its India Stack: the digital public infrastructure (DPI) used for payments, government transfers, establishing identity and data management. India invited 125 developing countries to a summit in Delhi in January 2023 to demonstrate the achievements of the Indian system and to market it overseas. In some African countries, Kenya and Nigeria especially, entrepreneurs have already developed sophisticated and efficient digital payment mechanisms, bypassing inefficient banks. The Stack could help to provide a public infrastructure for such innovative companies. A MOSIP is being trialled in several African countries, including Ethiopia. If it works well, the system will be rolled out free of charge (but with lucrative software contracts hoped to follow). Indian systems do not generate the same apprehensions about data control and manipulation associated with the Chinese Digital Silk Road, which were inflamed by a scandal involving Chinese exfiltration of data from the African Union headquarters in Addis Ababa.[40] In 2023, Huawei accounted for 70% of African 4G networks and cloud services for seventeen countries, including the African Union.[41]

Indian systems potentially offer low-cost digital alternatives which maintain access to an open global internet and data integrity. But the Indian offer is so far embryonic.

Latin America illustrates well the Chinese strategy of establishing a political base among like-minded countries of the Global South while simultaneously building raw material and food supply chains and manufacturing markets. The speed, coordination and thoroughness of the Chinese operation has alarmed Western governments, especially the USA.[42] Chinese trade with Latin America grew from $12 billion in 2010 to $445 billion in 2022, an increase from 5% to 18% of total trade for the region. That momentum may not be sustained, as the Chinese economic slowdown feeds through into weaker commodity demand and prices. But China has cemented the trade relationship by offering trade agreements (six so far), knowing that protectionist Congressional politics prevents the USA doing the same, while intrusive conditionality stands in the way of agreements with the EU.[43] China's strategic approach to the region can be seen in the attention it has lavished on Panama, the gateway connecting the Atlantic and Pacific oceans. Chinese private operators are involved in ports at both ends of the canal, a fact that has alarmed President Trump enough for him to threaten to invade the canal.[44]

A powerful catalyst of business dealings with China has been the fact that twenty-one countries in the region signed up to the BRI. Chinese bank loans for (mainly) infrastructure projects under the BRI totalled $138 billion from 2005 to 2020. And although the amount of Chinese finance has slowed, the number of projects has risen by a third from the five years 2013–18 to 2018–23. Moreover, Chinese activities are no longer dominated by big infrastructure projects (a significant number of which were suspended or cancelled) but are targeted in a more strategic way: telecoms and IT (cloud computing and data centres), critical minerals, green energy and electric vehicles. Major investments have also been made in electricity generation (Chile and Peru) and ports linked to food supplies (Peru), while $11 billion has been invested by Chinese companies in lithium, of which Latin America has 60% of world supplies in Chile, Argentina and Bolivia.

As a clear signal that China has major strategic ambitions in Latin America, trade has grown alongside the flag: President Xi visited the region eleven times after 2012; President Trump just once. Xi also participated in

three continental summits (without participation from the US). It is a measure of its growing influence that China has managed to reduce the Latin
American countries that recognise Taiwan to Paraguay and Guatemala plus
a handful of tiny Caribbean nations.[45] At least pre-pandemic, China also had
sky-high favourability ratings here in the Pew opinion surveys.

Arguably, the biggest success for the Chinese has been Brazil. Under
President Lula, Brazil has taken a leadership role in the BRICS and led
much of the campaigning for de-dollarisation, while Lula's predecessor
Dilma Rousseff now heads up the New Development Bank in Shanghai.
Even under the politically hostile Jair Bolsonaro trade blossomed, and China
accounts for 30% of Brazil's exports (soya beans, beef, crude oil and iron
ore). Brazil is also hosting a billion-dollar EV production plant which is in
the vanguard of China's attempt to circumvent American and European
trade barriers by building up markets in the Global South. Democracy
has, however, unpredictable outcomes. President Milei in Argentina has
upended China's – expensive – cultivation of his Peronist predecessors and
declined to join the BRICS group. But Argentina has been negotiating
for China's help to manage its debt and, so far, has left China's interest in
lithium resources intact.

A more reliable political ally has been the autocratic and anti-American
regime in Venezuela. The Maduro regime has been equipped with Chinese
weapons (which are being used to threaten neighbouring Guyana in a territorial dispute). But the government's economic failures have meant that
Venezuela has not been able to supply China with much crude oil or repay
large Chinese bank loans. The Venezuela experience has underlined one of
the flaws in the Chinese approach: that the most reliable political allies in the
Global South may be economically needy and costly, and the most economically significant or rewarding are politically unreliable, as when democratic
elections throw up leaders who identify more with the West. It is striking
that the list of countries expressing an interest in the BRICS group include
Venezuela, Cuba, Bolivia and Honduras, while Mexico and Argentina are
giving it a wide berth.

Mexico may prove to be the most important (and dangerous) country
for geopolitical competition, especially if President Trump chooses to escalate his dispute with newly elected President Sheinbaum over trade, drug
trafficking and undocumented migrants. So far, China's interests there

237

are minor compared to those in South America. But an obvious way of circumventing tariffs in the USA is to make Chinese EVs or car parts or other manufactures in Mexico, which has trade access to the US market. Mexico has limited bargaining power with the USA, but with China at her back – or even just the threat of deepening relations with China – that might change. The US also needs Mexican help to stem the flow of fentanyl from Chinese firms to the drug cartels operating across the US border. By contrast, India is largely absent from the competition for influence in Latin America.

But the real test of the different approaches to the Global South is in Asia itself. China has a strong presence in South Asia, though this is strongly related to India's own security vis-à-vis China and will be dealt with below. But Southeast Asia is a region of great economic importance and growth, as well as strategic significance. It is also where the battle for markets, raw materials and the hearts and minds of the Global South is being fought. The influential Singaporean thinker Kishore Mahbubani observed that 'from 2010 to 2020 the ASEAN bloc of SE Asian nations with its $3 trillion GDP contributed more to global economic growth than the EU with its $17 trillion economy'.[46]

China's approach of advancing trade and investment with support from the BRI is seriously complicated in this region by a long history of trade, migration and occasional dominance, territorial disputes in the South China Sea and the active presence not just of the USA but of its allies Japan and Australia (and potentially India). Relations range from the close and dependent (Cambodia and Laos) to the friendly (Malaysia, Brunei and Myanmar) to the carefully balanced (Indonesia, Thailand, Singapore) to outright hostility (Vietnam and the Philippines). But these dispositions vary as regimes and governments change. The Philippines swung from being a close ally to an adversary within a few months, following the election of Bongbong Marcos in 2022. Vietnam may now have swung in the opposite direction. Also, a state-centred view can be misleading, since the large Chinese (and smaller Indian) diasporas matter, as do the large numbers of – mainly Chinese – businesspeople, tourists, expatriates and criminal gangs.[47]

Generalisation is difficult in such a heterogeneous region, but the most striking feature in recent years has been the growing Chinese ascendancy relative to the USA. The Lowy Institute Asia Power Index has China with a growing lead in terms of perceived economic, military and political dominance.[48] China now accounts for 18% of ASEAN's trade, a figure that has doubled over a decade. It is an enthusiastic supporter of regional agreements, notably RCEP, unlike the USA, which has disengaged from the TPP and retreated into protectionism. The Lowy assessment is borne out by the annual ISEAS-Yusuf Ishak Institute survey of elite opinion, which asked which side decision makers would pick if forced to choose. In 2024, for the first time, the majority picked China.[49] China may not however be liked or trusted, and there is anxiety not only over the disputed areas of the South China Sea but also over what appears to be a major naval base in Cambodia. Crucially, the countries of the region are anxious to avoid a binary choice and to exercise as much agency as possible.[50]

Several examples illustrate this balancing act. Chinese-backed companies are mining Indonesia's large supply of cobalt and nickel, but the Indonesians have negotiated demanding conditions on processing. Chinese involvement has also been diluted to avoid losing US market access. The Indonesians have made good use of BRI financing to deliver key projects like the Jakarta–Bandung high-speed railway, but have avoided too close association with China, for example by not applying to join the BRICS. Recent Malaysian governments have challenged the value of BRI projects. But Malaysia ignored appeals from the USA not to award a 5G system to Huawei – and in the ensuing row decried 'China phobia'. President Duterte of the Philippines cultivated China and challenged the continuation of US bases, but his successor has abruptly reversed this policy and has strengthened military ties with the USA after clashes in the South China Sea with Chinese coastguard vessels that illegally entered Philippine waters.

The regional desire to avoid having to choose between China and the USA potentially opens the door to other powers. Japanese investment through the private sector or through its bilateral or multilateral aid channels is significant. There is also an opportunity for India, though India opted out of the regional economic agreement RCEP because of fear of Chinese trade competition. It did however land its biggest ever arms export contract with the Philippines and has openly supported the Philippines in its territorial dispute with China in the South China Sea.[51] India has also made arms deals with Vietnam and enhanced defence cooperation with Indonesia.[52] The survey of elite opinion cited above was dismissive of India's relevance,[53] but the country's importance in the long run is probably expressed through its membership of the Quad, which has the specific objective of offering a counter to China.[54]

The story emerging from the complex set of relationships described in this chapter does not correspond to the simple, polarised view of the world held in both Washington and Beijing. There is little sign of a situation in which the world's democracies, beyond those of the West, line up to confront the autocratic alliance of China, Russia, Iran and sundry allies. Many countries in the Global South value their relationships with Russia, China or both, while otherwise subscribing to democracy and values espoused by the West. Equally, there is a willingness to work with China in groups like the BRICS or through bilateral relationships, but not to be dominated by China. The word 'multi-alignment' best captures this complex and non-ideological world. It even extends to the relationship between China and India, to which I now turn.

9

China and India as frenemies

China and India work together in a variety of forums: the Non-Aligned Movement, the G77, the BRICS, the SCO. They also share common positions: the need for reform of the Bretton Woods institutions to reflect the growing importance of emerging economies in the Global South; reducing the role of the dollar in the international monetary system; a commitment to the UN-based COP process for dealing with climate change, while recognising the need for hydrocarbons – in particular coal – as transitional fuels. But that degree of overlap should not obscure the fact that there is a long-standing but live dispute over a long shared border, which is a source of continuing tension and considerable nationalistic passion on both sides: what has been called a 'hot peace' or 'armed coexistence'.[1]

The troubled frontier

An ill-defined 2,100-mile frontier has been a source of friction between China and India under successive governments. In essence, India claims that China is occupying 38,000 square miles of its territory on the western end of the border: Aksai Chin in Ladakh, part of Kashmir. China, meanwhile, claims that 90,000 square miles at the eastern end, in the Indian state of Arunachal Pradesh, belongs to China as 'South Tibet'.[2] The fact that this common frontier is high in the Himalayas, largely uninhabitable and unproductive, has not reduced the passion around it.

One problem is that a large section of the frontier is based on a 1914 agreement between the British colonial administration in India and the then independent government of Tibet, the so-called McMahon Line.

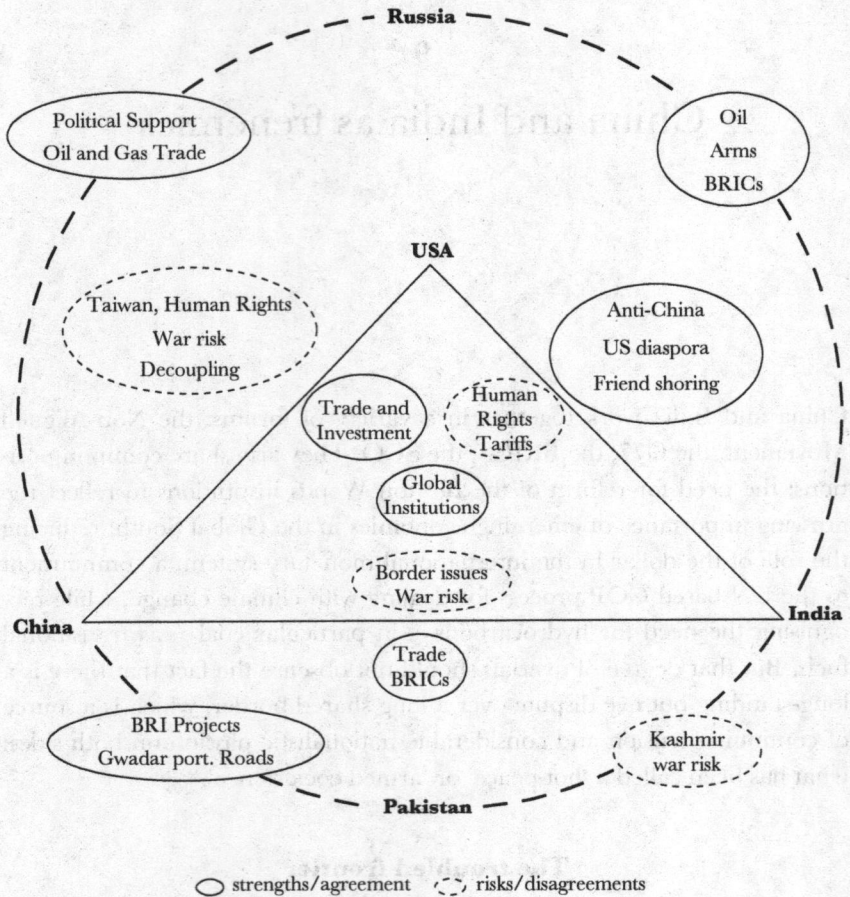

○ strengths/agreement   ⌐⌐ risks/disagreements

9.1 Frenemies

The uprising in Tibet in 1959 and the flight of the Dalai Lama, which the Chinese claimed India had provoked, complicated negotiations based on a Chinese proposal to drop its claim in the east in return for the Aksai Chin area in the west. The deal broke down, troops clashed on the frontier, and in 1962 full-scale war broke out. The Chinese inflicted a heavy and humiliating defeat on India, which lost 7,000 soldiers and saw a large area overrun. China then retreated behind the McMahon Line but kept the Aksai Chin. Sporadic clashes continued – most conspicuously in 1967 and 1975 – and the overall bilateral relationship festered.

Attempts were made from 1988 to try to improve the relationship and to separate the border dispute from wider cooperation. Prime Minister Rajiv Gandhi went to China and in 1993 there was agreement to park the border issue by creating a Line of Actual Control (LAC), effectively freezing the conflict. There was agreement, too, that in the event of fighting breaking out at the frontier, firearms would not be used (the terrain is highly inhospitable, notably around the Siachen Glacier in Ladakh). These practical steps enabled the wider relationship to move onto a better footing for the best part of twenty years. But the advent of a more assertive Chinese leadership under President Xi and a more nationalistic Indian leadership with Prime Minister Modi has increased tensions.[3]

After clashes in 2013, 2014 and 2015 there was serious confrontation in 2017 in the Doklam area in Sikkim, near the narrow area of land connecting most of India to the north-east, called the 'Chicken Neck'. The immediate flashpoint was a Chinese-built road in the disputed territory. But the presence of large numbers of troops – perhaps 100,000 in total – and growing infrastructure on both sides was bound to lead to conflict. Then in June 2020 there was a more serious clash. Chinese troops, claiming to have been provoked by Indian road building near the border, poured into the Galwan Valley in Ladakh. Serious fighting broke out. Both sides respected the agreement not to use firearms, resulting in a stone age confrontation involving sticks and stones. The fighting was bitter however, and twenty Indians were killed, as well as four Chinese – the first fatalities for forty-five years. The political ramifications in India were serious, with strong patriotic, anti-China feeling and moves to disengage economically. Since then there have been further clashes at different points along the frontier, but no more fatalities and some mutual withdrawal from sensitive points along the LAC to create buffer zones. At the 2024 BRICS summit in Russia agreement was reached on patrolling the frontier, which reduces the risk of conflict. But the level of distrust remains high.

These incidents, moreover, reflect deeper changes in both China and India. In China we have seen a consistently more nationalistic and aggressive response to neighbours who (in Chinese eyes) provoke trouble, as with the Philippines in the South China Sea and Taiwan under the DPP government. India's more nationalistic political rhetoric under the BJP government has also led to China interpreting events in India as threats, for example when some BJP politicians called for the invasion of Pakistan-occupied

Kashmir, through which runs a highway linking Pakistan and China. As a result, Sino-Indian relations went into deep freeze.[4] Some Indian commentators have concluded that terminal damage has been done to the bilateral relationship, with India moving closer to a military alliance with anti-China nations led by the USA: 'China has lost India'.[5] But that conclusion needs to be balanced against a more nuanced analysis which reflects some common interests in economic matters and on north–south issues.

The Chinese – perhaps ill-advisedly – do not appear to attach the same importance to India as an adversary as India does to China, even though both countries are nuclear weapon states.[6] The Chinese view appears to have been that India's deterrent is directed at Pakistan.[7] Indian governments, meanwhile, enjoy the popularity which comes from standing up to a militarily more powerful neighbour, in marked contrast to the humiliating defeat in 1962.[8] But a meaningful comparison of military capabilities can only be made by considering the triangular relationship involving Pakistan – quadrilateral if we include the USA.

The forever conflict with Pakistan

India's military and political focus has long been on its nuclear-armed neighbour Pakistan and associated problems, notably Islamist terrorism. Until recently, the big geopolitical picture, involving the USA and China, has been largely obscured by this regional conflict.

The origins of the seventy-five-year-old dispute lie in the 1947 Partition, when the Hindu maharajah of the largely Muslim Kashmir opted to be part of India. This led to wars in 1947, 1965, 1971 and 1999. Only one (1971) had a decisive outcome, when the intervention of India on the side of Bangladeshi rebels led to the splitting of Pakistan and the creation of Bangladesh. There have been several developments that have changed the nature of the conflict. The first was the acquisition of nuclear weapons. India first tested a weapon in 1974 and Pakistan in 1984. It is widely believed that the clashes in 1999 – the so-called Kargil War – came close to the use of nuclear weapons, but after Kargil India adopted a 'no first use' policy, which appears to have greatly reduced the risk.[9]

The second, and less manageable, development has been the emergence of Islamist terrorist groups, based in Kashmir and with roots in the Kashmiri population, but also motivated by events in Afghanistan and the Middle East. An early manifestation was the burgeoning resistance movement in Kashmir in 1989, when there was widespread communal violence. There were then several high-profile atrocities: an attack on the Indian parliament in 2001, the bombing of an express train in Pakistan and an attack on Mumbai in 2008 that left 166 dead. The Mumbai attack was attributed to the Kashmiri terrorist group Lashkar-e-Taiba, which was believed, certainly by the Indian authorities, to be operating with the backing of the Pakistani military intelligence group ISI. However, the Indians subsequently worked with the Pakistani authorities to track down members of the terrorist group, and there was some understanding that Pakistan itself was a victim of Afghan-related terrorism, which had mutated into the Pakistan Taliban.

A period of stability came to an end in 2016 when Kashmiri militants, also believed in India to be backed by ISI, attacked an Indian base, killing sixteen. There followed a long period of retaliatory strikes and counterstrikes until in February 2019 a suicide bomber killed forty Indian paramilitaries, leading to an escalation of cross-border fighting, including air strikes. Emotions were heightened further when the Indian government ended the special status of Kashmir and effectively locked down the state for a year, with large-scale detention of Muslim Kashmiris and alleged human rights abuses. India and Pakistan came close to war again. Since 2021 the relationship has stabilised, but it only requires another bad terrorist attack in India or an accidental border incident to inflame feelings in both countries. One of the long-term consequences of this constant insecurity and permanent militarisation has been the gradual decline of Pakistan's economy.

Pakistan's economic deterioration has coincided with India's sustained surge in growth. In the decades after independence it was Pakistan, not India, that was the economic success story. Military or military-dominated governments provided business-friendly policies. Also, during the Cold War era the United States saw Pakistan as a dependable ally, while India was seen as too close to the USSR, and this ensured a steady supply of aid to Pakistan. Pakistan's usefulness grew during the wars in Afghanistan. But in recent years it has become clear that India has the more resilient economy and, unlike Pakistan, responds to financial crises by pursuing policies that strengthen economic growth. India now has an economy which is not just ten times the size of Pakistan's but much richer (in 2022 with per capita incomes of $2,410 at market exchange rates, as against $1,390 in Pakistan). Especially humiliating for Pakistan is the fact that it has been overtaken economically by its once poorer former eastern province, Bangladesh (with per capita incomes of $2,688). Moreover, Pakistan has been unable to escape from a seemingly endless cycle of chronic economic weakness, financial and political instability, which has led it to seek bailout finance from the IMF no fewer than twenty-three times.

One practical consequence of Pakistan's economic failure is that it now has little to offer India in terms of market opportunities, so its attempts to normalise relationships through trade have been met with indifference. There is, however, a danger for India that Pakistan becomes a failed state, struggling to keep Islamist terrorists at bay and its nuclear weapons under control. Ironically, the country is most likely to be rescued from disaster by China, which has invested heavily in Pakistan's economic development, political stability and armed forces, and now has a strong motive to protect its investment.

China's engagement with Pakistan began with the 1962 Indo-China war, when the Chinese judged that their security position would be strengthened by having India distracted and tied down in a regional dispute.[10] Pakistan ceded disputed territory to China on the frontier, and in return China supplied armaments, development assistance and practical help for Pakistan's nuclear programme.[11] The Chinese were careful not to be drawn into confrontation with India on the back of Pakistan's 1971 and 1999 wars, but in the last decade collaboration with Pakistan has deepened. There is a jointly developed fighter aircraft (the JF-7), air force pilot training (of Chinese pilots) and a move to interoperability of military systems. The centrepiece of what is called an 'all-weather partnership' is the most ambitious of the BRI programmes: the China–Pakistan Economic Corridor (CPEC). The CPEC has involved $62 billion of investment in energy, infrastructure and economic zones. One of the main features has been the development of the Gwadar port on the Indian Ocean, directly linked by road to China, and there has been much speculation (albeit denied) about its potential military value.

Some BRI projects have been criticised, and the hopes of economic transformation have not been realised, but much of the Chinese-backed development has been welcomed. The real problem has been the legacy of debt, which has compounded Pakistan's dire economic position. Chinese debt accounts for around 30% of Pakistan's external debt. Pakistan's economic crisis will almost certainly draw China further in, since China's help is needed to restructure the debt.[12] China also stands ready to provide military equipment on a concessional basis, to help Pakistan maintain military parity with India. Security problems around the Gwadar port are also leading to a bigger Chinese security presence on the ground. The core of the bilateral relationship is the link with the Pakistan military, who continue to over-shadow Pakistan politics. From India's standpoint the worry is that it faces two cooperating adversaries on two fronts. And there are other fronts where China has built positions of influence in all India's neighbours, justifying Martin Jacques' judgement that India is 'constantly on the back foot in deal-ings with China'.[13]

China's friends in India's neighbourhood

A case in point is Bangladesh. Bangladesh is a natural friend and ally for India, since India's use of force was crucial to its liberation from Pakistan in 1971, during which India provided hospitality for one the great refugee movements in modern history. By contrast, China used its first veto in the United Nations Security Council to block Bangladesh's admission to the UN, to show its support for Pakistan. Yet despite this inauspicious start to their bilateral relationship, by 2006 China had replaced India as Bangladesh's largest trade partner. It is now also the largest supplier of direct foreign investment and of military hardware.[14] All this activity is underpinned by a 'strategic partnership of cooperation', agreed during a visit from President Xi in 2016 which also turbocharged a programme of infrastructure building.

China has been able to take advantage of India's neighbours' wish to maintain a balance in their external relationships and not to be dominated by India, often seen as the regional hegemon. Moreover, there was an early recognition by China of Bangladesh's progression from being the hopeless 'basket case' of half a century ago to being a serious economic and political power with rapid growth and progress in human development. Bangladesh now has the world's eighth largest population and fourth largest armed forces in terms of personnel.[15] The country's commitment to democracy was in doubt during the long reign of Sheikh Hasina, who was Prime Minister for twenty years. But that did not concern China. Rather, the overthrow of an unpopular leader closely tied to India now offers China the potential for even deeper relationships with her successor.

One concrete result of cultivating the Bangladeshi armed forces is that China is by far the largest supplier of military equipment, while Bangladesh has been the second largest purchaser of Chinese military equipment. China is the only country with which Bangladesh has a defence agreement (dating from 2002). There has been some anxiety in India about a possible Chinese submarine base in Bangladesh, but no hard evidence has emerged to support the fear. China has also given Bangladesh special trade – MFN – status, though trade is enormously imbalanced in China's favour. Any new government that emerges in Bangladesh following Sheikh Hasina's overthrow in a coup is however likely to try to maintain neutrality between India and China and between China and the USA.

China and India have also been jostling for influence in Myanmar, in the different context of a country whose repressive military junta is an international pariah, and which has been descending into a many-sided civil war. China dominated Burma – as it then was – for centuries, creating a relationship of dependence and resentment.[16] China's close links in recent decades to Myanmar's military governments have increased both the dependence, through trade and investment along a China–Myanmar Economic Corridor, and the resentment. There were major anti-Chinese riots in 2011. The military government identified itself with the nationalist protestors and cancelled big infrastructure projects, leading to an anguished debate in China on 'who lost Burma'.[17] Relations were rebuilt with the civilian government of Aung San Suu Kyi and, through trade and investment, China became once again the dominant influence in the country. It appears to have remained so under the post-2021 military dictatorship. To the alarm of India, China seems to have secured overland transport access to the Bay of Bengal and has established a surveillance facility on the Coco Islands.

The way that India has responded has not been, as one might expect, to support the imprisoned and exiled democratic opposition and their allies in the rebel 'Three Brotherhood Alliance' that is advancing across Myanmar. Rather its policy has been to support the junta.[18] One motive appears to be to counter Chinese influence with the military. But India is increasingly concerned by the war, since fighting in Myanmar is spilling over into India.

There have been around 60,000 refugees, who have caused friction in parts of north-east India. India has responded by constructing a 1,643 km border fence and by helping the Myanmar army restore order. A major setback resulting from the fighting is the failure to complete a big transport project, the Kaladan Multi-Modal Transit Project, linking north-east India to Myanmar port facilities and thence to Kolkata.[19] The end point, a port in Myanmar, has been overrun by the rebels. Neither India nor China wants a chaotic civil war on their doorstep, but that is where the country seems headed.

Nepal is anxiously seeking to maintain a position of neutrality with the Asian powers, between whom it is uncomfortably wedged as a buffer state. India has traditionally taken Nepal for granted, and critics have pointed to successive Indian governments' alienation of Nepali opinion through political meddling, attempts at micromanagement and the use of coercive boycotts. The same critics argue that Indian decision makers were labouring under a 'fog of misunderstanding' of China's intentions.[20] China was treated as an 'interloper', despite centuries of trade and political relationships. The challenge to both India and China has been to navigate through turbulent Nepali politics, passing from autocratic monarchy to parliamentary government to Maoist and other forms of Communist administration. The Chinese appear to have the advantage of deep links to a ruling Communist party.

China has been able to build up a significant presence through the supply of military equipment and military exercises, alongside BRI projects following a visit by Xi in 2019, opening up access and trade routes through China.[21] The closure of borders to Nepal during the Covid pandemic interrupted this build-up, but Chinese influence is still seen as a potential threat by India. Neighbouring and remote Bhutan is much more under Indian control (and accepts Indian 'guidance' on foreign policy).[22] But Bhutan has recently sought to settle its border with China, which could involve giving up territory in the Doklam area – strategically important to India and the subject of the border clashes in 2017 between Indian and Chinese troops.[23]

Another of India's neighbours trying to balance Chinese and Indian interests is Sri Lanka. India's interest is framed by what Shivshankar Menon describes as an 'aircraft carrier sitting 14 miles off the Indian coast. And sitting astride sea lines carrying much of India's trade and energy supplies.'[24]

Chinese geopoliticians make similar claims: that Sri Lanka sits on a major 'maritime silk road'. China has gone to some lengths to build up influence in Sri Lanka. Following the ending of the civil war, the Chinese cultivated the (then) popular Rajapaksa family, which dominated government at the time. Chinese banks invested large sums in Sri Lankan infrastructure – ports, an international airport and expressways – as part of the BRI.

The accumulation of Sri Lankan debt resulting from this wave of investment has often been cited as one example of 'debt trap diplomacy' – the Hambantota port development, which failed to generate the revenue to service loans.[25] Corruption may also have been involved. It has been alleged that Chinese creditors used default on the loans to forcibly acquire ownership of the port – though it appears to have been offered first to Indian investors. Accusations were also made around the operatorship of a container port, but the facts suggest that Indian and Chinese commercial interests were equally involved. What lay behind much of the controversy around ports was the suspicion that China was covertly seeking to establish a military base, though an analysis of warship movements into Sri Lanka does not bear this out.[26]

The contest for influence has reached an especially polarised level in the Maldives, where governments have alternated between pro-Chinese, anti-Indian administrations and anti-Chinese, pro-Indian ones. Given the Maldives' location in the Indian Ocean, in terms of naval access, the stakes are considerable. In 2024 the pro-Chinese tendency appeared to have prevailed, and the Maldives President visited China to sign up to an Action Plan for Strategic Cooperation, which has greatly alarmed the Indian government. Taken together with the other Chinese encroachments on the Indian neighbourhood, there is a pattern of expanding Chinese influence and strategic positioning which has led India to enter an embryonic pact with the USA, Australia and Japan: the Quad.

Head to head on the battlefield?

After the previous experience of fighting on the China–India border, and with the build-up of Chinese overall military capability, there has been much speculation as to the risks of conflict between the Asian superstates and, if it were to happen, what would be the result.

Both China and India have nuclear weapons as a deterrent against a nuclear strike. India and Pakistan each have an estimated 170 nuclear warheads, and it has been assumed that they were intended for mutual deterrence. It has only recently become apparent that China is a comparable or bigger threat. China had around 500 warheads in mid-2023 but was expanding its stockpile, the better to match the USA's much larger number of nuclear weapons (close to 5,000 including active, inactive and weapons being retired). However, India has recently developed an MIRV (multi-headed weapons) capability and the ballistic missiles (Agni 5) to deliver them, which is considered by experts to provide an effective second-strike deterrent to China.[27] Both countries also have a 'no first use' policy. The conclusion has been drawn that neither side has any incentive to use nuclear weapons but that, because of that security, both sides have a bigger incentive to embark upon conventional warfare.[28]

Other analysts, notably Ashley Tellis, have come to a different conclusion: that the dynamics of the situation are highly unstable.[29] Because China is rapidly expanding its nuclear arsenal to deter the USA – perhaps to 1,000 warheads by 2030 according to the Pentagon – the possibility arises that India no longer feels that it has an effective deterrent. Moreover, advances in Chinese surveillance and AI technology could lead to India's deterrent losing its credibility, which has already led to India hiding its weapons in two nuclear submarines. But these may not be sufficiently sophisticated to be truly credible. Tellis worries that the knock-on effect of the USA and Russia abandoning arms control may have been to create a cascade: China must escalate in response; India feels it must follow China; Pakistan feels it must follow India. At some point, someone miscalculates the risk. Armageddon.

The more sanguine view is that nuclear conservatism will prevail, and that warfare is much more likely to be restricted to conventional weapons. A plausible scenario centres on the disputed Himalayan frontier, in particular eastern Ladakh, where there have been clashes before.[30] China has an incentive to secure the transport route from Pakistan to China through Pakistan-occupied Kashmir and the valleys around it. And that incentive becomes greater if the Gwadar port in Pakistan starts to realise its potential as a major supply route to China, avoiding the South China Sea and the Malacca Strait. There is also potentially a gas pipeline route from Iran. For its part,

India will want to resist encroachments on its territory, having already lost the Aksai Chin area to China.

At first sight, India is heavily outgunned and outmanned, and spends much less on defence: $74 billion as against China's $230 billion in 2023/24. Based on statistics from the International Institute for Strategic Studies, India has just short of 1.5 million active service personnel, as against over 2 million for China (though India has bigger reserves – 1.2 million versus 0.5 million). The asymmetry is more obvious in equipment. India has 856 combat-capable fixed wing aircraft, compared to 2,800 for China. The Chinese have fifth-generation stealth fighters (the J-20 Chengdu), as against generally older, less advanced Indian planes from the 1980s and 1990s. There are also significant disparities in numbers and quality in relation to tanks and armoured vehicles. And the infrastructure on the Chinese side is better developed, permitting greater mobility. Moreover, in the event of war, Russia could no longer be relied upon to resupply India in a conflict with China, with whom it has strong political and economic links. And, arguably, the USA is already overstretched supplying Ukraine, Israel and Taiwan.

However, looking initially at a war in the Himalayas, it is far from clear that India would be at such a disadvantage.[31] India may well have an advantage in the high altitudes and frozen conditions. Only a tiny fraction of the Chinese People's Liberation Army is at the frontier with India; its priority is to be ready for conflict with the USA. Reinforcements would need acclimatisation. Some 70,000 troops and most of India's best planes and missiles are already stationed near the border, while only a small part of the Chinese air force is in Tibet and only a fraction of that facing India. In 1989 India was able to mobilise 200,000 troops quickly for the Kargil War with Pakistan in mountain terrain. Indian troops are also relatively more battle-hardened (China last fought, and lost, a land war almost half a century ago, in Vietnam). The Chinese army has been riven by politics and corruption, while India has a highly motivated, professional army which enjoys fierce competition to join. For these reasons, Christopher Colley of the United States Air War College argues that capability is different from numbers, though he acknowledges that China's growing technological sophistication means that asymmetry is moving in its favour.[32]

If China and India were to fight in the Indian Ocean there is a similar story. At first sight, India is totally outgunned at sea. In terms of major surface vessels and submarines, China has 145 and India 45 (aircraft carriers, cruisers, destroyers, frigates, submarines). Of India's two aircraft carriers, one has long-term maintenance issues and the other has not completed trials. A wider definition of the navy would have 730 Chinese vessels against 294. But Colley again makes the point that the number of vessels does not measure capability. China's navy is for use in the Pacific against the USA, around Taiwan and in the South China Sea, with no more than six to eight vessels in the Indian ocean – barely enough to contribute to anti-piracy operations in defence of merchant shipping.[33] India has a forward base in the Andaman and Nicobar Islands which could head off a task force from China. And a small number of modern submarines – eighteen – could do a lot of damage. India could also reasonably expect to rely on US intelligence to supply advanced warning. The advantage of fighting a naval war close to home bases would inevitably be lost, however, if China acquired Indian Ocean bases. But scares around Gwadar in Pakistan, Sri Lanka, Bangladesh and the Maldives have not yet led to a Chinese naval base (except in the well-established Djibouti facility). The United States also provides useful intelligence, and if the Quad develops a military capability through training and exercises it is likely to centre on the Indian Ocean.

The military asymmetry between India and China may not, therefore, be as great as the crude numbers suggest. But China is developing its armed forces rapidly, especially the navy, and its technological prowess is being translated into better weapons. And China and Pakistan may act in concert. For these reasons there is pressure on the Indian government to spend more on defence.[34] But that is not a straightforward matter. There is a classic 'guns and butter' choice, and the Modi government has been taught a chastening lesson at an election in which it underestimated the anger of poor people at low-quality public services and lack of government help. Furthermore, there is a conflict between pressures for indigenisation of defence equipment, which can be costly, slow and prone to technical failure (as recently with helicopters), as against dependence on overseas suppliers, who may not be wholly reliable. That in turn raises the question of whether India should engage with China on economic issues as well as preparing for military conflict.

Economic entanglement or disentanglement?

India's approach to trade and wider economic relations with China is ambiguous. The value of two-way trade has increased fourfold in a decade to $136 billion in 2022. But it is heavily unbalanced. Almost 90% of the trade by value consists of imports from China to India: either cheap consumer goods or inputs for India's high-tech activities, such as memory chips, integrated circuits and pharmaceutical ingredients. Yet exports to India are a tiny fraction of China's overall exports (around 3%), while China is India's third largest trade partner, with around 14% of India's imports by value. China matters a lot more to India, economically, than India does to China. It is deeply galling to many in India that the country imports from China large volumes of consumer goods such as toys and garments whose production requires low-cost, relatively unskilled labour, which India has in abundance. Moreover, India's current attempts to industrialise through advanced manufacturing rely heavily on Chinese inputs and experts.

Yet it is India that has been trying to minimise economic integration, for a mixture of protectionist and security reasons. Fear of Chinese manufacturing competition was a major reason for India's refusal to join the Asian trade liberalising group, RCEP. India has used tariffs to curb competition from Chinese mobile handsets and toys. And India is one of the countries to have banned telecommunications equipment from Huawei and ZTE. In response to the border hostilities in 2020, India acted against Chinese firms: 320 Chinese apps, including TikTok, WeChat and Shein, the fast-fashion retailer. Chinese companies have found that tax rules have been used to make them unwelcome: BYD, the electric vehicle makers and the handset-making company Xiaomi. Chinese companies' applications for foreign investment approval have been mostly rejected. And a programme of 'production-linked incentives' targets areas where Chinese suppliers dominate the market. Western companies are familiar with the obstacle course presented by Indian bureaucracy and its protectionist instincts. National security has created a whole new area for discretionary policymaking.

The partial thawing of relations around the frontier has led to a more relaxed view on economic relations. Indian businesses point out that if India is to develop its manufacturing sector this will often involve Chinese investment and the import of Chinese components and equipment. And a friend-shoring of investment away from China may well involve partially integrating Indian operations into Chinese supply chains. There is potentially a big inflow of Chinese investment into India, bringing jobs and technology transfer. Indian businesses have already been pushing for a more liberal visa regime which can allow more Chinese technical staff and engineers into India. There are business pressures to allow more Chinese imports where these can sustain successful Indian export industries such as pharmaceuticals. The two countries' main sources of comparative advantage in trade – China's advanced manufactures and India's traded business services – are complementary rather than competitive. A crudely nationalistic approach to Chinese imports and investment has costs, and there is some indication that Indian business lobbies are winning the argument for flexibility. But distrust of China means that economic security considerations will continue to loom large in policymaking.[35]

However, it should not be assumed that China's relationship with India is locked into a downward spiral. The Chinese may decide to stabilise the frontier, since it is a distraction from the confrontation with the USA, and to return to the cooperative relationship they had with India before the border clashes. They agree on much: global governance reform, diversifying from the dollar, climate change negotiations, curbing Islamic extremism, businesslike relations with Russia. They both bristle at Western finger-wagging on human rights and environmental standards. These irritations are likely to be less prominent under President Trump but his tariffs, while directed at China, have hit India too. Many Indians are not flattered to be used as a 'Western counterweight' to China, and value genuine multi-alignment.

It seems unlikely that coexistence could blossom into friendship, but it is possible. If so, 'friendship between China and India could transform geopolitics'.[36] At the very least there is, in the concept of 'frenemies', a complex balancing of interests with each other and with Pakistan and Russia, among others. That picture is more consistent with the idea of 'multi-alignment' than the simpler view of a world divided into two.

10

Conclusion: three possible futures

There is always a temptation to see the future as an extrapolation of the past. And there is an even bigger temptation to allow our perceptions of recent short-term events and trends to colour our views about the long term. At present, the wars in Ukraine and the Middle East, and memories – albeit fading – of the world financial crisis and Covid dominate much of our thinking. And the bigger, generation-shaping events like the collapse of the Soviet Empire and the rise of China continue to resonate; indeed, the latter is at the heart of this book. And there is much uncertainty, amid which the second Trump presidency looms large in the short run.

There are a few trends which are more certain than others. Demography is one. Falling fertility rates and an ageing population seem inevitable almost everywhere, together with a growing proportion of the world's population living in younger countries, notably in Africa, and a shrinking proportion in high-income countries and China. Although these trends seem unavoidable, small differences in population growth rates can have big cumulative effects in the long run. Population size also underpins the position of the two Asian superstates. Plausible UN projections to mid-century suggest that even a shrinking China will still have considerably more than three times as many people as the USA or rapidly growing Nigeria or Pakistan. Demography also influences differential economic performance. An expanding population of working age provides India with a potential long-term advantage over China in terms of economic growth, other things being equal (though, as discussed above, they are not equal, and India has chronic underutilisation of its labour force).

Economic growth rates are less predictable, though it seems reasonable to assume that the information and data processing revolution, and AI, will continue at pace, and that knowledge will spread rapidly through internet connectivity, enabling less developed countries to catch up. The trend over half a century, illustrated in Figure 0.1, of the 'advanced' economies being displaced in relative size by emerging economies of the Global South seems inexorable. But policy also matters – and, perhaps, political systems. There is much debate as to whether China's prodigious growth in the four decades after Deng's radical reforms is a better guide to the future, or the recent sharp slowdown following Covid, the collapse of the property market and the emergence of widespread excess capacity. In India too there is debate about how to raise growth from around 6% a year to the 10% experienced in parts of East Asia, including China. Differential growth rates give us a picture of future relative economic size. But future economic size also depends on whether and how quickly convergence in price levels takes place through real exchange rates. Figure 10.1 shows a plausible range of future economic sizes, based on modelling by the OECD as well as variations of the scenarios discussed below.[1] There is an enormous range of outcomes.

Economic growth projections to 2050 suggest that China and India are both likely – though not certain – to become pre-eminent economic powers, perhaps even surpassing the USA. With that pre-eminence will come military and political power (which China has already). They will almost certainly be, with the USA, the main centres of scientific discovery and technological innovation. And they will be both the main sources of and solutions to the planet's environmental threats, notably climate change. There are however many uncertainties. I summarise below some of the more obvious questions, before looking at several scenarios of how the future might evolve.

Is China stuck in a middle-income trap?

It matters enormously whether China can recapture the prodigious economic growth rates seen in earlier decades and become a high-income country, as its smaller neighbours, such as South Korea, have done. I reviewed this question in detail in Chapter 4. China is close to the threshold for a high-income country on World Bank definitions, and some of its coastal provinces are well above the threshold, though in rural areas there is much

OECD projected growth

(chart: Estimated GDP ($tn), years 2024–2049, lines for USA, China, India)

Scenario 1: Global West (PPP)

(chart: Estimated GDP ($tn), years 2024–2049, lines for USA, China, India)

Scenario 2: Multipolar (PPP)

(chart: Estimated GDP ($tn), years 2024–2049, lines for USA, China, India)

Scenario 3: Multilateral (PPP)

(chart: Estimated GDP ($tn), years 2024–2049, lines for USA, China, India)

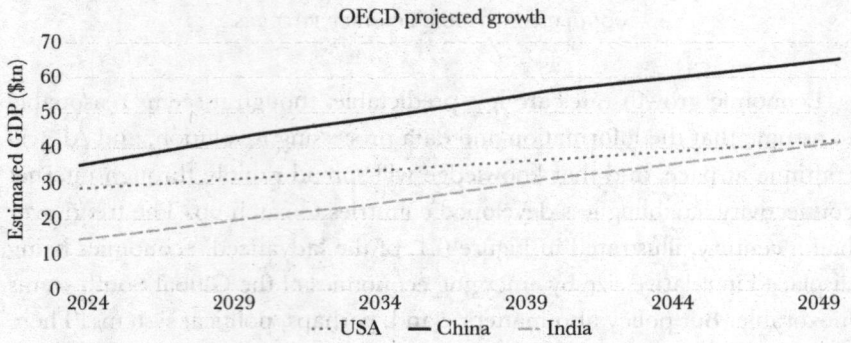

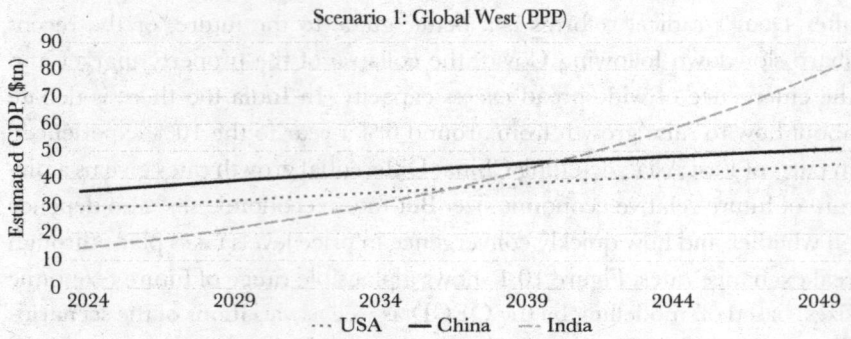

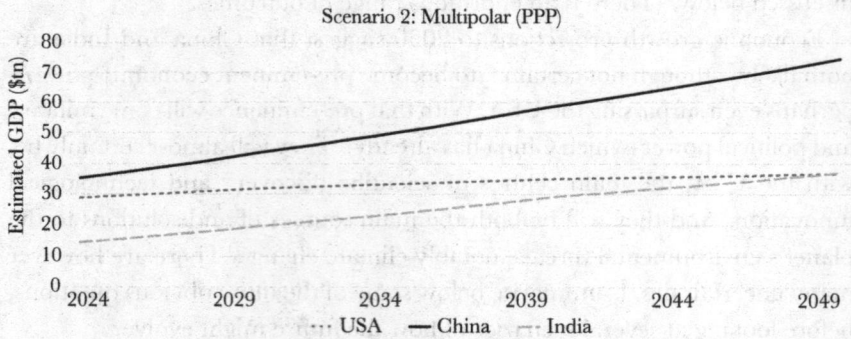

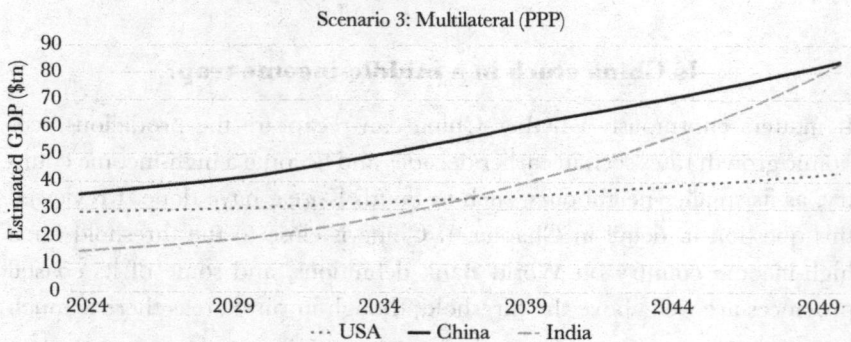

Source: Based on OECD long-term forecasts, Economic Outlook 2023

10.1 Projections to 2050

poverty, poor education and poor health. There is no overwhelming reason why China should be stuck at the middle-income threshold, though the experience of a significant number of middle-income countries is that failure to improve systems of governance inhibits future progress. China has seen a slowing of real economic growth from double-digit numbers earlier in the century to an officially estimated 5% in the two years after the Covid pandemic. There are arguments as to whether the official numbers can be trusted, but the major issue relates to the nature of China's slowdown and how deeply rooted its problems are.

To simplify, the key question is whether China suffers from a 'crisis of capitalism' or a 'crisis of Communism'. The 'crisis of capitalism' is in the form of a collapsed property market bubble. Overinvestment in residential property, boosted by speculation, led to the oversupply of property and the financial failure of leading property companies. Because the sector in its widest sense (including infrastructure building) is so big – on some estimates as much as 30% of the economy – this has caused serious repercussions for investor and consumer confidence. Pessimists have argued that China is fated to relive the experience of Japan after the collapse of a land and property asset bubble in 1989–90 led to a crisis in the banking system. The banks (and households) prioritised rebuilding their balance sheets, leading to a 'balance sheet recession'. Despite energetic, unorthodox monetary policy to head off deflation and (later) aggressive fiscal policy, Japan has stagnated ever since.[2]

Critics argue, furthermore, that China's property market crisis is not just a cyclical problem, but structural. It is difficult to see how the demand generated by investment in the vast property sector can be replaced. Infrastructure projects have reached the point of diminishing returns and, anyway, are heavily dependent on local government financing, and local government was left in a parlous financial state by the collapse in the property market. Arguably, China should shift to more consumer-driven growth (both private and public sector), but private consumers appear to lack confidence to spend, while the state regards itself as fiscally constrained by a weak tax base and manageable but potentially problematic public debt levels. Also, the regime appears to have an ideological preference for investment over consumption and manufacturing over services. It sees a way forward through export demand for innovative and cost-competitive manufactured products.

259

A state-backed, science-based industrial sector may be able to make up for the excesses of the property sector. But this assumes that the rest of the world will absorb the output. Protectionist policies, especially in the USA, suggest otherwise, and the return of President Trump has made the challenge even more difficult. The critics see no way out.[3]

Optimists argue that asset inflation in Japan was much more serious than in China, and that the government can use a wider range of policies – including coercion – to force banks and property companies to change behaviour and meet regulatory requirements. Moreover, the state can mandate expansionary policies if the private sector fails to invest. A combination of heavy investment in science, high-tech industries and infrastructure in less developed areas of China with controlled increases in public spending on health and education could provide a sufficient motor for continued growth. However, the critics respond by saying that it is precisely the extensive interventionism and micromanagement by the state which will prevent long-term recovery and sustained growth: what I call the 'crisis of Communism'. Their argument is that advanced capitalist countries are successful because democracy and the defence of individual freedoms nurture a culture of innovation and creative challenge. Acemoglu and Robinson won their Nobel Prize by developing this argument. The failure of the former USSR was widely attributed to the dead hand of the Soviet state: bureaucratic inertia, an inability to adapt to rapid technological change and discouragement of entrepreneurial talent. China, it is argued, will go the same way, even if not immediately.[4] From this analysis follows a prediction of slow and slowing economic growth.

The argument that China suffers from a crisis of Communism has some supporting evidence. One of the well-documented causes of the slowdown in recent years has been the declining efficiency of capital: rising incremental capital–output ratios. Some sectors of the economy – for example semiconductors, where much capital has been wasted – do not inspire much confidence in the state's capacity to pick winners. And many state-owned enterprises prioritise non-commercial objectives: the preferences of a particular party chief, job preservation, rewards for political insiders. The role of party committees in companies has been strengthened. Furthermore the 'common prosperity' philosophy of President Xi has involved reprimands or fines for some of China's most innovative and successful companies.

Flaunting wealth is unfashionable, even dangerous. Successful entrepreneurs are among the growing numbers of wealthy people moving to Singapore or the West. The economist George Magnus, among others, was warning, unfashionably, of 'red flags' a decade ago. Those flags are still waving.[5]

But China continues to defy expectations. Nicholas Lardy reminds us that despite slowdown, threats of deflation and much discussion of an economic crisis, 'China is still rising'.[6] A crisis-hit China has been growing in real economic terms at twice the rate of a booming USA supercharged by 'Bidenomics', let alone a moribund EU. Moreover, it is possible to construct an altogether more positive picture of the long-run growth outlook for China. In one crucial respect Chinese Communism has been fundamentally different from Soviet Communism. Chinese economic decision making (as opposed to Communist Party control) has been and remains highly decentralised. Undoubtedly much waste and duplication has resulted. But there is also a dynamism, willingness to experiment and energy, which is a powerful antidote to stagnation.

Furthermore, China's progress in science has been stunning, with more and more evidence of creative and rigorous research in a wide variety of fields, and results published and validated through international peer review. Chinese companies have long since ceased to be copiers of ideas from the West and have become genuine innovators across a range of sectors. Attempts to use sanctions and boycotts to stifle the growth of companies at the technological frontier have backfired spectacularly and appear to have made the companies stronger and more innovative. Trade protection has spurred China's efforts to make better, cheaper electric vehicles and develop new concepts like driverless vehicles and flying cars. Chinese companies have made themselves indispensable to the global green transition by relentlessly pushing down costs and maximising scale economies, and appear to be advanced in the next generation of technologies built around hydrogen. US sanctions on high-specification chips may have set back Chinese progress in AI, but this is likely to provide only temporary respite from Chinese competition. Nothing embodies this more optimistic view of China's future better than the emergence of DeepSeek, which has seemingly transformed the economics of AI language models.

Much capital may still be wasted, but China's stock markets and venture capital companies can make the allocation process more competitive and efficient. Where there is industrial excess capacity, incumbents fight it out through ferocious competition (rather in the manner of South Korean industrial policy). The end product is a series of formidable commercial 'national champions', with weaker companies allowed to fail. Indeed, one of the 'statist' President Xi's signature policies was more rigorous and predictable bankruptcy proceedings. The Chinese state can be inefficient, but it understands the role of markets and can also think and plan long term.

The more predictable drag on Chinese growth is demographic: a declining population of working age. Natalist policies are unlikely to succeed any better in China than in other ageing countries. But China may be able to navigate its way through the problem better than elsewhere.[7] Postponement of the retirement age will be unpopular, but an authoritarian regime is able to force through unpopular policies. Large-scale robotisation is well advanced in China as a means of raising labour productivity. There is also a large reserve of underemployed labour in rural areas that could be mobilised with more freedom of movement under the 'hukou' system and with greater investment in rural education and skills training.

Some China pessimists argue that, while Chinese living standards will continue to rise, slowly, we have essentially reached 'peak China'.[8] On this basis, China will struggle to achieve more than 1% to 2% annual growth, and, in terms of economic size, India will catch up and China will at best only just match the USA. There is however a more bullish view which dismisses the 'peak China' story as a bundle of Western myths.[9] In this view of the world, Chinese economic performance and resilience has been consistently underestimated. The problems that have arisen, from the property market collapse to demographic constraints, are exaggerated, and continued but evolving manufacturing dominance, combined with growing scientific and technological capacity, is bound to drive faster long-term growth: say 3.5% to 4% per annum. In that case, China will continue to pull away from the USA. I lean more to this latter view.

Can democratic India lift its growth tempo?

India has enjoyed a lot of plaudits for achieving growth rates of 6% to 7% since the turn of the twenty-first century. There is a degree of consensus that India could continue to grow at this rate for several decades and, whereas there are very different views about China's growth, India's is somewhat taken for granted. Indeed, the only real controversy is on the upside: whether India could realistically achieve the double-digit 'hyper-growth' which led to China's spectacular economic advance at the end of the last century and the beginning of this.

The basis of the belief in India's sustained growth rests on several fundamentals. The rate of investment of 34% over the last twenty years is very high by international (if not Chinese) standards. The labour force is growing (albeit much of it underemployed). There is a large pool of young STEM graduates. There is also a long entrepreneurial tradition, with a large business class that exhibits features of crony capitalism but also numerous innovative and successful companies. The productivity of the economy was increased through liberalising economic reforms, mainly under Manmohan Singh at the beginning of the 1990s, though some progress was made earlier and more since.

Several factors have increased India's growth potential. The creation of a national digital infrastructure linked to widespread mobile and internet access has not merely empowered individual Indians but also created a platform for business expansion. India's ICT (information and communications technology) sector has grown rapidly and may account for approaching 20% of the economy. India has seemingly developed a comparative advantage in internationally traded business services, which enjoys high income elasticity of demand and is mostly free of trade barriers. In addition, India's physical infrastructure – roads, rail, airports, ports, power supply – has greatly improved from previously dire levels, though there are still many deficiencies (certainly as compared with China). Critics of India's development to date focus on the fact that economic growth has failed to generate adequate employment. Yet the vast supply of underemployed labour (and economically inactive women) is a potential resource. Overall, however, a key feature of modern Indian development is the resilience of the economy. Despite numerous external and internal shocks, periods of political uncertainty and policy disasters like demonetisation and the Covid lockdown, the economy has continued to grow at over 6% per annum, and in per capita terms 4% per annum.

In terms of accelerating growth, essentially two approaches are advocated. One is to press ahead with further market liberalisation in product,

263

labour, capital and land markets. But that is not straightforward in a democracy. India is still protectionist in many aspects of trade policy and foreign investment, but economic nationalism appears to be politically popular and vested interests politically influential. Politics also explains the continued dominance of nationalised banks, and while these banks have moved a long way to clean up their balance sheets, they are far from being part of efficient, smoothly functioning capital markets. 'Labour market reform' – essentially a euphemism for making it easier to fire workers – is a particular favourite in the business community. And companies relocating from Chinese supply chains compare India adversely with China in terms of the flexibility of employment. There certainly used to be a serious problem in closing 'sick' enterprises because of labour resistance. But there is now an opposite problem of being stuck in a low-wage/low-productivity labour market; in any case, India's democratic politics makes it unfeasible to brush aside workers' rights and concerns. The same is true of farming, where protests saw off the Modi government's attempts to reform agriculture. As a result, the more successful farmers continue to enjoy expensive and environmentally damaging subsidies for fertilisers and irrigation, and artificially high support prices for their crops, while India continues to miss out on more efficient supply chains from farms to shops. There is often strong political resistance to further market liberalisation, however desirable it may be for economic efficiency and potential growth.

An alternative – or additional – approach, set out by the economists Raghuram Rajan and Karthik Muralidharan, among others, concentrates on improved governance.[10] India needs to decentralise more, from centre to states and from states to villages. There is a paradox here, as discussed above: the Leninists who rule China have been better at devolving economic decision making than the Indian democrats. A related shift is the need for development to prioritise education and health, which are largely state-level functions. India's potential greatest asset is its people, but they must enjoy better education at all levels to be employable and to maximise the country's role as a global supplier of traded services. Reformers such as Ashoka Mody argue that the problems are even deeper and more difficult, requiring higher levels of 'civic consciousness' of the kind seen in the burgeoning NGO movement across India and in experiments with radical decentralisation, as in Kerala.[11] Suffice it to say that there are no easy, quick solutions.

The big long-term challenge for India is to sustain a rapid tempo of eco-nomic development and poverty reduction alongside a democratic system of government. It is easy to point to the weaknesses of Indian democracy: the influence of divisive – Hindutva – identity politics, the corruption involved in party funding and election financing, the infiltration of serious criminals into political life in some states, the proliferation and instability of political parties. Until the general election of 2024 there was a widespread belief that India would inevitably travel down the authoritarian road. The Modi gov-ernment was bypassing democratic safeguards and advertising the benefits of 'strong man' and one-party rule. The surprise result, however, when some of the poorest voters in one of the poorest states turned against the BJP gov-ernment, delivered a powerful message: for all its messy compromises and unpredictability, democracy matters. It can signal distress and anger that governments would not otherwise hear or see. Democracy puts a brake on political overreach and is an effective course correction when governments make major errors. And, as the earlier administrations of Manmohan Singh illustrated, the most rapid growth spurt in India's history occurred under a seemingly weak coalition government, following reforms enacted under a minority government.[12] The dependence of weak governments in Delhi on regionally based parties may also be a factor driving initiative and experi-mentation at state level, which should help the more dynamic and reform-minded states to progress faster. Overall, Indian democracy has proved remarkably resilient and successful but, inevitably, it inhibits the ruthless decisiveness seen under the developmental dictatorships in South Korea, Taiwan and China. Overall, the mainstream forecast of solid and sustained but not spectacular growth in India – 6% to 7% per annum – seems about right.

How bad can the US–China relationship get?

Another major uncertainty is whether the current rift between the USA and China will widen further to a point where the world is effectively split between the two biggest economic superpowers and their allies in a new cold war. Economic decoupling could affect more and more goods and services and more countries. And the build-up of military capacity on both sides could result in outright conflict, most probably over Taiwan and the South

China Sea. But with the second Trump administration the range of uncertainties has widened from deepening conflict to a 'grand bargain' involving trade, Taiwan and much else.

A reason why this question is both uncertain and important is that China and the USA are the two biggest economies in the world and between them account for roughly 43% of the world economy at market exchange rates. If their allies are included, we may be talking double that. There is considerable potential for damage on a global scale. The degree of direct entanglement is much lower and has fallen in recent years – China now accounts for barely 10% of US trade – but there is much higher indirect involvement via supply chains and investment flows. The potential damage is even greater if we consider the fact that Taiwan accounts for a high proportion of the world's high-end chips, which are essential components for frontier technologies like AI and numerous other computer-based systems.

If war were to break out between heavily armed nuclear weapons states, the human and material damage is potentially incalculable. It is also difficult to see how the powers could continue to cooperate in areas of common endeavour. Climate change is among the issues that require both China and the USA to comply with global obligations, an understanding that would probably not survive wider conflict. There are, moreover, numerous regional or local, live or frozen conflicts – currently in Ukraine, Israel–Palestine and Lebanon, North and South Korea, Sudan, the Sahel, India and Pakistan and elsewhere – that could worsen if they were to become 'proxy' wars (like the Vietnam War). Much is at stake. So, what are the risks of the US–China relationship becoming much worse?

The main risk factor in the short run is the Trump administration. Trump has demonstrated from day one his belief in tariffs as a means of exerting pressure on allies and adversaries alike. While he has softened his earlier rhetoric on China, it seems sure that he will escalate tariffs on Chinese goods, though there is uncertainty over how much, on what products and for how long. Economic relations could deteriorate further, with a continuation and enlargement of more comprehensive technology competition and trade protection and a narrowing of the 'small yard, high fence' policy in relation to anything that can be construed as affecting economic security. Trump's administration includes ideologically driven 'China hawks' who wish to contain and confront China, and others like Elon Musk whose approach to

China is more pragmatic and commercially self-interested. Either could predominate. There is also uncertainty over how the Chinese will respond.

History is some guide. The political scientist Graham T. Allison has popularised the concept of the Thucydides Trap, which suggests, based on historical precedent, the near inevitability of conflict between a rising and a (relatively) declining superpower.[13] This framework of analysis is contentious, however, and the exceptions are arguably more instructive than the cases Allison cites to justify his thesis. They include the rise of postwar Germany within the constraints of the EU and the rise of the USA without (serious) conflict with Britain. Most important and relevant is the Cold War, where peace was maintained through mutually understood nuclear deterrence, supplemented by agreed 'guard rails' and lines of communication. In retrospect, the Cold War ended with a clear victory for the USA and its allies because the West had a superior economic and political model. But in the competition with China, the opposition is more formidable.

Pessimists point to one of those earlier examples of a 'trap' that did lead to war – the First World War – and see some ominous similarities.[14] A rapidly rising power, Germany, on the back of success in heavy industry, was overtaking the UK economically (as China has grown relative to the USA). Its greater economic strength gave it the capacity to build a formidable navy and to extend its reach into parts of the world assumed by the British to be part of their imperial sphere of influence (for which currently read the Chinese BRI and Chinese bases from the South China Sea to Djibouti). Anti-German narratives and propaganda grew in the UK and vice versa in Germany. Ideological differences were exaggerated. Insecurities arising from superpower competition led to destabilising alliances with fragile and unpredictable partners (Germany with Austria-Hungary, like China and Russia today). Little effort was put into creating diplomatic safety valves and 'trip wires', which meant that the two sides 'sleepwalked to war'.[15] It may be reassuring however that, while President Trump appears to relish the idea of tariff war, he seems to be genuinely averse to military conflict. His successors may not be.

The most plausible *casus belli* for a direct confrontation between the USA and China is Taiwan – if China were to seek reunification by force or Taiwan unilaterally declared independence: the two currently accepted red lines. There are deep political undercurrents on both sides. For the USA, Taiwan is a constant reminder of how America 'lost China' after the Second World War. Taiwan's emergence as a vibrant democracy and economic success story has won it many friends in the West. But these friends may not include President Trump, who has hinted that Taiwan does not deserve American protection and is one of those countries that have 'stolen America's lunch'. For its part, the Chinese leadership sees reunification as a fundamental policy objective. The CCP has always insisted that Taiwan must be returned to China and has set a deadline of a hundred years from the foundation of the People's Republic of China (PRC) (2047).

The political rhetoric is uncompromisingly hostile, but in practice there has been a lot of pragmatic accommodation, including a great deal of two-way travel, trade and foreign investment. There is also an agreed 'one country; two systems' formula which categorically excludes formal independence. The USA and all but a handful of countries have accepted the 'one China' formula, and Taiwan has virtually no international recognition. As for the current state of de facto independence, the USA has undertaken to protect Taiwan in the event of an attack but has done so in terms of 'strategic ambiguity'. US former National Security Advisor Jake Sullivan has described the maintenance of the peace as 'the greatest unclaimed success story in the history of US–China relations'.[16]

Several factors threaten to undermine this success story. One is the growth of a movement for independence in Taiwan, especially among young people. An estimated 60% of the population identify as Taiwanese, not Chinese, and the ruling party, the DPP, represents them. The collapse of the 'one country; two systems' model in Hong Kong does not encourage the Taiwanese to trust it. Second, there is a strong Taiwanese lobby in the USA, which may encourage what the Chinese regard as 'provocation'. A US president could well be tempted to cross red lines, especially if he or she judges that the Chinese are planning to do the same. President Trump seems disinclined to fight, but he is unpredictable and will not want to look weak in any confrontation. That element of uncertainty and instability is aggravated by periodic aggressive comments and deeds that suggest the Chinese are running out of patience. President Xi will want to resolve the matter before leaving office. At first sight, a frontal amphibious invasion and then occupation of Taiwan is a massive and improbable task for the Chinese armed forces, who have no relevant battle experience. The element of dangerous uncertainty lies in a wide range of possible 'grey' activities: a partial or total blockade of the sea and air routes to Taiwan, disruption of communications, harassment of offshore islands. It is far from clear how the USA would react to these, or what would constitute an impassable red line – hence the risk of a major war by accident and misunderstanding.

By 2050 the issue of Taiwan will have been resolved, peacefully or not. It should be clear much earlier whether the process of 'decoupling' from China has continued and, if so, in what form. There is evidence that, for over a decade, there has been some retreat from the highs of 'hyperglobalisation', in part due to reactions to the financial crisis of 2008.[17] Since then, Trump's tariffs and their continuation under Biden, Covid, the Ukraine War, protectionist industrial policy and a Trump Mark II focused on curbing Chinese exports have all added momentum to calls for decoupling. So far decoupling is more talked about than real, and global supply chains continue to link China to the rest of the world economy.[18] Some analysts describe deglobalisation as a 'dangerous myth'.[19] But there is clearly a political appetite for more decoupling, as evidenced by Trump's tariff proposals and growing protectionist sentiment towards Chinese exports in the EU and elsewhere. Chinese economic nationalism and the preoccupation with security are also discouraging engagement. The attempt by China and many emerging market economies, including India, to de-dollarise, while ineffective in the short run, also indicates an intention to prepare for a fragmented global economy. What form this takes is explored in the scenarios below.

Attempts to look into the future run into one obvious problem: the wholly unexpected. The further we try to look, the greater the uncertainties – the greater the possibility of 'left field' or 'black swan' events, or of fundamentally different technologies and political or economic trends developing.

Tales of the unexpected

A major premise of the book is that size matters in international economics and politics: hence the role of the 'superstate', a category of nation for which there are three obvious candidates discussed here. In the long term, however, one or more of these could fail. After all, this is what happened to the Soviet Union. In none of the three cases do centrifugal forces appear that strong, but that cannot be assumed, and the governments of China and India certainly take nothing for granted. Alternatively, there could be a new, unified force. There is one obvious candidate: the European Union. Those of us who are Europhiles and supporters of the European project might wish it so. It is possible that the EU could become an even bigger entity with enlargement to the east and/or the reabsorption of the UK. But for the EU to become a superstate would require a step change from a confederal to a federal organisation, which currently looks remote. An entity whose common budget is just 1% of its combined economic strength falls well short of any definition of a state. It would also require a strong upward move in the economic growth trajectory, which also appears unlikely at present.

It is also possible that looking at the world through the lens of nation states is simply rather retro, and that the future lies with transnational entities based on technology or ideology. In the 1980s and 1990s there was a belief that the internet would create a global communication medium independent of governments. The impact of the internet has been huge, but one of China's 'achievements' has been to control it and to create a separate Chinese internet. Today's leading technology platforms and media companies are global in reach and influence, but when powerful owners overreach themselves – from Jack Ma and Rupert Murdoch to Elon Musk – governments eventually move to reel them in. And while global belief systems have enormous transnational influence – from the Catholic Church to militant Islam to Communism – none are transcendent. Even the organisations that were established to provide global governance – the UN, the WTO, the IMF – struggle to justify their existence and continue largely on sufferance from the major powers.

If there is a major twist, it is likely to be because one or other of the three superstates fails to overcome its specific challenges: to escape the – lower or upper – middle-income trap, or to sustain efficient autocracy in the case of China or functioning democracy in India and the USA. Like Japan, seen a quarter of a century ago as a serious threat to US economic dominance, any one of them might subside into relative obscurity. And if the CCP or the elected leaders of India were to fail to deliver the promise of greater prosperity (and, in China's case, national reunification) by the middle of the century, there might well be a strong and messy domestic reaction. In the case of the USA, there is the question of how the country will react to seriously diminished relative power and prestige. The MAGA phenomenon does not suggest an acceptance of genteel decline. It may accelerate it.

One way of addressing these uncertainties is to look at alternative stories of the future, or possible scenarios. Scenario planning is a process of examining plausible and logical alternative narratives about the future built around different assumptions about variables which are both uncertain and important (I was a practitioner in the Shell scenario planning team in the 1990s).[20] The approach adopted here is necessarily crude but serves to bring out the challenge of considering different futures which may be unfashionable or uncomfortable. Figure 10.2 summarises the key elements in the scenario stories that I develop below.

Scenario 1: the Global West

The narrative recently favoured in much of the West and promoted by the G7 governments is that the world will increasingly polarise around different political systems: democracy versus autocracy. The Global West scenario is essentially one in which this dichotomy becomes the organising principle for international relations, not just in the political and military sphere but also governing economic integration. A key turning point was the Ukraine War,

Themes	Global West	Multipolar world	Multilateral world
Big picture	New cold war West-led coalition to contain China and its allies (ideological)	Fragmentation Superstates dominate and compete (transactional)	From disaster to cooperation (trust)
China	Peak China Low and declining growth	China outperforms US	Davos China
India	Joins Global West Liberalisation and rapid growth	New superstate Redistribution	India as the new China
USA	Hegemon	No hegemon Regional powers	Reformed postwar order
Europe	Junior partner to USA	Weakest of regional powers	Big player

10.2 Scenario summaries

271

which finally shredded any illusions about China's willingness or ability to work constructively with the West. It has helped to define an axis of hostile powers that have embraced autocratic forms of government and are disruptors of the 'liberal international order'. The core of the hostile axis consists of Russia, China and Iran, with various lesser allies or dependents North Korea, Belarus, Venezuela, Cuba, Zimbabwe among others.

In opposition to this axis is a coalition of countries which can be called the Global West. In this scenario the United States takes the lead in what is essentially an ideological approach to the world, bringing together like-minded democratic countries. This includes not just the traditional US allies in the 'developed' world but also democracies in the Global South, including Nigeria, Argentina, Indonesia, the Philippines, Mexico, Kenya and – crucially – India, together with many small states in the Caribbean and the Pacific. The definition of 'democracy' is far from settled, and some countries that might see themselves as part of this group are best described as 'semi-democratic': Turkey, also a NATO member; Singapore; and until the 2024 election, even India. In the Global West scenario, the return of Trump introduces a more transactional and less ideological view of allies and adversaries, but only to the extent that allies are expected to contribute more to their defence and balance their trade with the USA. There is also a more elastic view of common values. We see the re-emergence of the (old) Cold War doctrine attributed to Secretary of State John Dulles: 'It doesn't matter if he is a son of a bitch provided he is our son of a bitch.'

In this scenario, the Global West expands its reach as companies and governments, however reluctantly, are forced into making choices. Huawei cannot operate in the West and neither can companies like Shein and TikTok, whose identity is ambiguous. The German 'zeitenwende' – turning away from Russian energy supplies and the Chinese export market – could serve as a model for countries finding themselves under pressure to cut commercial and political links with China as well as Russia and Iran. Leadership comes from the USA, as successive administrations manage to find a common purpose in one of the few issues on which there is cross-party agreement: confronting the economic, technological and military threat from China and its unsavoury allies. They expect their European and Pacific allies to follow suit as part of a quid pro quo for military protection. There is also sustained 'decoupling' from China using discriminatory tariffs and other barriers, controls over foreign investment and restrictions on technology transfer. The USA can mobilise support for this mission using both its 'soft power' – as a democracy with a successful, innovative economy and with the backing of a global currency – and the 'hard power' of global military reach. There is the Biden 'soft cop' approach through alliance building or the Trump 'hard cop' routine of economic coercion. In the end they amount to the same thing. Allies and neutrals can be forced to choose by using the threat of tariffs or secondary sanctions. Early tests will include the threats to impose stronger sanctions on Iran to enforce controls on nuclear proliferation and to exert pressure on Russia to end the Ukraine War, should Russia prove to be the main stumbling block.

The divergence between the Global West and the China-led club of autocracies is not just confined to coalitions of the like-minded and economic decoupling. In this scenario the world splits, much as it did in the Cold War with the Soviet Union. There is a divergence in technical standards. Rules governing AI, data flows and the infrastructure of undersea cables, maritime and aviation transport operate under different regimes. There is also a continuing arms race based around different technological platforms. The aim of defence policy, as in the Cold War, is not just to contain and isolate the 'bad actors' but to use deterrence and diplomacy to prevent conflict. That balancing act is put under strain on the Chinese periphery. The deliberately ambiguous commitment to defend Taiwan must be made less ambiguous. Countries which hitherto preferred to hedge and to maintain good relations with China – like the Philippines – are driven, by territorial threats, to embrace a military alliance with the USA. Even old adversaries like Vietnam come to accept that, ideology apart, their interests are best served by defence arrangements with the Global West.

The crucial state is India, not least because of its growing weight in the world economy. The long, disputed border with China and continued Chinese occupation of, and claims on, territory regarded as Indian, represent a major security threat. This is especially so as China has a close economic and defence partnership with Pakistan, India's long-standing, nuclear-armed adversary. In these circumstances, the attractions of a close alignment with the Global West for security reasons, through the Quad (Japan, Australia, the USA and India), become overwhelming. Sentimental attachment to 'non-alignment' becomes secondary to security imperatives,

273

and increasingly close economic ties are formed through companies 'de-risking' from China. These top-down influences are supported by bottom-up pressures from the influential Indian diaspora in the West and the aspirations of the Indian middle class for Western lifestyles (and visas). Indeed, the closer links to the West help to open up markets to India's successful traded services sectors and supercharge India's already impressive growth.

Much of China's behaviour in the Xi era is based on the premise that the West is in terminal decline. In this scenario he is proved wrong. Rather, there is a vindication for those in the West who believe that democracy plus capitalism must be stronger and more durable than an authoritarian system with a state-led economy. China, they maintain, will fail, and they see evidence in the form of China's property crisis and economic slowdown. China's economy is much stronger and more sophisticated than that of the former USSR and is unlikely to collapse. But the country has reached its peak. Economic failure means that the regime faces a frustrated and disillusioned middle class who feel that the regime is not delivering on its 'social contact'. More and more resources must be devoted to internal security to ensure the survival of the CCP. China's relative economic failures also mean that it can no longer afford expensive overseas investment programmes like the BRI, which will disappoint erstwhile allies in Africa, Latin America and the rest of the Global South. The burden of carrying Russia, a failed petro-state, badly damaged by war, and other failed states like Venezuela and Pakistan, becomes insupportable. Recognising reality, the Chinese leadership is forced by circumstances to seek accommodation and settle for a more circumscribed role. The new Cold War peters out. The End of History happens again.

The numerical simulations summarised in Figure 10.3 represent, in a somewhat caricatured form, what could happen in a business environment that is highly supportive of growth in India and highly unfavourable to China. The power of compound interest rates is such that by mid-century India could have overtaken both the USA and China in terms of the size of its economy (at least in PPP terms): Figure 10.4. However wildly improbable this might seem today, the consequences of Chinese growth seemed equally improbable a quarter of a century ago. Moreover, there is a certain internal logic to a world in which a highly successful India reinforces the narrative of the democratic 'West' prevailing over Communist China, albeit to the

		USA	India	China
Base year GDP,	PPP	30.3	17.4	39.4
2025 est. ($ trillion)	Market	30.3	4.3	19.5
OECD scenario	2025–30	1.6	5.9	3.7
(% growth)	2030–40	1.45	4.3	2.5
	2040–50	1.35	2.9	1.5
Global West	2025–30	1.8	8.0	2.0
	2030–40	1.6	7.0	1.5
	2040–50	1.5	6.0	1.0
Multipolar world	2025–30	1.6	5.0	3.5
	2030–40	1.0	4.0	3.0
	2040–50	0.5	2.5	2.5
Multilateral world	2025–30	1.0	5.0	3.0
	2030–40	1.5	8.0	4.0
	2040–50	2.0	8.0	3.5

Sources: IMF Economic Outlook April 2024; OECD long-term forecast (central forecast) www.oecd.org > economicprojections and > OECD> Data> Indicators

10.3 Scenario growth assumptions

	China	India	USA
Base year (2025)	130	57	100
OECD 2050	151	98	100
Global West	113	182	100
Multipolar	203	100	100
Multilateral	195	193	100

10.4 Summary of 2050 projections (GDP–PPP as a ratio of USA)

benefit of the leading democratic emerging market economy rather than the West as traditionally understood.

This scenario, in one form or another, is a popular one in the West. It describes not only what elite opinion thinks ought to happen but what it believes will happen. It does however stretch plausibility on several counts. First, it assumes that the coalition-building approach of the Biden administration can somehow be married with Trump's bluster and bullying to keep the Global West united. But the MAGA movement of Trump (and like-minded successors) has a different view of the world: more inward-looking and protectionist, less committed to democratic processes at home let alone abroad, more 'realistic' in foreign policy, recognising that the

275

USA no longer dominates the global economy and cannot afford to be the world's policeman. Make America Great Again and variants such as forms of Christian nationalism are not readily exportable ideas. It has been a major struggle even to sustain domestic support for Ukraine. And in relation to the key relationship with the world's biggest democracy, there has been a certain rapport between Trump and Modi but it seems improbable that such amity could be sustained for a generation with India increasingly calling the shots.

Second, the strength of the Global West depends not just on the USA but on its main allies. The other major pillar of the Global West is the EU, which faces severe internal challenges from nationalist movements and has a weakening commitment to common projects. Slow economic growth does not permit a big expansion of defence commitments alongside the maintenance of a welfare state for an ageing population. Within the loosely structured decision making of Europe there are also disagreements as to the desirability of disengagement from China and/or Russia. If one of the main pillars of the Global West is wobbly, the whole edifice becomes insecure.

Furthermore, neither the USA nor the EU has much to offer the Global South to bring wavering countries on board, especially those countries currently hedging their bets in the BRICS grouping. Fiscal problems, like the dangerously large US debt, mean that there is little scope for aid to help with the massive, continuing problems of poverty in the Global South and climate finance. Failure to deliver on Covid vaccines was a warning signal. And, with the priority given to security and to excluding adversaries through primary and secondary sanctions, there is little appetite – especially in the USA – for free trade agreements, multilaterally or regionally. Also, one of the West's main domestic political concerns is how to keep out dark-skinned migrants from the Global South, which can be regarded as offensive by the countries affected – as with President Trump's attacks on Mexicans. The ideal of a rules-based and open 'liberal international order', underwritten by the USA, is no longer on offer.

With the Global West organised to confront and contain China and its allies, it is also far from clear how it would be possible to make progress in areas where their active cooperation is required. This is especially true of global environmental issues, as with climate change. For countries being 'contained', regime survival comes first. That would inevitably lead to the prioritisation of national security concerns. In the energy sector that would mean more coal being burned as a 'safe' indigenous resource. It is difficult to see how a Global West scenario built around the 'containment' of China and its allies would ever secure active cooperation on global issues from its lead adversary.

Then, as we have seen from failed efforts to get the main countries of the Global South to sign up for the West's position on Ukraine, there is strong resistance to being co-opted into a Global West agenda. That is even more true in the light of the West's backing for Israel, especially after the Gaza war, seen in the Islamic world and beyond as a serious case of double standards. Attempts to use the threat of sanctions to get countries into line would also have the counterproductive effect of accelerating the push to de-dollarisation. The refusal of the West to surrender its dominant role in international financial institutions is another continuing source of grievance. And, in the case of India, there remains a commitment to multi-alignment, which is given concrete expression in the determination to retain strong ties with Russia. Other democracies such as Brazil and South Africa see themselves, for ideological or historical or national interest reasons, as committed members of the Global South.

It is also far from clear that China (and its fellow 'bad actors') will fail economically. Western critics consistently underestimate the resilience of China's economy, the scale and creativity of its science and innovation, its pragmatic use of markets and the competitiveness of state-backed business. It will take far bigger economic setbacks than the post-Covid slowdown and the property crash to dislodge China from its position as the world's largest manufacturing economy and trade partner to far more countries than the USA. The countries of East and Southeast Asia will continue to see China as their major economic partner, and the oil exporters of the Middle East know that China (with India) is their main market. Even the more fragile, energy-based Russian economy has shown itself to be remarkably resilient in the face of sanctions and war losses.

Attempts to recreate the Cold War in a new form are therefore unlikely to succeed. End of History II is a fantasy. The reality is a much more fragmented, multipolar world. I try to capture this world in Scenario 2.

277

Scenario 2: a multipolar world

It is not too difficult to imagine a future in which the USA no longer wants, or is willing, to be the world's policeman – the hegemon. Nor is any other country. Arguably that point has now been reached. China, but also India and 'middle powers' like Saudi Arabia, Brazil and Indonesia – and, of course, Russia – have agency to act independently based on economic size or resource wealth or military potential.

The main significance of Trump's return is that it represents an honest reappraisal of America's role based on hard-headed realism in external relations: steering clear of unnecessary military entanglements and alliances; concentrating on America's economic interests, pursued through greater self-sufficiency and tough mercantilist trade policies; being sceptical of globalisation and global institutions; Making America Great Again through economic competition and deal making. As voters have shown, there is a short-term appeal for the USA in this world, given the size of America's home market, the strength of its entrepreneurial and innovative economy and its energy self-sufficiency. But in the longer term the underlying trend is towards relative US decline and the continued inexorable – relative – rise of China, India and the 'middle powers'. The simulations in Figures 10.3 and 10.4 capture a world in which by mid-century China has far outgrown the USA and India has caught up in terms of size (in PPP terms).

The rhetoric on military matters may be belligerent, and the USA will continue to need the deterrent power of military superiority – or at least parity. But in this scenario, there is little interest in picking a fight with China and Russia, provided they respect core US interests. China is, in fact, mainly an adversary to the extent that it operates an 'unfair' and 'aggressive' trade policy which it can adapt by switching to domestic sources of demand. In this hard-headed, zero-sum world, ideology is not an issue. 'Realism' also dictates that Russia is not necessarily an adversary at all but has common interests, including support for hydrocarbon industries and avoiding undue dependence on China.

In this scenario, much of the world suffers economic damage from the spread of protectionist measures, capricious economic policy largely geared to the domestic priorities of the USA, and a lack of clear and consistent economic rules. There is a strong advantage in being big enough to be reasonably self-reliant and to be able to exercise leverage. The EU is hit by the impact of a more protectionist world on Germany, but it can fall back on its single market and customs union, and its network of special preferential trade agreements. Other well-organised regional groupings, as with the ASEAN countries in Southeast Asia, or perhaps the Chinese-led RCEP or the Asia-Pacific CGTPPT, are energised. But small states are seriously exposed, as are open, medium-sized economies like the UK.

This situation suits the two Asian superstates reasonably well. The dream of a multipolar world built around national sovereignty is being made real. Although President Xi has sketched out a bigger vision around his Global Development, Global Security and Global Civilisation initiatives, actions speak louder than words and China's behaviour under his leadership is nationalistic and preoccupied with security and domestic stability. China can adjust to a more self-sufficient, inward-looking environment and is already preparing for this. It must pivot towards growth based on domestic consumption, but it has a vast home market, which soon becomes unambiguously the world's biggest, and its economic reach is supported by a network of preferential trading relationships in the Global South. Competition with the USA is tough, but China's science and innovation complex can keep pace and already is doing so in green transition technologies particularly. In this scenario, China seeks a dominant position in its neighbourhood, but in a multipolar world the aim is coexistence and respect for spheres of influence.

For India, too, a protectionist world is no stranger. There is a cost, but the country can absorb it, as it did during the global financial crisis. In any event, India's services exports are not much affected by tariffs. The Indian economy is sufficiently large and diverse to absorb external shocks and, while growth is a little slower, the government can concentrate on a better balanced form of development: emphasising poverty reduction and employment. India's economy is big and strong enough to dominate the subregion. Economic dominance translates into military and political dominance, and India is unquestionably the hegemonic power in its subregion. But the lack of trust in relations with China, originating in the disputed border, means that a multipolar world is also fraught with suspicion, latent conflict and an arms race. Another key objective is to build a network of relationships in the Middle East and with Russia and the USA to secure imported energy supplies as oil and gas are crucial transitional fuels. Demanding reform of the global system, however, becomes pointless since the USA is no longer interested in running global bodies like the WTO, the IMF and World Bank. And since economic sanctions are no longer being used for geopolitical purposes, there is less urgency to de-dollarise – though, as part of a fragmenting system, India is able to have its currency used for a growing amount of business.

This is a transactional world where old sentimental alliances no longer count for a great deal. The Ukraine War ends with a US-mediated peace agreement that leaves Russian territorial gains largely intact but ensures that postwar reconstruction prioritises US, rather than Chinese, companies. Once the Chinese leadership has been persuaded that the US has no interest in trying to displace the CCP, it can settle into the role of regional hegemon. It is careful not to threaten the security interests of the USA, to meddle in Latin America or to provoke unnecessary conflict in East and Southeast Asia. In return, its neighbours, from Japan to Australia, accept a modern version of 'tribute' status. Taiwan is supported by the USA for as long as its advanced chips are essential for the US economy but is then quietly abandoned to negotiate a degree of nominal independence within the PRC.

In a multipolar world, global problems – the trading system, climate, rules around data and AI, weapons proliferation, humanitarian crises – depend for resolution on 'consensus' within the UN system. And this is rarely reached since there is no global leadership and there are too many interests to reconcile. China, India and the EU have their own self-interested reasons for wanting to stop climate change and are willing to take some action to abate GHG emissions. But energy-rich USA, Russia and the Gulf states prioritise their interests as energy producers, and they can successfully resist collective action.

Just as the Global West is the fantasy of G7 summits, a multipolar world is the fantasy of BRICS summits. And there is a contradiction at the heart of it. Because the common denominator of the proponents of a multipolar world is the protection of their national sovereignty, they find it impossible to cooperate over much. The problem of the global commons is a basic challenge in this scenario. If there is no meaningful action on climate change (for example) there will be, within the next few decades, dangerous tipping points. We are already seeing extreme climatic events affecting individual countries, including China, India and the USA, but so far they have not been enough to create a strong consensus for common action. Also, there is little inclination to work together on shared problems like preserving ocean fisheries or the fragile ecosystem of Antarctica. Self-interested competition also produces many points of friction and potential conflict.

That conflict poses another global threat that is potentially graver than climate change: nuclear proliferation. Iran is one step away from acquiring a weapon and could become a breakout country if the current set of concerted international pressures weaken. That in turn could lead to Saudi Arabia feeling the need for its own nuclear capability. In Asia, Japan and South Korea might feel sufficiently exposed by US loss of interest in the region that they also feel the need for a nuclear deterrent. And so on and on.

What makes nuclear proliferation particularly dangerous is that a multipolar world can incubate lethal conflict at a regional level. Northeast Asia has the unexploded bomb that is the ruling family of nuclear-armed North Korea. It is restrained, if at all, by China, and is a threat to both South Korea and Japan. At some point, the unstable chemistry of the region might create an explosion, and the process of disengagement by the USA could be a trigger. Another highly dangerous set of relationships is in the Persian Gulf, where there is an unstable set of interactions between Iran and its rivals. With the USA self-sufficient in energy, it has every incentive to leave these problems to someone else. And potentially most dangerous of all is the China–India border. Even if the USA and China avoid the Thucydides Trap, China and India may not. Any of these regional fault lines could trigger disaster – which leads to the third scenario.

Scenario 3: from disaster to multilateralism

In the first two scenarios, multilateral cooperation does not loom large. Either the world is split into blocs with competing and adversarial systems (Global West), or we have a fragmented multipolar world. At present we can see many signs of a weakening order. The WTO is no longer functioning. The IMF and the World Bank are struggling to find a role, with inadequate resources and a governance structure which richer members refuse to reform. The UN provides an umbrella under which countries, large and small, can sit, but its power to act is tightly constrained by the veto powers and its treaties and conventions are widely disregarded. The Law of the Sea,

281

for example, has been undermined by one superpower refusing to sign it and another refusing to accept its legal rulings. To take another example, the International Criminal Court represents an attempt to establish humanitarian standards at times of military conflict. But the major powers, including China and the USA, do not accept that it applies to them. Global governance is weak and seemingly weakening. This raises the issue of how common problems can be addressed: the Kindleberger Trap.

In today's world there is no obvious escape from this trap. To suggest that governments should live by the UN Charter and its universal system of law would be considered extremely naive. But either of the two scenarios outlined above could well lead to global disaster. So I suggest a third scenario, in which the levels of cooperation necessary to deal with major global challenges are reached, however implausible it may seem now. The mechanism by which this happens is learning through experience of disaster. As described above, it is not difficult to conceive of a disaster on a sufficient scale to shake the major powers out of narrow and short-term calculations. The current cold war between China and the USA could spiral out of control in the form of economic or military conflict. Various regional rifts have a similar potential for escalation and conflict. The consequences could include a major economic depression, a sequence of devastating climate events, the use of nuclear weapons in one of several conflicts or an inability to cooperate over a pandemic more deadly than the last.

It is easy to sketch out many actual and potential disasters in a world of fragmenting authority, conflict and weak rules. It is more difficult to see how a cooperative approach to shared problems could become the norm. The Second World War led to such a paradigm change, thanks to American leadership and a reconciliation within Western Europe. It may require a major disaster – if not necessarily on the scale of a world war – to establish a new system of rules and international order.

In reality, an assembly of more than two hundred countries is unlikely to reach common ground quickly. The G20 is the most representative global body we currently have. But what is required in the first instance is for a smaller group to act as a catalyst and to set the broad framework of agreement: the USA, China, India (and perhaps the EU, if it can speak with one voice.) For that to happen, the USA must accept that it is no longer the hegemonic power, but one of several; China must accept that it has obligations as well as opportunities; India must realise that it also has obligations as a major economic power (and the EU must become a more meaningful political entity if it is to count).

Not every global problem can be solved, let alone all at once, but there are several priorities. The first is to ensure that the mechanisms of economic cooperation and coordination are adapted to the new reality: that the world's centre of economic gravity has moved to what used to be regarded as the poor world, particularly in Asia. The prospect of sustained poverty reduction and economic stability is the common ground. But authority must be restored to the main multilateral institutions and rule-setting bodies. It then becomes possible to envisage a new and improved stage of globalisation.

The WTO is a key body, and there are many technical papers suggesting how its rules can be adapted to a world dominated by 'state capitalist' economies like China, India and other emerging economies. It will also be necessary for rules to reflect the reality that data is now the main traded commodity.[21] The current international financial institutions are not lacking in technical excellence or economic understanding, but do lack legitimacy. The governance reforms required to improve legitimacy are already well understood. The big technical challenge will be to maintain stability in a multi-currency world, or even to adopt a new global currency, which Keynes and others anticipated decades ago.

One crucial challenge is climate change. Fortunately, there are structures in place, through the UN COP (Conference of the Parties). There is an understanding, based on sound science, of what must be done and the timescales for doing it, and there are some encouraging models for successful implementation, such as the Montreal Protocol. But success requires the commitment of the big future emitters, notably China and India, with the rapid phasing out of coal. And that is unlikely to happen in a cold war environment where the priority is national security, or in a world of mercantilist, beggar-my-neighbour economic policy. But where there is confidence that a system of rules will hold, braver policies are possible.

The deadliest threat is from nuclear proliferation. The former Cold War was – just about – contained by active and intelligent bilateral detente between the two superpowers. The position now is more complex and multidimensional, and cannot be managed without multilateral cooperation. There is a multilateral framework of inspection and monitoring in place,

283

but to function it requires the active cooperation of the future 'big three': the USA, China and India. The USA has a degree of restraining influence on some 'breakout' countries (Japan, South Korea, Saudi Arabia) and its NATO allies. China has leverage over Iran, North Korea, Pakistan and possibly Russia. India is on the nuclear front line, facing China and Pakistan. The nuclear genie cannot now be put back in the bottle, but active, genuine multilateral cooperation can head off the worst outcomes.

Those possibilities by no means exhaust the list of lethal common problems. There is also the danger of AI development spinning out of control without strict shared protocols. And Covid is sufficiently recent to remind us of the risks around pandemics. To achieve a more cooperative outcome requires some degree of convergence in values, which seems improbable in a world of competitive nationalism and cynicism about human rights. But the UN treaties contain a comprehensive body of rights and obligations that governments have (mostly) signed up to. As late as 2005, even China actively supported intervention to counter genocide and war crimes and, with India, has continued to play a role in international peacekeeping.[22] There are grounds for optimism, albeit slender. But what is the alternative?

Conclusion: a world with three superstates

The scenarios sketched out above are caricatures. Many others are possible, and we are likely to see elements of all three. There is already an attempt to frame US relations with China as a mixture of containment, competition and cooperation. But such subtlety requires implausible levels of political sophistication. One or other scenario will soon emerge as the dominant trend.

I have sought to add some hypothetical numbers to illustrate the qualitative stories. Figure 10.3 summarises the assumptions behind the numerical simulations. Figure 10.4 summarises the results, which are also shown in graphical form in Figure 10.1. A major problem in making alternative projections is deciding what assumptions to make about the base year. As discussed in the Introduction, there are large disparities between GNP calculated on a PPP or market prices basis. This particularly affects India, which is over three times 'bigger' if we correct for greatly different price levels between India and the USA. The speed at which different price levels converge through exchange rate movements and relative inflation rates is as important in extrapolating long-term GNP numbers as real economic growth. I use PPP numbers here, as is common in the work of the IMF and World Bank. But I recognise that some will feel that this means the importance of India and China is overstated. For this reason, the results of the projections should not be taken too seriously, though the broad picture is of some interest.

If we accept that the PPP measure of economic activity is a 'true' measure of the baseline, China is already 'bigger' than the USA, and the differential widens in all but one of the scenarios. More strikingly, India catches up with the USA in terms of economic size, and on plausible growth rate assumptions has an economy in 2050 of at least the same size as the USA and, on some not very extreme assumptions, twice the size. On the most favourable set of assumptions for India relative to China, India has an economy over 60% bigger than China, and on another scenario they are the same size. That is an outcome that is plausible if China does not escape from its current malaise and if India maintains the strong but not extreme tempo of the last two decades. In China the idea that it might be overtaken by India will be regarded with incredulity, but it is perfectly conceivable.

On any plausible assumptions, by mid-century we will have two Asian economies that are as big as or substantially bigger than the USA in economic terms. Because of the importance of economic size in defining output and demand and the capacity of states to arm and exercise influence, the days of US hegemony are well and truly over, though market exchange rates could be used to argue that the process would be longer and less certain. (The recent appreciation in the value of US stocks and in the value of the dollar against other currencies, which is almost certainly a 'bubble' phenomenon, has persuaded some that relative US decline has been stopped and perhaps reversed, though data on relative real economic growth gives little support for this.) The Asian superstates nonetheless remain relatively poor. The UN population forecasts to 2050 envisage an increase in the Indian population of around 17%, in the USA an increase of 11% and a decline in China by 8%. On the most favourable set of assumptions China gets to around 60% of American per capita incomes in PPP terms and India to 40%.

The broad story that emerges is that we are heading to a world where there will be three economic superpowers: the USA, China and India. With economic power will go political influence, military capability and environmental responsibility. I have tried to sketch out how these factors could play out, recognising the vast uncertainties. It is possible that one or more of the three may experience major convulsions (as did the USSR). It is also possible that there could be major new forces at work – if the EU gets its act together or if Africa develops economic and political structures to channel its potential – though neither looks likely.

The most profound change is the virtual inevitability that, within a generation, the main states of the West will have to coexist as dominant economic and political powers in the world with new superstates. For Westerners, this world is bound to be uncomfortable and threatening. After all, what we call 'Western civilisation' has been dominant for centuries, and the Anglo-Saxon variant for at least two hundred years. That world is ending.

The most challenging of the three scenarios, and the one to which least attention is currently being paid, is the third. At the heart of it is the idea of the Kindleberger Trap: that with a disappearing or diminished hegemonic power there comes a neglect of international public goods. The most important of these are global economic rules and institutions; environmental protection, notably on climate; peacekeeping and control over nuclear proliferation. The Global West story is, in effect, a new cold war with military security and ideological difference at its core, leading to a split in the global economy and in responsibility for global systems. A multipolar world with assertive superstates and a crop of middle-sized aspiring powers is transactional and inward-looking, and global public goods are neglected. There is no obvious way forward. That is why my scenario assumes global disaster of some kind to trigger a more cooperative approach.

Multilateralism does not require heroic idealism. It does require enlightened realism. The institutional and policy responses do not entail the reinvention of the wheel. There are endless tracts setting out the reforms needed in the UN, the Bretton Woods institutions, the WTO and other institutions of global governance, to provide an overarching set of rules and principles that better reflect the growing importance of the Global South and the existence of new superstates. Far from beginning with a blank sheet of paper, there is already a dense network of global and regional crossnational cooperation to build on: business supply chains and services, industrial, financial and data-based standard setting, transnational charitable and non-government organisations, scientific and academic collaboration, sporting activities and more. Much of what we call globalisation is non-governmental and success-fully self-regulating. But there are some basic tasks for which cooperating national governments are essential. The glue that is needed is the capacity and will to enforce agreed international rules and standards. That was dif-ficult enough with one hegemonic power. In future there will probably be three.

Figures

Abbreviations

AIIB	Asia Infrastructure Investment Bank
API	application programming interface
BJP	Bharatiya Janata Party
BPO	business process outsourcing
BRI	Belt and Road Initiative
BRICS	Intergovernmental organisation consisting of ten countries: Brazil, Russia, India, China, South Africa, Egypt, Ethiopia, Indonesia, Iran and the United Arab Emirates
CAT	Climate Action Tracker
CCP	Chinese Communist Party
CIDCA	China International Development Cooperation Agency
CMIE	Centre for Monitoring Indian Economy
COP	Conference of the Parties – the supreme governing body of an international convention
CPEC	China–Pakistan Economic Corridor
DAC	Development Advisory Committee (OECD)
EEZ	exclusive economic zone
EV	electric vehicle
FDI	foreign direct investment
FOCAC	Forum on China–Africa Cooperation
G7	Group of Seven – an intergovernmental political and economic forum consisting of Canada, France, Germany, Italy, Japan, the United Kingdom and the United States

G20	Group of Twenty – an intergovernmental forum comprising nineteen sovereign countries, the European Union and the African Union
G77	Group of 77
GATT	General Agreement on Tariffs and Trade
GDP	gross domestic product
GHG	greenhouse gas
GNP	gross national product
GST	goods and services tax
IDA	International Development Association
IEA	International Energy Agency
IMF	International Monetary Fund
IOR-ARC	Indian Ocean Rim Association for Regional Cooperation
IP	intellectual property
IPCC	Intergovernmental Panel on Climate Change
LAC	Line of Actual Control (India–China)
LGFV	local government financing vehicle
LSE	London School of Economics
MAGA	Make America Great Again
MES	market economy status
MFN	most-favoured-nation
MOSIP	modular open-source identity platform
NAM	Non-Aligned Movement
OBCs	other backward castes
OCA	optimum currency area
ODI	Overseas Development Institute
OECD	Organisation for Economic Co-operation and Development
OPEC	Organization of the Petroleum Exporting Countries
PPP	purchasing power parity
PRC	People's Republic of China
Quad	Quadrilateral Security Dialogue – a strategic security dialogue between Australia, India, Japan and the United States
RBI	Reserve Bank of India
RBIO	rules-based international order
RCEP	Regional Comprehensive Economic Partnership
RSS	Rashtriya Swayamsevak Sangh

SAARC   South Asian Association for Regional Cooperation
SASAC   State-owned Assets Supervision and Administration
           Commission of the State Council
SBI   State Bank of India
SCO   Shanghai Cooperation Organisation
SEZ   special economic zone
SMEs   small and medium-sized enterprises
SOE   state-owned enterprise
TFP   total factor productivity
TPP   Trans-Pacific Partnership
TSMC   Taiwan Semiconductor Manufacturing Company
TVEs   Township and Village Enterprises
UNCTAD   United Nations Trade and Development organisation
VPN   virtual private network
WIPO   World Intellectual Property Organization
WTO   World Trade Organization

Notes

Prologue

1 'Chinese President Xi Jinping's India Visit: After Six Decades, a Chinese Leader gets Public Welcome', *Times of India*, 18 September 2014.
2 'Xi Visits Modi's Home State, Extends Birthday Wishes', *China Daily*, 18 September 2014.
3 'China's Xi Jinping Signs Landmark Deals on India Visit', *BBC News*, 18 September 2014.
4 'PM Modi's Meetings with China's Xi Jinping: A Timeline', *Times of India*, 8 June 2018.
5 'Indian Protesters Burn Effigies of President Xi after China Border Clash', *Guardian*, 17 June 2020.

Introduction: the new superstates

1 Anthony Giddens, *Runaway World: How Globalisation is Reshaping Our Lives* (New York: Routledge, 2003); Vincent Cable, *Globalisation and Global Governance* (London: Royal Institute of International Affairs, 1999).
2 Kenichi Ohmae, *The End of the Nation State* (New York: Free Press, 1995).
3 Parag Khanna, *The Future is Asian: Global Order in the Twenty-First Century* (London: Weidenfeld and Nicholson, 2019).
4 Fred Bergsten, *The United States and China: The Quest for Global Economic Leadership* (Cambridge, MA and Cambridge, UK: Polity Press, 2022).
5 Nicholas Kitchen (ed.), *India: The Next Superpower*, LSE IDEAS Special Report (London: LSE, 2012); Martin Wolf, 'Why India Will Become a Superpower', *Financial Times*, 9 July 2024.
6 Alasdair Roberts, *Superstates: Empires of the Twenty-First Century* (Cambridge: Polity Press, 2022).
7 Graham Allison, *Destined for War: Can America and China Escape the Thycidides's Trap* (London and Melbourne: Scribe, 2017).

8 Biden press conference quote from 25 March 2021; Xi in Ian Easton, *The Final Struggle: Inside China's Global Strategy* (Manchester: Eastbridge Books, 2022); Matt Pottinger, Matthew Johnson and David Feith, 'Xi Jinping in His Own Words', *Foreign Affairs*, 30 November 2022.

9 Robert Harris and Jenny Harris, *War by Other Means: Geoeconomics and Statecraft* (Cambridge, MA: Harvard University Press, 2016).

10 Joseph Nye, 'The Kindleberger Trap', Project Syndicate, 9 January 2017, www.project-syndicate.org/commentary/trump-china-kindleberger-trap-by-joseph-s--nye-2017-01 (accessed 17 March 2025); Charles Kindleberger, *The World in Depression 1929–1939* (Los Angeles: University of California Press, 1973).

11 Sam Olsen, 'China, America and the Kindleberger Trap', *Critic*, 9 November 2020.

12 Michael Beckley, *Unrivaled: Why America Will Remain the World's Sole Superpower* (Ithaca, NY: Cornell University Press, 2018), chapter 3; and Bergsten, *The United States and China*, chapter 3.

13 George Magnus, *Red Flags: Why Xi's China is in Jeopardy* (New Haven, CT: Yale University Press, 2018), pp. 208–9.

14 Chris Giles, 'Sorry America, China has a Bigger Economy than You', *Financial Times*, 6 December 2023; also Tim Callen, 'PPP Versus the Market: Which Weight Matters?', *IMF Finance and Development Magazine*, 44:1 (2007), pp. 50–1.

Chapter 1

1 Sarwar Lateef, *China and India: Economic Performance and Prospects*, IDS Discussion Paper 118 (1976); Vincent Cable, *China and India: Economic Reform and Global Integration* (London: Royal Institute of International Affairs, 1995).

2 Jawaharlal Nehru, *The Discovery of India* (Calcutta: Signal Press, 1946).

3 Angus Maddison, *Monitoring the World Economy, 1820–1992* (Paris: OECD Paris, 1995), p. 24.

4 Adam Smith, *An Inquiry into the Nature and Causes of the Wealth of Nations*, ed. Edwin Cannon (Chicago, IL: Chicago University Press, 1977), p. 70.

5 There is an extended discussion of the 'plunderers' of India on pp. 747–52, Volume 2 of the original text edited by R. H. Campbell and A. S. Skinner, published by Liberty Fund, Indianapolis in 1981.

6 Prasannan Parthasarathi, *When Europe Grew Rich and Asia Did Not: Global Economic Divergence 1600–1850* (Cambridge: Cambridge University Press, 2011).

7 Maddison, *Monitoring the World Economy*, table A-3e describes a fall in population of 64 million between 1850 and 1870, the years of the Taiping Rebellion.

8 S. Sivasubramonian, *The National Income of India in the Twentieth Century* (New Delhi: OUP India, 2000).

9 Angus Deaton, *The Great Escape: Health, Wealth and the Origins of Inequality* (Princeton, NJ: Princeton University Press, 2014).

10 B. Chandra, 'The Colonial Legacy', in Bimal Jalan (ed.), *The Indian Economy: Problem and Prospects* (Delhi: Viking/Penguin, 1992), pp. 1–33.

11 Estimates by D. W. Perkins (medium growth estimate for 1913–52), Yeh (low) and
    Ravski (high) in Maddison, Monitoring the World Economy, p. 145.
12 Jung Chang and Jon Halliday, *Mao: The Unknown Story* (London: Jonathan Cape,
    2005), pp. 496–7.
13 Lateef, *China and India.*
14 Zuhiu Hu and Mohsin Khan, 'Why is China Growing so Fast?', *IMF Economic Issues*,
    8 (1997), pp. 103–31.
15 C. H. Hanumantha Rao, 'Agriculture: Policy and Performance', in Jalan (ed.), *The
    Indian Economy*, pp. 116–41.
16 'Modi has driven growth and helped poor but record on jobs is wanting', *Financial
    Times*, 10 January 2024.
17 Arvind Subramanian, '"We are not a big market": Former CEA Arvind Subramanian
    calls domestic base peg a "fatal" error', *Business Today India*, 15 March 2024.
18 Hu and Khan, 'Why is China Growing so Fast?'
19 Eswar Prasad, 'China Stumbles but Unlikely to Fall', *IMF Finance and Development
    Magazine*, December 2023, pp. 54–8.
20 Arvind Virmani, *Sources of Indian Growth; Trends in Total Factor Productivity*, ICRIER
    Working Paper no. 131 (2004); B. Bosworth and S. Collins, 'India's Growth
    Slowdown: End of an Era?', *India Review*, 14:1 (2015), pp. 8–25.
21 Dani Rodrik and Arvind Subramanian, *From 'Hindu Growth' to Productivity Surge: The
    Mystery of India's Growth Transition*, NBER Working Paper 103:76 (2004).
22 Surjit Bhalla and Karan Bhasin, 'India–China: Reversal of Fortunes?', Brookings
    Institution paper, September 2023, www.brookings.edu/articles/india-china-rever
    sal-of-fortunes/ (accessed 1 April 2025).
23 International Labour Organization, *India Employment Report 2024: Youth Employment,
    Education and Skills* (New Delhi: ILO, 2024).
24 Ashoka Mody, *India is Broken: A People Betrayed, Independence to Today* (Stanford, CA:
    Stanford University Press, 2023).
25 Richard Baldwin, 'India vs China: Trade's Role in their Industrialisation', IMD
    Business School (15 March 2024), www.linkedin.com/pulse/india-vs-china-trades-
    role-industrialisation-richard-baldwin-q2xmf (accessed 11 March 2025).
26 WTO data as in Mody, *India is Broken*, p. 10.
27 World Population Review, 2024, https://worldpopulationreview.com/ (accessed
    11 March 2025), based on manufacturing production data from UN Statistics
    Division.
28 Share of manufacturing in GDP from World Bank Open Data.
29 Loren Brandt and Thomas Rawski, *China's Great Economic Transformation* (Cambridge:
    Cambridge University Press, 2018); China Development Foundation (ed.), *Chinese
    Economists on Economic Reform* (Abingdon: Routledge, 2018).
30 Bank of International Settlements data in *Financial Times*, 7 August 2023.
31 Richard Baldwin, *The Great Convergence: IT and the New Globalisation* (Cambridge, MA:
    Harvard University Press, 2006).
32 Dan Wang, 'China's Hidden Tech Revolution', *Foreign Affairs*, 28 February 2023.
33 Vijay Joshi, *India's Long Road: The Search for Prosperity* (New York: Oxford University
    Press, 2017), p. 71, based on Asian Development Bank data.

34 V. Cable, L. C. Jain and Ann Weston, *The Commerce of Culture: Experience of Indian Handicrafts* (Delhi: Lancer International, 1986).

35 Yasheng Huang, 'Human Capital Development: The Reason Behind China's Growth', *Economic Times*, December 2009, discussed in Raghuram Rajan and Rohit Lamba, *Breaking the Mould: Reimagining India's Economic Future* (Delhi: Penguin Random House, 2024), p. 14.

36 Scott Rozelle and Natalie Hell, *Invisible China: How the Urban–Rural Divide Threatens China's Rise* (Chicago, IL: Chicago University Press, 2020).

37 'ASER Survey', *Economist*, 1 July 2023.

38 Maria Ana Lugo, Martin Raiser and Ruslan Yemtsov, 'What's Next for Poverty Reduction Policies in China?', Brookings Institution, 24 September 2021, www.brookings.edu/articles/whats-next-for-poverty-reduction-policies-in-china/ (accessed 11 March 2025).; 'Extreme Poverty is History in China, Officials Say', *Economist*, 2 January 2021.

39 Himanshu, Peter Lanjouw and Nicholas Stern, *How Lives Change: Palanpur, India and Development Economics* (Oxford: Oxford University Press, 2018).

40 Surjit Bhalla and Karan Bhasin, 'Poverty in India Over the Last Decade', *Economic and Political Weekly*, 59:28 (2024).

41 'Global Multidimensional Poverty Index (MPI): 2020 revision', Oxford Poverty and Human Development Initiative, Oxford University.

42 National Early Health Survey: multidimensional poverty.

43 Yashwant Sinha quoted by Arun Kumar, *Indian Economy's Greatest Crisis: Impact of Coronavirus and the Road Ahead* (Delhi: Penguin Random House, 2020).

44 Findings of Fred Hutchison Cancer Centre, Seattle, reported by NBC News, 29 August 2023.

45 W. Msembuni et al., 'WHO Estimates of Excess Mortality Associated with the COVID 19 Pandemic', *Nature* 613:7942 (2023), pp. 130–7.

46 Arvind Subramanian, *Of Counsel: The Challenges of the Modi–Jaitley Economy* (Delhi: Penguin Random House, 2018), pp. 225–9 and 235–8.

47 Rajan and Lamba, *Breaking the Mould*, pp. 107–10.

48 Christian Alonso et al., *Stacking up the Benefits: Lessons from India's Digital Journey*, IMF Working Paper 2023/078 (March 2023).

49 Alicia Herrero and Jianwei Xu, *How Big is China's Digital Economy?*, IMF Working Paper WP04 (2017).

50 Arvind Subramanian, speech to Centre for Global Development, Washington, DC, October 2014.

51 L. Chancel et al., *World Inequality Report 2022* (Paris: World Inequality Lab, 2021), https://wir2022.wid.world (accessed 1 April 2025).

52 Maria Ana Lugo et al., *How Redistributive is Fiscal Policy in China*, World Bank Policy Research Working Paper 10887 (September 2024).

53 'World's Billionaires List', Forbes, 2024, www.forbes.com/billionaires/ (accessed 2024).

54 Hurun Global Rich List, 2022, London, Shanghai, Mumbai.

55 Matthew Klein and Michael Pettis, *Trade Wars are Class Wars* (New Haven, CT: Yale University Press, 2020).

56 Ezra Vogel, *Deng Xiaoping and the Transformation of China* (Cambridge, MA: Belknap Press, 2013), p. 600.
57 Enwar Prasad, 'The People's Bank of China has a Transparency Problem', *Financial Times*, 26 August 2024.
58 Claire Xiao, 'How China keeps its debt in order', Fidelity International, 25 January 2024, www.fidelityinternational.com/editorial/article/how-china-keeps-its-debt-in-order-e1feea-en5/#:~:text=Industry%20estimates%20indicate%20that%20the, capability%20in%20the%20near%2Dterm (accessed 11 March 2025).

Chapter 2

1 Chalmers Johnson, *MITI and the Japanese Economic Miracle* (Stanford, CA: Stanford University Press, 1982).
2 Rainer Zittelman, 'State Capitalism? No, the Private Sector was and is the Main Driver of China's Economic Growth', *Forbes Magazine*, 30 September 2019. Numbers are from the All China Federation of Industry and Commerce.
3 Franklin Allen et al., *Centralization or Decentralization? The Evolution of State-Ownership in China*, Wharton University paper, 5 December 2022, revised 22 October 2024, https://papers.ssrn.com/sol3/papers.cfm?abstract_id=4283197 (accessed 1 April 2025).
4 Stein Ringen, *The Perfect Dictatorship: China in the 21st Century* (Hong Kong: Hong Kong University Press, 2016), p. 15.
5 Government of India Economic Survey 2021–22.
6 Gurcharan Das, *India Grows at Night: The Liberal Case for a Strong State* (Mumbai: Penguin/Allen Lane, 2012).
7 Tianlei Huang, Nicolas Véron and David Xu, *The Private Sector Advances in China: The Evolving Ownership Structure of the Largest Companies in the Xi Jinping Era*, Peterson Institute of International Economics Working Paper 22–3 (March 2022) (and revised paper in October).
8 J. I. Cheng (ed.), *Economics and Foreign Investment in China* (New York: Nova Science Publishers, 2007).
9 Nicholas Lardy, 'Foreign Investment is Exiting China, New Data Show', Peterson Institute of International Affairs, 17 November 2023, www.piie.com/blogs/realtime-economics/2023/foreign-direct-investment-exiting-china-new-data-show (accessed 11 March 2025).
10 Kimberly Long, 'China's Shadow Banking Sector Pushed into the Light', The Banker, 29 March 2021, www.thebanker.com/content/e57783ae-4b19-5620-b416-b6ef7de0b75f (accessed 1 April 2025).
11 Kellee Tsai, 'The Rise of Shadow Banking in China: The Political Economy of Modern Chinese State Capitalism', Hong Kong University of Science and Technology Thought Leadership Brief 10, 2015.
12 Guofeng Sun, *China's Shadow Banking: Bank's Shadow and Traditional Shadow Banking*, Bank of International Settlements Working Paper 822 (November 2019).

13 Hazel Sheffield, 'The Real Reason so many Asset Managers are Struggling in China', Institutional Investor, 7 November 2023, www.institutionalinvestor.com/article/2cf3e6oxr5pdpnjo2u3nk/corner-office/the-real-reason-so-many-asset-managers-are-struggling-in-china#:~:text=Foreign%20asset%20managers%20have%20been,institutions%20play%20an%20important%20role (accessed 11 March 2025).

14 Tianlei Huang and Nicolas Véron, 'Share of China's Top Companies in the Private Sector Continued to Steadily Decline in 2023', Peterson Institute of International Economics, PIIE Charts, 8 January 2024, www.piie.com/research/piie-charts/2024/share-chinas-top-companies-private-sector-continued-steadily-decline-2023 is slightly different (accessed 1 April 2025).

15 Ibid.

16 Yingzhi Yang, 'China Surpasses North America in Attracting Venture Capital Funding for First Time', *South China Morning Post*, 5 July 2018.

17 Jo-Ann Suchard, Mark Humphery-Jenner and Xiaping Cao, 'Government Ownership and Venture Capital in China', *Journal of Banking and Finance*, 129 (2021), article 106164.

18 'The Rise of China's Venture Capital Industrial Complex', *Economist*, 27 June 2022.

19 Gregory Stein, 'What will China do when Land Use Rights Begin to Expire?', *Vanderbilt Journal of Transnational Law*, 50:3 (2017), pp. 625–72.

20 Tony Saich and Kunling Zhang, *Institutional Change and Adaptive Efficiency: A Study of China's Hukou System* (Singapore: World Scientific Publishing Co., 2023); Kam Wing Chang (ed.), *Urbanization with Chinese Characteristics: The Hukou System and Migration* (Abingdon and New York: Routledge, 2019).

21 Jonathan Spence, *The Search for Modern China* (New York: W.W. Norton, 1990); Richard Evans, *Deng Xiaoping and the Making of Modern China* (New York: Viking, 1994); Peter Nolan, *Transforming China: Globalization, Transition and Development* (London: Anthem Press, 2004).

22 Vogel, *Deng Xiaoping*, p. 391 (on 'cat theory'). Also Chinadaily.com.cn, 2 August 2018.

23 Jikun Huang, Keijiro Otsuka and Scott Rozelle, 'Agriculture in China's Development: Past Disappointments, Recent Successes, and Future Challenges', in Brandt and Rawski, *China's Great Economic Transformation*, pp. 467–505.

24 Rakesh Mohan, 'Industrial Policy and Controls', in Jalan (ed.), *The Indian Economy*, pp. 85–116; Isher Ahluwalia, *Productivity and Growth in Indian Manufacturing* (Delhi: Oxford University Press, 1991).

25 Vijay Joshi and I. M. D. Little, *Indian Economic Reforms 1991–2001* (Oxford: Oxford University Press, 1996).

26 Vincent Cable, 'Manmohan Singh, the Quiet Reformer', in *Money and Power* (London: Atlantic Books, 2021), chapter 13; Shankar Acharya and Rakesh Mohan (eds), *India's Economy: Performance and Challenges: Essays in Honour of Montek Singh Ahluwalia* (Delhi: Oxford University Press, 2010).

27 The phrase originated with the 'free-market' Swatantra Party in the 1950s. Arvind Subramanian, in Aditya Balasubramanian, 'Contesting "Permit-and-License *Raj*": Economic Conservatism and the Idea of Democracy in 1950s India', *Past and Present*, 251:1 (2021), pp. 189–227.

28 Joshi, *India's Long Road*, p. 26 inter alia.

29 Ibid.

30 Deepak Lal, *India and China: Contrasts in Economic Liberalisation*, UCLA Economics Working Papers 706 (1993).

31 Yuen Yuen Ang, *China's Gilded Age: The Paradox of Economic Boom and Vast Corruption* (Cambridge: Cambridge University Press, 2020).

32 Magnus, *Red Flags*.

33 'India Must Abandon Protectionism', *Economist*, 17 August 2023.

34 Arvind Subramanian, keynote address to the Competition Commission of India, 2 March 2017.

35 Mody, *India is Broken*, p. 147.

36 Cable, *Globalisation and Global Governance*.

37 Joseph Stiglitz, *Globalization and its Discontents* (New York: W.W. Norton, 2002); Kimberly Elliott and J. David Richardson, *Assessing Globalization's Critics: 'Talkers Are No Good Doers???'*, Peterson Institute for International Economics Working Paper 02-5 (2002).

38 *fDi Report 2023*, fDi Insights, 16 May 2023, www.fdiinsights.com/fdi/report2023 (accessed 11 March 2025).

39 James Griffiths, *The Great Firewall of China: How to Build and Control an Alternative Version of the Internet* (London: Zed Books, 2019); Margaret Roberts, *Censored: Distraction and Diversion Inside China's Great Firewall* (Princeton, NJ: Princeton University Press, 2018).

40 Elizabeth Economy, *The Third Revolution: Xi Jinping and the New Chinese State* (New York: Oxford University Press, 2018).

41 World Bank, *Private Participation in Infrastructure (PPI): 2022 Annual Report* (Washington, DC: World Bank, 2022).

42 Emin Dinlersoz and Zhe Fu, 'Infrastructure Investment and Growth in China: A Quantitative Assessment', *Journal of Development Economics*, 158:2 (2022), article 102916.

43 L. Lakshmanan, *Public–Private Partnership in Indian Infrastructure Development: Issues and Options*, Reserve Bank of India Occasional Papers, 29 (2008).

44 World Economic Forum, *Global Country Ranking by Quality of Infrastructure*, Annual Report (Geneva: WEF, 2021).

45 'Corruption Perceptions Index: 2022', Transparency International, www.transparency.org/en/cpi/2022 (accessed 17 March 2025).

46 World Economic Forum, *The Global Risks Report 2022* (Geneva: WEF, 2022).

47 Desmond Shum, *Red Roulette: An Inside Story of Wealth, Power, Corruption and Vengeance in Today's China* (London: Simon & Schuster, 2021).

48 Daren Acemoglu and James Robinson, *Why Nations Fail* (New York: Crown Business, 2012).

49 Yuen, *China's Gilded Age*.

50 S. Sukhtankar and M. Vaishnav, 'Corruption in India: Bridging Research Evidence and Policy Options', *India Policy Forum*, 11:1 (2015), pp. 193–276.

51 D. Kapur, 'Addressing the Trilemma of Indian Higher Education'. Seminar paper quoted in Joshi, *India's Long Road*; also in the novel Chetan Bhagat, *Revolution 2020* (Delhi: Shalimar Publications, 2011).

52 Robert Wade, 'The System of Administrative and Political Corruption: Canal Irrigation in South India', *Journal of Development Studies*, 18:3 (1982), pp. 287–328.

53 Milan Vaishnav, *When Crime Pays: Money and Muscle in Indian Politics* (New Haven, CT: Yale University Press, 2017).

54 Yongnian Zheng and Wei Shan, 'Xi Jinping's "Rule of Law" with Chinese Characteristics', *East Asian Policy*, 7:2 (2015), pp. 5–19.

55 Sarwar Lateef, 'Reforming India's Governance and Ins Genocide Watch titutions', in Radicha Kapur, *A New Reform Paradigm* (India: Rupa Publications, 2022), pp. 508–56.

56 Lan Xiaohuan, blog post, Pekingnology, 20 March 2024 (extract from Lan Xiaohuan, *How China Works: Introduction to China's State-led Economic Development* (New York: Springer Link, 2021).

57 Karthik Muralidharan, *Accelerating India's Development* (Delhi: Viking Penguin, 2024).

Chapter 3

1 'Democracy Index 2024', Economist Intelligence Unit, 14 February 2024, www.eiu.com/n/campaigns/democracy-index-2024/ (accessed 17 March 2025). Based on assessments of electoral processes, civil liberties, the functioning of government, political participation and political culture.

2 Mody, *India is Broken*, p. 15.

3 V-Dem Institute *Democracy Report 2021: Autocratization Turns Viral* (Gothenburg, Sweden: V-Dem Institute, University of Gothenburg, 2021), pp. 20–1.

4 Freedom House, *Freedom in the World 2023* (Washington, DC: Freedom House, 2023).

5 Raymond Zhang et al., 'Micro-Manager-in-Chief: Modi Upends How India is Run', *Wall Street Journal*, 10 March 2017.

6 B. R. Ambedkar, cited in Roberts, *Superstates*, p. 85.

7 Milan Vaishnev, 'The Decay of Indian Democracy', *Foreign Affairs*, 18 March 2021.

8 Christophe Jaffrelot, *Modi's India: Hindu Nationalism and the Rise of Ethnic Nationalism* (Princeton, NJ: Princeton University Press, 2021).

9 'Worldwide Governance Indicators 2023', World Bank, www.worldbank.org/en/publication/worldwide-governance-indicators (accessed 17 March 2025).

10 Jayati Ghosh, C. P. Chandrasekhar and Prabhat Patnaik, *Demonetisation Decoded: Critique of India's Demonetisation Experiment* (London: Routledge, 2017).

11 Kumar, *Indian Economy's Greatest Crisis*.

12 William Joseph, 'Ideology and China's Political Development', in William Joseph (ed.), *Politics in China* (Oxford University Press, 2019), pp. 157–200.

13 Chang and Halliday, *Mao: The Unknown Story*.

14 Manfred Elfstrom and Sarosh Kuruvilla, 'The Changing Nature of Labour Unrest in China', *Industrial and Labor Relations Review*, 67:2 (2016), pp. 453–80.

15 Kerry Brown, *Xi: A Study in Power* (London: Icon Books, 2022).

16 Maksyan Ivanyna and Anwar Shah, *How Close is your Government to the People?: Worldwide Indicators of Localisation and Decentralisation*, World Bank Policy Research Working Paper 6138 (2012).

17 Jens Presthus, 'Some Positives Leading up to the National People's Congress', Macro Insights, 2 March 2024, https://jenspresthus.substack.com/p/some-positives-leading-up-to-the (accessed 12 March 2025).
18 Roberts, *Superstates*, p. 95.
19 Cai Xia, 'The Party that Failed', *Foreign Affairs*, January/February 2021.
20 19th Party Conference, Beijing, 18–24 October 2017.
21 Document 9 of the Party Central Committee ('Communique on the Current State of the Ideological Sphere', distributed in 2012 by the General Office of the Chinese Communist Party).
22 Steve Tsang and Olivia Cheung, *The Political Thought of Xi Jinping* (New York: Oxford University Press, 2024).
23 Wang Huning, 'The Structure of China's Changing Political Culture' (introduction by Matthew Johnson), Reading the China Dream, www.readingthechinadream.com/wang-huning-ldquothe-structure-of-chinarsquos-changing-political-culturerdquo.html (accessed 11 March 2025)
24 Kerry Brown, *The World According to Xi* (London: Icon Books, 2022), p. 48.
25 Steve Tsang and Olivia Cheung quoted in Katie Stallard, 'Inside the Mind of Xi Jinping', *New Statesman*, 26 January 2024.
26 Rana Mitter, 'The Real Roots of Xi Jinping Thought', *Foreign Affairs*, March/April 2024.
27 Mark Leonard, 'Sunset of the Economists', *China Books Review*, 23 February 2024. Also in 'What is Xi Jinping Thinking', *China Books Review*, 18 January.
28 Mody, *India is Broken*.
29 V. D. Savarkar, *Hindutva: Who is a Hindu?* (Mumbai: Asia Publishing House, 1961).
30 N. Gardels, 'Two Concepts of Nationalism; An Interview with Isaiah Berlin', *New York Review of Books*, November 1991.
31 Hartosh Singh Bal, 'The End of Secular India', *Foreign Affairs*, 12 April 2024.
32 Jaffrelot, *Modi's India*, p. 84.
33 Genocide Watch, www.genocidewatch.com (accessed 11 March 2025).
34 Data from Public Policy Research Centre, Delhi.
35 Freedom House, *Freedom in the World 2023*.
36 *India's Civil Society Under Pressure*, Newsreel Asia Insight 95, 6 January 2024, www.newsreel.asia/articles/indias-civil-society-under-pressure (accessed 17 March 2025); Rahul Mukherji and Aditya Shrivastava, 'Civil Society Under Siege, in India', *The Hindu*, 5 January 2024.
37 Abhadian Sukhri, 'News Laundry', *Economist*, 27 January 2024.
38 Anirudh Burman, 'Considering India's Encryption Policy Dilemma', Carnegie India, 15 November 2023, https://carnegieindia.org/research/2023/11/considering-indias-encryption-policy-dilemma?lang=en (accessed 17 March 2025).
39 Various reports from Reporters sans Frontieres (RSF), also from *The Wire*.
40 RSF, '2023 World Press Freedom Index', 21st edition, May 2023, https://rsf.org/en/2023-world-press-freedom-index-journalism-threatened-fake-content-industry (accessed 17 March 2025).
41 Discussed in Chun Han Wong, *Party of One: The Rise of Xi Jinping and China's Superpower Future* (London: Corsair, 2023). As reviewed by Rana Mitter in *Literary Review*, December 2023/January 2024.

42 Roberts, *Censored*.

43 Griffiths, *The Great Firewall of China*.

44 Kieran Green et al., *Censorship Practices of the Peoples Republic of China* (Vienna, VA: CIRA, for US–China Economic and Security Review Commission, 2024).

45 Indian Government Central Statistical Office, *Final Report on Non-profit Institutions in India* (New Delhi: Central Statistics Office, 2012).

46 Rahul Mukherji, 'India's Civil Society is Under Attack', *Economist*, 24 February 2024.

47 'Why Bother Counting?', *Economist*, 16 January 2012, p. 51; Vince Cable, *The Chinese Conundrum* (London: Alma Books, 2021), p. 193.

48 Brown, *The World According to Xi*, p. 99.

49 Mark Leonard, *What Does China Think?* (London: 4th Estate, 2008).

50 Carolyn Hsu et al., 'The State of NGO's in China Today', Brookings Commentary, 15 December 2016, www.brookings.edu/articles/the-state-of-ngos-in-china-today/ (accessed 17 March 2025).

51 Kevin O'Brien (ed.), *Popular Protest in China* (Cambridge, MA and London: Harvard University Press, 2008); Teresa Wright, *Popular Protest in China* (Cambridge: Polity Press, 2018).

52 Abbey Heffer, 'Authoritarian Practices with Adjectives in China', The Loop: European Council for Policy Research blog, 6 January 2023. https://theloop.ecpr.eu/authoritarian-practices-with-adjectives-in-china/ (accessed 17 March 2025).

53 Data recorded in the Wickedonna database, https://ciass.uni-konstanz.de/wickedonna/; also China Dissent Monitor, https://freedomhouse.org/report/china-dissent-monitor (both accessed 17 March 2025).

54 Samson Yuen and Edmund Cheng, 'Neither Repression nor Concession: A Regime's Attrition Against Mass Protests', *Political Studies*, 65:3 (2017), pp. 611–30.

55 Peter Lorentzen, 'Regularizing Rioting: Permitting Public Protest in an Authoritarian Regime', *Quarterly Journal of Political Science*, 8:2 (2013), pp. 127–58.

56 Jing Vivian Zhen, 'Repress or Redistribute: The Chinese State's Response to Resource Conflicts', *China Quarterly*, 248:1 (2021), pp. 987–1010.

57 Abbey Heffer, 'Popular Protest won't Bring Down the Chinese regime', LSE blog, 9 August 2023, https://blogs.lse.ac.uk/cff/2023/08/09/popular-protest-wont-bring-down-the-chinese-regime/ (accessed 11 March 2025).

58 Ibid.

59 Lin Zi, 'From Smog to Carbon: Chinese NGOs in Transition', China Dialogue, 4 January 2023, https://dialogue.earth/en/climate/from-smog-to-carbon-chinese-ngos-in-transition/ (accessed 11 March 2025).

60 Heffer, 'Popular Protest'.

61 Minxin Pei, *The Sentinel State* (Cambridge, MA: Harvard University Press, 2024).

62 Bruce Dixon, *The Party and the People* (Princeton, NJ: Princeton University Press, 2021).

63 Manfred Elfstrom, *Workers and Change in China: Resistance, Repression, Responsiveness* (Cambridge: Cambridge University Press, 2021).

64 Ivan Franceschini and Elisa Nesossi, 'State Repression and Chinese Labour NGOs: A Chilling Effect?', *China Journal*, 80:1 (2018), pp. 111–29.

65 *China Labour Bulletin*, Hong Kong 2024 edition, https://clb.org.hk (accessed 1 April 2025).

66 Hsin Hsien Wang and Yun Shi Shan, 'Comprehensive Law-based Governance in China? Legislating Authoritarianism in the Xi Jinping Era', *Journal of Contemporary East Asian Studies*, 11:2 (2022), pp. 195–213.

67 World Justice Index, World Justice Project (a non-profit organisation based in Washington, Mexico and Singapore).

68 Jaffrelot, *Modi's India*, chapter 8: 'The Supreme Court from Resistance to Surrender'.

69 Ibid.

70 Xi Jinping, *The Governance of China* (Beijing: Foreign Languages Press, 2014), p. 162.

71 Boston Database of Religions, 2020, www.bu.edu/cura/research-programs/world-religion-database/ (accessed 11 March 2025).

72 Martin Jacques, *When China Rules the World: The Rise of the Middle Kingdom and the end of the Western World* (London: Allen Lane, 2009).

73 Bill Hayton, *The Invention of China* (New Haven, CT: Yale University Press, 2005).

74 Aaron Glasserman, 'Is Assimilation the New Norm for China's Ethnic Policy?', Epicentre blog, Weatherhead Centre for International Affairs, Harvard University, 25 February 2022. https://epicenter.wcfia.harvard.edu/blog/assimilation-new-norm-chinas-ethnic-policy (accessed 11 March 2025).

75 Office of the Human Rights High Commissioner, 'OHCHR Assessment of Human Rights Concerns in the Xinjiang Uyghur Autonomous Region, People's Republic of China', 31 August 2022, www.ohchr.org/en/documents/country-reports/ohchr-assessment-human-rights-concerns-xinjiang-uyghur-autonomous-region (accessed 11 March 2025).

76 Contrasting views in Charles Parton, 'The Truth about Chinese Genocide against the Uyghurs', *Spectator*, 3 February 2021; Colum Lynch, 'State Department Lawyers Concluded Insufficient Evidence to Prove Genocide', *China Foreign Policy*, 19 February 2022; 'Xinjiang: The Evidence' (unpublished), hard copy in author's possession.

77 Edelman, '2024 Edelman Trust Barometer', www.edelman.com/trust/trust-barometer (accessed 11 March 2025).

78 Tony Saich and Edward Cunningham, Ash Center Research Team, cited in Dan Harsha, 'Taking China's Pulse', *Harvard Gazette*, 9 July 2020, https://news.harvard.edu/gazette/story/2020/07/long-term-survey-reveals-chinese-government-satisfaction/ (accessed 1 April 2025).

79 David Daokui Li, *China's World View: Demystifying China to Prevent Global Conflict* (New York: W.W. Norton, 2024).

80 Dixon, *The Party and the People*.

81 Scott Rozelle et al., *The Myth of the Social Volcano*. Reported in Big Data China, Stanford University, 9 July 2024, https://bigdatachina.csis.org/is-it-me-or-the-economic-system-changing-evaluations-of-inequality-in-china/ (accessed 11 March 2025).

82 P. Jha, *How the BJP Wins: Inside India's Greatest Electoral Machine* (Delhi: Juggernaut, 2017).

83 Mody, *India is Broken*, pp. 333–5.
84 N. P. Ullekh, 'Gujarat Promises Continued and Accelerated: Jagdish Bhagati and Arvind Panagaria', *Economic Times*, 3 January 2013.
85 Mody, *India is Broken*, p. 334.
86 *Analysing Governance*, BJP White Paper on a comparative study of the UPA and NDA eras, 2024.
87 James Crabtree, *The Billionaire Raj* (London: Oneworld Publications, 2018).
88 Jaffrelot, *Modi's India*, pp. 132–3.
89 Mody, *India is Broken*, pp. 352–3.
90 Kumar, *Indian Economy's Greatest Crisis*.
91 Acemoglu and Robinson, *Why Nations Fail*, pp. 231–2.
92 Ramachandran Guha, 'India's Feet of Clay: How Modi's Supremacy will Hinder his Country's Economic Rise', *Foreign Affairs*, March/April 2024.
93 Martin Wolf, *The Crisis of Democratic Capitalism* (London: Allen Lane, 2023), p. 356.

Chapter 4

1 Clark Kerr, *Industrialisation and Industrial Man* (Cambridge, MA: Harvard University Press, 1960).
2 Paul Johnson and Chris Papageorgiou, 'What Remains of Cross-country Convergence?', *Journal of Economic Literature*, 58:1 (2018), pp. 129–75.
3 Ehsan Choudhry and Mohsin Khan, *Real Exchange Rates in Developing Countries: Are Balassa-Samuelson Effects Present?*, IMF Working Paper WP/04/188 (2004).
4 Roland Rajah and Alyssa Leng, 'Revising Down the Rise of China', Lowy Institute Analysis, Australia, 14 March 2022, www.lowyinstitute.org/publications/revising-down-rise-china (accessed 11 March 2025).
5 Mohammed El-Erian, 'China is no Longer Sure to Become the Largest Economy', *Financial Times*, 7 September 2023, p. 14.
6 Indermit Gill and Homi Kharas, *An East Asia Renaissance: Ideas for Economic Growth* (Washington, DC: World Bank, 2007); 'The Middle-Income Trap has Little Evidence Going for it', *Economist*, 5 October 2017.
7 'Is Chinese Power About to Peak?', *Economist*, 13 May 2023. For a contrary view: Martin Wolf, 'We Shouldn't Call "Peak China" Just Yet', *Financial Times*, 19 September 2023.
8 Justin Lin, 'The Economics of China's New Era', Project Syndicate, 1 December 2017, www.project-syndicate.org/onpoint/the-economics-of-china-s-new-era-by-just in-yifu-lin-2017-12 (accessed 17 March 2025).
9 Lant Pritchard and Lawrence Summers, *Asiaphoria Meets Regression to the Mean*, NBER Working Paper 20573 (October 2014).
10 Rajah and Leng, 'Revising Down the Rise of China', p. 3.
11 Muralidharan, *Accelerating India's Development*.
12 OECD, *OECD Economic Outlook*, vol. 2022, issue 2, no. 112 (Paris: OECD, 2022), www.oecd.org/en/publications/oecd-economic-outlook/volume-2022/issue-2_f6d a2159-en/full-report.html (accessed 1 April 2025).

13 Daniel Rosen et al., 'Through the Looking Glass; China's 2023 GDP and the Year Ahead', Rhodium Group, New York, 29 December 2023, https://rhg.com/research/through-the-looking-glass-chinas-2023-gdp-and-the-year-ahead/ (accessed 17 March 2025).

14 Joanna Chua referred to in Leo Lewis, 'Investors Ponder the Japanification of China', *Financial Times*, 7 September 2023. On Japan, Richard Koo, *Japan's Struggle with Uncharted Economics and its Global Implications* (Singapore: John Wiley, 2003).

15 Klein and Pettis, *Trade Wars are Class Wars*.

16 'How Economists have Underestimated Chinese Consumption', *Economist*, 14 October 2023.

17 Nicholas Lardy, 'China is Still Rising', *Foreign Affairs*, 2 April 2024.

18 Ernst & Young, *India@100: Realising the Potential of a US$26 Trillion Economy* (Kolkata: Ernst & Young, 2023).

19 Angus Deaton, 'Franco Modigliani and the Life Cycle Theory of Consumption', Princeton University, 2005, www.princeton.edu/~deaton/downloads/romelecture.pdf (accessed 11 March 2025).

20 Ronald Lee and Andrew Mason, *Population Aging and the Generational Economy: A Global Perspective* (Cheltenham and Ottawa: Edward Elgar and IDRC, 2011); Ronald Lee and Andrew Mason, 'What is the Demographic Dividend?', *IMF Finance and Development Magazine*, 43:3 (2006), pp. 16–17.

21 Xin Meng, *China's 40 Years of Demographic Dividend and Labor Supply: The Quantity Myth*, IZA Discussion Paper 16207, Institute of Labour Economics (June 2023).

22 Claudia Goldin, *The U-Shaped Female Labour Force Function in Economic Development and Economic History*, NBER Working Paper 44707 (April 1994).

23 Rajah and Leng, 'Revising Down the Rise of China', p. 13 (low estimate). Higher figure in Martin Wolf, 'China Faces a Demographic Deficit', *Financial Times*, 3 October 2023.

24 Rozelle and Hell, *Invisible China*.

25 Cai Fang, 'Breaking the "Fertility Paradox"', CSIS Interpret, published in Economic Perspectives, 26 March 2022, https://interpret.csis.org/translations/breaking-the-fertility-paradox/ (accessed 1 April 2025).

26 Cited in Li, *China's World View*, p. 180.

27 Mody, *India is Broken*, p. 7.

28 Rajan and Lamba, *Breaking the Mould*.

29 Goldin, *The U-Shaped Female Labour Force Function*.

30 International Monetary Fund, PRC Article 4 Consultation, 2 February 2024, www.imf.org/en/Publications/CR/Issues/2024/02/01/People-s-Republic-of-China-2023-Article-IV-Consultation-Press-Release-Staff-Report-and-544379 (accessed 1 April 2025).

31 Richard Herd, *Estimating Capital Formation and Capital Stock by Economic Sector in China: The Implications for Productivity Growth*, World Bank Policy Research Working Paper 9317 (2020).

32 Kenneth Rogoff and Yuanchen Yang, *Peak China Housing*, NBER Working Paper 27697 (August 2020).

33 Cited by *Economist*, 17 November 2022. Also in Tianlie Huang, *Why China's Housing*

Policies Have Failed, Peterson Institute for International Economics Working Paper 23–5 (2023).

34 Indian Brand Equity Foundation (IBEF), 'Indian Residential Real Estate', IBEF, November 2024, www.ibef.org/industry/real-estate-india (accessed 1 April 2025).

35 National Housing Bank, *Report on Trend and Progress of Housing in India in 2023* (New Delhi: National Housing Bank, 2024).

36 International Transport Forum, *Comparing Transport Infrastructure Investment Policies Around the Globe*, Statistics Brief (Paris: OECD, 2023).

37 Presthus, 'Some Positives'.

38 Edward White and Cheng Leng, 'Xi's Plan to Rescue China's Economy', *Financial Times*, 27 March 2024.

39 Martha Lawrence, Richard Bullock and Ziming Liu, *China's High Speed Rail Development* (Washington, DC: World Bank, 2019).

40 'Putting Wheels on the Elephant', *Economist*, 18 March 2023, p. 57; Dewangi Sharma, 'India's Push for Infrastructure Development', Invest India, 23 February 2024, www.investindia.gov.in/blogs/indias-push-infrastructure-development#:~:text=The%20government's%20commitment%20is%20evident,Railways%20and%20Urban%20Public%20Transport (accessed 11 March 2025).

41 Rajah and Leng, 'Revising Down the Rise of China', appendix 2, p. 40.

42 Gerard DiPippo et al., 'Red Ink: Estimating Chinese Industrial Policy Spending in Comparative Perspective', CSIS, 23 May 2022, www.csis.org/analysis/red-ink-estimating-chinese-industrial-policy-spending-comparative-perspective (accessed 11 March 2025); F. Bickenbach et al., *Foul Play? On the Scale and Scope of Industrial Subsidies in China*, Kiel Institute for the World Economy Policy Brief 173 (April 2024).

43 Dan Wang, 'How Beijing Threatens US Dominance', *Foreign Affairs*, March/April 2023.

44 Rana Foroohar, 'Shipbuilding: The New Battleground in the US–China Trade War', *Financial Times*, 12 March 2024.

45 Estimates vary from 35% of global production to 29% of global value added. Based on analysis of OECD's TIVA database by Richard Baldwin, Centre for Economic Policy Research (CEPR), 17 January 2024.

46 Huang Yiping and Lu Feng, 'Is China's State-led Industrial Policy on a Perilous Path?', *South China Morning Post*, 15 March 2024.

47 Robert Solow, 'A Contribution to the Theory of Economic Growth', *Quarterly Journal of Economics*, 70:1 (1956), pp. 65–94; Paul Romer, 'The Origins of Endogenous Growth', *Journal of Economic Perspectives*, 8:1 (1994), pp. 3–22.

48 Thomas Philippon, *Additive Growth*, NBER Working Paper 29950 (2022).

49 Gill and Kharas, 'The East Asian Renaissance'; Daniel Rosen, 'How China's Economic Slowdown Could Hurt the World', *Foreign Affairs*, April 2023.

50 Magnus, *Red Flags*, p. 57.

51 Loren Brandt et al., 'Recent Productivity Trends in China', *China: An International Journal*, 20:1 (2022), pp. 93–113; Loren Brandt et al., *China's Productivity Slowdown and Future Growth Potential*, World Bank Policy Research Working Paper 9298 (2020).

52 'China's Better Economic Growth Hides Reasons to Worry', *Economist*, 14 April 2024.

53 Bhalla and Bhasin, 'India–China: Reversal of Fortunes'.

54 Rajah and Leng, 'Revising Down the Rise of China', p. 22 and figure 7.

55 Henry Storey, 'Is China Finally Getting Serious About Hukou Reform?', the Interpreter, Lowy Institute, 7 September 2023, www.lowyinstitute.org/the-inter preter/china-finally-getting-serious-about-hukou-reform (accessed 11 March 2025); Eduardo Jaramillo, 'China's Hukou Reform in 2022: Do they Mean it this Time?', CSIS, 20 April 2022, www.csis.org/blogs/new-perspectives-asia/chinas-hukou-reform-2022-do-they-mean-it-time-0 (accessed 11 March 2025).

56 International Monetary Fund, PRC Article 4 Consultation.

57 Gene Grossman and Elhanan Helpman, *Innovation and Growth in the Global Economy* (Cambridge, MA: MIT Press, 1991).

58 Linsu Kim and Richard Nelson, *Technology Learning, and Innovation: Experiences of Newly Industrializing Economies* (Cambridge: Cambridge University Press, 2000); Robert Wade, *Governing the Market: Economic Theory and the Role of Government in East Asian Industrialization* (Princeton, NJ: Princeton University Press, 1990).

59 Linsu Kim, *Imitation to Innovation: The Dynamics of Korea's Technological Learning* (Boston, MA: Harvard University Press, 1997).

60 Australian Policy Research Institute, 'China has Become a Scientific Superpower', *Economist*, 12 June 2024, p. 66.

61 World Bank Open Data, https://data.worldbank.org/indicator/IP.JRN.ARTC.SC (accessed 12 March 2025).

62 World Intellectual Property Organization, 'Global Innovation Index', WIPO, 2023, www.wipo.int/en/web/global-innovation-index (accessed 12 March 2025).

63 '80% of India's Urban Population have Access to High-speed Internet', *The Hindu*, 28 October 2023.

64 Deepak Mishra et al., *State of India's Digital Economy Report 2024* (Delhi: ICRIER, 2024).

65 Inter alia, 'Digital Transformation (DX) Market Size, Companies, Trends and Industry Growth (2025–2030)', Mordor Intelligence, 13 February 2023, www.mor dorintelligence.com/industry-reports/digital-transformation-market (accessed 1 April 2025).

66 Jonathan Hillman, *The Digital Silk Road* (London: Profile Books, 2021), chapter 4.

67 Zeyi Yang, 'China Just Announced a New Social Credit Law: Here is What it Means', *MIT Technological Review*, 22 November 2022.

68 Katja Drinhausen and John Lee, in *The CCP's Next Century: Expanding Economic Control, Digital Governance and National Security*, MERICS Papers on China 10 (Berlin: MERICS, 2021), citing the story in Xinhua of 12 July 2020.

69 Nasscom and Zinnov estimate 1,580 GCC operations in India with 1.7 million employees. Nasscom and Zinnov, *Weathering the Challenges: The Indian Tech Start-up Landscape Report* (Noida, India: Nasscom, 2023).

70 Rob Waugh, 'The Skeptics Who Believe AI is a Bubble – Could They be Right?', Technopedia, 19 January 2024, www.techopedia.com/the-skeptics-who-believe-ai-is-a-bubble-could-they-be-right (accessed 12 March 2025).

71 There is a comprehensive review of AI capacity, including data consumption, in Bhaskar Chakravorti, Ajay Bhalla and Ravi Shankar Chaturvedi, 'Charting the Emerging Geography of AI', *Harvard Business Review*, 12 December 2024.

72 Dennis Wang, *Reigning the Future: AI, 5G, Huawei, and the Next 30 Years of US–China Rivalry* (Potomac, MD: New Degree Press, 2020).

73 Chakravorti et al., 'Charting the Emerging Geography of AI'.

74 Rajah and Leng, 'Revising Down the Rise of China', p. 24.

75 Diego Cerdeiro et al., *Sizing up the Effects of Technological Decoupling*, IMF Working Paper 50125 (March 2021).

76 Peking University Institute of International and Strategic Studies, cited in Cable, *The Chinese Conundrum*, p. 178.

77 Nicholas Chaillan, 'The Pentagon Needs a New AI Strategy to Catch Up With China', *Financial Times*, 22 November 2021.

78 Douglas Fuller, *Paper Tigers, Hidden Dragons: Firms and the Political Economy of China's Technological Development* (Oxford: Oxford University Press, 2016).

79 *Financial Times* report, 29 November 2023.

80 'Global Chips Battle Intensified with $81 billion Subsidy', Bloomberg, 12 May 2024.

81 Daniel Rosen and Logan Wright, 'China's Economic Collision Course', *Foreign Affairs*, 27 March 2024.

Chapter 5

1 Dwight Chaplin cited in *Economist*, 28 February 2022, p. 80.

2 Quoted in Jonathan Fenby, *The Penguin History of Modern China* (London: Penguin, 2008), p. 506.

3 Vogel, *Deng Xiaoping*, chapter 7.

4 Ibid., p. 487.

5 Ibid., p. 649.

6 Bob Davies and Lingling Wei, *Superpower Showdown: How the Battle Between Trump and Xi Threatens a New Cold War* (London: Harper Collins, 2020), p. 59.

7 A phrase attributed to Robert Zoelick at the 2015 National Committee Gala.

8 Stephen Moore and Arthur Laffer, *Trumponomics: Inside the America First Plan to Revive our Economy* (New York: St Martins Publishing Group, 2018); Cable, *Money and Power*, chapter 16: 'Trumponomics, Economic Nationalism and Pluto-populism'.

9 Donald J. Trump and Tony Schwarz, *Trump: The Art of the Deal* (London: Arrow Books, 1989).

10 Peter Navarro and Greg Autry, *Death by China: Confronting the Dragon – A Global Call to Action* (Upper Saddle River, NJ: Pearson Prentice Hall, 2011).

11 David Autor, David Dorn and Gordon Hanson, *The China Syndrome: Local Labour Market Effects on Import Competition Effects in the USA*, NBER Working Paper 18054 (May 2022).

12 Davide Furceri et al., *The Macroeconomic Consequences of Tariffs*, IMF Working Paper 2019/009 (January 2019).

13 Biden, quote from 25 March 2001.

14 Michael Pillsbury, *The Hundred-year Marathon: China's Secret Strategy to Replace America as a global Superpower* (New York: Henry Holt, 2014); Rush Doshi, *The Long Game: China's Grand Strategy to Displace American Order* (New York: Oxford University Press, 2023).

15 Vogel, *Deng Xiaoping*.

16 US Chamber of Commerce, *Made in China 2025: Global Ambitions Built on Local Protections* (Washington, DC: US Chamber of Commerce, 2017).

17 Davis and Wei, *Superpower Showdown*, p. 293; Carsten Holz, 'Industrial Policies and the Changing Patterns of Investment in the Chinese Economy', *China Journal*, 81 (2018), pp. 23–57.

18 Swarnali Ahmed, Maximiliano Appendino and Michele Ruta, *Global Supply Chains and the Exchange Rate Elasticity of Exports*, IMF Working Paper 15/252 (2015).

19 Michael Pettis, 'Can Trade Intervention Lead to Freer Trade?', Carnegie Endowment for International Peace, 23 February 2024, https://carnegieendowment.org/china-financial-markets/2024/02/can-trade-intervention-lead-to-freer-trade?lang=en (accessed 12 March 2025).

20 Remarks by Jake Sullivan, National Security Adviser on Reviewing American Economic Leadership, Brookings Institution, 27 March 2023.

21 Dani Rodrik, 'Has Globalization Gone Too Far?', *Challenge*, 41:2 (1998), pp. 81–94.

22 Speech by Janet Yellen at Johns Hopkins School of Advanced International Studies, 20 April 2023.

23 Speech by Ursula van der Leyen, 20 June 2023.

24 Speech by Ursula van der Leyen, 24 January 2024.

25 Katja Drinhausen and Helena Legarda, *'Comprehensive National Security' Unleashed: How Xi's Approach Shapes China's Policies at Home and Abroad* (Berlin: MERICS, 2022).

26 Samuel Huntington, 'Why International Primacy Matters', *International Security*, 17:4 (1993), pp. 68–83, on p. 72.

27 Edward Luttwak, 'Disarming the World's Economies', Centre for Strategic and International Studies, 1990 (unpublished).

28 Lester Thurow, *Head to Head: The Coming Economic Battle Among Japan, Europe and Africa* (New York: Morrow, 1992).

29 Vincent Cable, 'What is International Economic Security?', *International Affairs*, 71:2 (1995), pp. 305–24.

30 Raymond Vernon, *Multi-national Enterprise and National Security*, Adelphi Papers 74 (London: International Institute for Strategic Studies, 1971).

31 Michael Franklin and Jonathan Ockenden, *European Agriculture Policy: Ten Steps in the Right Direction*, RIIA (Chatham House) Briefing Paper 14 (November 1994).

32 Daniel Yergin, *The Prize: The Epic Quest for Oil Money and Power* (New York: Free Press, 2009); John Mitchell, *An Oil Agenda for Europe* (London: RIIA (Chatham House), 1994).

33 Marc D. Lax, *Selected Strategic Minerals: The Impending Crisis* (Lanham, MD: University Press of America, 1989).

34 DeAnne Julius, 'Britain's Changing International Interests', *International Affairs*, 63:3 (1989), pp. 375–93, on p. 390.

35 Paul Krugman (ed.), *Strategic Trade Policy and the New International Economics* (Cambridge, MA: MIT Press, 1986); Barbara Spencer and James Bredner, 'Strategic Trade

Policy', in S. N. Durlauf and L. Blume (eds), *The New Palgrave Dictionary of Economics* (Basingstoke: Palgrave MacMillan, 2008); Marc Fasteau and Ian Fletcher, 'Industrial Policy for the United States', Coalition for a Progressive America (unpublished), 2024.

36 Laura Tyson, *Who's Bashing Whom?: Trade Conflict in High-technology Industries* (Washington, DC: Institute for International Economics, 1992).

37 Paul Krugman, 'Competitiveness: A Dangerous Obsession', *Foreign Affairs*, 73:2 (1994), pp. 28–44, on pp. 41–2.

38 R. Kuttner, *The End of Laissez-faire: National Purpose and the Global Economy After the Cold War* (New York: Knopf, 1991).

39 Eben Kaplan and Lee Hudson, 'Foreign Ownership of US Infrastructure', Council on Foreign Relations, 3 February 2007, www.cfr.org/backgrounder/foreign-owner ship-us-infrastructure (accessed 12 March 2025).

40 FIRRMA, or the Foreign Investment Risk Review Modernization Act of 2018, strengthens and modernizes the Committee on Foreign Investment in the United States (CFIUS).

41 Alex Brummer, *Britain for Sale: British Companies in Foreign Hands* (London: Penguin Random House, 2012); Des Cohen, 'Who Owns Britain?', Open Democracy, 24 February 2018, https://neweconomics.opendemocracy.net/index.html%3Fp=2472. html (accessed 12 March 2025).

42 Attributed to Lawrence Summers; Brad Setser, 'The Balance of Financial Terror Circa August 9, 2007', Council on Foreign Relations', 9 August 2007, www.cfr.org/ blog/balance-financial-terror-circa-august-9-2007 (accessed 12 March 2025).

43 Niall Ferguson and Moritz Schularick, *The End of Chimerica*, Harvard Business School Working Paper 10-037 (2009).

44 Chris Miller, *Chip War: The Fight for the World's Most Critical Technology* (New York: Scribner, 2023).

45 Barry Eichengreen, review of Miller's *Chip War* in *Foreign Affairs*, 28 February 2023.

46 Fuller, *Paper Tigers, Hidden Dragons*.

47 Gregory Allen, *China's New Strategy for Waging the Microchip Tech War* (Washington, DC: CSIS, 2023).

48 Angela Zhang, *High Wire: How China Regulates Big Tech* (New York: Oxford University Press, 2024).

49 Xiangrong Yu, 'Who's Winning the US–China Chip War?', Citigroup, 11 October 2023, www.citigroup.com/global/insights/who-s-winning-the-us-china-chip-war- (accessed 12 March 2025).

50 Tobias Mann, 'Teardown finds Huawei's 5nm Notebook Processor was Made in Taiwan, not China', The Register, 5 January 2024, www.theregister.com/2024/01/ 05/huawei_5nm_chip_tsmc/ (accessed 12 March 2025).

51 Kevin Xu, various entries in Muck Rack, and Chris Miller, 'Chip War Could Turn into a Cloud War', *Financial Times*, 30 July 2024.

52 Chris Miller, 'Western Nations Must Plan for when China Floods the Chip Market', *Financial Times*, 28 January 2024.

53 House of Lords, '20th Report of the Select Committee of the European Community (Strategic Minerals)', 1982; Lax, *Selected Strategic Minerals*.

54 China Power Project, 'Does China Pose a Threat to Global Rare Earth Supply Chains?', ChinaPower, July 2020 (updated 2021), https://chinapower.csis.org/china-rare-earths/ (accessed 12 March 2025).

55 Sophia Kalanzakos, *China and the Geopolitics of Rare Earths* (New York: Oxford University Press, 2018).

56 OECD, *Raw Materials Critical to the Green Transition*, Trade Policy Paper 269 (April 2023); IEA, *The Role of Critical Minerals in Clean Energy Transitions* (Paris: IEA, 2021).

57 Rodrigo Castillo and Caitlin Purdy, *China's Role in Supplying Critical Minerals for the Global Economy Transition: What Could the Future Hold?* (Washington, DC: Brookings Institution, 2022).

58 Stephen Roach, *Accidental Conflict: America, China and the Clash of False Narratives* (New Haven, CT: Yale University Press, 2022), pp. 118–19.

59 Isobel Hilton, 'The Huawei Dilemma', *Prospect Magazine*, August–September 2019.

60 Wang, *Reigning the Future.*

61 Hillman, *The Digital Silk Road*, chapter 4.

62 Roach, *Accidental Conflict*, p. 120.

63 Demetri Sevastopulo, James Fontanella-Khan and Tabby Kinder, 'The Battle Over TikTok', *Financial Times*, 16 March 2024.

64 Vinod Khosla, 'America is Right to Target TikTok', *Financial Times*, 9 April 2024.

65 'Why Politicians are Obsessed by Mythical Chinese Land Grabs', *Economist*, 27 January 2024, p. 35.

66 Mabel Banfield-Nwachi, 'Foreign States Targeting Sensitive Research at UK Universities, MI5 Warns', *Guardian*, 26 April 2024.

67 Jenny Lee and John Haupt, 'The "China Threat" and the Future of Global Science', *Scientific American*, 7 January 2020; Andrew Silver, Jeff Tollefson and Elizabeth Gibney, 'How US–China Political Tensions are Affecting Science', *Nature*, 18 April 2019; Liming Li et al, 'US–China Health Exchange and Collaboration Following Covid', *Lancet*, 397:10291 (2021), pp. P2304–8.

68 Ana Gross and Alexandra Heal, 'The Subsea Fight over Internet Plumbing', *Financial Times*, 16 June 2023.

69 Hillman, *The Digital Silk Road*, chapter 5.

70 Speech by Janet Yellen at Johns Hopkins School of Advanced International Studies, 20 April 2023.

71 Amar Breckenridge, 'Will the EU's Approach to Strategic Autonomy 'prove to be self-defeating?', Frontier Economics, 2 December 2024, www.frontier-economics.com/uk/en/news-and-insights/news/news-article-i9919-will-the-eu-s-approach-to-strategic-autonomy-prove-to-be-self-defeating (accessed 1 April 2025).

72 Marijn Bolhuis, Jiaquan Chen and Benjamin Kett, 'The Costs of Geo-economic Fragmentation', *IMF Finance and Development Magazine*, June 2023, pp. 34–7.

73 Chad Brown and Yilin Wang, *Five Years into the Trade War, China Continues its Slow Decoupling from US Exports*, Peterson Institute for International Economics blog, 2023, www.piie.com/blogs/realtime-economics/2023/five-years-trade-war-china-continues-its-slow-decoupling-us-exports (accessed 11 March 2025).

74 Greg Guyott, 'Globalisation's New Economic Networks', HSBC Global Banking and Markets, 8 April 2024, www.gbm.hsbc.com/en-gb/insights/facilitating-trade/globalisation-new-economic-networks (accessed 12 March 2025).

75 Caroline Freund et al., *Is US Trade Policy Reshaping Global Supply Chains?*, World Bank Policy Research Working Paper 10593 (October 2023).

76 James Kynge and Keith Frey, 'China's Plan to Reshape World Trade', *Financial Times*, 27 February 2024; and FT research.

77 Subrahmanyam Jaishankar, *Why Bharat Matters* (New Delhi: Rupa Publications, 2024).

Chapter 6

1 Joseph Nye, *The Kindleberger Trap: Soft Power and Great Power Competition* (Singapore: Springer, 2023), based on Charles Kindleberger, 'International Public Goods Without International Government', *American Economic Review*, 76:1 (1986), pp. 1–13.

2 Paul Samuelson, 'The Pure Theory of Public Expenditure', *Review of Economics and Statistics*, 36:4 (1954), pp. 387–9.

3 Inge Kaul, Isabelle Grunberg and Marc Stern (eds), *Global Public Goods: International Cooperation in the 20th Century* (New York: Oxford University Press, 1999).

4 Joseph Stiglitz, *The Theory of International Public Goods and the Architecture of International Organisations*, World Institute for Development Economics Research, Background Paper 7 (1995).

5 Benjamin Cohen, *International Political Economy: Intellectual History* (Princeton, NJ: Princeton University Press, 2008); Robert Gilpin, *War and Change in World Politics* (Cambridge: Cambridge University Press, 1981); Kindleberger, *The World in Depression 1929–1939*.

6 Garnett Hardin, 'The Tragedy of the Commons', *Science*, 162:3859 (1968), pp. 1243–8.

7 Fikret Berkes, *Fishermen and the Tragedy of the Commons* (Cambridge: Cambridge University Press, 2009). Originally an article in *Environmental Conservation*, 12:3 (1985), pp. 199–206.

8 Chris Alden and Sergio Chichava, 'Chinese Overseas Fishing Fleet and the Global South', LSE blog, 27 June 2022, https://blogs.lse.ac.uk/cff/2022/06/27/chinas-overseas-fishing-fleet-and-the-global-south/ (accessed 12 March 2025); Ian Urbina, 'How China's Expanding Fishing Fleet is Depleting the World's Oceans', Yale Environment 360, 17 August 2020, https://e360.yale.edu/features/how-chinas-expanding-fishing-fleet-is-depleting-worlds-oceans (accessed 12 March 2025).

9 Anne-Marie Brady, *China as a Polar Great Power* (Cambridge: Cambridge University Press, 2017).

10 Richard Cooper, *International Approaches to Global Climate Change*, Working Paper 99-03, Weatherhead Center for International Affairs, Harvard University (1999).

11 'Climate Change Performance Index', German Watch, www.germanwatch.org/en/CCPI#:~:text=The%20Climate%20Change%20Performance%20Index%20(CCPI)%20compares%2059%20countries%20and,progress%20of%20the%20countries%20analysed (accessed 12 March 2025).

12 Nick Stern, 'Public Lecture on Climate Change: China and India', LSE, 26 March 2024.

13 Martina Caretta et al., 'Water', in IPCC, *Climate Change 2022: Impacts, Adaptation and Vulnerability*, contribution of Working Group II to the Sixth Assessment Report of the Intergovernmental Panel on Climate Change (New York and Cambridge, UK: Cambridge University Press, 2022), pp. 551–712, www.ipcc.ch/report/ar6/wg2/downloads/report/IPCC_AR6_WGII_Chapter04.pdf (accessed 12 March 2025).

14 Robert McSweeney, 'China Tops New List of Countries Most at Risk from Coastal Flooding', Carbon Brief, 25 September 2014, www.carbonbrief.org/china-tops-new-list-of-countries-most-at-risk-from-coastal-flooding/ (accessed 12 March 2025).

15 R. J. Nicholls et al., *Ranking Port Cities with High Exposure and Vulnerability to Climate Extremes: Exposure Estimates*, OECD Environment Working Papers 1 (2008).

16 Judy Lawrence et al., 'Australasia', in IPCC, *Climate Change 2022*, pp. 1581–1688, www.ipcc.ch/report/ar6/wg2/downloads/report/IPCC_AR6_WGII_Chapter11.pdf (accessed 12 March 2025).

17 Sharfaa Hussein et al., 'Navigating the Impact of Climate Change in India: A Perspective on Climate Action (SDG13) and Sustainable Cities and Communities (SDG11)', *Frontiers in Sustainable Cities*, 5 (2024); ESCAP, *2023 Review of Climate Ambition in Asia and the Pacific* (Bangkok: ESCAP, 2023).

18 R. Debnath, Ronita Bardhan and Michelle Bell, 'Lethal Heatwaves are Challenging India's Sustainable Development', PLOS Climate, 2:4 (2023), article e0000156.

19 '2023 World Air Quality Report', IQ Air, 19 March 2024, www.iqair.com/gb/newsroom/waqr-2023-pr?srsltid=AfmBOorT1978tgBSMqHyvIdLpwikB9o91_baJa4pPshTMFe4laTyqeyw (accessed 12 March 2025).

20 'Aqueduct', World Resources Institute, 2025, www.wri.org/aqueduct#:~:text=The%20latest%20iteration%20of%20Aqueduct,access%20to%20underlying%20hydrological%20models (accessed 12 March 2025).

21 Arpita Das Gupta, 'Water Security in India', Earth.org, 6 August 2019, https://earth.org/water-scarcity-how-climate-crisis-is-unfolding-in-india/ (accessed 12 March 2025).

22 United Nations, *Drought in Numbers 2022 – Restoration for Readiness and Resilience* (Bonn: UN Convention to Combat Desertification, 2022), www.unccd.int/sites/default/files/2022-05/Drought%20in%20Numbers.pdf (accessed 12 March 2025).

23 'Aqueduct', World Resources Institute.

24 Global Energy Monitor, Covina, California, https://globalenergymonitor.org/ (accessed 12 March 2025).

25 Climate Action Tracker, https://climateactiontracker.org/ (accessed 12 March 2025).

26 Global Energy Monitor, Covina, California.

27 'Coal Information', International Energy Agency (IEA), updated July 2024, www.iea.org/data-and-statistics/data-product/coal-information-service (accessed 12 March 2025).

28 Global Energy Monitor (GEM), reported in an article by Molly Lempriere: 'China Responsible for 95% of New Coal Power Construction in 2023, Report Says',

Carbon Brief, 11 April 2024, www.carbonbrief.org/china-responsible-for-95-of-new-coal-power-construction-in-2023-report-says/ (accessed 12 March 2025).

29 Rahul Tongia and Anurag Sehgal (eds), *Future of Coal in India: Smooth Transition or Bumpy Road Ahead?* (Chennai: Notion Press and Brookings, 2020).

30 'India Says 5 Million Directly Depend on Coal Mining', *Indian Express*, 15 May 2023.

31 Rohit Chandra (Indian Institute of Technology) in *Financial Times*, 26 September 2023, quoting from 'India wants Transition on its own Terms – Without Phasing Coal Out and with More Grants', *The Hindu*, 26 September 2023.

32 See report of China's renewable capacity: 'China Leads Global Renewables Race with Record-breaking 230 GW Installations in 2023', Wood McKenzie, 28 November 2023, www.woodmac.com/press-releases/china-leader-in-renewables/#:~:text=Mark%20Thomton-,China%20leads%20global%20renewables%20race%20with%20record,230%20GW%20installations%20in%202023&text=Currently%20on%20target%20to%20reach,leads%20the%20global%20renewables%20market. (accessed 1 April 2025).

33 IEA, *Renewables 2023: Analysis and Forecast to 2028* (Paris: IEA, 2024).

34 David Fickling, 'India is Finally Becoming a Clean Energy Superpower', Bloomberg, 14 October 2024, www.bloomberg.com/opinion/articles/2024-10-14/india-is-finally-becoming-a-clean-energy-superpower (accessed 1 April 2025).

Chapter 7

1 Stephen Cohen, *India: Emerging Power* (Washington, DC: Brooking, 2001).

2 Amrita Narlikar, *India's Role in Global Governance: A Modi-fication* (London: Chatham House, 2007).

3 Jashenkar, *Why Bharat Matters*.

4 David Dollar, 'Reluctant Player: China's Approach to International Economic Institutions', Brookings Institution, 14 September 2020, www.brookings.edu/articles/reluctant-player-chinas-approach-to-international-economic-institutions/ (accessed 12 March 2025).

5 Council on Foreign Relations, *China's Approach to Global Governance*, briefing note (New York: CFR, 2024).

6 Paulo Nogueira Batista, 'How the IMF can be Reformed to Better Represent Developing Countries', LSE Blog, 10 May 2024, https://blogs.lse.ac.uk/europpblog/2024/05/10/how-the-imf-can-be-reformed-to-better-represent-developing-countries/#:~:text=For%20the%20poorest%20countries%2C%20the,to%20deal%20with%20economic%20challenges (accessed 12 March 2025).

7 Jeffrey Frankel, 'The Plaza Accord, 30 Years later', in Fred Bergsten and Russell Green eds, *Currency Policy Then and Now: 30th Anniversary of the Plaza Accord* (Washington, DC: Peterson Institute for International Economics, 2016).

8 Marcus Noland, *China and the International Economic System*, Peterson Institute for International Economics Working Paper 95 (January 1993).

9 Niall Ferguson, *The Ascent of Money: A Financial History of the World* (New York: Penguin-Putnam, 2009), pp. 337–40.

10 Eric Helleiner and Jonathan Kirschner, *The Great Wall of Money* (Ithaca, NY: Cornell University Press, 2014); Adam Tooze, *Crashed: How a Decade of Financial Crises Changed the World* (London: Penguin Books, 2019).

11 Eswar Prasad, *The Dollar Trap: How the USA Tightened its Grip on Global Finance* (Princeton, NJ: Princeton University Press, 2014); Kynge and Frey, 'China's Plan to Reshape World Trade', and FT research.

12 Sebastian Horn et al., *China as an International Lender of Last Resort*, Aiddata Working Paper 124 (March 2023).

13 Deborah Brautigam and Yufan Huang, *Integrating China into Multilateral Debt Relief: Progress and Problems in the G20 DSSI*, China–Africa Research Initiative Briefing Paper 9 (2023).

14 Matthew Mingay and Logan Wright, *China's External Debt Renegotiation After Zambia*, Rhodium Group paper (June 2023).

15 Comment by Ms Georgieva, *Economist*, 8 April 2023, p. 62.

16 David Malpass et al., 'China is Winning the Belt and Road Battles', Hudson Institute, 21 March 2024, www.hudson.org/economics/china-winning-belt-ro ad-debt-battles-david-malpass-joshua-meservey-thomas-duesterberg (accessed 12 March 2025).

17 Kindleberger, 'International Public Goods Without International Government'.

18 Barry Eichengreen, *Exorbitant Privilege: The Rise and Fall of the Dollar and the Future of the International Monetary System* (New York: Oxford University Press, 2011).

19 Michael Pettis, 'An Exorbitant Burden?', *Foreign Policy*, 7 September 2011.

20 Ferguson, *The Ascent of Money*, chapter 6.

21 Barry Eichengreen, 'War Accelerates Stealth Erosion of Dollar Dominance', *Financial Times*, 27 March 2022.

22 Zhou Yu, 'The Weaponization of Global Financial Public Goods and its Formational Mechanism', CSIS interpretations from *Journal of International Relations*, 28 August 2022, https://interpret.csis.org/translations/the-weaponization-of-global-financial-public-goods-and-its-formation-mechanism/ (accessed 12 March 2025); Robert Greene, 'How Sanctions on Russia will Alter Global Payments Flows', Carnegie Centre for International Peace, 4 March 2022, https://carnegieendowment.org/posts/2022/03/how-sanctions-on-russia-will-alter-global-payments-flows?lang=en (accessed 12 March 2025).

23 Eswar Prasad, *The Future of Money: How the Digital Revolution is Transforming Currencies and Finance* (Cambridge, MA: Belknap Press, 2021).

24 Anita Hauser, 'Russian Sanctions Bring Non-dollar Currencies to the Fore in International Trade', The Banker, 15 May 2024, www.thebanker.com/content/86b559b7-b89f-5531-acf9-05deda502c13 (accessed 12 March 2025).

25 Niels Graham and Hung Tran, *Dedollarization is not just Geopolitics, Economic Fundamentals Matter*, Atlantic Council, 22 January 2024, www.atlanticcouncil.org/blogs/econo graphics/sinographs/dedollarization-is-not-just-geopolitics-economic-fundamenta ls-matter/ (accessed 1 April 2025).

26 Camilo E. Tovar and Tania Mohd Nor, *Reserve Blocs: A Changing International Monetary System*, IMF Working Paper 18/20 (January 2018).

27 Gillian Tett, 'Prepare for a Multi-Polar Currency', *World Financial Times*, 30 March

2025; Wolfgang Munchau, 'China and its Allies are Well Placed to Topple the Dollar as the World's Leading Currency', *New Statesman*, 5–11 May 2023.

28 Robert Wade, 'The Beginning of the End for the US Dollar's Global Dominance', LSE blog, 29 February 2024, https://blogs.lse.ac.uk/internationaldevelopment/2024/02/29/long-read-the-beginning-of-the-end-for-the-us-dollars-global-dominance/ (accessed 1 April 2025).

29 Rajshri Jayaraman and Ravi Kanbur, 'International Public Goods and the Case for Foreign Aid', in Kaul et al. (eds), *Global Public Goods*, pp. 418–35; Kerri Elgar et al., *Development Co-operation and the Provision of Global Public Goods*, OECD Development Co-operation Working Paper 111 (May 2023).

30 D. J. Nordquist, 'China is Using the World Bank as its Piggy Bank', The Hill, 17 May 2023, https://thehill.com/opinion/international/4006228-china-is-using-the-world-bank-as-its-piggybank/#:~:text=Our%20firms%20garner%20less%20than,other%20democracies%20footing%20the%20bill (accessed 12 March 2025).

31 Yunnan Chen, Keyu Jin and Weiwei Chen, 'Development or Dependence?: China's Investment and Development Finance in Africa', LSE Seminar, series 4, episode 8 of *Cutting-edge Issues in Development Thinking and Practice*, 4 December 2023, https://cuttingedgeissues.transistor.fm/episodes/s4-e8-development-or-dependence-chinas-investment-and-development-finance-in-africa (accessed 12 March 2025).

32 Yunnan Chen and Kanyi Lui, *The Evolution of China's Lending Practices on the Belt and Road*, (London: ODI, 2021).

33 Tom Miller, *China's Asian Dream: Empire Building Along the New Silk Road* (London: Zed Books, 2019); Andrew Chatzky and James McBride, 'China's Massive Belt and Road Initiative', Council on Foreign Relations, 28 January 2022 (updated 2 February 2023), www.cfr.org/backgrounder/chinas-massive-belt-and-road-initiative (accessed 12 March 2025).

34 Yuen Yuen Ang, 'Demystifying Belt and Road: The Struggle to Define China's Project of the Century', *Foreign Affairs*, 22 May 2019.

35 AEI data, discussed in Fredrik Sjoholm, *The Belt and Road Initiative: Economic Causes and Effects*, Research Institute of Industrial Economics Working Paper 1439 (2022).

36 Joseph Leahy, James Kynge and Benjamin Parkin, 'The Legacy of China's Belt and Road', *Financial Times*, 23 October 2013.

37 'China's Belt and Road Initiative Heightens Debt Risks in Eight Countries, Points to Need for Better Lending Practices', press release, Centre for Global Development, 4 March 2018.

38 Lee Jones and Shahar Hameiri, 'Debunking the Myth of Debt-trap Diplomacy', Chatham House, 23 October 2020, www.chathamhouse.org/2020/08/debunking-myth-debt-trap-diplomacy (accessed 12 March 2025).

39 Junhua Zhang, 'What is the Future of the Belt and Road Initiative?', GIS Reports, European Institute for Asian Studies, Berlin 19 February 2024, www.gisreportsonline.com/r/what-is-the-future-of-chinas-belt-and-road-initiative/ (accessed 12 March 2025).

40 Xue Gong, 'The BRI is Still China's "Gala" but Without as Much Luster', Carnegie China, 3 March 2023, https://carnegieendowment.org/posts/2023/03/the-belt-and-road-initiative-is-still-chinas-gala-but-without-as-much-luster?lang=en (accessed 12 March 2025).

41 Samir Saran, 'India Sees the Belt and Road Initiative for what it is: Evidence of China's Unconcealed Ambition for Hegemony', Observer Research Foundation, 19 February 2018, www.orfonline.org/research/india-sees-the-belt-and-road-initi ative-for-what-it-is-evidence-of-chinas-unconcealed-ambition-for-hegemony (accessed 12 March 2025); Pramit Pal Chauduri, 'India Nudges China Toward Belt and Road Changes', GIS Reports, 4 January 2019, www.gisreportsonline.com/r/ belt-road-initiative-dangers/ (accessed 12 March 2025).

42 'India's Digital Belt and Road Initiative', *Economist*, 10 June 2023.

43 Kirsten Hopewell (ed.), *Breaking the WTO: How Emerging Powers Disrupted the Neo-liberal Project* (Stanford, CA: Stanford University Press, 2016).

44 Camille Gijs, 'Don't Just Blame the US: India is Blocking WTO Reform', *Politico*, 16 February 2024, www.politico.eu/article/world-trade-organization-india-united-states-protectionism-agriculture/ (accessed 12 March 2025).

45 Hai Feng, *The Politics of China's Accession to the World Trade Organization: The Dragon Goes Global* (New York: Routledge, 2012).

46 Ann Harrison et al., *Can a Tiger Change its Stripes?: Reform of China's State-owned Enterprises in the Penumbra of the State*, NBER Working Paper 25475 (January 2019).

47 Petros Mavroidis and André Sapir, *China and the WTO: Why Multilateralism Still Matters* (Princeton, NJ: Princeton University Press, 2021).

48 Davies and Wei, *Superpower Showdown*.

49 Kynge and Frey, 'China's Plan to Reshape World Trade'.

50 Alex He, *The Digital Silk Road and China's Influence on Standard Setting*, CIGI Papers no. 264, Centre for International Governance Innovation (April 2022).

51 Arjun Gargeyas, *Navigating the Geopolitics of Technical Standards for India*, Takshashila Discussion Document 2021-08, Takshashila Institution, 21 October 2021, https:// static1.squarespace.com/static/618a55c4cb03246776b68559/t/622863c86cf2fe0 9c50252d7/1646814172781/TDD_The-Geopolitics-of-Standards_AG_V1-1.pdf (accessed 12 March 2025).

52 Marianne Schneider-Petsinger et al., *US–China Strategic Competition: The Quest for Global Technological Leadership* (London: Chatham House, 2019).

53 Rudra Chaudhuri, 'India's Role in Technology Standards', Carnegie Endowment for International Peace, 9 September 2020, https://carnegieendowment.org/ posts/2020/09/on-indias-role-in-technology-standards?lang=en (accessed 12 March 2025).

54 Nikki Teo, *The United Nations in Global Tax Coordination* (Cambridge: Cambridge University Press, 2023).

55 'Chinese Nuclear Weapons, 2025: Federation of American Scientists Reveals Latest Facts on Beijing's Nuclear Buildup', press release, 12 March 2025, Federation of American Scientists.

56 Raphael Cohen et al., *Assessing the Prospects of Great Power Cooperation in the Global Commons* (Santa Monica, CA: Rand Corporation, 2023).

57 Ted Bromund, James Carafano and Brett Schaefer, '7 Reasons US Should not Ratify UN Convention on the Law of the Sea', Heritage Foundation, 4 June 2018, www.heritage.org/global-politics/commentary/7-reasons-us-should-not-ratify-un-convention-the-law-the-sea (accessed 12 March 2025).

Chapter 8

1 Subrahmanyam Jaishankar, *The India Way: Strategies for an Uncertain World* (Gurugram: HarperCollins, 2024).

2 Nataša Mišković, Harald Fischer-Tiné and Nada Boškovska, *The Non-aligned Movement and the Cold War* (Abingdon and New York: Routledge, 2017); Jürgen Dinkel, *The Non-aligned Movement: Genesis, Objectives, Politics* (Leiden: Brill, 2018).

3 Navdeep Suri and Jhanvi Tripathi, 'The BRICS Summit: Seeking an Alternative World Order?', Council on Foreign Relations, 31 August 2023.

4 Randy Mulyanto, 'Why Indonesia did not Join the BRICS', The China Project, 5 October 2023, https://thechinaproject.com/2023/09/15/why-indonesia-did-not-join-brics/ (accessed 12 March 2025).

5 Hung Tran, *Institutions for Policy Coordination in the Global South*, Atlantic Council Policy Center policy brief 18/24, April 2024.

6 Jim O'Neill, 'Does an Expanded BRICS Mean Anything?', Chatham House, 27 August 2023, www.chathamhouse.org/2023/08/does-expanded-brics-mean-anything/ (accessed 12 March 2025).

7 Daniel Azevedo et al., 'An Evolving BRICS and the Shifting World Order', Report of Boston Consulting Group, 29 April 2024, www.bcg.com/publications/2024/brics-enlargement-and-shifting-world-order (accessed 12 March 2025).

8 UNCTAD, *BRICS Investment Report 2023* (Geneva: UNCTAD, 2024), p. 6.

9 Joe Sullivan, 'A BRICS Currency Could Shake the Dollar's Dominance', *Foreign Policy*, 24 April 2023.

10 R. A. Mundell, 'A Theory of Optimal Currency Areas', *American Economic Review*, 51:4 (1961), pp. 657–65.

11 O'Neill, 'Does an Expanded BRICS Mean Anything?'

12 Robert Greene, 'The Difficult Realities of the BRICS' Dedollarization Efforts – and the Renminbi's Role', Carnegie Endowment for International Peace, 5 December 2023. https://carnegieendowment.org/research/2023/12/the-difficult-realities-of-the-brics-dedollarization-effortsand-the-renminbis-role?lang=en (accessed 12 March 2025).

13 Riya Sinha and Niara Sareen, *India's Limited Trade Connectivity with South Asia* (New Delhi: Brookings India, 2020).

14 Ashley Tellis, '"What is in Our Interest": India and the Ukraine War', Carnegie Endowment for International Peace, 25 April 2022. https://carnegieendowment.org/research/2022/04/what-is-in-our-interest-india-and-the-ukraine-war?lang=en (accessed 12 March 2025).

15 Nivedita Kapoor and Tanvi Madan, 'Why India Cares About China–Russia Relations', Global India Podcasts, Brookings India, 10 January 2024, www.brookings.edu/articles/why-india-cares-about-china-russia-relations/ (accessed 12 March 2025).

16 Mohamed Zeeshan, 'India Turns the Page on Tie with Russia after Ukraine War', The Diplomat, 3 January 2024, https://thediplomat.com/2024/01/india-turns-the-page-on-ties-with-russia-after-ukraine-war/ (accessed 12 March 2025).

17 Jeff Smith, 'India, Russia, and the Ukraine War', Heritage Foundation, 14 June 2022, www.heritage.org/global-politics/commentary/india-russia-and-the-ukraine-war (accessed 12 March 2025).

18 Sheena Chestnut Greitens, 'China's Response to War in Ukraine', *Asian Survey*, 62:5–6 (2022), pp. 751–81; Evan Feigenbaum and Adam Szubin, 'What China has Learned from the Ukraine War', *Foreign Affairs*, 2 February 2024.

19 Quoted in the *New York Times*, 6 April 2023.

20 Sam Olsen, 'The Depressing Reason for China's Support of Russia: How Beijing is Planning its Defences Against Future American Action', What China Wants blog, 22 March 2022, https://whatchinawants.substack.com/p/the-depressing-reason-for-chinas (accessed 12 March 2025).

21 Jude Blanchette and Ryan Haas, 'The Taiwan Long Game: Why the Best Solution is No Solution', *Foreign Affairs*, February/March 2023.

22 Angela Stent, Yun Sun and Adrianna Pita, 'The Dynamics of the Russia–China Partnership', Brookings podcast, 22 May 2024, www.brookings.edu/articles/the-dynamics-of-the-russia-china-partnership/ (accessed 12 March 2025).

23 Kristina Spohr, 'Arctic Analysis Frozen in Cold War Thinking', *Financial Times*, 21 November 2023.

24 'War on Ukraine: China's Domestic and Diplomatic Balancing Act', Chatham House podcast, 17 May 2022, www.chathamhouse.org/events/all/members-event/war-ukraine-chinas-domestic-and-diplomatic-balancing-act (accessed 12 March 2025).

25 Sebastian Horn,Carmen Reinhart and Christoph Trebesch, 'China's Overseas Lending and the War in Ukraine', CEPR, 11 April 2022, https://cepr.org/voxeu/columns/chinas-overseas-lending-and-war-ukraine (accessed 12 March 2025).

26 Wang Wen Report (unpublished), Zhongyang Institute of Financial Studies, Renmin University, 2023, based on a study in twenty-one Russian cities.

27 Xavier Romero Vidal, David Evans and Roberto Foa, 'Global Public Opinion is Divided on Russia and China', UK in a Changing Europe, 15 December 2022, https://ukandeu.ac.uk/global-public-opinion-is-divided-on-russia-and-china/ (accessed 1 April 2025).

28 Laura Silver et al., 'Comparing Views of the US and China in 24 Countries', Pew Research Centre, 6 November 2023, www.pewresearch.org/global/2023/11/06/comparing-views-of-the-us-and-china-in-24-countries/ (accessed 1 April 2025).

29 Christine Huang, Moira Fagan and Sneha Gubbala, 'Views of India Lean Positive Across 23 Countries', Pew Research Centre, 29 August 2023, www.pewresearch.org/global/2023/08/29/views-of-india-lean-positive-across-23-countries/ (accessed 12 March 2025).

30 Jon Alterman, 'China and the Middle East', Congressional testimony, Center for Strategic & International Studies, 19 April 2024, www.csis.org/analysis/china-and-middle-east (accessed 12 March 2025).

31 Viraj Solanki, 'The Gulf Region's Growing Importance for India', International Institute of Strategic Studies, 21 February 2024, www.iiss.org/online-analysis/online-analysis/2024/02/the-gulf-regions-growing-importance-for-india/ (accessed 12 March 2025).

32 Chietigj Bajpaee, 'India's Engagement with the Middle East Reflects New Delhi's Changing Worldview', War on the Rocks, 22 May 2024, https://warontherocks.

com/2024/05/indias-engagement-with-the-middle-east-reflects-new-delhis-chang
ing-worldview/ (accessed 12 March 2025).

33 Donald Berlin, *India–Iran Relations: A Deepening Entente* (Honolulu: Asia-Pacific Center for Security Studies, 2004).

34 Deborah Brautigam, *The Dragon's Gift: The Real Story of China in Africa* (Oxford: Oxford University Press, 2009).

35 Li Anshan, *China and Africa in a Global Context* (Cape Town: Ace Press, 2020).

36 Chris Alden, *China in Africa* (London: Zed Books, 2017).

37 Laura Silver et al, 'Views of China and Xi Jinping', Pew Research Centre, 9 July 2024, www.pewresearch.org/global/2024/07/09/views-of-china-and-xi-jinping/ (accessed 1 April 2025).

38 Data sourced from International Peace Research Institute, Stockholm, 2024, in 'Chinese Arms Sales in Sub-Saharan Africa', IISS, December 2024, www.iiss.org/publications/strategic-comments/2024/12/chinese-arms-sales-in-sub-saharan-afri ca/#:~:text=At%20least%2021%20countries%20in,now%20operate%20Chinese %20armoured%20vehicles (accessed 1 April 2025).

39 Kristina Kironska, 'How Taiwan Lost Africa', Central European Institute of Asian Studies, 21 December 2022, https://ceias.eu/how-taiwan-lost-africa/ (accessed 12 March 2025).

40 Hillman, *The Digital Silk Road*, p. 13.

41 Ibid., p. 14.

42 Alicia Garcia-Herrero, 'China's Growing Presence in Latin America is a Problem for the West', *Breughel Newsletter*, 28 September 2023.

43 Ángel Melguizo and Margaret Myers, 'Ahead of the Curve: Why the EU and US Risk Falling Behind China in Latin America', European Council on Foreign Relations (ECFR), 10 May 2024, https://ecfr.eu/article/ahead-of-the-curve-why-the-eu-and-us-risk-falling-behind-china-in-latin-america/ (accessed 12 March 2025).

44 Helen Thompson, 'The New Great Game', *New Statesman*, 24 May/6 June 2024.

45 Diana Roy, 'China's Growing Influence in Latin America', Council on Foreign Relations, 15 June 2023, www.cfr.org/backgrounder/china-influence-latin-america-argentina-brazil-venezuela-security-energy-bri (accessed 12 March 2025).

46 Kishore Mahbubani, 'It's Time for the West and the Rest to Talk as Equals', *Financial Times*, 12 December 2023.

47 Enze Han, *The Ripple Effect: China's Complex Presence in Southeast Asia* (New York: Oxford University Press, 2024).

48 Susannah Patton and Jack Sato, 'China and the United States in Southeast Asia', Lowy Institute, 20 April 2023, www.lowyinstitute.org/publications/asia-power-snapshot-china-united-states-southeast-asia (accessed 12 March 2025).

49 Based on ISEAS, *The State of Southeast Asia 2024 Survey Report* (Singapore: ISEAS, 2024), www.iseas.edu.sg/category/centres/asean-studies-centre/state-of-southeast-asia-survey/ (accessed 1 April 2025).

50 Prashanth Parameswaran, 'Southeast Asia and US–China Competition: Contours, Realities, and Implications for the Indo-Pacific', Wilson Centre, 21 December 2023, www.wilsoncenter.org/article/southeast-asia-and-us-china-competition-contours-re alities-and-implications-indo-pacific (accessed 12 March 2025).

51 Viraj Solanki, 'India's Increased Defence and Security Engagement with Southeast Asia', International Institute of Strategic Studies, 1 May 2024, www.iiss.org/online-analysis/online-analysis/2024/04/indias-increased-defence-and-security-engagem ent-with-southeast-asia/ (accessed 12 March 2025).

52 Derek Grossman, 'India is Becoming a Power in Southeast Asia', *Foreign Policy*, 7 July 2023.

53 Rahul Mishra and Yanitha Meena Louis, 'Why India's Global South Ambitions Must Turn to Southeast Asia', The Interpreter, Lowy Institute, 29 April 2024, www. lowyinstitute.org/the-interpreter/why-india-s-global-south-ambitions-must-turn-so utheast-asia (accessed 12 March 2025).

54 Premasha Saha, 'India Wants Strategic Engagement with Southeast Asia – but How?', The Strategist, Australian Strategic Policy Institute, 18 April 2024, www. aspistrategist.org.au/india-wants-strategic-engagement-with-southeast-asia-but-how/ (accessed 12 March 2025).

Chapter 9

1 Vijay Gokhale, *The Long Game: How the Chinese Negotiate with India* (Delhi: Penguin Random House, 2021).

2 Manoj Joshi, *Understanding the India–China Border: The Enduring Threat of War in the High Himalaya* (Gurugram: HarperCollins, 2022); report of the International Crisis Group, *Thin Ice in the Himalayas: Handling the India–China Border Dispute* (Brussels: International Crisis Group, 2023); Tanvi Madan, 'Emerging Global Issues: The China–India Boundary Crisis and its Implications', Brookings Institution, 9 September 2020, www.brookings.edu/articles/emerging-global-issues-the-china-india-boundary-cri sis-and-its-implications/ (accessed 12 March 2025).

3 Samir Saran and Wang Dong, 'There's a Standoff Between China and India in the Himalayas. Both Sides Explain', World Economic Forum, 16 August 2017, www. weforum.org/stories/2017/08/there-s-a-standoff-between-china-and-india-in-the-himalayas-both-sides-explain/ (accessed 12 March 2025).

4 Rajeswari Rajagopalan, 'India–China Relations are Unlikely to See Much Progress', ChinaPower Project, Center for Strategic and International Studies, 15 February 2024, https://chinapower.csis.org/analysis/rajagopalan-india-china-relations/ (acc essed 12 March 2025).

5 Tanvi Madan, 'China has Lost India', *Foreign Affairs*, 4 October 2022.

6 Vijay Gokhale, 'A Historical Evaluation of China's India Policy: Lessons for India–China Relations', Carnegie Endowment for International Peace, 13 December 2022, https://carnegieendowment.org/research/2022/12/a-historical-evaluation-of-chinas-india-policy-lessons-for-india-china-relations?lang=en (accessed 12 March 2025); Lora Saalman (ed. and trans.), *The China–India Nuclear Crossroads* (Washington, DC: Brookings Institution Press, 2012).

7 C. Raja Mohan, *Samudra Manthan: Sino-Indian Rivalry in the Indo-Pacific* (Washington, DC: Carnegie Endowment for International Peace, 2012).

8 Samir Saran, 'How India has Actually Done a Great Job in Dealing with the Dragon', *Hindustan Times*, 1 November 2017.

9 Center for Preventive Action, 'Conflict Between India and Pakistan', Global Conflict Tracker, Council on Foreign Relations, 9 April 2024, www.cfr.org/global-conflict-tracker/conflict/conflict-between-india-and-pakistan (accessed 14 March 2025).

10 Manjari Chatterjee Miller, 'How China and Pakistan Forged Closer Ties', Council on Foreign Relations, 3 October 2022, www.cfr.org/article/how-china-and-paki stan-forged-close-ties (accessed 14 March 2025); Andrew Small, *The China–Pakistan Axis: Asia's New Geopolitics* (London: Hurst and Co., 2015).

11 Gautam Babawale and Tanvi Madan, 'How India Sees China's Ties with Pakistan and Bhutan', Brookings Institution podcast, 1 November 2023, www.brookings.edu/articles/how-india-sees-chinas-ties-with-pakistan-and-bhutan/ (accessed 14 March 2025).

12 Uzair Younus, 'With Pakistan's Economy in Freefall, China's Economic and Military Influence is Likely to Grow in the Country', SouthAsiaSource blog, Atlantic Council, 9 March 2023, www.atlanticcouncil.org/blogs/southasiasource/with-pakistans-eco nomy-in-freefall-chinese-economic-and-military-influence-is-likely-to-grow-in-the-country/ (accessed 14 March 2025).

13 Jacques, *When China Rules the World*, pp. 339–40.

14 Anu Anwar, 'China–Bangladesh Relations: A Three Way Balance Between China, India and the US', MERICS Mercator Institute for China Studies, 18 August 2022, https://merics.org/en/china-bangladesh-relations-three-way-balance-between-chi na-india-and-us/ (accessed 14 March 2025).

15 Lailufar Yasmin, 'Understanding Bangladesh–China Relations: Bangladesh's Rising Geopolitical Agency and China's Regional and Global Ambitions', *Journal of Contemporary East Asian Studies*, 12:1 (2023), pp. 87–109.

16 Peter Church, *A Short History of Southeast Asia* (Singapore: John Wiley, 2009).

17 Tom Miller, *China's Asian Dream: Empire Building on the New Silk Road* (London: Zed Books, 2017).

18 Ophelia Yumlemban, 'Is Myanmar Impeding India's Act East Policy?', Raisina Debates, Observer Research Foundation, Delhi, 27 March 2024, www.orfonline.org/expert-speak/is-myanmar-impeding-indias-act-east-policy (accessed 17 March 2025).

19 Rajeev Bhattacharyya, 'Has the Indian Flagship Kaladan Project in Myanmar Hit a Dead End?', The Diplomat, 27 February 2024, https://thediplomat.com/2024/02/has-the-indian-flagship-kaladan-project-in-myanmar-hit-a-dead-end/ (accessed 1 April 2025).

20 Vijay Gokhale, 'India's Fog of Misunderstanding Surrounding Nepal–China Relations', Carnegie Endowment for International Peace, 4 October 2021, https://carnegieendowment.org/research/2021/10/indias-fog-of-misunderstanding-surro unding-nepal-china-relations?lang=en (accessed 17 March 2025).

21 Atul Kumar, 'China–Nepal Military Relations: Risks and Opportunities for India', Observer Research Foundation, 20 April 2024, www.orfonline.org/expert-speak/china-nepal-military-relations-risks-and-opportunities-for-india (accessed 17 March 2025).

22 John Pollock and Damien Symon, 'China Takes More Lead in Bhutan Before Expected Border Deal', *World Today*, 21 December 2023.

23 Shibani Mehta, 'On Thin Ice – Bhutan's Diplomatic Challenge Around the India–China Border Dispute', Carnegie Endowment for International Peace, 23 April 2024, https://carnegieendowment.org/posts/2024/04/on-thin-ice-bhutans-diplomatic-challenge-amid-the-india-china-border-dispute?lang=en (accessed 17 March 2025).

24 Shivshankar Menon, *Indian and Asian Geopolitics: The Past, Present* (Washington, DC: Brookings Institution, 2021).

25 Shakthi De Silva, 'Tightrope Balancing in a Time of Rising Great Power Competition: An Assessment of Sri Lanka's Relations with India and China', *Oasis*, 37 (2023), pp. 47–68.

26 Ibid.

27 Debak Das, 'How India's Restricted Rocket Force Makes Conflict with China More Likely', *Bulletin of the Atomic Scientists*, 22 April 2024.

28 Ibid.

29 Ashley Tellis, *Striking Asymmetries: Nuclear Transitions in Southern Asia* (Washington, DC: Carnegie Endowment for International Peace, 2022).

30 Samir Tata, 'War Clouds Over the Indian Horizon', RUSI (Royal United Services Institute), 6 March 2024, https://rusi.org/explore-our-research/publications/commentary/war-clouds-over-indian-horizon#:~:text=While%20wars%20elsewhere%20hold%20the,and%20China%20in%20Eastern%20Ladakh (accessed 17 March 2025).

31 Christopher Colley and Prashant Suhas, 'India–China and their War-making Capabilities', *Journal of Asian Security and International Affairs*, 8:1 (2021), pp. 33–61.

32 Christopher Colley, *The Nexus of Naval Modernization in India and China* (Oxford: Oxford University Press, 2023).

33 Prashant Suhas and Christopher Colley, 'It's Still the Indian Ocean: Parsing Sino-Indian Competition Where it Counts', War on the Rocks, 7 May 2020, https://warontherocks.com/2024/05/its-still-the-indian-ocean-parsing-sino-indian-naval-competition-where-it-counts/ (accessed 17 March 2025).

34 John Reed and Chloe Cornish, 'India's Plan to Build up Military Muscle', *Financial Times*, 13 December 2022.

35 Harsh Pant and Kalpit Mankikar, 'The Fatal Flaw in India's China Strategy', *Foreign Affairs*, 14 November 2024.

36 'Asia's Biggest Beasts', *Economist*, 22 July 2023, pp. 51–2.

Chapter 10

1 Use of OECD model baseline case for 'business as usual' in OECD, *Long Term Scenarios: Incorporating the Energy Transition*, OECD Economic Policy Paper 33 (December 2023), www.oecd.org/content/dam/oecd/en/publications/reports/2023/12/long-term-scenarios-incorporating-the-energy-transition_0be911c4/153ab87c-en.pdf (accessed 17 March 2025).

2 Richard Koo, *The Holy Grail of Macro-economics: Lessons from Japan's Great Recession* (Singapore: John Wiley, 2009); and Richard Koo, *Escape from Balance Sheet Recession and the QE Trap* (Singapore: John Wiley, 2014).

3　Zongyuan Zoe Liu, 'China's Real Economic Crisis', *Foreign Affairs*, 6 August 2024; Rosen and Wright, 'China's Economic Collision Course'.
4　Acemoglu and Robinson, *Why Nations Fail*.
5　Magnus, *Red Flags*.
6　Lardy, 'China is Still Rising'.
7　Li, *China's World View*.
8　Hal Brands and Michael Beckley, *Danger Zone* (New York: W.W. Norton, 2023); 'Is China's Power About to Peak?', *Economist*, 11 May 2023.
9　Wang Wen, 'Six Peak China Myths', *Diplomat*, 9 March 2024.
10　Muralidharan, *Accelerating India's Development*; Rajan and Lamba, *Breaking the Mould*.
11　Mody, *India is Broken*.
12　Cable, *Money and Power*, chapter 13.
13　Allison, *Destined for War*.
14　Odd Arne Westad, 'Sleepwalking to War', *Foreign Affairs*, July/August 2024.
15　Ibid.
16　Kurt Campbell and Jake Sullivan, 'Competition without Catastrophe', *Foreign Affairs*, 13 September 2019.
17　Pinelopi Goldberg and Tristan Reed, *Is the Global Economy Deglobalizing?*, World Bank Policy Research Working Paper 10392 (2023).
18　Guy Erb and Scott Sommers, 'Why Claims of Deglobalisation are Overblown', LSE blog, 11 May 2024, https://blogs.lse.ac.uk/usappblog/2024/05/11/why-claims-of-deglobalisation-are-overblown/ (accessed 17 March 2025).
19　Brad Setser, 'The Dangerous Myth of Globalization', *Foreign Affairs*, 4 June 2024.
20　Peter Schwarz, *The Art of the Long View* (New York: Crown, 1991).
21　Mavroidis and Sapir, *China and the WTO*.
22　Claude Lambert, 'Small Eagle, Big Dragon: China's Expanding Role in UN Peacekeeping', RUSI, 19 July 2024, www.rusi.org/explore-our-research/publications/commentary/small-eagle-big-dragon-chinas-expanding-role-un-peacekeeping (accessed 17 March 2025).

Acknowledgements

I am indebted to a variety of individuals and institutions who made this book possible.

The origins of the book lie in discussions with a colleague at the Overseas Development Institute (ODI) fifty years ago – Sarwar Lateef – who published an excellent Institute of Development Studies Discussion Paper (number 118, 1976) on economic growth in China and India. I was able to take the work forward when asked by Chatham House, where I headed the International Economics Programme, to produce a published research paper in 1995 (*China and India: Economic Reform and Global Integration*). The interest was revived when I was invited, as a Distinguished Fellow, to lead a roundtable discussion on the subject at the ODI (now ODI Global) by the Chief Executive, Sara Pantuliano, in February 2023.

I was helped in developing the ideas by the School of Public Policy at the London School of Economics (LSE), where I was a Professor in Practice, and in particular its Dean, Andres Velasco, when the School helped me in organising a series of public lectures around the main themes of the book: economic growth (Keyu Jin and Rathin Roy); international governance (Niall Ferguson and Rebecca Nadin); environmental impacts (Isabel Hilton and Nick Stern); politics and decision making (Mukulika Bannerjee and Kerry Brown). I would like to express thanks to the speakers, to my colleagues who chaired the sessions (Alexander Evans and Tony Travers) and to the administrative team, especially Carolina Stern.

A special debt is due to Leo Chen, a postgraduate at the LSE, for his help with the charts and quantification in the book and for his insights on today's China.

I wish to thank Shivshankar Menon, who invited me to give a lecture on the book at Ashoka University in Sonipat, Haryana. I am also thankful for helpful discussions with Harsh Pant at the Observer Research Foundation and Shibani Mehta at Carnegie India, both in New Delhi. I am particularly grateful to Vikram Doraiswami, Indian High Commissioner in London, for reading a draft and for his comments.

I am also grateful to Wang Wen and his colleagues at the Institute for Financial Studies at Renmin University, Beijing, for the invitation to visit them and for discussions around the book.

Georgina Capel, my literary agent, gave valuable advice and help in locating an excellent publisher: Manchester University Press. Alun Richards, Associate Editor at MUP, and his team did the hard work of editing the text and producing the many charts, for which I am very grateful.

As always, I relied heavily on moral and practical support from my family: my wife Rachel, especially, and my grandson Ayrton for help with graphics.

Index

Page numbers in *italic* refer to figures.
Titles of books can be found after authors' names.

EU authorised representative for GPSR:
Easy Access System Europe, Mustamäe tee 50,
10621 Tallinn, Estonia
gpsr.requests@easproject.com

www.ingramcontent.com/pod-product-compliance
Lightning Source LLC
Chambersburg PA
CBHW011537260326
41914CB00036B/1975/J